Professional Microsoft® SharePoint® Server 2007 Reporting with SQL Server 2008 Reporting Services

Property of Dewpoint

Professional
Microsoft® SharePoint® Server 2007 Reporting with SQL Server 2008 Reporting Services

Professional

Microsoft® SharePoint® Server 2007 Reporting with SQL Server 2008 Reporting Services

Coskun Cavusoglu

Jacob Sanford

Reza Alirezaei

Wiley Publishing, Inc.

Professional Microsoft® SharePoint® Server 2007 Reporting with SQL Server® 2008 Reporting Services

Published by
Wiley Publishing, Inc.
10475 Crosspoint Boulevard
Indianapolis, IN 46256
www.wiley.com

Copyright © 2009 by Wiley Publishing, Inc., Indianapolis, Indiana

Published simultaneously in Canada

ISBN: 978-0-470-48189-9

Manufactured in the United States of America

10 9 8 7 6 5 4 3 2 1

For general information on our other products and services please contact our Customer Care Department within the United States at (877) 762-2974, outside the United States at (317) 572-3993 or fax (317) 572-4002.

Wiley also publishes its books in a variety of electronic formats. Some content that appears in print may not be available in electronic books.

Library of Congress Control Number: 2009931749

I dedicate this book to my wonderful wife, Kader, and our daughter, Tuana.
—Coskun Cavusoglu

I dedicate this book to my wife, who has never once complained about not having a book dedicated to her in the past, and to my kids, Matthew, Hayden, and Wendy, for continually inspiring me to be better than I was yesterday.
—Jacob J. Sanford

I dedicate this book to my parents, who gave me my past and continue to encourage and support me towards my vision of the future. I am enormously thankful to have been allowed to follow in their footsteps.
—Reza Alirezaei

About the Authors

Coskun Cavusoglu is the Director of Consulting Services and the Chief Solution Architect of Captaré Consulting, LLC. He has been architecting and implementing technology solutions for more than 10 years in both large, enterprise organizations and fast-growth midmarket firms. As a Software Engineer specializing in the .NET Framework and the Office Server System, specifically Windows SharePoint Services and Microsoft Office SharePoint Server, he has extensive experience designing, implementing, and supporting Internet solutions using Microsoft technologies. Coskun is a technology writer, blogger, and published author on Microsoft server products. His latest book which he co-authored with fellow SharePoint experts is *Professional Microsoft SharePoint 2007 Design* by Wrox Publishing. He also is a speaker who attends various community events both locally and internationally where he talks about SharePoint topics and his past and future engagements can be found at his blog, www.Share-PointCoskun.com. Coskun is a Microsoft Certified Professional and is also an MCTS for SharePoint Portal Server 2003 and Microsoft Office SharePoint Server 2007.

Jacob J. Sanford is a senior consultant with Resolute Solutions Corporation, a Microsoft Gold Certified Partner and a National Systems Integrator. He has been working with web application development using Microsoft technologies for more than 10 years, specializing in .NET solutions since the 1.0/1.1 Framework. Jacob is a frequent speaker at local and regional .NET and SharePoint events and is the creator of the Tallahassee SharePoint Experts Exchange for Developers (SPEED), a SharePoint User Group in Tallahassee, FL. He has written two previous books for Wrox Press: *ASP.NET 2.0 Design* (September 2007) and *Professional Microsoft SharePoint 2007 Design* (September 2008). Jacob is a Microsoft Certified Technology Specialist in the .NET Framework 2.0 (Web Applications) and a Microsoft Certified Technology Specialist (Microsoft Dynamics CRM 4.0 Customization and Configuration).

Reza Alirezaei is an independent consultant and Microsoft Office SharePoint Server MVP with a focus on developing custom solutions with SharePoint, Office, Reporting Services, and the .NET platform. As a technical leader with more than 10 years of experience in software, he has helped many development teams architect and build large-scale, mission-critical applications. This former SQL Server Reporting Services MVP has been also nominated and awarded three times as one of the Top 20 Contributors to the Microsoft Developer Network (MSDN) Wiki since 2006. In addition to consulting, Reza is a SharePoint instructor and speaker. He speaks at many local and international conferences. Reza frequently blogs at http://blogs.devhorizon.com/reza and can be reached at reza@devhorizon.com.

Credits

Acquisitions Editors
Paul Reese
Katie Mohr

Project Editor
Kelly Talbot

Technical Editors
Darrin Bishop
Kanwal Khipple

Production Editor
Rebecca Anderson

Copy Editor
Christopher Jones

Editorial Director
Robyn B. Siesky

Editorial Manager
Mary Beth Wakefield

Production Manager
Tim Tate

Vice President and Executive Group Publisher
Richard Swadley

Vice President and Executive Publisher
Barry Pruett

Associate Publisher
Jim Minatel

Project Coordinator, Cover
Lynsey Stanford

Proofreader
Carrie Hunter, Word One
Dr. Nate Pritts, Word One

Indexer
Robert Swanson

Acknowledgments

Coskun, Jacob, and Reza would like to first thank everyone at Wrox that helped make this book happen. To Katie Mohr, the Acquisitions Editor who first green-lighted the project, and to Paul Reese who carried the torch when she took a new position at Wiley, thanks for getting us going and having faith in us to get this book out. To Kelly Talbot, the Development Editor that has worked with both Coskun and Jacob in the past, thanks for working with us again and for keeping us motivated. You put the pressure on when we needed it and told us everything was going to be okay when we needed that. You have been a constant friend and source of great support and guidance throughout this entire process. Again.

To Darrin Bishop and Kanwal Khipple, the Technical Editors for this book, we thank you for your time and expertise. Without your keen observations and technical recommendations, this book would not be as strong. You made us rethink our original ideas and helped us improve upon them. This book is much better because of your involvement.

To all of our friends and families, thank you so much for your continued support and understanding. Writing a book is so time consuming and, at times, frustrating that it's amazing that all of our relationships are still intact. You are the reasons we do it and we don't thank you enough for allowing us to do this time and time again.

To our clients, colleagues, and employers, we thank you for providing the experience and training that enables us to do what we do. None of us would be where we are today without your assistance and encouragement.

And, finally, to anyone reading this book, we thank you for patronage. We hope you get as much out of reading this book as we did in writing it.

Contents

Contents

Contents

Contents

Introduction

Microsoft Office SharePoint 2007 is a great technology. It is the fastest growing product in the Microsoft suite of applications. It provides an easy to use portal interface that conveniently integrates document management and a collaborative environment for intranet and Internet web applications. Users without any technical background can easily create lists of data, alerts, and collaborative tools that enable colleagues, no matter how far apart, to work together to get their jobs done. And, with a little knowledge and motivation, users can even set up workflows and design elements to really make their portal come to life.

However, one of the things that could be improved in SharePoint is its reporting capabilities. While it is certainly true there are some reporting functions that come with SharePoint, they are fairly limited in use and extensibility. Fortunately, though, this is where Microsoft SQL Server Reporting Services (SSRS) comes in.

SSRS provides a very rich environment to create stunning reports that quickly and accurately report data from your line of business applications. You can pull lists directly from your legacy systems and databases or even directly from SharePoint itself. You can present this data in tabular style reports with a matrix look and feel and full drill-down capabilities, or you can simply provide graphical representations of your data through the use of gauges and charts. Designing dashboards and similar reporting interfaces has never been simpler than with the latest version of SSRS, Microsoft SQL Server 2008 Reporting Services.

This book will take you through the nuances and caveats of setting up your SharePoint environment to take full advantage of SSRS 2008. You will see how to create your environment, how to plan and develop your reports, and how to deploy them to your current SharePoint environment. At the end of this book, you should have all the tools necessary to take data reporting in your SharePoint environment to the next level.

Who This Book Is For

This book is intended for the SharePoint professional who wants to learn more about integrating Reporting Services into their SharePoint environment. The book is mostly targeted towards the individual who has familiarity with SharePoint and has at least been exposed to Reporting Services in some capacity. However, special attention was paid to try to ensure that if you are pretty new to either technology (or both of them) that you can still follow along with the examples and concepts in this book.

What This Book Covers

This book covers all the concepts of running Microsoft SQL Server 2008 Reporting Services in SharePoint Integrated mode in your Microsoft Office SharePoint 2007 environment. You will see how to take your existing SharePoint environment and set up reporting services to be an integral part of the farm. You will actually go through the process of setting up SQL Server 2008 from scratch and setting its properties so that it runs in SharePoint Integration mode, which you will also learn about.

You will find out what goes into planning a good report and what features are available so that you know how to think about the final report while still in the design and planning phase. You will get an overview of the tools used to create reports in SSRS and how to create a simple report using the integrated report wizard.

You will learn how to create more complicated reports by learning how to replicate much of the wizard functionality manually. You will see how to include data from different data sources and how to make it all work together under the hood to make useful reports for your own projects.

Next, you will get into deployment for your reports. You will see some basic deployment steps and then get into much more advanced deployment techniques, such as deploying through PowerShell and Managed Code.

Finally, you will get into different ways to display your reports once they are deployed. You will get exposed to the web parts that come with SSRS that are specifically intended to help display your reports in your SharePoint environment. You will also see some cool things SharePoint can do with displaying reports that you may have never even considered.

However, one thing that is intentionally not covered in this book is setting up your initial installation of SharePoint. This books begins with the assumption that you have a SharePoint environment already set up and active. This book just shows you how to make SSRS 2008 an integrated part of that environment.

How This Book Is Structured

The audience for technical books typically falls into one of two categories. The first category is the person that will read the book cover to cover and try all the examples to try to get a really deep understanding of a new (at least to them) technology. The second category is the group that will use the book simply as a reference guide that they pull out when they have a specific issue they need help resolving. This book was written in the hopes that it could satisfy both audiences.

The book flows in a logical sequence to developing reports. First, you will see how to set up your reporting development/production environment, including server requirements and detailed installation instructions for setting us SSRS 2008 to run in your SharePoint environment. Next, you will discover best practices and guidance for planning your report and gathering requirements for your report projects. You will move on to gain an overview of setting up your development tools and how to use them. At this point you will be prepared to create your reports and, as such, you will spend three chapters doing exactly that. The next chapters will target the deployment and display of your reports so that you can make your reports to be viewable to the right people.

However, the authors of this book wanted to make sure that each and every chapter could stand on its own. For the most part, you don't need to have the end product of one chapter to start the next chapter. In other words, you don't have one report from Chapter 5 that you need to have at a certain point in its development before you can start Chapters 6 or 7. This way, if you want to learn a specific technique from, say, Chapter 9, you don't have to read the preceding eight chapters to follow the examples in that chapter.

Of course, this autonomy isn't always completely possible. The first chapters are about setting up SSRS to run in your SharePoint environment, and all subsequent chapters rely in some part on that being in place. So, if you don't have SSRS set up properly, you may have difficulty deploying reports to your server. But, as much as was possible, the authors tried to make the book as solid a desk reference as it is a page-by-page manual.

What You Need to Use This Book

The most important thing you need for this book is the motivation and desire to get deep into a combination of technologies that not a lot of people are very deep in.

But more related to general prerequisites, you should be at least moderately technical in some capacity. This doesn't mean that you have to be well versed in SharePoint or SSRS. Having a .NET background, for example, would be perfectly suitable. But much of the discussion in this book is technical, and if you don't have something of a technical background, you may find it hard to follow the examples. For many of the critical ideas presented in this book, the authors tried to at least give a cursory explanation or a link where you can learn more, even if a detailed discussion of the topic was deemed out of this book's scope. So, even without a really strong technical background, the initiated reader should be able to follow along.

As far as specific hardware and software requirements are concerned, the book begins with the premise that you have WSS 3.0 or MOSS 2007 already installed and available for use as the development environment for the projects in this book. So, before getting too far into this book, you need to make sure you have that in place.

You will also need to have some version of SQL Server 2008 installed with its tools to get the development tools you will use in this book.

Finally, for at least one of the chapters in this book, you will need a copy of Visual Studio 2008.

In at least the first chapter when an application is needed, the authors will point out where you can get the application and, if a known free version exists, how to get it for free.

Conventions

To help you get the most from the text and keep track of what's happening, we've used a number of conventions throughout the book.

> Boxes like this one hold important, not-to-be forgotten information that is directly relevant to the surrounding text.

Notes, tips, hints, tricks, and asides to the current discussion are offset and placed in italics like this.

As for styles in the text:

❏   We show keyboard strokes like this: Ctrl+A.

❏   We show URLs and code within the text like this: `persistence.properties`.

❏   We present code in two different ways:

```
We use a monofont type with no highlighting for most code examples.
We use gray highlighting to emphasize code that's particularly important in the
present context.
```

Source Code

As you work through the examples in this book, you may choose either to type in all the code manually or to use the source code files that accompany the book. All of the source code used in this book is available for download at `http://www.wrox.com`. Once at the site, simply locate the book's title (either by using the Search box or by using one of the title lists), and click the Download Code link on the book's detail page to obtain all the source code for the book.

> *Because many books have similar titles, you may find it easiest to search by ISBN; this book's ISBN is 978-0-470-48189-9.*

Once you download the code, just decompress it with your favorite compression tool. Alternately, you can go to the main Wrox code download page at `http://www.wrox.com/dynamic/books/download.aspx` to see the code available for this book and all other Wrox books.

Errata

We make every effort to ensure that there are no errors in the text or in the code. However, no one is perfect, and mistakes do occur. If you find an error in one of our books, such as a spelling mistake or faulty piece of code, we would be very grateful for your feedback. By sending in errata you may save another reader hours of frustration and at the same time you will be helping us provide even higher-quality information.

To find the errata page for this book, go to `www.wrox.com` and locate the title using the Search box or one of the title lists. Then, on the book details page, click the Book Errata link. On this page you can view all errata that has been submitted for this book and posted by Wrox editors. A complete book list, including links to each book's errata is also available at `www.wrox.com/misc-pages/booklist.shtml`.

If you don't spot "your" error on the Book Errata page, go to `www.wrox.com/contact/techsupport.shtml` and complete the form there to send us the error you have found. We'll check the information and, if appropriate, post a message to the book's errata page and fix the problem in subsequent editions of the book.

p2p.wrox.com

For author and peer discussion, join the P2P forums at p2p.wrox.com. The forums are a Web-based system for you to post messages relating to Wrox books and related technologies and interact with other readers and technology users. The forums offer a subscription feature to email you topics of interest of your choosing when new posts are made to the forums. Wrox authors, editors, other industry experts, and your fellow readers are present on these forums.

At http://p2p.wrox.com you will find a number of different forums that will help you not only as you read this book but also as you develop your own applications. To join the forums, just follow these steps:

1. Go to p2p.wrox.com and click the Register link.

2. Read the terms of use and click Agree.

3. Complete the required information to join as well as any optional information you wish to provide and click Submit.

4. You will receive an email with information describing how to verify your account and complete the joining process.

You can read messages in the forums without joining P2P, but in order to post your own messages, you must join.

Once you join, you can post new messages and respond to messages other users post. You can read messages at any time on the Web. If you would like to have new messages from a particular forum emailed to you, click the Subscribe to this Forum icon by the forum name in the forum listing.

For more information about how to use the Wrox P2P, be sure to read the P2P FAQs for answers to questions about how the forum software works as well as many common questions specific to P2P and Wrox books. To read the FAQs, click the FAQ link on any P2P page.

Professional

Microsoft® SharePoint® Server 2007 Reporting with SQL Server 2008 Reporting Services

1

An Introduction to SQL Server Reporting Services

If you have been doing web application development or design for any amount of time, you have almost assuredly been asked to create reports. Maybe you have created dashboard reports that show very high-level snapshots of productivity or other key measures. Perhaps you have created drill-down employee utilization reports so that managers can see how employees are spending the majority of their time. Or maybe Human Resources has needed to create summary reports for annual performance reviews. Whatever the reason, as a developer, creating data reports has probably been required of you.

To this end, you have many options. You can obviously create a custom reporting solution using something like C# and its related controls to provide the intended information. And depending on the size and requirements of the data, this might be a very attractive solution.

However, what if the report features a large amount of data spanned over an extensive amount of time? And what if management wants drill-down capabilities or, even worse, graphical representations such as charts and graphs? While it is certainly possible to accomplish this in C#, it also adds a level of complexity that many developers either do not want to deal with or, quite frankly, do not have the time to deal with.

To address this need, several server-side reporting technologies have been introduced over the years. If you have been in the developer community long enough, you have probably heard of some of the big names such as Oracle Reports or Crystal Reports. In the last few years, however, Microsoft has introduced its own server-based report generation software: SQL Server Reporting Services (SSRS). While there are plenty of similarities between SSRS and its competitors, SSRS has at least one glaring advantage over any other game in town; it is free. Well, sort of. It is tightly integrated within the SQL Server infrastructure, and if you have SQL Server installed, you can also have SSRS for free. (The *sort of* part of *free* is that you have to have pay for SQL Server, obviously. But once you do, SSRS is free.)

If you grasp the importance of reporting in a business environment, you can probably see how valuable this technology can be within a SharePoint installation. After all, SharePoint is first and foremost a web portal and, as such, is full of reportable data. Whether the data consists of tasks assigned to employees in a given time span or the number of active discussion boards employees participated in this month, there is plenty of data for any SharePoint installation. But beyond that, it is also fair to state that many organizations that deploy SharePoint have other business data they would like to report within SharePoint. Maybe they have an inventory and sales system used for tracking the ongoing business of their operations. Wouldn't it be great to be able to report this data within SharePoint without having to import the data directly into your SharePoint lists or libraries?

However, integrating SSRS and SharePoint provides some unique challenges and architecture. This book will walk you through these considerations and give you a good idea of how to best use these two technologies to make awe-inspiring reports that will accurately provide the information that decision makers want and will even allow decision makers to easily manipulate the parameters of the reports to meet their needs.

This chapter will start you on your journey by giving you an understanding of exactly what SSRS is and providing an overview of some of the obstacles you will face as you develop reports in your SharePoint environment.

And with that, it's time to get started.

What Is SQL Server Reporting Services (SSRS)?

SQL Server Reporting Services (SSRS) is a server-based reporting platform that allows you to deploy professional-looking and powerful reports fairly easily (once everything is set up). You get the drag-and-drop functionality that you may be familiar with if you have used any version of Visual Studio over the years. You can literally drop a chart onto your report, drag some data fields to the chart, and then deploy the report. You can also do more powerful things such as create pie charts where each pie segment, when clicked, takes the user to a related matrix of data where they can drill down even further to find more detail.

One of the nicer details about SSRS is that it will allow you, as a developer, to access a variety of data sources to feed the report. Of course, since it is a SQL Server product, you can easily tie into your SQL Server database. But beyond that, you can connect to a whole slew of other data objects, as seen in the following table (obtained from `http://msdn.microsoft.com/en-us/library/ms159219.aspx`):

Source of Report Data	Reporting Services Data Source Type	Version of Data Source
SQL Server relational database	Microsoft SQL Server	SQL Server 2008
		SQL Server 2005
		SQL Server 2000
		SQL Server 7.0
SQL Server relational database	OLEDB	SQL Server 2008
		SQL Server 2005
		SQL Server 2000
		SQL Server 7.0
SQL Server relational database	ODBC	SQL Server 2008
		SQL Server 2005
		SQL Server 2000
		SQL Server 7.0
Analysis Services multidimensional database	Microsoft SQL Server Analysis Services	SQL Server 2008 Analysis Services
		SQL Server 2005 Analysis Services
		SQL Server 2000 Analysis Services
Analysis Services multidimensional database	OLEDB	SQL Server 2008 Analysis Services
		SQL Server 2005 Analysis Services
		SQL Server 2000 Analysis Services
XML	XML	XML Web Services or documents
Report Server Model	Report Model	Models can be created from:
		SQL Server 2008
		SQL Server 2005
		SQL Server 2000
		SQL Server 2005 Analysis Services
		Oracle 9.2.0.3 or later
		Teradata v12 and v6.2
SAP multidimensional database	Sap BI NetWeaver	SAP BI NetWeaver 3.5
Hyperion Essbase	Hyperion Essbase	Hyperion Essbase 9.3.0
Oracle relational database	Oracle	Oracle 10g, 9, 8.1.7

(continued)

Source of Report Data	Reporting Services Data Source Type	Version of Data Source
Oracle relational database	Part of OLEDB	Depends on version of MDAC
Teradata relational database	Teradata	Teradata v12
		Teradata v6.20
DB2 relational database	Customized registered data extension name	.
Generic OLEDB data source	OLEDB	Any data source that supports OLEDB
Generic ODBC data source	ODBC	Any data source that supports ODBC

When you see things like "Any data source that supports ODBC," the field is pretty wide open. Any data source that supports ODBC? That is pretty encompassing.

One of the more interesting items on this list is the XML data source. This data source allows you to connect to pretty much any web service out there (given that you have the correct connection information and credentials). So anything not in this list? Well, you can create a web service on your server, grab the data you need, and send it back in a DataTable or DataSource object, and reporting services can read it. That is pretty powerful.

Is SSRS just Microsoft's Version of Crystal Reports?

When looking at SSRS, it is not difficult to begin drawing comparisons to other similar products, especially something like Crystal Reports, if you have ever worked with those technologies in the past. They are very similar, at least as far as they both are tools that allow you to create reports on your business data.

So which is better? Has more features? Is easier to use? That probably depends on who you ask. If you do a Live Search for something like "SSRS versus Crystal Reports," you will find page and page of hits and, depending on what camp the author comes from, the winner will be different on every page. Many people will say Crystal Reports is more powerful; others will argue that SSRS has better handled the primary functions of the reporting interface. Most people will probably say it also depends on how you plan to deploy your reports (web reports or standalone). However, at least in the world of SharePoint, SSRS wins.

For one thing, if you are using SharePoint, you already have access to SSRS. SSRS came as a free add-in for SQL Server 2000 and has been included with both SQL Server 2005 and SQL Server 2008. So, since you are most likely using a SQL Server technology for your data backend for SharePoint, it is a fair bet that you already have SSRS, even if you don't have it set up yet.

Additionally, SSRS has two specific modes that can be installed: Native and SharePoint Integrated Mode. That's right; one of the two SSRS modes that can be installed is specifically targeted toward SharePoint. Installing SSRS in this manner, as you will see in Chapter 2, will give you access to special Web Parts specifically meant to handle SSRS reports. It will also allow you to deploy your reports directly to libraries in your SharePoint site collection (as opposed to deploying them directly to the Reporting Services server).

Finally, another huge advantage is that, if you are a SharePoint developer (or any .NET developer, for that matter), you are already intimately familiar with the SSRS designer, which is called the Business Intelligence Development Studio (BIDS). This is because BIDS is simply an add-on to Visual Studio 2008, and all development work, as such, is done within the Visual Studio application. So when you begin development of your SSRS 2008 reports, you will be designing them within Visual Studio 2008, which you probably are already familiar with. To verify this, you need only to glance at Figure 1-1.

You will get an overview of BIDS, including where to get it and how to install it, in Chapter 4.

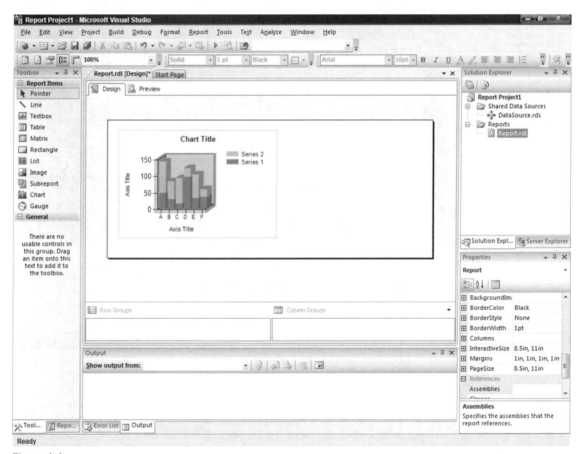

Figure 1-1

It is worth mentioning at this point that there is another option for developing SSRS 2008 reports: the Microsoft SQL Server 2008 Reporting Services Report Builder 2.0. You can download this product from the following location: http://www.microsoft.com/downloads/details.aspx?FamilyID=9f783224-9871-4eea-b1d5-f3140a253db6&displaylang=en. Alternatively, you could just use the following shortened reference to the same URL: http://tinyurl.com/ReportBuilder2-0.

This application, also free, is a standalone report designer that has all of the same features of BIDS in an arguably better Microsoft Word-like format, as can be seen in Figure 1-2.

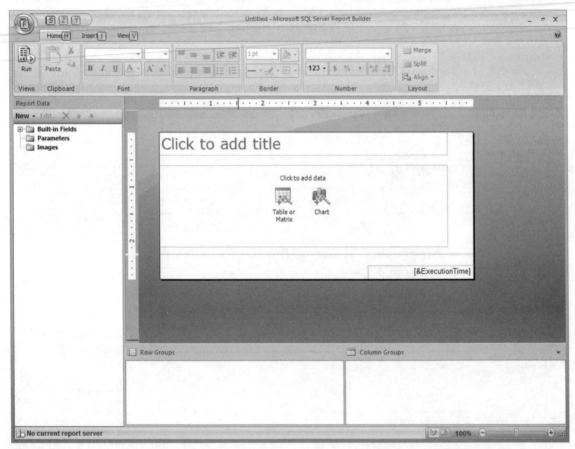

Figure 1-2

While this might be a viable option for your own report development and certainly warrants your own evaluation, it will not be used for this book. Since BIDS is just using the Visual Studio 2008 shell, it will be familiar to a lot of SharePoint developers. And even if you are not a SharePoint developer, there is still a chance you have used Visual Studio in your experience in development. So the interface won't be entirely new. Although Report Builder might work for you, it would be easier to explain BIDS within the

Visual Studio context than it would be to explain an entirely new concept. And if you are already using Visual Studio, you will probably be more comfortable staying there. Thus, it isn't really feasible to show how to create reports generated in both platforms throughout the entire book; using only one platform is more practical, and BIDS wins out. Much of the planning and development you do in BIDS, however, will transfer (knowledge-wise) in your future attempts to use Report Builder if you should so choose.

What Are Some of the New Features of SSRS 2008?

As with any new software release, SSRS 2008 has some very cool new features that appeal not only to the developers who create the reports but to the end users who will use them in their decision-making strategies. These include things like enhanced rendering extensions and graphs for the end user, as well as a simplified development experience with better integration to your current server infrastructure.

A Better User Experience

One of the most discussed new features of SSRS 2008 is the incorporation of Dundas charts bundled as part of the development environment. These include both radial and linear graphs, as well as some pretty neat "slider" charts. You will see a lot more of these charts in later chapters but, to give a small tease, look at a simple dashboard report that can now be easily created using the new Dundas Radial chart as seen in Figure 1-3.

Figure 1-3

While these new charts and graphs are impressive on their own, it is also worth noting that Microsoft has added 3D rendering to all of its previously included charts. For example, in SSRS 2005, you could produce an exploded pie chart similar to the one shown in Figure 1-4.

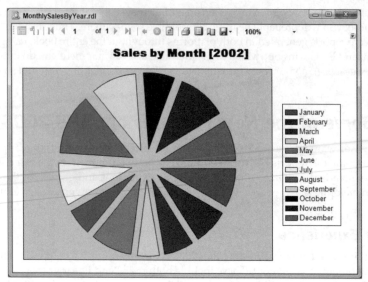

Figure 1-4

However, with the exact same data and with no additional formatting (i.e., using the default settings), you can now also produce a 3D version of the exploded pie chart, shown in Figure 1-5.

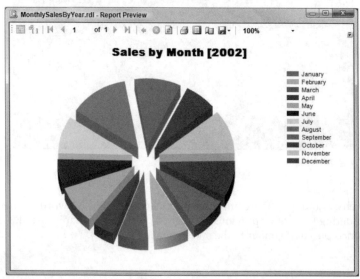

Figure 1-5

While the difference may be hard to see in the black-and-white constraints of this manuscript, it will become very apparent in the charts you create. Along with the Dundas gauges, your reports will have a level of elegance and professionalism not available out of the box in earlier versions.

In addition to all of the enhanced graphs and charts discussed in this section, it is also worth noting that reports can be exported in several different formats. As has been possible since at least the SSRS 2005 release, you can export your report directly from the web version to formats such as PDF, Excel, and CSV. With SSRS 2008, however, you can also export directly to Microsoft Word. This provides a new level of flexibility for generating and distributing your reports to those who need them.

As a final note with regard to a better user experience, users now have better integration with their SharePoint environment for reports deployed in SharePoint integrated mode (you can read more about SharePoint integrated mode in Chapter 2). For example, users can now create data-driven subscriptions for their reports deployed to a SharePoint library.

While there are several other features that directly apply to the end user, the ones highlighted in this section are surely some of the biggest and will get users excited about upgrading to the new SSRS 2008.

A Simplified Development Experience

While there are several new developer enhancements in SSRS 2008, the biggest one is probably the fact that SSRS no longer requires Internet Information Services (IIS) to run. And yet, even with this being true, none of the functionality of previous versions has been lost. This is done through the use of native support for HTTP.SYS and ASP.NET; URL management for site and virtual directory names; a new authentication layer; and health monitoring through new memory-management features. This is a pretty impressive change in the architecture of SSRS and will get a lot of developers buzzing.

Perhaps the most exciting part of diving into the developer experience in SSRS 2008 for the first time is that once you get started you will feel at home, especially if you are used to creating web applications using .NET technologies. If you are used to creating your web application pages in Visual Studio, guess what? You will be creating your reports in Visual Studio. If you are used to modeling your data backend in SQL Server, you can still do that, too. Maybe you are used to accessing web services to mash up data to display on your pages. You have the power to do that in SSRS as well.

While this is still going to be a little intangible this early in the book, if you have done web application development using tools like Visual Studio and SQL Management Studio, you will find yourself thinking "hey, I've done something very similar to this in the past," or "this is much easier than I thought it would be," several times as you read the following chapters.

However, at the same time, you will be able to tap into a power that you generally don't get in your other applications. You will have a fairly easy way to create eye-catching graphical interfaces that pretty much all management loves to see. You will be able to take your data and, rather than just report it, you can showcase it. You will find how easy it is to create dazzling reports with simple drag-and-drop controls and intuitive designers. You will take what is familiar and go with it to a new and exciting place.

While the end users will get a lot out of the reports and the managers will certainly enjoy the end product, the development experience will be one that is familiar and, hopefully, a lot of fun to work with.

SSRS Deployment

While this will be covered in much more detail later in this book, deployment warrants at least a mention in this introductory chapter, as it is a crucial part of the reporting process. After all, if your users can't get to the reports, what value do they have?

When SSRS is set up in SharePoint integrated mode (see Chapter 2), a couple of things happen. First, you actually deploy your reports and their related data sources directly to SharePoint libraries hosted in your target site collection. This means that, at any given time, you can navigate to your site, find your reports library, and see a listing of the currently deployed reports. You can even run the reports directly from the library simply by clicking them.

Another thing that happens is that you get new Web Parts installed on your server that will be available to all site collections that utilize SSRS. These Web Parts will allow you to set up a report to be hosted directly on any page within your site collection. This way, the reports will look as though they are a seamless part of your existing page, as shown in Figure 1-6.

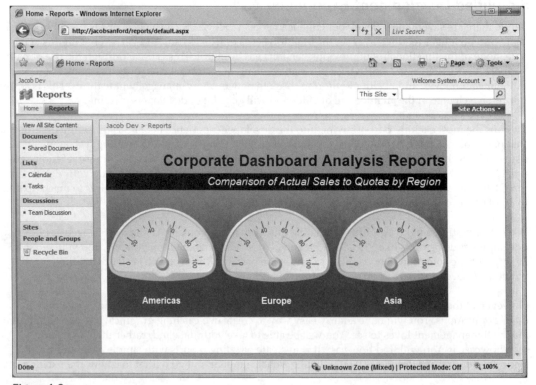

Figure 1-6

Summary

This chapter has provided a basic overview of SSRS and the new features available in SSRS 2008. You have seen the basic development tools available to create new reports and some of the enhancements to the user and development experience that make SSRS 2008 much better than any of its predecessors. You have also been given a brief glimpse of how your reports integrate with your SharePoint installation and how your reports will look and feel once deployed to your site collection.

This chapter was meant to provide an SSRS 2008 and SharePoint integration. It was meant to foreshadow a bit for future chapters and to offer at least a cursory understanding of SSRS so that subsequent chapters will be more accessible. And with that it is time to get to the fun stuff: making reports.

2

Setting up SQL Server Reporting Services for SharePoint 2007

This chapter mainly details how you can install SQL Server Reporting Services in SharePoint integrated mode. The chapter starts with the benefits of SharePoint integrated mode and dives into the steps you must take before installing SQL Server Reporting Services in SharePoint integrated mode. The chapter also features a step-by-step installation guide with screenshots that will provide guidance for your installation.

Let's start the installation process by answering a big question: Why SharePoint integrated mode?

Why SharePoint Integrated Mode?

When you have SharePoint in your organization, this is one of the main questions you will find yourself trying to answer. The short answer is that it's easier to maintain, easier to secure, and easier to access reports when you already have a SharePoint installation.

Microsoft first introduced SharePoint integrated mode capabilities with SQL Server 2005 SP2. Before integrated mode was available, there was partial integration provided by two web parts: Report Viewer and Report Explorer. Although these web parts offered an easy way to display SQL Server reports within SharePoint, this was not a full integration of technologies. In reality, the major components of both SharePoint and SQL Server Reporting Services, such as security and storage, were not integrated. SharePoint and SSRS handled their storage needs separately by having distinct databases for storage. Security was another component handled separately on both SharePoint and SSRS, so the web parts just provided a window to the report server, not true integration.

With SharePoint integrated mode, users gain several benefits. The following sections detail some of the key features of the integration.

❑ **Integrated storage:** With SharePoint integrated mode, administrators can manage, secure, and deliver reports to end users using SharePoint. Reports, data models, and data sources are all stored in a document library that enables users to go to one place to get data. You no longer need to send users one URL for project workspaces and another URL for project reports. Since integrated mode provides seamless access to the reports through a SharePoint site, you also get full SharePoint functionality such as check-in, check-out, versioning, alerts, and workflow. Although storage is integrated for files, the report server still maintains its own database for reporting capabilities. Files are stored in SharePoint document libraries, but report metadata such as schedules, cache, and subscriptions are stored only in the report server database. When a user requests a report, data model, or data source in SharePoint, data is synchronized to the report server database by reporting services.

❑ **The report viewer web part:** The new report viewer web part, which is enabled once the reporting services add-in is installed on the SharePoint server, supports the consumer interfaces of SharePoint. The web part can get data from filter web parts or can connect to other SharePoint web parts that can provide data to be consumed by the report viewer web part.

❑ **Integrated security:** Reporting Services provides security by mapping to SharePoint permissions defined in the SharePoint web application. Administrators can easily provide security to their reports by using the existing SharePoint security groups and security defined by the existing governance.

While we gain several new advantages through these features when using integrated mode, not all SharePoint features are available for report document files hosted in SharePoint integrated mode. For example, Reporting Services integrated mode does not support web applications that use Anonymous access. Personalization is also a feature that is not supported for report document files in integrated mode. This is explained further in "Features Supported by Reporting Services in SharePoint Integrated Mode" at http://technet.microsoft.com/en-us/library/bb326290.aspx.

To summarize, having true integration between SharePoint and SSRS allows administrators to easily maintain technologies and end users to access the data they need without having to use several applications.

Planning for SharePoint Integration

Before installing Reporting Services, you must plan for a successful deployment. Let's say that you've sold your internal management team on the benefits of having report server installed in SharePoint integrated mode, and they loved it and gave you the green light. You will next find yourself needing to answer questions such as:

❑ What are the requirements for Reporting Services?

❑ What servers will you install Reporting Services on?

- ❏   Will it work with the current SQL server?

- ❏   Will installing it on the existing SQL server bring down the performance?

- ❏   Can you create a standalone server just for Reporting Services?

- ❏   Better yet, do you need another server?

- ❏   What are the hardware requirements?

Where do you start? Not knowing where to start and what to do could result in an environment that might not be suitable for you. To answer these questions you need have a good grasp of the following topics:

- ❏   How integration works

- ❏   Deployment topologies

- ❏   Requirements for SharePoint integration

The following sections will give you a high level understanding of how SharePoint integrated mode works, what deployment topologies are out there, and the requirements for deploying SharePoint integrated mode to guide you during your planning phase.

How Integration Works

While planning for Reporting Services SharePoint integrated mode, knowing how SharePoint integrated mode works will help you. Once you understand all of the required components that make up the integrated mode, you will need to make some decisions about your physical architecture. But to determine what you need on the hardware side, you should first consider how the integration works so you know what you're dealing with.

At a high level, the integration between the Reporting Services and SharePoint is done through two components:

- ❏   Reporting Services add-in for SharePoint technologies

- ❏   Report Server Web Service

The Reporting Services Add-In is installed to your SharePoint farm and brings several key components needed for the integration to your SharePoint environment. The Report Server Web Service sits on the report server and allows the report server to talk to SharePoint as shown in Figure 2-1.

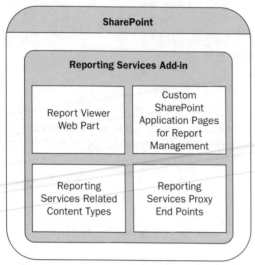
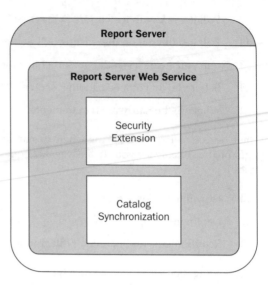

Figure 2-1

Now look at what these components provide to integration. On the report server, there is the Report Server Web Service, which comprises a big part of the integration. The report server also has custom security and delivery extensions. The Reporting Services Add-In for SharePoint provides four key components when deployed to a SharePoint environment:

❑   **Report Viewer Web Part:** The add-in, once installed on the SharePoint web front end server, provides a Report View web part. This web part allows SharePoint users to display reports on their sites using the web part technology.

❑   **Reporting Services Related Content Types:** Along with the web part, the reporting services add-in also includes the following new content types for SharePoint: Report Definition file (.rdl), Report Model (.smdl), and Shared Data Source (.rsds)

❑   **Custom Application Pages:** The custom application pages allow you to manage reports in SharePoint. These pages are hosted under the SharePoint 12 hive located at `[DriveLetter]:\Program Files\Common Files\microsoft shared\Web Server Extensions\12\TEMPLATE\LAYOUTS\ReportServer`. Just like all of the other SharePoint application pages, the report server application pages are available to all sites via the /_layouts/ReportServer folder. There are more than 20 application pages that come with the add-in. A few of the application pages that help you manage reports include:

   ❑   DataDrivenSubscriptionWizard.aspx

   ❑   RSViewerPage.aspx

   ❑   ScheduleProperties.aspx

❑   **Reporting Services Proxy End Points:** The final key component that is deployed to SharePoint with the add-in is the report server proxy endpoints. These endpoints will allow you to develop reporting solutions that are integrated with SharePoint. Similar to the custom application pages, the endpoints are also deployed to the 12 hive, but this time they are under the ISAPI folder with all of the other web services: `[Drive letter]:\Program Files\Common Files\ microsoft shared\Web Server Extensions\12\ISAPI\ReportServer`. Similar to the application pages, using the SharePoint technology, the endpoints are available to all sites via the /_vti_bin/ReportServer folder. The end points that get installed with the reporting services add-in are as follows:

- ❏ **ReportExecution2005.asmx:** Provides the APIs for execution and navigation of reports.

- ❏ **ReportService2006.asmx:** Provides the APIs for managing a report server that is configured for SharePoint integrate mode. You can get more information on this endpoint at `http://msdn.microsoft.com/en-us/library/reportservice2006.aspx`.

- ❏ **ReportServiceAuthentication.asmx:** Provides the APIs for authenticating users against a report server when the SharePoint Web Application is configured for Forms Authentication.

❏ There are two databases that hold the report information: the SharePoint content database and the report database. The SharePoint content database is where the report files are saved. Information such as the subscriptions and schedules are saved on the report server database. The report server communicates with the SharePoint server using the WSS object model.

Deployment Topologies for SharePoint Integration

To determine the best topology for your environment, it's always good to know how other people are deploying SharePoint integrated mode. You don't want to reinvent the wheel, right? What you would want to know is what's out there and what the downsides and advantages of each method (topology) are. As you learn more about each topology you will be able to determine which topology fits your needs the most.

Every organization has different requirements, which makes each environment unique. But at a high level when you look at most of the environments that have deployed report server in SharePoint integrated mode, you'll see that they fall within one of the following three main deployment topologies.

- ❏ **Standalone Server Deployment:** All components run on a single server.
- ❏ **Distributed Server Deployment:** Several servers host different components.
- ❏ **Scalable Deployment:** Components on different servers and multiple servers host the same component.

Standalone Server Deployments

In this topology, all components are running on a single server, as shown in Figure 2-2. This is not the way to go when you are going to use this for production. If you're at a point where you are looking into reporting services and your SharePoint and SQL server share a server, you are ready for a new server. This is typically used for proof of concepts or as development servers by most organizations.

- ❏ **Pros:** Very easy to install and get running.
- ❏ **Cons:** Single point of failure. All components running on one machine would result in performance issues.

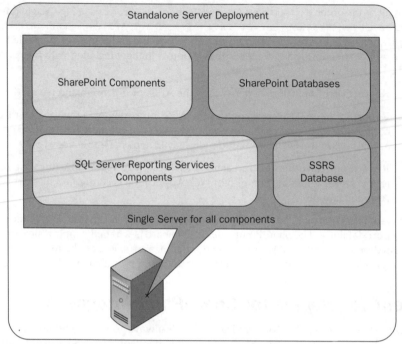

Figure 2-2

Distributed Server Deployments

In this topology several servers host different components. This is the deployment topology most organizations use when deploying SSRS in SharePoint integrated mode. As this deployment model can have several servers, the possibilities are endless. In this section, we detail the most common two scenarios: the two-server topology and the three-server topology.

The Two-Server Scenario

In this scenario, one server hosts the SharePoint components, and the second server is the database server that hosts the SharePoint database, the SSRS database, and the Reporting Services Components, as shown in Figure 2-3. Because of installation requirements, the database server is also configured as a SharePoint web front end and is joined to the farm.

This approach is the next step up from the one server approach. It performs much better and is the topology that should be used at a minimum when it's used for a production deployment. With the two server approach, although you install SharePoint on the database machine, SharePoint will not use that server for anything since you will not install or run any services on the database machine. Reporting services only needs the SharePoint bits on the machine so that it can use the SharePoint object model to access the reports that are hosted in SharePoint sites.

By separating the two layers and giving them their own resources, we have improved performance greatly. We have one server doing SharePoint-related work and the other server is doing database-related work. This is the minimum required setup if you are going to use reporting services in production.

- ❏ **Pros:** Better performance. SharePoint and database layers are separated.

- ❏ **Cons:** Need more hardware compared to the one server approach. Potentially more SharePoint licensing.

Licensing can be a tricky topic and this topic is out of this book's scope. We strongly encourage you talk to your licensing specialist who will guide you through the licensing process.

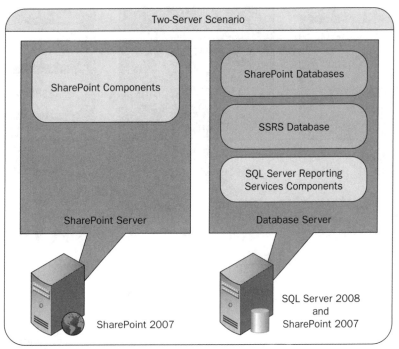

Figure 2-3

The Three-Server Scenario

With the three server approach, report server will get its own server. In this scenario, one server hosts the SharePoint components, one server hosts SSRS, and the last server hosts the database engine, as shown in Figure 2-4. The second server, which hosts SSRS, is also configured as a SharePoint web front end and is joined to the farm. This approach is used when you do not want to install SharePoint bits on the SQL server. This way SharePoint will only be installed on the machine that hosts the SQL Reporting Services components.

Another scenario for the three server approach is when you want to have SSRS 2008 and yet SharePoint is hosted on SQL 2005. With the three servers in hang, the third machine will have SQL 2008 and SSRS installed on it, which would be the report server machine for SharePoint. The three server approach allows you to have a mixed environment when you don't want to upgrade the existing SQL 2005 instance.

❑ **Pros:** The report server gets its own machine, allowing for better performance. Can be used for mixed environments.

❑ **Cons:** Need more hardware compared to the two server approach. Potentially more SharePoint licensing.

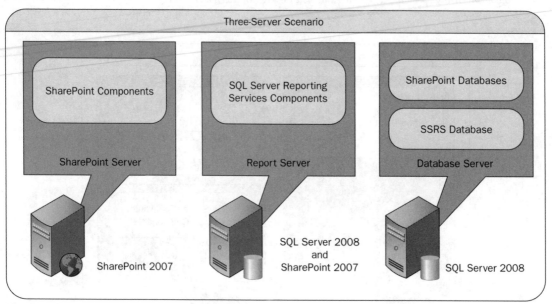

Figure 2-4

Scalable Server Deployments

In this topology, several servers host different components. This is the deployment topology that you must use when thousands of users need access to reports on a SharePoint site. In this type of deployment, for the report server you can have two or more report servers that share a single report server database. And for the SharePoint server you can have several servers hosting SharePoint components. For example, a SharePoint farm can have two web front ends and one application server for a total of three servers. Finally, the database server can also have a mirrored or clustered setup where you would have at a minimum two database servers.

Requirements for SharePoint Integration

Now that we have covered the topologies, we are ready to review the installation requirements before we start installation.

❑ **Report Server Requirements:** The server hosting the report server must have SharePoint installed, and the server must be joined to the SharePoint farm that will host the reports. The report server can be installed before or after SharePoint is installed. Reporting Services in SharePoint integrated mode cannot be installed in the SQL Server Express edition.

❑ **SharePoint Server Requirements:** Reporting Services in SharePoint integrated mode can be installed with Windows SharePoint Services 3.0 or MOSS 2007 Standard or Enterprise editions. The Reporting Services add-in must be installed on each web front end, and the web front end servers must have at least 2GBs of RAM. Reports cannot be hosted on a SharePoint site that is set for anonymous access.

❑ **Database Server Requirements:** Reporting Services in SharePoint integrated mode cannot use the SQL Express Edition or the embedded edition installed with WSS as its database. The Reporting Services Add-in requires that the report server is hosted on SQL Server 2008.

These requirements apply to all approaches. Some of the approaches can easily accommodate these requirements compared to others, but overall it doesn't matter if you have a single server or a multiple server deployment plan. In all cases you will need to make sure you've met the above requirements in your environment. More information on the requirements can be found at http://msdn.microsoft .com/en-us/library/bb283190.aspx.

Installing Reporting Services in SharePoint Integrated Mode

As detailed earlier in this chapter in the "Deployment Topologies for SharePoint Integration" section, Reporting Services can be installed either on a standalone server or on multiple servers. The recommended SharePoint deployment approach for most organizations will at a minimum have two servers, where one server is used for SharePoint and the other server is for the database server. Therefore, in this section, we will detail the steps to install Reporting Services in SharePoint integrated mode on multiple servers, assuming that you have SharePoint already deployed at your organization.

Assuming that we have two servers, the following sections detail the steps to install reporting services in SharePoint integrated mode.

The installation process includes the following steps:

1. Install Reporting Services on SQL Server 2008.

2. Configure Reporting Services using the configuration wizard.

3. Install SharePoint on the report server.

4. Install the Reporting Services Add-in for SharePoint.

5. Activate Reporting Services Integration Services Feature.

6. Configure Report server integration on SharePoint Central Administration.

We'll start by looking at the first two steps in more depth.

Installing and Configuring Reporting Services for SharePoint Integration

When SQL is initially installed, you can choose not to install Reporting Services; install it using the files-only option, or install it using the default configuration for SharePoint integrated mode.

In this section, we will assume that Reporting Services was never installed, but please note that even if you have an existing Reporting Services installation, you can change it to be SharePoint integrated using the Reporting Services Configuration Tool.

As you have one database server in the SharePoint farm, you will install Reporting Services to the SQL server that is the database server of the farm. To install Reporting Services, connect to the SQL server using the remote desktop. Because you are going to install reporting services from scratch, in this example you will need to start the SQL installation. Once you're connected to your SQL server, you will need to start the SQL installation by inserting the SQL 2008 Installation CD on the SQL server.

Initiating the Installation

Once the installation CD is inserted and the installation wizard starts, follow these steps to initiate the installation:

1. Click the New SQL Server stand-alone installation or add features to an existing installation option, as shown in Figure 2-5.

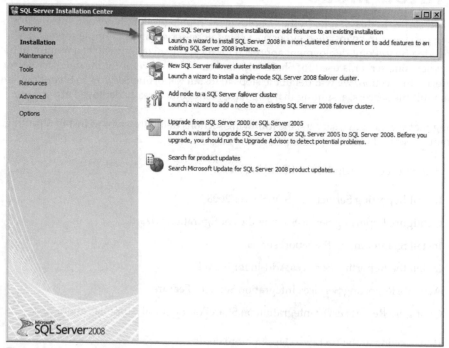

Figure 2-5

2. Click OK once the Setup Support Rules screen states the Operation has completed.

3. On the Setup Support Files screen, click Install to initiate the installation.

When the installation process finishes instantiation, you should return to the Setup Support Rules screen.

Installing Reporting Services on the SQL Server

Now that we have initiated the installation process, we will continue to install Reporting Services on the SQL Server. There are 11 steps in the installation process. In this section we will walk through these installation steps.

1. On the Setup Support Rules screen, wait until all of the rules are checked. Once all of the rules pass, click Next, as shown in Figure 2-6. In this installation there are two warnings: The first warns us that the server is running as a domain controller, and the other is the firewall warning. If you receive any errors, click the status and read a detailed report that explains the actions you must take to fix the issue. You can rerun the rules. Once all failures are fixed and there are no more failures, the Next button will be enabled.

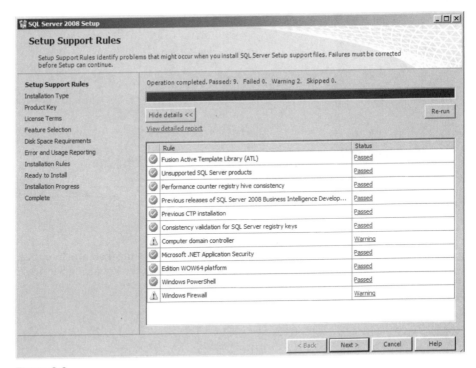

Figure 2-6

2. On the Installation Type screen, we can either perform a new installation of SQL Server 2008 or add features to an existing instance. To install Reporting Services to an existing SQL instance, select the "Add features to an existing instance of SQL Server 2008" radio button. Once the radio button is selected, you will also select the SQL Server 2008 instance you wish to add the feature to using the drop-down, as shown in Figure 2-7. In our example, we will select the default instance named MSSQLSERVER and click Next to continue.

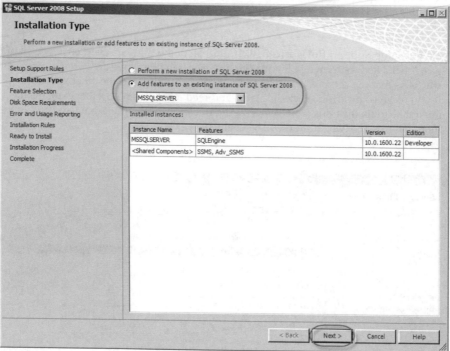

Figure 2-7

3. The next step is to select the feature we want to add to the existing instance. In our case, we will add the Reporting Services. To accomplish this, we will check the Reporting Services checkbox on the Feature Selection screen and click Next, as shown in Figure 2-8.

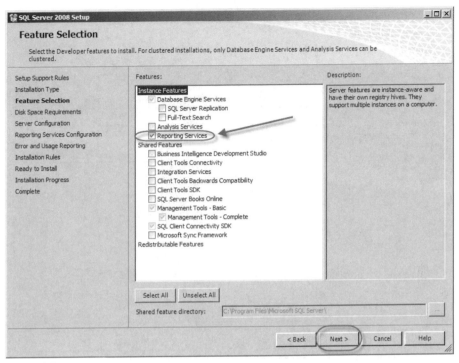

Figure 2-8

4. On the Disk Space Requirements screen, you will verify that the disk space is sufficient. When ready, click Next.

5. On the Server Configuration screen, type the account information you wish to have Reporting Services use and click Next, as shown in Figure 2-9. It is recommended that you create a service account for Reporting Services to run the service (for instance, YourDomain\ReportServiceAcnt).

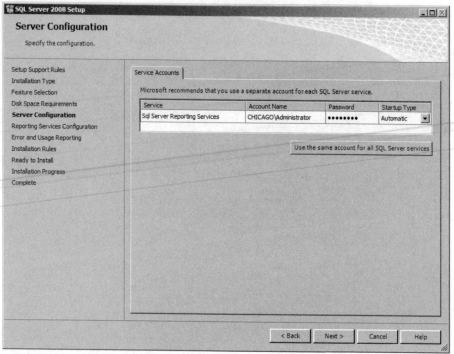

Figure 2-9

6. On the Reporting Services Configuration screen, select Install, but do not configure the report server option and click Next. This option will allow us to configure the report server using the Reporting Services Configuration Manager.

7. On the Error and Usage Reporting screen, check the checkboxes that apply and click Next.

8. Wait until the Installation Rules screen completes; then click Next.

9. On the Ready to Install screen, verify the SQL Server 2008 features to be installed and click Install, as shown in Figure 2-10.

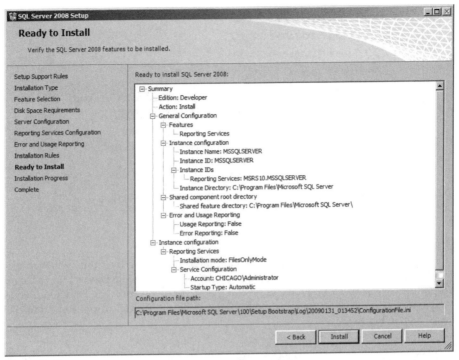

Figure 2-10

10. On the Installation Progress screen, wait until the installation completes. Once the installation is complete, click Next.

11. On the Complete screen, click Close to complete your installation.

Configuring Reporting Services on the SQL Server

As you remember from step 6 of the installation process, we select Install, but do not configure the report server option and click Next. At this point, since Reporting Services is installed but not configured, we will use the Reporting Services Configuration Manager. The next section details the steps that configure the report server.

1. The Reporting Services Configuration Manager is located under All Programs ⇨ Microsoft SQL Server 2008 ⇨ Configuration Tools, as shown in Figure 2-11.

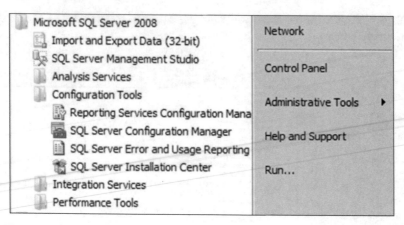

Figure 2-11

2. Once you click the Reporting Services Configuration Manager, the utility will start up and wait for you to select the server and report server instance you wish to connect to. To list all of the report server instances, you have to type in the server name and click Find. Once you see the report server instance you wish to configure, select it from the drop-down and click Connect, as shown in Figure 2-12.

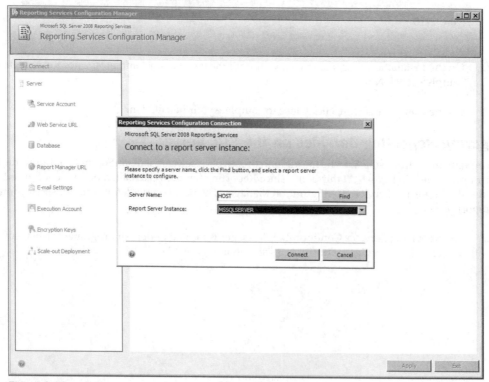

Figure 2-12

3. Once you are connected to the report server instance, you will be directed to the Report Server Status screen. This screen only allows you to start and stop the SQL Reporting Services Service.

This is the first screen that you will see when you connect to the report server. Note that all of the other settings are also accessible through the left hand menu on the configuration manager. In the following sections we will click on the relevant corresponding menu item on the left to see its settings.

The Service Account Screen

The next screen in the configuration manager is the Service Account screen. To see this screen click on the Service Account menu item that is listed at the left of the configuration manager. On this screen, you can view or set the account that Reporting Services windows will run under, as shown in Figure 2-13. This is the account you entered in step 5 of the installation process, as shown in Figure 2-9.

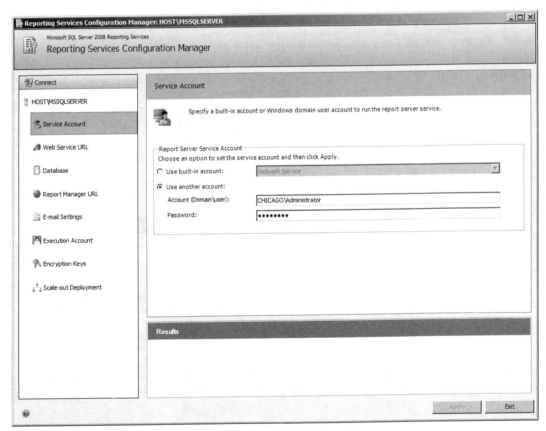

Figure 2-13

The Web Service URL Screen

The next screen is the Web Service URL screen. On this screen, you are able to view or set the Web Service URL used by the Reporting Services web service. This screen also allows you to select the port and SSL information for the web application. In this case, we accept the default and click Apply, as shown in Figure 2-14.

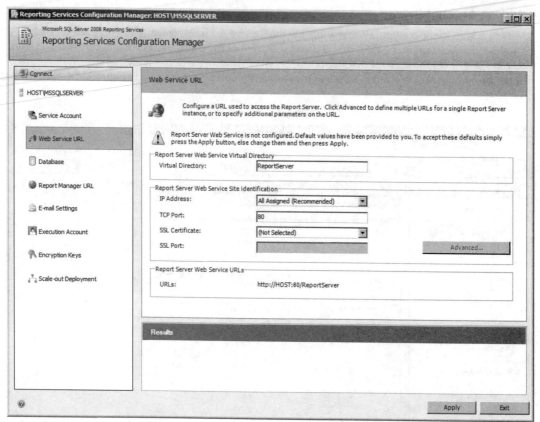

Figure 2-14

Once you click the Apply button, you will see the results in the results section. The configuration manager creates a virtual directory named ReportServer and reserves the URL, as shown in Figure 2-15.

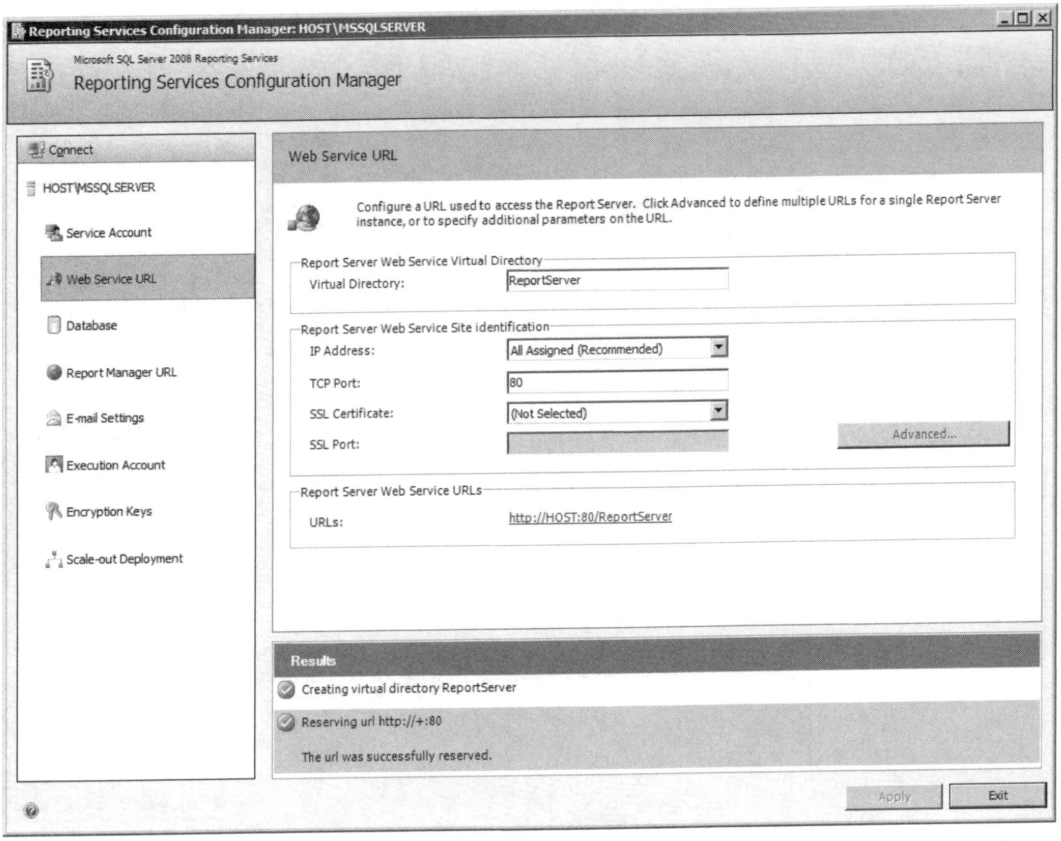

Figure 2-15

The Database Screen

The next step is to configure the database. Click the next screen to continue your configuration. On the Database screen, you have the option to create or change a database. By default, this page will be empty.

1. To start the configuration, click the Change Database button, as shown in Figure 2-16.

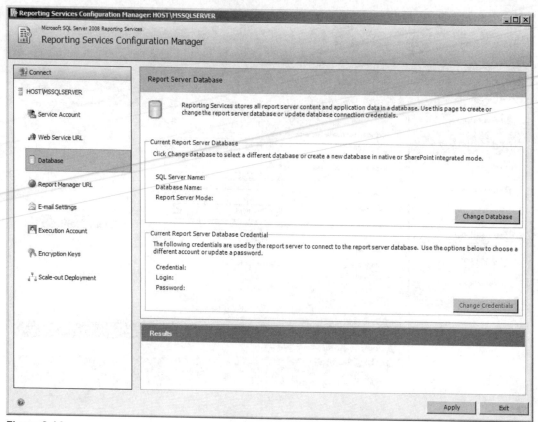

Figure 2-16

2. Once you click the Change Database button, you will see a new wizard that allows you to create a database. On the screen that appears, you can create a new database or select an existing report server database. To create a new database, select the Create a new report server database option and click Next, as shown in Figure 2-17.

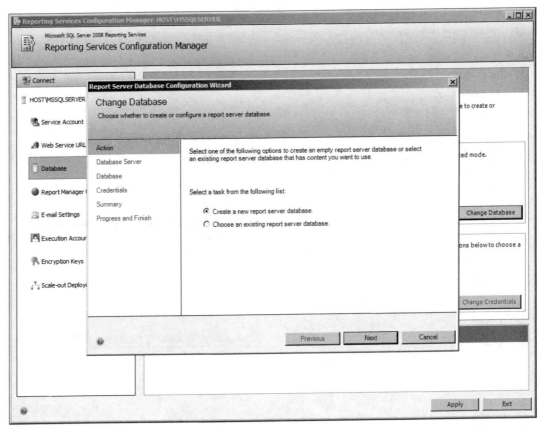

Figure 2-17

3. On the next screen, select the SQL Server Database engine and specify credentials that have permission to connect to that server. While doing the configuration, being logged in to the server with an account that has access to the database server is beneficial. In this scenario, you are logged in as the administrator, so choose Current User – Integrated Security for the Authentication Type, as shown in Figure 2-18, and click Next.

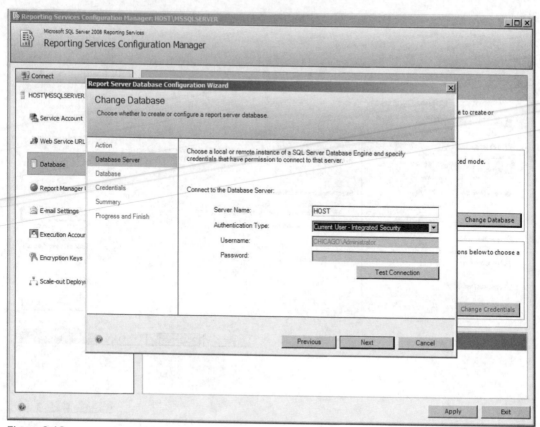

Figure 2-18

4. This is the screen where you select the SharePoint integrated mode. In this screen, you enter a name for the database, select a language, and finally select the report server mode. For the database name, enter something easy to identify. In this scenario, you will use the default name ReportServer. Once you select your language, select SharePoint Integrated Mode under the Report Server Mode option and click Next, as shown in Figure 2-19.

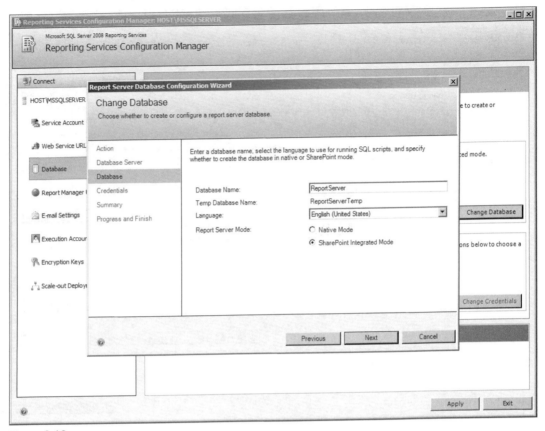

Figure 2-19

5. For the Authentication Type, select the Service Credentials option and click Next.

6. On the Summary screen, verify that the information is correct and click Next, as shown in Figure 2-20.

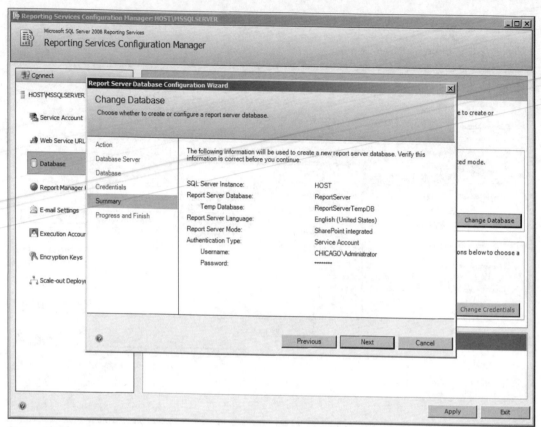

Figure 2-20

7. Wait until the configuration of the database is complete. Then click the Finish button.

8. After you create the database you will be redirected to the Report Server Database screen. You can click on the Change Database button and go through the steps to either create a new database or modify the existing one. You can also update the credentials after your database is created using the Change Credentials button without needing to create a new database. For this example, this isn't necessary. Click Apply, as shown in Figure 2-21. The configuration wizard will grant access rights to report server accounts and set the connection information.

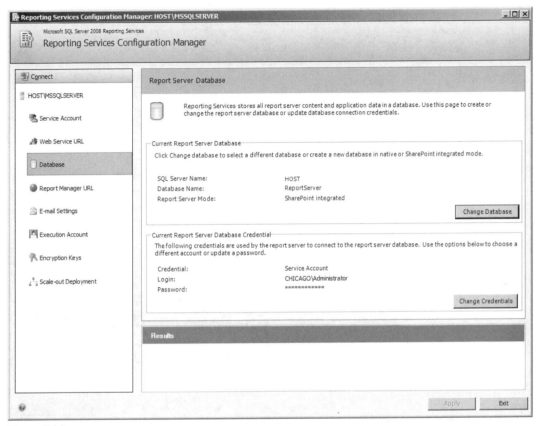

Figure 2-21

The Report Manager URL Screen

At this point, you're half way through the configuration and your next step is to create the virtual directory that will host your report server web site. To continue with the configuration, click the Report Manager URL section on the left menu.

On the Report Manager URL screen, enter the name of the Virtual Directory and click Apply, as shown in Figure 2-22. In this case, you use the default name Reports for your Virtual Directory.

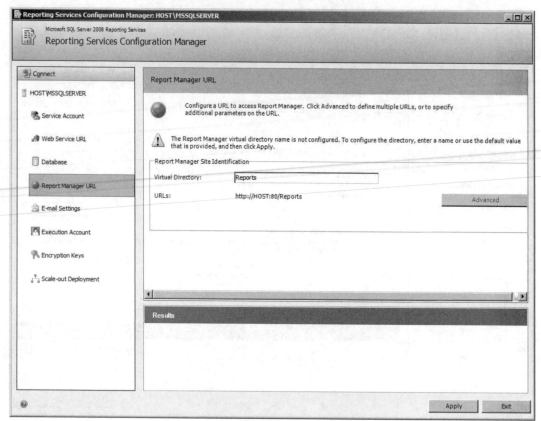

Figure 2-22

As you click Apply, the configuration wizard will create the virtual directory and reserve the URL for the report manager website, as shown in Figure 2-23.

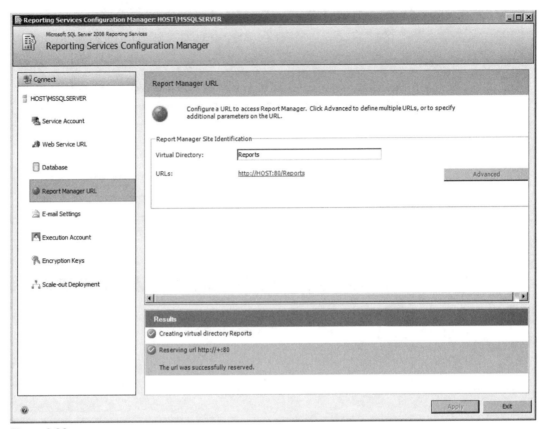

Figure 2-23

The Email Settings Screen

The email settings for the report server allow users to subscribe to reports via email. When you enter the information for email settings, users will be able to subscribe to reports and receive reports via email.

On this screen, you enter the name of the SMTP server, as shown in Figure 2-24. You can also enter an email for the Sender Address, the address from which users receive email.

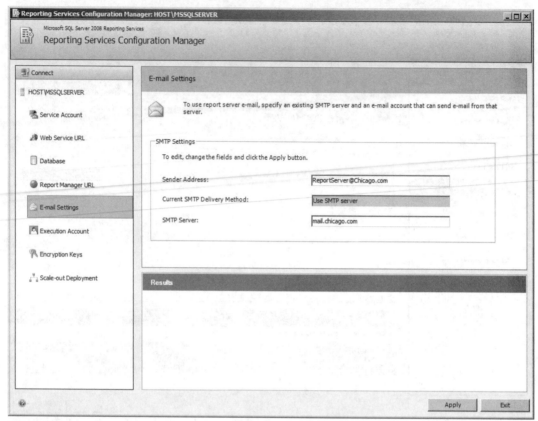

Figure 2-24

Once you enter the SMTP server and the sender email information, click Apply. When you click Apply, the configuration wizard will apply the sender email settings to the report server.

The Execution Account Screen

This screen allows you to configure the user account that Reporting Services will use when it needs to access a file. If you don't have the need to access files such as images in your reports, you do not need to setup this account. In this case, you use the default administrator account.

When adding an account, make sure it is a domain account and does not have network administration rights. Read-only rights to the files are sufficient for the execution account. Once you have entered the account information, click the **Apply** button. You will then receive an update on the results pane, letting you know that the execution account has been set, as shown in Figure 2-25.

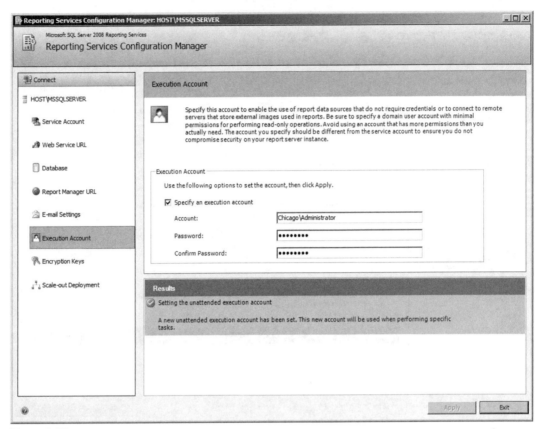

Figure 2-25

The Encryption Keys Screen

All sensitive data such as the account login and password information and shared data sources are encrypted with report server. Report server uses the encryption key to decrypt and encrypt this information, and this key is created as a part of the report server installation.

On the Encryption Key screen, you can back up the encryption key to avoid situations where you have a corrupt key. Since report server heavily relies on the encryption key, it will become inoperable if there is no encryption key, and making a backup of the key can help you bring back report server from the dead in these situations. The Backup button will allow you to make a backup of the key, and the Restore button will allow you to restore the backed-up key in a situation where you might have a corrupt key. The Change button will allow you to create a new key if you feel that the existing key has been compromised.

If you do not have a backup and your key is corrupt, you can use the Delete button in the Delete Encrypted Content section, as shown in Figure 2-26. Once you delete the encrypted information, you must go back and provide all of the credentials to the report configuration wizard. Until you reset all of the credentials, report server will not be able to serve reports for your environment.

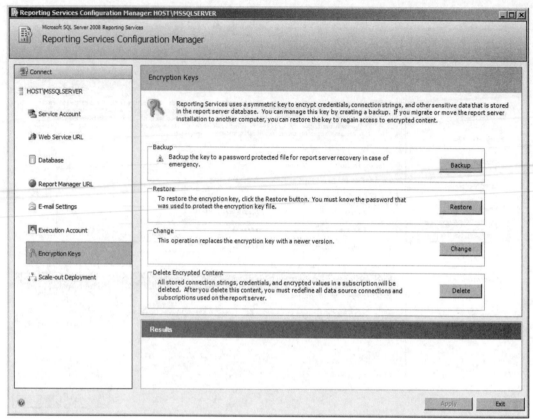

Figure 2-26

To make a backup, click the Backup button and select the file location where you wish to save the backup key on your server. Enter the password to protect your key and click OK.

The Scale-out Deployment Screen

The Scale-out Deployment screen allows users to add report servers to the existing deployment, as shown in Figure 2-27. All servers share the encrypted data. This way, the data can be encrypted or decrypted by any report server in the scale-out deployment.

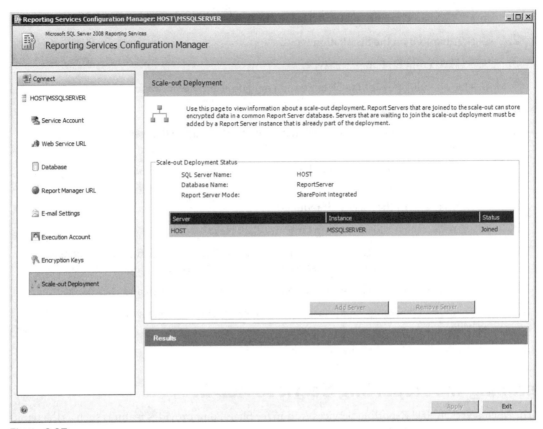

Figure 2-27

Installing a SharePoint Web Front-end on a Report Server Computer

At this point, you must install SharePoint on the SQL Server, as Reporting Services needs to access the SharePoint API in order to host reports in SharePoint integrated mode.

If your SharePoint farm uses WSS 3.0, you must install WSS 3.0 on the report server. If it uses MOSS 2007, you must install MOSS 2007, as all servers must have the same version of SharePoint on them.

You must be logged in as a SharePoint administrator to the report server in order to install SharePoint, and after SharePoint is installed and the server is joined to the farm, you must turn off the report server as a web front-end using SharePoint 3.0 Central Administration.

The following steps are only required for multiserver farms and will install SharePoint on the report server and detail how to add the server to the farm.

1. Insert the SharePoint installation CD and Run SharePoint setup on the report server.

2. Click Advanced on the installation types.

3. Select Web Front End on server type.

4. Use the default value for the Data location or choose another location.

5. Click Install Now.

6. Once the Setup is complete, the next thing you do is configure the web front-end to join it to the farm.

7. Once installation is complete, run the SharePoint Products and Technologies Configuration Wizard and click Next on the welcome screen.

8. Click Yes to restart the services if required.

9. Select Yes to connect to an existing farm and click **Next**.

10. Specify the SQL Server Database instance where the SharePoint configuration database is hosted; then click Retrieve Database Names and select the configuration database.

11. Enter the username and password to connect the server to the farm and click Next.

12. Click Advanced Settings on the last screen and select Do not use this machine to host the website.

13. Click OK, click Next, and then finish the wizard.

Installing the Reporting Services Add-in

The Microsoft SQL 2008 Reporting Services Add-in for SharePoint provides features such as the report viewer web part, application pages to manage reports, and other report server content on a SharePoint site. This add-in is required for the SharePoint integrated mode.

> *If your SharePoint farm includes more than one front-end, this add-in must be installed on all web front-end servers.*

In order to install the Reporting Services Add-in on the SharePoint server, you must log in as the SharePoint Administrator and use the following steps.

1. Locate rsSharePoint.msi on your setup CD by navigating to [Drive Letter]:\x86\Setup and double-click it to start the installation, as shown in Figure 2-28.

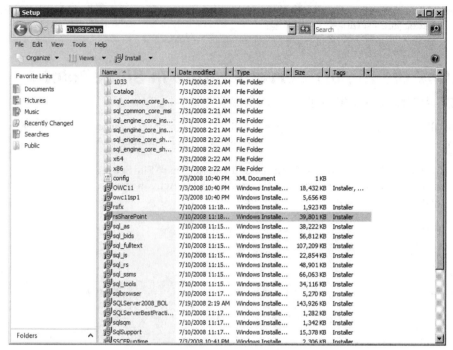

Figure 2-28

Please note that if you have a 64-bit machine, you will navigate to [Drive Letter]:\x64\Setup.

2. Once the wizard starts, click Next on the welcome screen.

3. Accept the license agreement and click Next.

4. Enter the Registration Information and click Next.

5. On the Ready to Install the Program, screen click Install.

6. Once you click Install, the installation will quickly start to copy files and deploy assemblies. This might take several minutes.

Please note that once the installation reaches the status of "Removing backup files," it does take several minutes before it completes the installation. Some installations might take up to 30 minutes to complete this screen. Please be patient while the installation is completing.

7. Once the installation completes, click the Finish button to complete the setup.

Installing the Reporting Services add-in is the first step to integrating SharePoint with Report Server. By installing the Reporting Services add-in, you've completed a major part of the integration, but there are two other steps you need to perform to complete the SharePoint integration with the Report Server.

After you install Reporting Services, you then need to activate the Report Server feature and configure the settings for the integration. After the Reporting Services add-in is installed, a new feature is deployed to SharePoint. In the following sections you will see how to activate this feature, after which a new configuration section will appear in the Central Administration. Then you will see how to configure the SharePoint integration settings.

Activating the Report Server Feature in SharePoint Central Administration

After installing the add-in, your next step is to activate the report server integration feature, which will enable you to configure the report server integration in SharePoint Central Administration.

1. To activate the report server feature, go to Site Actions ⇨ Site Settings ⇨ Site Collection Features on the SharePoint Central Administration. Click the Activate button next to the Report Server Integration Feature, as shown in Figure 2-29.

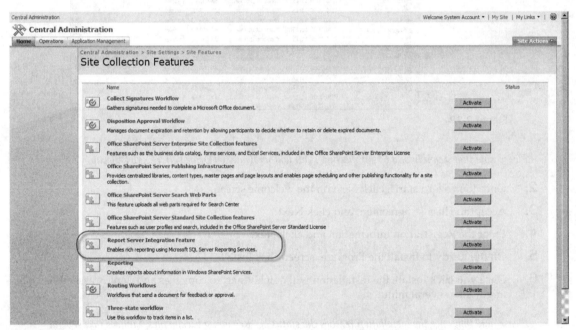

Figure 2-29

2. After clicking Activate, verify that the report server integration feature is Active, as shown in Figure 2-30.

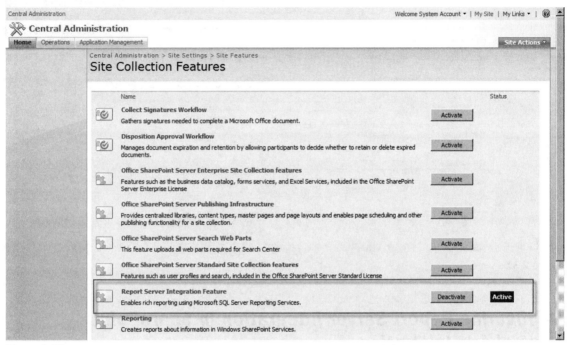

Figure 2-30

3. Once the report server integration feature is activated, go to Application Management and locate the Reporting Services section to verify the activation, as shown in Figure 2-31.

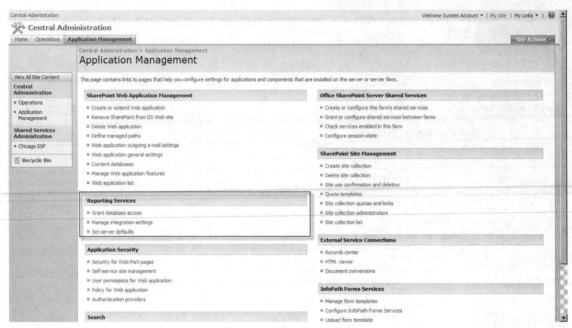

Figure 2-31

Configuring Report Server Integration in SharePoint Central Administration

The final step in installing the report server in SharePoint integrated mode is to configure the report server integration in SharePoint Central Administration.

1. On the Application Management page, locate the Reporting Services section and click Manage integration settings, as shown in Figure 2-32.

Figure 2-32

2. In the report server Web Service URL page, you will need to specify the report server site.

If you do not remember the URL , you can find your URL by going to the Reporting Services Configuration Manager and clicking on Web Service URL, as shown in Figure 2-33. In this example, the URL is `http://HOST:80/ReportServer`.

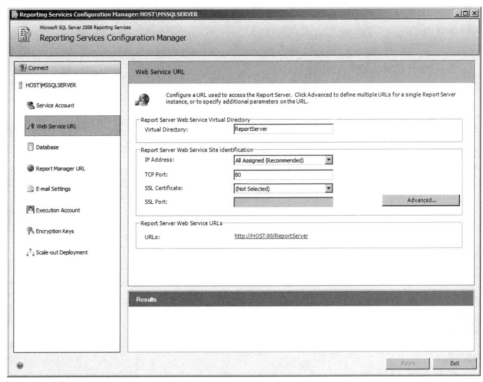

Figure 2-33

3. Once you enter the URL, you will need to select the Authentication Mode. You can select Windows Authentication or Trusted Authentication. If Kerberos is not used, you can select Trusted Authentication mode and click OK, as shown in Figure 2-34.

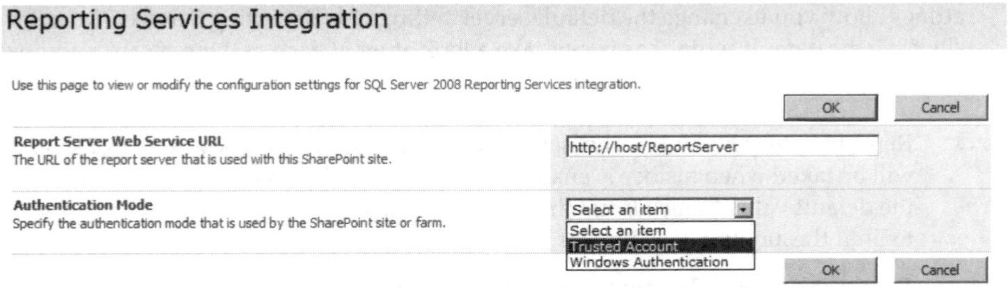

Figure 2-34

4. Once you have set up the integration, you need to grant access to the database. By doing this, you enable SharePoint to get the report server service account and grant it access to the SharePoint configuration database. First, click the Grant Database **Access** link. Next, enter the name of the report server in the Server Name textbox and click OK. In this case, you enter HOST as the name of the server, as shown in Figure 2-35.

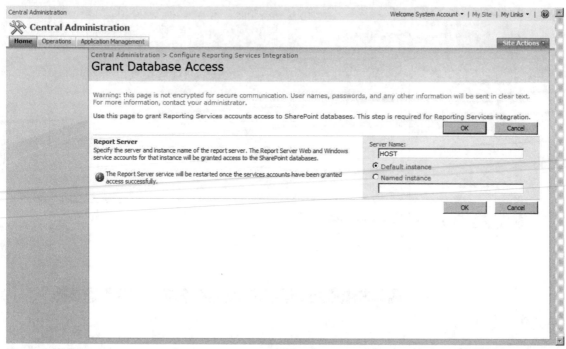

Figure 2-35

5. The next step is to provide credentials for database access. For SharePoint to give the report server service account access to the configuration database, it needs you to provide it with the SharePoint farm administrator account. On the credentials dialog, enter the SharePoint farm administrator account and click OK.

6. For the final step, you can set up your report server defaults by clicking the Set server defaults link. Now you see that the Reporting Services Server Defaults has several settings. These settings allow you to change the default server settings for Reporting Services. Most installations will leave the default settings as is, but take a look at what each of them means and how it will affect your environment.

    ❑   **Report History Default** – This setting allows you to control the number of snapshots that will be taken when history is enabled. There are two options: You can choose not to change the default value (which is not limiting the number of snapshots), or you can set a number to limit the amount of snapshots.

    ❑   **Report Processing Timeout** – This setting allows you to control the timeout time interval in seconds. The default value is set so that the report server that is handling the request will time out after 30 minutes, which includes both the data processing and report processing time. If you have queries that will take longer than 30 minutes, you must plan for the data processing time and the report processing time when setting this value.

    ❑   **Report Processing Log** – The log keeps a record of when every report is processed. Information about the report that is being processed (such as the user who ran the report) will also be stored in the log. With this setting you can either enable or disable the log. By default log keeping is enabled and the log will be kept for 60 days, but you can change this

number. The logs are stored on the report server in the folder `\Microsoft SQL Server\`
`MSSQL.n\ReportServer\Log`.

❑ **Enable Windows Integrated Security** – With this setting you specify whether a connection
to a report data source can support integrated security.

❑ **Enable Ad Hoc Reporting** – With this setting you specify if Report Builder can be used in
your environment. Setting this property sets the EnableLoadReportDefinition property on
the report server. If this property is not enabled, you lose the report builder functionality,
and report server will not generate clickthrough reports for reports that use a report model
as a data source.

❑ **Custom Report Builder launch URL** – With this option you can specify the custom
URL you wish to use for report builder. With the Service Pack 1 release for SQL 2008 you
have ClickOnce support for Report Builder 2.0. By default SharePoint will use Report
Builder 1.0. And if you are using SQL 2008 SP1 for your reporting services, you can set up
SharePoint to open reports in Report Builder 2.0 by setting the custom URL to:
`/_vti_bin/ReportBuilder/ReportBuilder_2_0_0_0.application`.

Make sure you use the updated version of the reporting services add-in that includes the Report Builder
2.0 ClickOnce update.

Once you are done with your settings, click OK to save your changes, as shown in Figure 2-36.

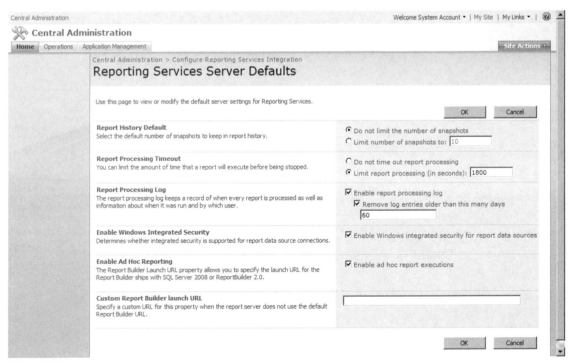

Figure 2-36

Summary

We began this chapter with the question of why we even consider SharePoint integration, and we end it with a successful SharePoint integrated mode install. With step-by-step walkthroughs, this chapter provided the details of each step and things to consider when configuring your servers.

You should now have a report server that is in SharePoint integrated mode, and with your new setup, you will immediately start getting the benefits of SharePoint integrated mode.

Even though there aren't a lot of steps in installing reporting server in integrated mode, things have to be done in a certain order. As long as the installation requirements are met, installing Reporting Services will be pretty easy after your install, as it will be the same thing over and over again.

Now that your server is set up in SharePoint integrated mode, enjoy having reports on SharePoint document libraries and maintaining one central location for your content and reporting needs.

3

Planning Your Report Project

Often, when a new reporting system is available, the most popular approach is to migrate the existing reports from a line of business applications such as the mainframe to the new reporting system selected by the organization. In fact, not too long ago, I performed this exact task when I was architecting a custom .NET solution running on SharePoint 2007 for a client that had been using mainframe reports for the past 10 years.

Until a few years ago, the client was using a batch process that would print reports on paper. Then someone would manually go through the reports to review each page to make sure things added up. Some reports were very long and not user friendly, and some people were only interested in bits and pieces of the report and didn't need the whole print out. The training for a new employee was very long, as each report had nonintuitive names such as the 710 report or the 514-D report. Knowing what report you needed wasn't easy, as you needed to know the report's name and request the report from your mainframe person.

> *The nonintuitive names of these reports always amused me, as they reminded me of the TPS reports in the comedy film Office Space. But I can assure you it was no joke for employees, since they had to know what was in each report.*

As I continued to gather requirements, I was assured by the CFO that a lot of paper and time was wasted with this process, as each report was literally a 500-page booklet. In the last few years, though, the client has improved the process by using Excel, since upgrading the mainframe system allowed them to dump the data to comma separated value (.csv) format.

Upgrading mainframes, creating 500-page reports that need to be printed, looking for reports with names that are not intuitive, and migrating reports to platforms that display data that is not real time-these are just a few of the reasons that you might find yourself migrating reports.

Migrating reports is one of the most common scenarios when creating reports. Migration brings the following questions to mind: What is the best practice for migrating reports? Do you bring them over as is? Do you create them from scratch? Do you even need to migrate them? Can you combine them? All these questions lead to one conclusion: Don't blindly convert reports to new technologies. You have to adequately plan for migration.

In this chapter, you see methods that help you prepare for your next report project. This chapter is intended for SharePoint professionals who are planning and designing a report for the first time. If you are a report developer, you can use the content in this chapter as reference to educate your client on reports and what goes into planning for their requirements.

Educating Your Clients about SSRS Reports

Let's use the migration scenario mentioned in the introduction to this chapter to help determine the best practice for migrating reports. Say you are converting the mainframe report that is dumped into a .csv format file to a SSRS report. Do you just copy the text-based report and convert it to a Reporting Services report, or do you try to identify opportunities to make it better? The best practice is to identify the opportunity for change and present it to your client. However, this is not easy to accomplish unless you plan for it.

Even though this sounds like a no-brainer, believe it or not, when there is not a good plan for the report project, mistakes happen over and over again. One of my clients hired a contractor to work directly with the business user to develop custom reports. Since we were using SSRS for the solution we were working on, they decided to use SSRS for these reports since SharePoint 2007 was installed in integrated mode and it was easy to host these reports on their intranet. Since this was not a part of the project, the contractor was managed by the business user who needed the reports. The key part to remember here is that they didn't have a good plan. They just gave the developer the existing report and asked him to convert the report with no guidance.

The contractor doing the reporting development had a formatting question, and as the business user was not technically savvy in SSRS, he pointed the contractor in my direction. Once the contractor showed me the report he was working on, I was surprised to see that his questions were centered on how to create a tabular report that looked exactly like the mainframe report, which had dashes for lines and plus signs to make it look pretty. The contractor was spending over 20 hours (thousands of consulting dollars) to make the new report look like the old one, which didn't look good in the first place. This is a very good example of what can happen if you don't have good requirements established for your developers.

At that point, we went to the client and demonstrated how SSRS reports look and feel out of the box. They were immediately impressed with what SSRS had to offer, and they were now saying that this was exactly what they needed. Before you start developing any report, you must not only define what the client wants but also educate them on what is available with SSRS.

Most business users/clients will not know what SSRS can provide them if they've never worked with it before. Part of the requirements-gathering process and a best practice is to educate clients on what's available to them with SSRS after the initial requirements are received.

But what is the best way to educate the client on SSRS features? One of the things I always recommend is to have several sample reports you can show your clients before you start gathering requirements.

So how do you get these prebuilt reports that will help demonstrate SSRS functionality to clients? One way is to build them from scratch, but you rarely have enough time in your budget to build sample reports. If you are in the same boat as the rest of us and do not have a budget to create sample reports, no need to worry, as this chapter explains how you can have the newest and greatest reports in your environment in a matter of minutes without having to build them.

SQL Server Reporting Services Product Samples

A project has been created on CodePlex.com, an open-source project hosting site, which contains Reporting Services samples released by Microsoft with SQL Server 2008.

To demonstrate SSRS functionality to clients, you will use these open-source reports provided by Microsoft with SQL Server 2008. To get these reports working on your servers, all you have to do is download the product samples and install them on your machine.

The SQL Server Reporting Services product samples site is located at `http://www.codeplex.com/MSFTRSProdSamples`.

Once you navigate to the site, you will see that the product samples are grouped in five main categories:

- Application Samples
- Extension Samples
- Model Samples
- Report Samples
- Script Samples

Each of the categories has several items. You're interested in the Report Samples category, which has the following samples:

- Adventure Works Sample Reports
- Adventure Works Offline Report Samples
- Report Builder Report Samples
- Server Management Samples Reports

You can use any of the preceding report samples to demonstrate to your client the different types of reports that you can develop. This way you do not have to spend valuable time creating reports to show the client the SSRS features.

In this chapter, you will be using the Adventure Works sample reports, which can be downloaded from `http://msftrsprodsamples.codeplex.com/Release/ProjectReleases.aspx?ReleaseId=21472` (`http://tinyurl.com/cp5mnb`) and can be installed using the instructions located at `http://msftrsprodsamples.codeplex.com/Wiki/View.aspx?title=SS2008%21AdventureWorks%20Sample%20Reports&referringTitle=Home` (`http://tinyurl.com/c8lfgq`).With Adventure Works sample reports, you get several reports that allow you to demonstrate SSRS functionality to your clients. Once you download the sample reports, you can examine them and the features they demonstrate to the end user, which we will discuss next.

Please note that this section assumes that you have the sample database installed on your server. If you have not installed the sample databases on your server, you can advance to Chapter 5 as it will walk you through installing the sample database on your server. You can also visit the following URL to learn more about installing the Adventure Works sample database: `http://msftdbprodsamples.codeplex.com/Wiki/View.aspx?title=Installing%20Databases&referringTitle=Home` (`http://tinyurl.com/daeofm`)*.*

The sample reports display product and sales information accessed by employees throughout the fictitious bike company named Adventure Works. Since these reports present data in a variety of formats, educating the client with these reports becomes easier. The list of Adventure Works sample reports available to you follows:

- ❑ Company Sales 2008
- ❑ Employee Sales Summary 2008
- ❑ Product Catalog 2008
- ❑ Sales Order Detail 2008
- ❑ Product Line Sales 2008
- ❑ Territory Sales 2008
- ❑ Store Contacts 2008
- ❑ Sales Trend 2008

Let's walk through these reports to get a better understanding of what should be demonstrated to the client in each report. Once the samples are installed, you can access these reports from `C:\Program Files\Microsoft SQL Server\100\Samples\Reporting Services\Report Samples\ AdventureWorks Sample Reports`.

In this section, you will open each report in Visual Studio and render the report from the Business Intelligence Development Studio. Once you have demonstrated the preceding reports to your client, you will have successfully demonstrated most of the SSRS features that any report will need or have. Following are some of the features highlighted in the sample reports:

- ❑ Grouping
- ❑ Drilldown
- ❑ Look and feel
- ❑ Charts
- ❑ Drillthrough
- ❑ Paging
- ❑ Header and footer
- ❑ Subreports
- ❑ Calculations
- ❑ Conditional font, color, and images

The Company Sales 2008 Report

This sample report displays the Adventure Works Cycles sales by quarter and product category. This is a great example of explaining groupings to your client. With this report, you can also demonstrate how matrix data regions work with drilldown capabilities. Using the collapse and expand icons, you can demonstrate how to expand the summary view and show hidden rows of data. Also with this report, you can demonstrate embedded background images, as shown in Figure 3-1.

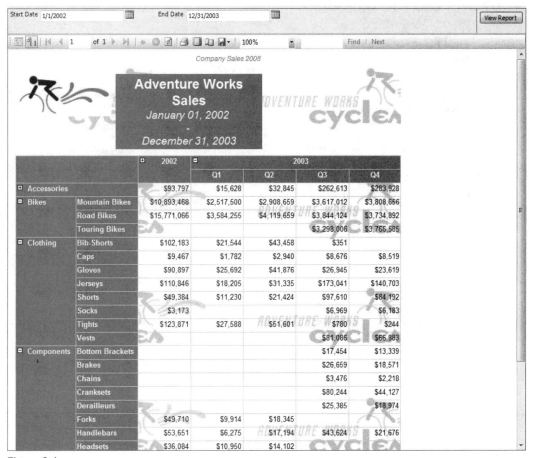

Figure 3-1

The Employee Sales Summary 2008 Report

This sample report will display Adventure Works Cycles sales for an individual employee. This report is a great example of the charting features in SSRS, as it displays the Sales Comparison and Current Month Sales Comparison, as shown in Figure 3-2.

It also includes a Current Month Order Summary table, with drillthrough to individual orders. Once you click the SalesOrder ID, you will see that a new report is shown to the end user, displaying the details of the sales order, as shown in Figure 3-3.

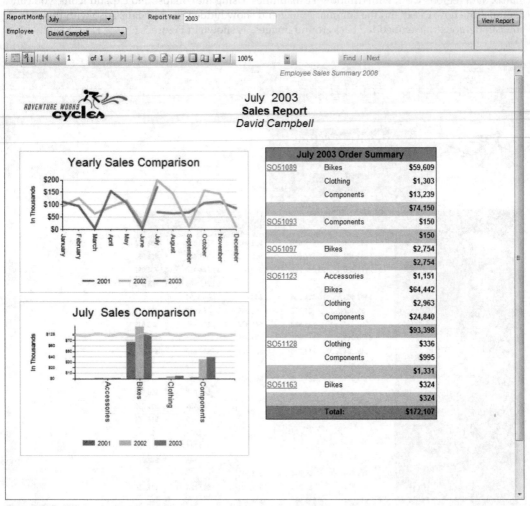

Figure 3-2

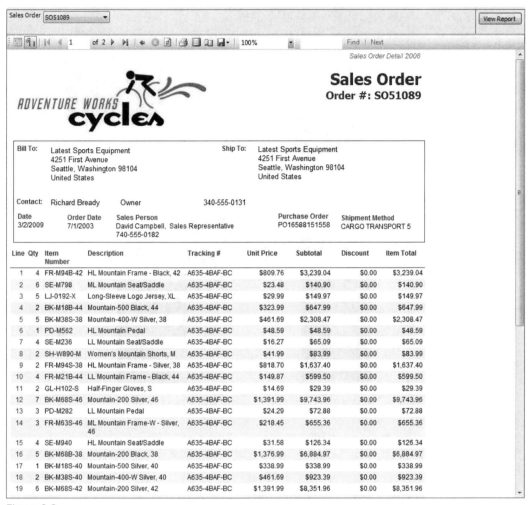

Figure 3-3

The Product Catalog 2008 Report

This sample report displays the Adventure Works Cycles full product catalog with pictures. This report allows you to demonstrate the power of embedded images, page breaks, page footers, conditional formatting, and a document map, as shown in Figure 3-4 and Figure 3-5.

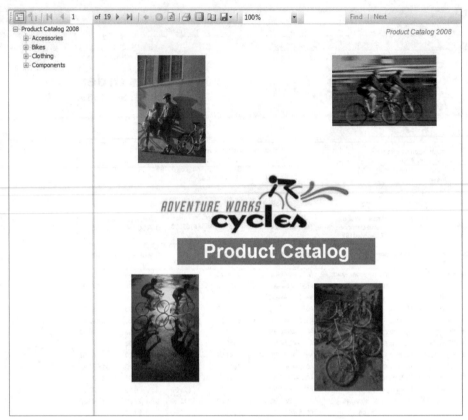

Figure 3-4

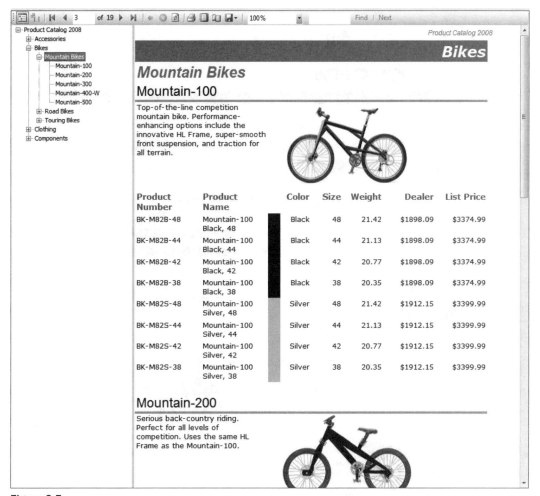

Figure 3-5

The Sales Order Detail 2008 Report

This is the detail report that was shown in Figure 3-3. This report can be accessed as a drillthrough report from the Employee Sales Summary and Territory Sales drilldown report.

The Product Line Sales 2008 Report

This sample report displays the Adventure Works top five sales people and stores. This report will help you demonstrate sorting, tables, charts, and calculated fields, as shown in Figure 3-6.

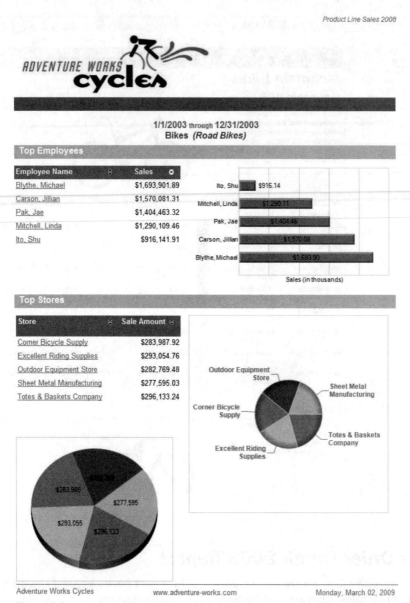

Figure 3-6

The Territory Sales 2008 Report

Similar to other drilldown reports, this sample report displays the Adventure Works sales by territory. This report will allow you to drill down to a salesperson and see his or her order numbers, which are connected to the individual orders. This report will help you demonstrate the two-level grouping on the rows, as shown in Figure 3-7.

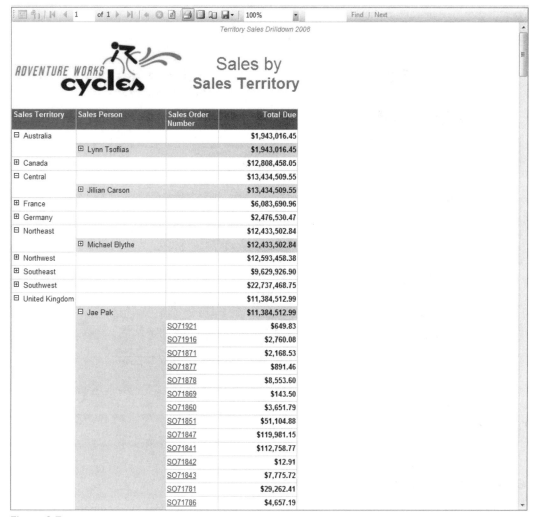

Figure 3-7

The Store Contacts 2008 Report

This sample report displays the Adventure Works store contacts and is a subreport that displays all the contacts for a selected store on the sales order report, as shown in Figure 3-8. You will see that there is no border, header, or footer for the contact report, since it is used as the subreport to the sales order report.

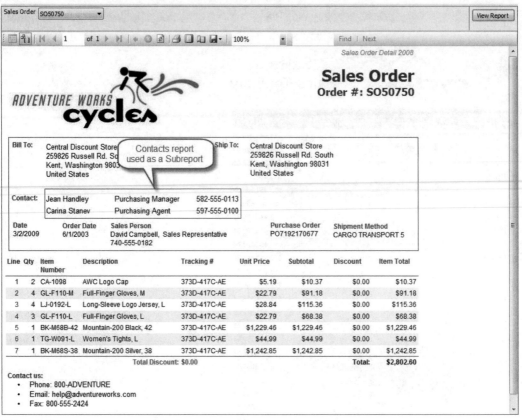

Figure 3-8

The Sales Trend 2008 Report

This final sample report displays the Adventure Works sales-trend analysis that compares year over year (Y/Y) growth for products by category and subcategory, as shown in Figure 3-9. This report demonstrates the new tablix format, which will have conditionally hidden static columns, repeat columns, and row headers. In this report you will see features such as conditional formatting, custom code, and drillthrough parameters demonstrated.

Products by Subcategory, Quarter & Trend		2002			2003						2004			
		Q3	Q4	Total	Q1	Q2	Q3	Q4	Total	Y/Y%	Q1	Q2	Total	Y/Y%
Accessories	Bike Racks						$75,920	$60,863	$136,804		$37,150	$63,094	$100,234	-36 %
	Bike Stands						$6,996	$11,925	$18,921		$8,268	$10,653	$18,921	0 %
	Bottles and						$11,854	$15,968	$27,822		$16,105	$18,659	$34,764	20 %
	Cleaners						$5,137	$4,724	$9,862		$3,358	$4,949	$8,307	-19 %
	Fenders						$7,649	$11,759	$19,408		$11,583	$13,276	$24,859	22 %
	Helmets	$33,653	$24,871	$58,724	$11,660	$25,524	$81,538	$89,595	$208,317	72 %	$72,597	$101,789	$174,386	-19 %
	Hydration Packs						$31,577	$27,110	$58,687		$17,904	$28,254	$46,158	-27 %
	Locks	$6,325	$3,780	$10,105	$2,205	$3,939		$15	$6,159	-54 %				
	Pumps	$5,157	$3,226	$8,383	$1,763	$3,362			$5,145	-63 %				
	Tires and Tubes						$41,940	$61,948	$103,889		$61,519	$66,817	$128,337	19 %
Bikes	Mountain Bikes	$3,141,467	$2,837,647	$5,979,114	$2,517,500	$2,908,659	$3,617,012	$3,608,656	$12,651,826	53 %	$3,473,750	$4,268,134	$7,741,684	-86 %
	Road Bikes	$4,930,693	$4,189,622	$9,120,315	$3,584,255	$4,119,659	$3,844,124	$3,734,892	$15,282,929	40 %	$3,391,876	$4,001,737	$7,393,614	-107 %
	Touring Bikes						$3,298,006	$3,766,585	$7,064,592		$3,414,027	$4,066,455	$7,480,482	6 %
Clothing	Bib-Shorts	$66,860	$35,323	$102,183	$21,544	$43,456	$351		$65,353	-56 %	$234	$234	$468	-13,866 %
	Caps	$3,991	$3,076	$7,066	$1,762	$2,940	$8,670	$9,519	$21,917	66 %	$7,319	$9,265	$16,584	-32 %
	Gloves	$52,537	$38,360	$90,897	$25,992	$41,876	$25,945	$23,619	$118,132	23 %	$14,214	$22,079	$36,293	-225 %
	Jerseys	$49,992	$35,495	$84,397	$18,205	$31,335	$173,041	$140,793	$383,264	77 %	$102,317	$144,044	$246,362	-47 %
	Shorts	$26,287	$23,177	$49,384	$11,230	$21,424	$97,610	$84,192	$214,457	77 %	$65,637	$86,668	$152,305	-41 %
	Socks						$6,969	$6,163	$13,152		$4,160	$5,629	$9,992	-32 %
	Tights	$67,688	$56,792	$123,871	$27,588	$51,601	$780	$244	$80,212	-54 %		$292	$292	-27,327 %
	Vests						$91,086	$66,863	$147,968		$45,492	$67,871	$113,353	-31 %
Components	Bottom Brackets						$17,454	$13,339	$30,793		$7,727	$13,307	$21,034	-45 %
	Brakes						$26,659	$18,571	$45,231		$8,115	$12,716	$20,831	-117 %
	Chains						$3,476	$2,218	$5,694		$1,542	$2,149	$3,692	-54 %
	Cranksets						$80,244	$44,127	$124,371		$35,461	$44,233	$79,693	-56 %
	Derailleurs						$25,385	$18,974	$44,359		$8,872	$18,032	$25,903	-71 %
	Forks	$26,167	$23,543	$49,710	$9,914	$18,345			$28,259	-78 %				
	Handlebars	$35,341	$18,309	$53,651	$6,275	$17,194	$43,624	$21,876	$88,769	40 %	$8,345	$21,892	$28,298	-214 %
	Headsets	$19,702	$16,362	$36,064	$10,650	$14,102			$25,052	-44 %				
	Mountain	$608,353	$443,599	$1,051,952	$236,070	$440,261	$827,288	$565,230	$2,068,849	49 %	$309,890	$563,954	$873,844	-137 %
	Pedals						$54,185	$39,901	$94,086		$15,784	$37,681	$53,445	-76 %
	Road Frames	$567,746	$468,890	$4,416,908	$132,890	$467,690	$755,931	$596,360	$1,922,702	46 %	$79,169	$271,826	$1,368,608	-56 %

Figure 3-9

Gathering Requirements for Reports

Once your client has seen what can be done with SSRS, the next thing is to understand the client's requirements. Gathering requirements is the most important part of planning because the information collected in this phase will allow you to determine how the report will work and how it will look and feel. So where do you begin? What do you ask the client when gathering requirements? One of the things I hear over and over again is that there is really not a good requirements-gathering template for reports. As reports are an area where business analysts need a database background, organizations generally end up using developers to gather business requirements.

The goal of this section is to help business analysts and business users learn what questions to ask when collecting requirements without needing to know much about databases and development. Using the topics discussed in this section, a business analyst will be able to create a detailed functional design document that will allow developers to create exactly what the client needs.

So let's start gathering requirements for a report project.

Naming Your Report

You should start your requirements-gathering session by naming your report. Assuming that you have a list of reports stored in a SharePoint document library, the name is the first thing the business user will see. So which report do they need? You don't want them to click through all of the reports in the document library to find the one they need, so you must focus on the name of the report.

The name of the report should tell the business user what data is being displayed in the report. While it's important to explain what the report does with the name you pick, you don't want the name to be a paragraph long. When naming your report, select a name that is no longer than five words, and make sure it is intuitive.

The name should be self-explanatory so that when business user reads it, he or she should be able to guess what the report will display. Don't name your report the 514-S Report. Name it the Yearly Spending Budget for Marketing Report or the Territory Sales Report. Some other example names of reports are Company Sales, Employee Sales Summary, Product Catalog, Product Line Sales, Sales Order Detail, Store Contacts, and Sales Trend.

The Purpose of the Report

The next thing you need to define is the purpose of the report. In this section of your requirements document, answer the following questions:

❑   What does the report display?

❑   What is the report's purpose? Does the data on the report kick-off any processes?

❑   Who uses the report?

An example of the purpose section of the requirements document is as follows:

```
The purpose of the Territory Sales report is to display the Adventure Works
Cycles sales by territory. The Sales manager for each territory utilizes the
report to update their forecast and manage their sales force.
```

The Report Type

Now that you have given the report a name and defined its purpose, the next step is to define how the data will be displayed in your report. Before you begin determining what data will be displayed in your report, it is important to establish what kind of report you will be creating. Several types of reports can be created with SSRS:

❑   Parameterized reports

❑   Linked reports

❑   Snapshot reports

❑   Cached reports

❑   Ad hoc reports

❑ Clickthrough reports

❑ Drillthrough reports

❑ Subreports

Please note that there might be times when one report can have the characteristics of more than one report type. For example, you can have a parameterized report that has subreports. Let's review the report types, which will allow you determine the type of report you will be creating.

Parameterized Reports

A parameterized report requires the end user to provide the report interface with a parameter to render a report. In parameterized reports, the output varies based on the value selected when the report runs. These reports are mostly used for subreports, drillthrough reports, and linked reports, but they are also used when the dataset needs to be filtered. Almost all reports accept parameters since this allows developers to create one report and have the end user select the information they would like to see.

For example, when creating for a quarterly profit report instead of creating a report for every quarter, you will design the report so that it accepts parameters. Say your report will accept two parameters, Year and Quarter. Once the report is enabled to accept parameters, all the end user would have to do is select the quarter and the year as a parameter before they run the report. The end user will do this by using the report interface that provides the parameters. You can see that the example reports provided in Figures 3-1, 3-2, and 3-3 all allow you select a parameter.

When the user selects the parameters Year and Quarter and they run the report, the report will generate data specifically for the specified year and quarter. If you were to select 2009 as your year and Q3 as your quarter, the report would return only the data that corresponds to Q3 2009.

This is why parameterized reports are extremely powerful. With this type of filtering, the developer does not need to create a report for each quarter and year, as this would be a waste of time. So instead of creating four reports for each year, they create one parameterized report that will accept a parameter, and at runtime end users will be able to get the data for any year and any quarter by selecting the parameter.

Linked Reports

A linked report uses a report server item that provides a link to an existing report. The report server item is no different from a typical link on a website; it connects to reports via a link. One of the biggest advantages of a linked report is that it is derived from an existing report and inherits the original report's data source and layout properties.

This report is mostly used when there is an existing report that will be updated to display the data in a filtered way. If you have a report that displays national sales, for instance, you can create linked reports to display regional data using a single regional sales report.

One thing to remember is that linked reports are not supported in SharePoint integrated mode.

Snapshot Reports

Snapshot reports allow users to have a view of a snapshot in a scheduled manner. This type of report runs on a schedule. In accordance with the schedule, the report is processed and the results are saved to the report server. Whenever a user wants to see data that was run at a particular time, he or she can do so without running the report at that exact time.

For example, if the report needs to run at 12:00 A.M. on the first day of every month, you can create a snapshot report so that users don't have to be on their computers 24 hours a day.

With snapshot reports, you get three main benefits:

❑ **Report history:** You can run a report the first day of every month or week or even at the beginning of each day automatically with a snapshot report, which will give you a historical view of how data changes over time.

❑ **Consistency:** Snapshot reports provide the same data to all users running the report. If the data changes throughout the day, an on-demand report can display different results to each user running the report if it isn't a snapshot report. With snapshot reports, however, you can provide consistent reports for all users.

❑ **Performance:** Reports that have a high impact on server resources can be run during off-peak hours to reduce the processing impact on the server during core business hours.

Cached Reports

Cached reports are similar to snapshot reports, with one big difference: the expiration period. Cached reports save the report, but in the end it expires. Using this report reduces the time it takes to render large reports. Typically, reports are cached for 20 minutes, but this can be changed based on requirements.

Ad Hoc Reports

Add Hoc reports are reports that are created on the fly by the end user. This is similar to the Pivot tables in Excel: Once the end user has rows of data, they pick the columns they wish to see on the fly.

In reporting services, Report Builder is used to allow end users to easily create and update the reports. The user can click on a report that is deployed to SharePoint and Report Builder will pop up, allowing the user to update the report.

Clickthrough Reports

A clickthrough report displays the detailed version of the original report. When a user clicks the data, the clickthrough report is displayed and is generated by the report server on the fly. For example, you could create a report that lists all of the sales orders, and when you click on one of the sales orders (interactive data), this will generate new data by the report server.

Also note that clickthrough reports are only available with the Enterprise version of SQL Server 2008.

Drillthrough Reports

Drillthrough reports are similar to clickthrough reports, with one main difference: With drillthrough reports, data is not autogenerated by the report server; instead, it opens another report file, which is saved on the report server.

For example, you could create a report that lists all of the sales orders, and when you click on one of the sales orders it will redirect you to another report that shows the details of the sales order. This way you connect two reports with one click, creating a drillthrough report. These types of reports are typically used in dashboards allowing users to access data by drilling down.

Subreports

With subreports you can display another report inside the main report. It's very helpful when you are embedding different views of the same data, as you can set up the subreport where it gets its parameters from the main report.

Subreports are different than clickthrough and drillthrough reports because with subreports you do not have to click on anything to see the subreport. The subreport when added to the report is directly viewable. You can think of subreports as the iframes in HTML.

Now that you have a good understanding of the reports with SSRS, you should be able to determine the type of report the client needs.

Data for the Report

Once you select the report type, the next thing is to determine what data you will display in the report. This section of the requirements document will help the developer create the SQL query. There are five major questions you must answer to define the data requirements for the report:

- ❑ What is the name or the IP address of the database server?
- ❑ What is the name of the database catalog/model that should be used for the data?
- ❑ What is the username and password that can be used to access the data?
- ❑ What are the names and types of the data columns you need to display?
- ❑ What parameters need to be passed in to the report to filter the data?

Once you have established the IP address of the database server, the database model that will be used for the data, and the username and password, you are ready to begin creating a mockup of the data for the report, inlcuding the columns and parameters.

If you are a business analyst and you've made it this far in the requirements gathering process, this is where you would want to include a database expert in your requirement meetings. It's always best to get the database expert/developer involved at this stage since this will help them determine how they need to create their SQL queries.

And if you are a developer, you should make sure that you create the mockup of the data set with the end user before you start thinking about creating your SQL queries. Creating the mock-up will allow the business user to have a visual understanding of what data they will get back with the report you are developing.

Creating a Mockup of the Data Set

Assuming that you note the name of the server and the database with its credentials, you can define the data set that will be accessed in the report. All reports are generated using the the data set, which is the rows of data that are in SSRS reports. The data set is the data that is returned back from the database based on a SQL query. Each row in the data set will have one or more columns and in order to create the SQL query developers need to know the columns and the type of data each column holds.

The business analyst who is writing the requirements for the data set needs to provide the developer with a list of columns and the type of data each column represents. This is one of the most important parts of the requirements section of the report as this is where most of the miscommunication happens between the business user and the developer. So this part needs extra attention and should be well thought out before any development begins.

Most business analysts do not have database development experience, so how does a business analyst create the requirements for a data set? This is a real concern and a very common question among business analysts who are tasked with creating requirements for reports.

The most effective way for a business analyst to create requirements for a data set is to create a mock-up of the data that the business is expecting to report on. A mock-up of the data set can be created with no SQL knowledge by using a tool such as Excel, which is a tool that many business analysts are very efficient in using. Data sets have several columns and rows, which makes them similar to the tables you would create in Excel. Therefore, when designing the data set, it is easy to use Microsoft Excel to collect the data and design the look and feel of a table.

Working with the business user, a mockup of the data set should be created. At this point no SQL knowledge is required since all you would be doing is creating an example of the data set you wish to report on. Using Excel, you should create rows and columns of the sample data. If the report already exists and is being migrated, things are much easier, since the columns are already defined. But if you don't know what data you need to report on, you will have to work with the business user to understand their needs and recommend the columns they should have in their data set.

Once you create the mockup of the report data set, you should have something similar to Figure 3-10. You can see that the mock-up will show exactly how you wish the data to be displayed on your report, including the formatting and spacing of the columns. You can see that in Figure 3-10 the mock-up is letting the report developer know that the Line column should be centered, and the Unit Price column should be right justified and formatted as a currency type.

Without any SQL knowledge and report development experience, the business analyst has given almost 90% of the requirements to the developer by creating the mock-up shown in Figure 3-10. This is why it's very important to start with a mock-up before the development begins, since this will save a lot of valuable development time.

Line	Qty	Item Number	Description	Tracking #	Unit Price	Subtotal	Discount	Item Total
1	2	CA-1098	AWC Logo Cap	373D-417C-AE	$5.19	$10.37	$0.00	$10.37
2	4	GL-F110-M	Full-Finger Gloves, M	373D-417C-AE	$22.79	$91.18	$0.00	$91.18
3	4	LJ-0192-L	Long-Sleeve Logo Jersey, L	373D-417C-AE	$28.84	$115.36	$0.00	$115.36
4	3	GL-F110-L	Full-Finger Gloves, L	373D-417C-AE	$22.79	$68.38	$0.00	$68.38
5	1	BK-M68B-42	Mountain-200 Black, 42	373D-417C-AE	$1,229.46	$1,229.46	$0.00	$1,229.46
6	1	TG-W091-L	Women's Tights, L	373D-417C-AE	$44.99	$44.99	$0.00	$44.99
7	1	BK-M68S-38	Mountain-200 Silver, 38	373D-417C-AE	$1,242.85	$1,242.85	$0.00	$1,242.85
				Total Discount: $0.00			Total:	$2,802.60

Figure 3-10

Defining Columns

Once the mock-up is created, the business analyst has now created a list of the columns that need to be returned by the data set. Although the mock-up gets almost all of the requirements across, you still need to provide the developer with more detailed information on your columns. The best way to do this is to create a table that defines these columns. Again, this can be easily accomplished using Excel or Word, which are the two most commonly used tools by business analysts.

This table will note the name of the column in the database in the tablename.column name format, the column name that will appear on the report for that column and its description, as shown in the table that follows:

Column Name in the Database	Column Name to appear on the report	Description
N/A	Line	Automatically numbered line number.
Product.Quantity	Qty	The quantity purchased on the SalesOrder.
Product.ItemNumber	Item Number	The item number of the product.
Product.Description	Description	The description of the item.
Shipping.Tracking	Tracking #	The tracking number of the item ordered.
Product.Price	Unite Price	The Unit Price of the product.
N/A	Subtotal	This is a calculated field. Formula = Qty × Unit Price.
Customer.Discount	Discount	This is a calculated field. The discount amount = SubTotal × Customer.Discount/100.
N/A	Item Total	This is a calculated field. Formula = Qty × (Unit Price – Discount).

Having the preceding table in your requirements document will allow developers to understand how each column works in the mockup you have created with the client. As the business analyst you will need help from the developer when defining the names of the tables and columns in the database when filling out the Column Name in the Database column of your table, since this requires access to the database and knowledge of the database structure.

By providing the mock-up and the column definition table, the business analyst will have provided all of the needed information for a developer to create the SQL query that will generate the data set. Without exaggerating much, the mock-up and the column definition will bring down the development time at least 75% based on my personal experience, because at this point there is no room for error and the developer will focus on creating the query.

> It is best practice to use stored procedures when querying the database. The developer should use stored procedures when creating reports since this allows you to keep the business logic in SQL and not on the report itself. With this approach if your business rules change at any given time, all you would have to do is update your stored procedure and your report will consume the new data. In this way you would not have to make changes to the report and re-deploy to SharePoint.

At this point you have defined the columns that the data set will store, but you are not done with designing the data set. The next important thing to define the parameters the report will accept. As defined earlier in this chapter, parameterized reports are very powerful and almost all reports accept parameters. This next section will go over the ins and outs of defining the parameters for your reports.

Defining Parameters

Allowing your report to accept parameters makes the report very powerful since it allows the user to change the data that is returned at runtime based on their needs. With SSRS there are several different ways your report can accept parameters. Before you determine what parameters the data set will accept, let's review how parameters are selected in reports. Most commonly used approaches to display parameters are dropdowns, multi-select check boxes, text boxes, and date selectors.

The simplest way to provide a parameter to a report is by using a text field. This is the default way to provide a parameter if you don't make any changes to the parameter settings in SSRS. For example if you had a report that accepted a Product Name as its parameter, you could simple type the name of the product into the text box and run the report. Although this approach allows you to create a parameter rather quickly, it's not intuitive and provides a lot of room for mistakes to happen, since users might not know how the product name is stored in the database.

Another way in collecting the parameter data in a report is using dropdowns. You can create a SQL query that will generate a list of all of the products that will populate the dropdown. Doing this leaves no room for mistakes and the user does not have to type in the product name when they are selecting the parameter. All they would have to do is select the product they are looking for and run the report.

The enhanced version of collecting the parameter information with a dropdown is to use cascading dropdowns. With cascading dropdowns you can allow the user to pick the first dropdown option, which will populate the second option. This comes in quite handy when you have relational data and you want to enhance the user experience.

For example, assume that you have several hundred products. When you create a dropdown that displays all the products, it can be very hard to use. When selecting a parameter, you will have to scroll through hundreds of items to find the product you're looking for. This is when using cascading dropdowns make sense. If you add another dropdown called Category that populates the Products dropdown, you can very quickly enhance the user experience.

Take a look at the example shown in Figure 3-11. The way the cascading dropdown will work is that the end user will first select a Category (in this case Bikes); then the second dropdown will display the subcategories of that category. This way the end user will be able to easily sort through tens of products instead of all of the products.

Another type of parameter that SSRS provides is the multiple selection option. As shown in the second example in Figure 3-11, when multiselect is enabled, the user can select both Mountain Bikes and Touring Bikes.

Figure 3-11

Now that you have seen the different ways you can collect the paramenter information, you are ready to define the parameters. When defining parameters, you should use a table similar to the one you use to define the columns:

Parameter Name	From Database? If so, what stored procedure will be used to populate?	Parameter Type	Required?
Category	Yes. spGetCategories()	Dropdown	Yes
SubCategory	Yes. spGetSubCategories(CategoryId)	Dropdown	Yes
StartDate	No	Date/Time	No
EndDate	No	Date/Time	No

Layout of the Data

In this part of the requirements, you will determine the layout of the data. Each report you create will have a different layout based on the information being displayed. Oftentimes, you will find yourself showing the same data in different layouts, where each layout is considered a new report.

The SSRS toolbox provides several ways display data in reports. The report items that can be added to your report are Text Box, Line, Table, Matrix, Rectangle, List, Image, Subreport, Chart, and Gauge, as shown in Figure 3-12.

Figure 3-12

Text boxes, lines, rectangles, and images are basically used for look and feel. The layout of the actual data is controlled by the following data regions:

❏ **Table:** This is the tabular format where the data is displayed in rows and columns. It is similar to the mockup shown earlier in Figure 3-10. This data region supports grouping rows and can display group totals. The bracket in the first column in Figure 3-13 denotes that the rows can be grouped in the table data regions.

Figure 3-13

❏ **Matrix:** Similar to the table data region, it displays data in rows and columns. The main differentiator is that it allows grouping between rows and columns. However, no fixed rows or columns can be added. This form of layout is very similar to the Pivot tables in Excel. The brackets in Figure 3-14 denote that columns and rows can be grouped, and in a matrix data region there will be at least one row and at least one column group.

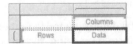

Figure 3-14

- ❑ **List:** This is a free-form data region. The list is typically used when you need to have a custom look and feel. This is the best data region to use when the data you wish to display is not in tabular format.

- ❑ **Chart:** This is a graphical representation of the data as bars, pies, or other chart types.

- ❑ **Gauge:** This new feature has been introduced to SSRS with the release of SSRS 2008 and gives you the ability to add linear or radial gauges.

- ❑ **Tablix:** Although this is not shown in the toolbox you should know that list, table, and matrix are all derived from the new tablix data region. This new feature was added to SSRS with the release of SSRS 2008.

Since the tablix is the new concept introduced with this version of SSRS, you'll start by reviewing the tablix data region to get a better understanding of its capabilities, which will help you to determine what data region to use in your report's data layout.

The Tablix Data Region – Welcome to the Region with No Restrictions!

Let's take a look at what's so great about the tablix data region. Its biggest advantage is that it combines the best characteristics of the matrix and table data regions. With the tablix data region, you have the ability to do things you couldn't do before. To understand the benefits of the tablix data region, think about how the table and matrix data regions work.

As mentioned earlier, in a table data region the rows of the report are dynamically repeated and can be grouped, whereas the columns in a table data region are static and cannot be grouped. In a matrix report, both rows and columns are dynamic, but no fixed rows or columns can be added.

With tablix data regions, you get the best of both worlds and no restrictions. The tablix data region provides the flexibility to include both dynamic and fixed rows, as well as dynamic and fixed columns. To better illustrate the differences of these data regions, the following table is a representation of the features that come with each data region.

	Column		Row	
	Dynamic	Static	Dynamic	Static
Table	No	Yes	Yes	No
Matrix	Yes	No	Yes	No
Tablix	Yes	Yes	Yes	Yes

The Chart Data Region

Charts provide a graphical summary view of your data. But before creating a chart report, you must design your data, as the chart will become useless if the data you feed it is incorrect, as you know in Garbage In, Garbage Out.

A chart, like the other data regions such as a matrix or table, can only use a single data set. In a report, you can add as many as reports as you need, and in this section you will review the types of charts available so you can determine if the report will need a chart and, if so, which one you should use.

- ❏ Area Charts
- ❏ Bar Charts
- ❏ Column Charts
- ❏ Line Charts
- ❏ Pie Charts
- ❏ Polar Charts
- ❏ Range Charts
- ❏ Scatter Charts
- ❏ Shape Charts
- ❏ Stock Charts

Some of the previews of the charts are shown in Figure 3-15. The best way to see how these charts work is to be able to edit them in Report Designer. This way you can demonstrate how each chart works to your client. The sample reports you've downloaded also come with chart examples, although the name of the project doesn't say anything reports, `AdventureWorksOffline Sample Reports`, there are chart examples in that project. To get a hold all of the examples shown in Figure 3-15 and many more, load the project located at `%Drive Letter%:\Program Files\Microsoft SQL Server\100\Samples\ Reporting Services\Report Samples\AdventureWorksOffline Sample Reports`.

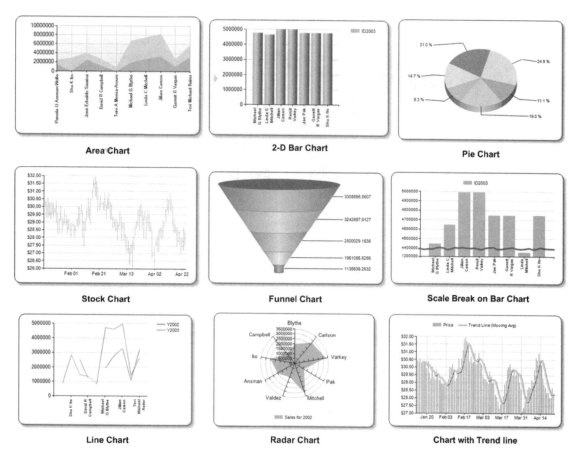

Figure 3-15

The Gauge Data Region

Several types of chart types are available to you when creating reports, as discussed in the earlier section, but with the new version of SSRS, you now have the new graphical view into data called gauges. You no longer need third-party tools to create linear and radial gauges, such as shown in Figure 3-16, which is one of most widely used gauges when developing business intelligence reports.

Figure 3-16

You can create several types of gauges, as shown in Figure 3-17.

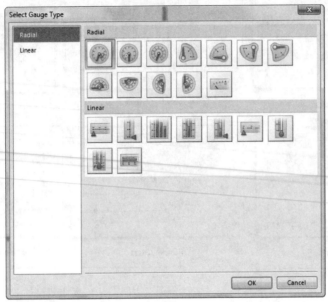

Figure 3-17

The different types of radial gauges you can add to your report are as follows:

- ❏ Radial
- ❏ Radial with Mini Gauge
- ❏ Two Scales
- ❏ 90 Degrees Northeast, Northwest, Southeast, and Southwest
- ❏ 180 Degrees North, South, East, and West
- ❏ Meter

The different types of linear gauges you can add to your report are as follows:

- ❏ Horizontal
- ❏ Vertical
- ❏ Multiple Bar Pointers
- ❏ Two Scales

- ❏ Three Color Range
- ❏ Logarithmic
- ❏ Thermometer
- ❏ Thermometer Fahrenheit/Celsius
- ❏ Bullet Graph

Grouping Your Data

Most reports that use the table and matrix data regions group their data into a visual hierarchy that makes sense to the consumer of the data. And most of the time the groupings are accompanied by calculated totals. It is important to understand how grouping works to design reports that work for the client. In this section, you will review how grouping works to establish the basics of grouping.

The Company Sales 2008 Report shown in Figure 3-1 is a perfect example of how groupings add value to a report. To get a better understanding of how groupings work, you will use Report Builder 2.0, which allows you to modify the report.

Open the Company Sales 2008 Report in Report Builder. As you see in Figure 3-18, the interfaces are very similar when it comes to grouping.

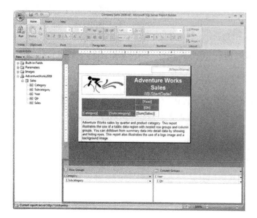
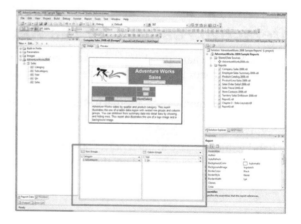

Figure 3-18

So now that you have the report open, let's see how reporting works for this report. You can see that two panes allow you to set up grouping properties for a tablix data region: Column Groups and Row Groups. The sample report currently has grouped the data using a parent group and an inner group for both the row and the column. The columns are grouped by year, and within that they are grouped by quarter, as shown in Figure 3-19.

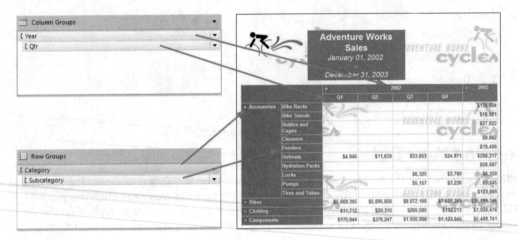

Figure 3-19

Also you see in Figure 3-19, the rows are grouped by category, and within the category the data is grouped by subcategory. An example of how you collect requirements for grouping is as follows:

Group rows first by Category then by SubCategory and also group columns first by Year then by Quarter.

Interactive Features for the Report

With SSRS you have the ability to make a report interactive. Having an interactive report will allow the end user to control what's being rendered in the report.

The most commonly used approach when you need to bring interactivity to a report is to modify the properties of a text box, since each of the cells in a matrix, table or list are all text boxes.

To bring interactivity to the report, you can simply right-click on a cell on a table, matrix, or list and select its properties. You will get the Text Box Properties window, as shown in Figure 3-20.

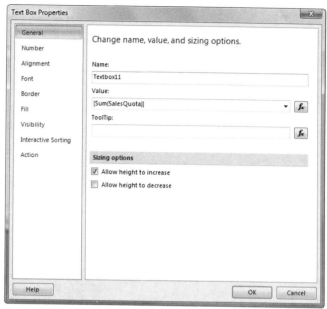

Figure 3-20

The features provided by SSRS 2008 to add interactivity to reports are shown in this window. With this window, you have the ability to update the general properties of the textbox such as name, value, and sizing options. But you also get the ability to set up the number, alignment, font, border, fill, visibility, interactive sorting, and actions for the textbox.

In this section, you will review a few of the features that allow you to make the report interactive, which will allow you to determine whether you need any of the following:

❑ Visibility

❑ Interactive Sorting

❑ Action

With the Visibility pane in the textbox properties window, you can select whether you want to show or hide the report item. You can also show or hide the report based on an expression, as shown in Figure 3-21. And the last option is to provide the ability to show or hide the item based on another item in the report. For example, groupings in reports use this functionality; when you click the expand icon, it triggers the report to show the item.

This is one of the most common ways end users will interact with the report. You can by default have all of your groupings collapsed, and the end user can simply click on the plus icon to expand the section they wish to see. You can also use expressions to hide or display report items based on the parameters the end user selected when running the report.

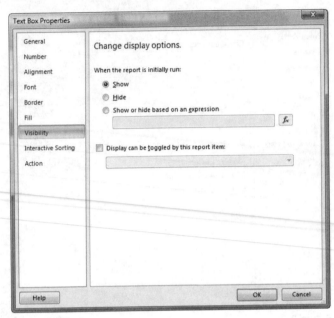

Figure 3-21

When adding the interactive sorting feature to a report, you must define what to sort, what to sort by, what context to sort in, and what data regions you want the sorting to affect when the user clicks the Sort button.

The Interactive Sorting pane allows you to define these parameters when setting up sorting. As shown in Figure 3-22, you can sort Detail rows or groups and select what to sort by.

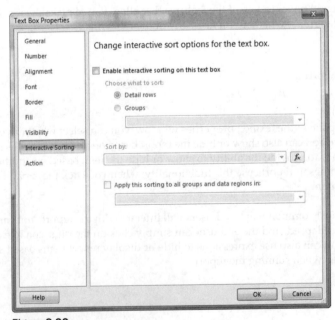

Figure 3-22

By enabling sorting on your reports, you quickly allow the end users to interact with the data and sort the data based on their needs. You might sort by default all of the sales orders so that the latest sale is on the top, but if you enable sorting the user can easily change to have the oldest one on the top if this is what they like to see. This way you are not forcing the user to see the data a certain way and you allow them to customize the report on the fly based on their needs.

So when you are creating requirements for sorting, saying that you want to sort by date isn't enough. You need to give more details to developers when they have the ability to set up all of these features. And as long as you know what exists, you have the chance to make a more educated request on sorting.

And finally in the Action pane of the textbox properties, you have the ability to make a textbox a link to take the user to another report, make it a bookmark, or just use it as a plain URL.

The Report Layout

Once you have defined the data-related items, the next thing to work on is the report layout. A report has a header, a body, and a footer. In the above sections you have defined how the body will look and what it can contain. Now that you have the body defined, the next thing you need to define is how your header and footer will look in your report.

The header and footer of a report are very similar to the header and footer in Microsoft Word. Once you add a header and footer to a report, they will always appear in their corresponding places. Having headers and footers enhances the look and feel of the report and is very important when you have reports that have multiple pages.

Typically in the header you will include information such as the company logo, the name of the report, and the date and time it was executed. In footers, most reports have the page number and notes such as the department that owns the report, the version of the form, and maybe even a short summary of the purpose of the form. Although these are the most common things you will see in the headers and footers of a report, there are no hard rules as to what you should and should not have in these sections. But it is very important that you include the design of the header and footer if you need them in your requirements document since it will take up space in a report and the developer can design the paging of the report accordingly.

One of the best tools to use when creating this design is Microsoft Visio. In your requirements document, you should include a layout mockup, such as the one shown in Figure 3-23, that you've created working with the client. This mockup template is available with the materials provided with this book. Be sure to take a look at the files provided for requirements gathering.

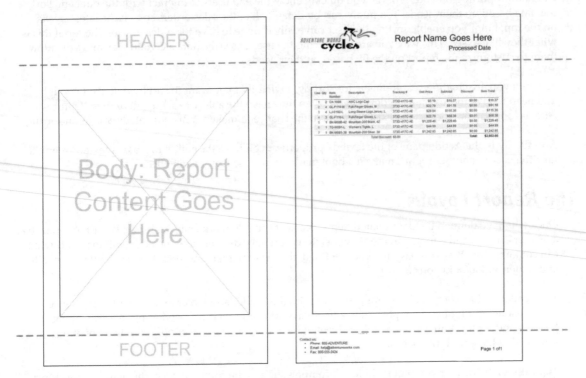

Figure 3-23

Accessing and Delivering Reports

There are two main ways users can access a report created and published to SharePoint:

❑ **On-Demand:** Users can directly access the report through the document library or see their report via a report viewer web part.

❑ **Subscription:** With the subscription model, the report is delivered automatically by the report server in the format of an email, saved into file share or a SharePoint document library.

When selecting the subscription model, you must select the type of delivery and schedule, as shown in Figure 3-24. The report can be rendered in several formats, and the subscription panel gives you the ability to update the write mode, which enables autoincrementing the name of the document versus overwriting it.

Also, as shown in Figure 3-24, parameters can be submitted manually, and overriding the report's default values is a powerful feature.

For example, say you work for a consulting company and you need to provide a timesheet to all of your clients for the hours you've worked on their projects and each of them has a site on your extranet. If you didn't have a better way to do this, you would have to create a separate report for each client and deploy their reports to their sites. This would be a maintenance nightmare since updating the timesheet report would mean redeploying it to all client sites.

Instead, what you could do is create one report, deploy it centrally on your extranet and then create different subscriptions that have custom parameters using the overriding the report's default values approach. This way each subscription will have a different parameter, in this case the Client name. The subscription will use the parameter that you entered and create the reports and send them to your client sites on the fly. With this approach each client will get their own reports and you will only manage one report file. Combining the subscriptions and parameter overriding is very powerful and can be applied to several real life scenarios.

Subscriptions will be covered in greater detail Chapter 11, which discusses managing reports in SharePoint.

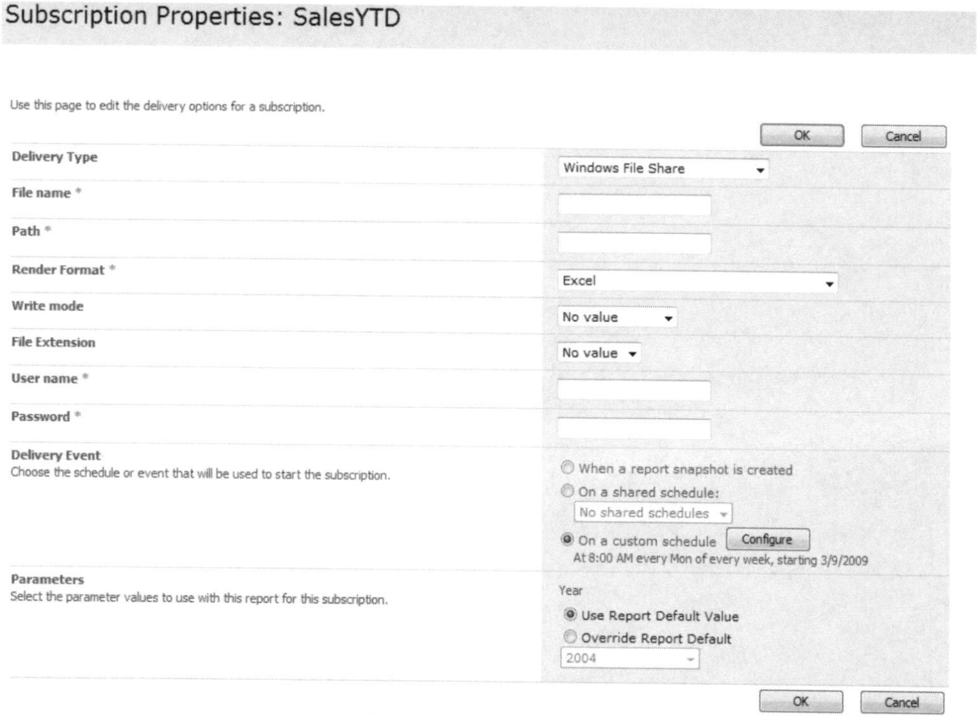

Subscription Properties: SalesYTD

Use this page to edit the delivery options for a subscription.

	OK Cancel
Delivery Type	Windows File Share ▾
File name *	
Path *	
Render Format *	Excel ▾
Write mode	No value ▾
File Extension	No value ▾
User name *	
Password *	

Delivery Event
Choose the schedule or event that will be used to start the subscription.
	○ When a report snapshot is created
	○ On a shared schedule:
	   No shared schedules ▾
	◉ On a custom schedule Configure
	   At 8:00 AM every Mon of every week, starting 3/9/2009

Parameters Select the parameter values to use with this report for this subscription.	Year ◉ Use Report Default Value ○ Override Report Default 2004 ▾
	OK Cancel

Figure 3-24

Summary

To create an easy-to-use report, you must create a plan. In this chapter, we went over the different types of reports available. We discussed what types of reports best fit various business needs and uses. And we mostly went over the steps for gathering requirements for a report project by answering these questions:

- ❑ What is the report for?
- ❑ What is the data layout (tablix, matrix, table, or list)?
- ❑ What do you want the report to look like?

Having read this chapter, you will now be able to better plan for your report project and get better results.

Overview of Business Intelligence Design Studio (BIDS) 2008

Before introducing BIDS 2008 and its capabilities, let's start by answering what BIDS 2008 is and why you should care about it. BIDS 2008 is short for Business Intelligence Development Studio 2008 and is a development tool that allows you to build reports and deploy them to the report server. The tool comes with SQL Server 2008 and is almost always referred to as BIDS 2008.

Although when we talk about BIDS it sounds as though it is a product that Microsoft has created just for report development, in all reality BIDS is just a slimmed-down version of Microsoft Visual Studio 2008 that has only the Business Intelligence project templates such as the reporting services project templates, analysis services project templates, and integration services project templates.

In this chapter, you walk through the different parts of BIDS, such as the Toolbox, Report Data, Server Explorer, and Solution Explorer. With the help of a walkthrough, you use the new report project wizard to create a new project report. This chapter demonstrates the report layout and preview views in BIDS. You also briefly go over the new functionality such as gauges, now available with BIDS 2008.

Since the audience of this book includes SharePoint professionals, not just report developers, this chapter exists so that readers who do not have experience with BIDS or report development can get a quick start in developing reports that reside in SharePoint using BIDS 2008. If you're already a BIDS user, most of the information in this chapter will reiterate what you already know and will highlight things you do in your day-to-day job.

Should you read this chapter if you're a seasoned report developer who has used BIDS before? The answer is yes, because this chapter also includes new features of SQL 2008. So if you're not familiar with the new version of SQL Reporting Services and what it has to offer, this chapter will give you what you need.

This chapter will use the Adventure Works database and report samples that Chapter 3 highlighted. Although you do not need these components installed on your development machine to follow along, you can use Chapter 3 to get more information on the report examples. Also, Chapter 5 will walk you through installing the AdventureWorks database if you haven't already installed it.

Introduction to BIDS 2008

BIDS 2008 is a report-authoring tool hosted within Microsoft Visual Studio 2008. BIDS 2008 looks very similar to Visual Studio 2008, as shown in Figure 4-1. With the exception of a few extra tools on the toolbox and new tool windows such as report data, report designer, and preview you can consider BIDS as Visual Studio for Business Intelligence. BIDS consists of several tool windows. The one mostly used when developing reports are:

- ❑ Server Explorer
- ❑ Solution Explorer
- ❑ Report Data
- ❑ Toolbox
- ❑ Properties Window
- ❑ Report Designer Surface
- ❑ Report Preview
- ❑ Grouping
- ❑ Errors List and Output Windows

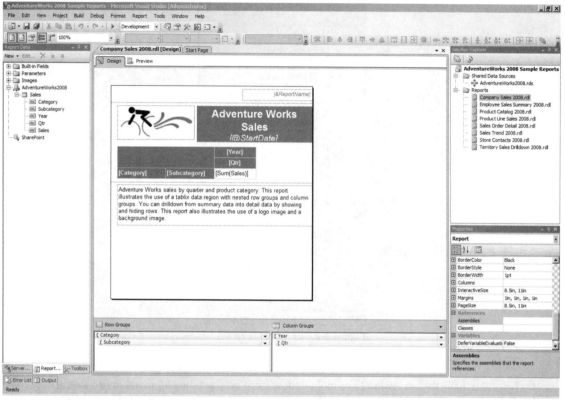

Figure 4-1

The Server Explorer

This tool window allows you to connect to different servers you will use in your data connections. It allows you create data connections directly to the database server. On this tool window, you can see all the database tables, views, stored procedures, and functions without having to log in to SQL Management Studio, as shown in Figure 4-2. You can also directly modify the tables, columns, and data on the database server through this tool window.

With the Server Explorer, you can get direct access to your database and make modifications as needed without having to leave BIDS. To enable the Server Explorer, click on View ⇨ Server Explorer or perform the following key combination: Ctrl+Alt+S. Although it's convenient to make changes to your database through BIDS, it's not where you spend most of your time. Developers new to BIDS tend not to add it to their workplace.

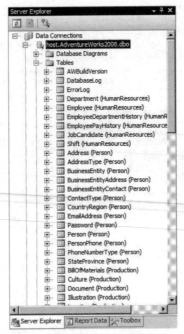

Figure 4-2

It is helpful to have the Server Explorer tool window open on your development environment. If you don't use it that much, you can put it under an active tab. To save time when developing reports, you could use the left pane to keep the Server Explorer window. The Report Data window is almost always active, and the Server Explorer resides under it, but this way, when you need to make a change to a column in your database, you can just click the Server Explorer tab next to the Report Data tab. This way you don't have to open SQL Management Studio to make a change while you're in the middle of developing a report, as shown in Figure 4-2.

The Solution Explorer

The Solution Explorer is where all of the reports, data sources, and models in a solution are shown. The Solution Explorer displays the physical files you have in your project. By default, there will be two folders, named Shared Data Sources and Reports, as shown in Figure 4-3. When you open the Adventure Works sample report project, you will see that the sample solution has several files.

The files ending with the .rds extension are your data sources and are kept under the Shared Data Sources folder. The files ending with the .rdl extension are report files and are kept under the Report folder in the Solution Explorer, as shown in Figure 4-3.

Figure 4-3

You can add a new or existing report to a solution by right-clicking the Reports folder and clicking the action you wish to perform, as shown in Figure 4-4. Similarly, you can add a new Data Source to the project by right-clicking the Shared Data Sources folder and clicking the action you wish to perform.

Figure 4-4

When a new project is created in BIDS, it will automatically create a solution for that project. A solution can have more than one project attached to it. Using the Solution Explorer, you can view all projects attached to the solution. To add a new project to the solution, click File ⇨ Add ⇨ New Project, as shown in Figure 4-5.

Figure 4-5

Once you click New Project from the menu, the new project window will appear. In this window you can select the type of the new project you wish to add, then name it and click OK. This will add a project to your solution, and the Solution Explorer will display all of the solution files, which now include a new project, as shown in Figure 4-6.

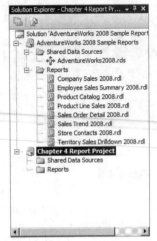

Figure 4-6

To enable the Solution Explorer click View ➪ Solution Explorer or perform the following key combination: Ctrl+Alt+L.

Report Data

This tool window allows you to create and manage data items used in your reports. In most cases, for a report you will need to create a dataset in BIDS, and all of your datasets will be presented to you in this window. Although datasets are what you mostly manage in this window, you can manage other items with the Report Data window. The Report Data window presents the following groupings, as shown in Figure 4-7.

❑ Built-in Fields

❑ Parameters

❑ Images

❑ Dataset(s)

To enable the Report Data window, click View ➪ Report Data. This is the last option on the list.

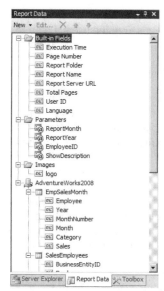

Figure 4-7

Built-in Fields

The Built-In Fields grouping has a list of predefined report information provided by Reporting Services. Built-in fields become handy when you need to display or use information. The fields available to you are the Execution time of the report, Total pages of the report, the current page number on a report, Report folder, Report name, report server URL, User ID, and Language.

When do you use the built-in fields? Built-in fields are used quite frequently when developing reports to enhance the user experience. For example, when a report is deployed to SharePoint, it can be secured using the SharePoint security model, but this means you require separate reports per user group to secure the information being displayed. This works out when you create one report for managers and another for employees, but what if you need to create a report for your clients?

You don't really want all clients to see other client's information, and you most definitely don't want to create a copy of the same report for all of your clients, but with SharePoint security that's what you have to do, right? Not really. You can create a single report but use a built-in field to secure the information displayed in your report. To accomplish this, you create your SQL query in a way where it takes in the User ID as a parameter and returns data only that User ID can see. At runtime, you pass in the User ID built-in field as a parameter to the query, which secures the data. This allows you to create a single report that allows different types of users to consume their personalized data, since the report shows only the information that the users have access to based on their User ID.

Execution Time is another built-in field commonly used on reports. It becomes very handy when you display the timestamp on reports, as this give the users a way to tell when the report was last executed and how fresh the data is.

Parameters

The Parameters grouping has a list of the parameters being used in the report. Parameters are typically used to filter data on a report and mostly are generated on the SQL query statements. If the SQL query used as the dataset has a parameter named ReportYear, the parameter will appear under the Parameters grouping as @ReportYear. You can consider these types of parameters to be query parameters.

Although mostly parameters come from your SQL query, you can still go ahead and create your own. To add a new parameter, right-click the Parameters grouping and click Add Parameter. As you click Add Parameter, you will get a new dialog box, as shown in Figure 4-8. The parameter you're creating can have a type of Text, Boolean, Date/Time, Integer, or Float. Also, once you determine the type of parameter, you can specify the visibility settings of the parameter. You can make your parameter visible, hidden, or internal.

For example, going back to the example used in built-in fields, where you needed to create a report for your clients using the User ID built-in parameter. That example could use a hidden parameter where the value of the parameter is equal to the logged-in users' ID. To assign the User ID to the parameter as a value, you click the Available Values section of the Report Parameter Properties dialog. Using the expression builder, you can select the built-in field User ID, as shown in Figure 4-9. In this example, you use the expression builder to select your value, but the values can also be populated using a dataset. So if you need to, you can easily show a list of all employees as a parameter. This also helps when cascading parameters are needed on a report.

Although this section does not go into the details of expression builder, you will find references to the expression builder throughout this chapter and you can find more details on the expression builder in the upcoming chapters.

You can also use expressions on a report to do conditional formatting based on the parameter's value. For example, assume that you have a parameter named Status and you're showing the status of all projects. Using conditional formatting you can change the background color of the row based on the status of the project. For example if the Status parameter is marked Critical, you can give it a red background, and if it's marked Complete, you can give it a green background. Depending on your requirements, you can even add images based on a condition you define using the parameter's value.

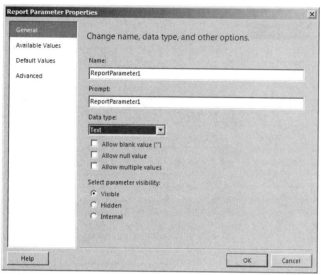

Figure 4-8

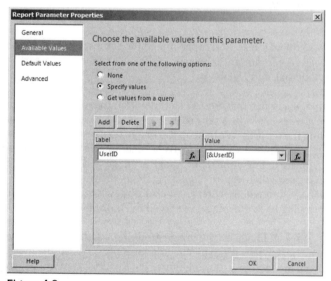

Figure 4-9

Images

The Images grouping has a list of the images available for use in the report. Images typically used in reports are logos and/or backgrounds. Although images can exist in a report in many forms, the Report Data window (or pane) does not show the source of the image directly under the Images grouping. To learn the source of the image, right-click the image in the report designer and click Image Properties. Also, if you're adding an image to a report for the first time, you will be presented with the Image Properties dialog box, shown in Figure 4-10.

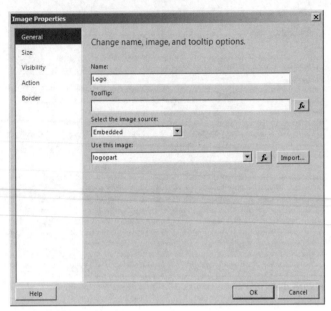

Figure 4-10

As shown in Figure 4-10, there is a section in the Image Properties dialog box that allows for an image source, and this value is very important when adding images to the report. The options you can select from are Embedded, External, and Database.

If you select Embedded, the image then will be stored within the report definition. This option is mostly used when the image always has to be a part of the report and does not need to be shared. If you select External, you are telling the report sever to keep the image on the server, and this option is particularly useful when displaying static images such as logos or other images shared across reports. And finally, if you select Database, you are telling your report that the image you are using is binary data stored in a database. This option is used when you're displaying items such as products in a product catalog report. When you select Database, you will then get another dropdown that will allow you to select the field in your dataset that is bringing back the image, as shown in Figure 4-11.

So to summarize, if you see an image on the Image grouping, that doesn't necessarily mean you are using it in your report. It just means it's available to your report. To add the image to your report, drag and drop the image from the toolbox grouping under the Report Data Window to your report design surface. When an image is added to the report, the Image Properties dialog box will automatically open and you get all the bells and whistles, since you have the ability to customize the image properties using the Image Properties dialog box.

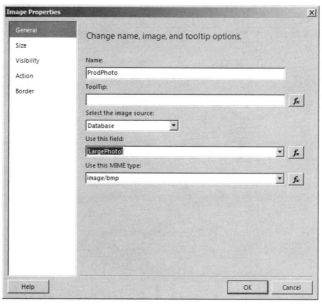

Figure 4-11

Datasets

Although there is no group header named Datasets, you do have datasets in your report data tool window. The datasets used in your report are typically grouped under the data source name the dataset is using. Datasets are the source of information to your reports, and typically you have one dataset for your report, but there are times when you will have multiple datasets. For example, if you open the Product Line Sales report from the Adventure Works sample reports solution, you will see that it has several datasets, as show in Figure 4-12.

In Figure 4-12, under the AdventureWorks2008 data source, you have the following datasets: Top Employees, ProductCategories, TopCustomerStores, and ProductSubCategories. Each dataset returns its own set of fields. For example, the ProductSubCategories dataset has the following fields: ProductSubCategoryID, ProductCategoryID, and Name, as shown in Figure 4-12.

So why do you need multiple datasets? In some cases you might not want to create several reports to show different segments of your data. Sometimes it makes sense to bring all information into one report, giving it a dashboard look and feel. In cases such as this, you might have different sections on a report that all need their own dataset. When you look at the Product Line Sales report example that is a part of the Adventure Works solution, you will see that there are multiple parts of the report, as shown in Figure 4-13.

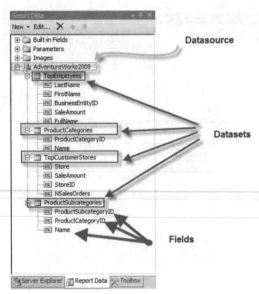

Figure 4-12

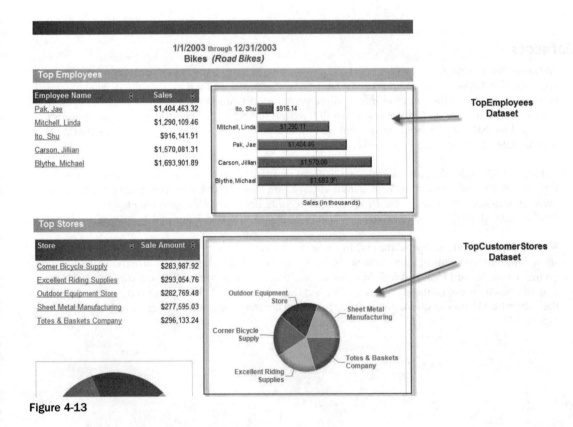

Figure 4-13

To create a new dataset, you can click on the New button located on the top left of the Report Data tool window, as shown in Figure 4-12, or you can simply right-click the data source and add a new dataset. Although you will not walk though how you can create a dataset now, this will be covered later in this chapter.

When designing a report, this tool window will be used frequently because once you have your datasets and fields accessible, you drag and drop the fields into your report.

The Toolbox

This is one of the most important tool windows you will use when developing reports. This tool window allows you to add report-design elements when creating reports. The report items available through the Toolbox tool window are:

- ❏ **Text box:** Displays labels, fields, or values calculated from expressions.
- ❏ **Line:** Draws a line from one point to another. Mainly used for look and feel.
- ❏ **Table:** Displays data in a grid view that has a fixed number of columns and a variable number of rows.
- ❏ **Matrix:** Displays aggregated data in a grid but has a variable number of columns and rows.
- ❏ **Rectangle:** Draws a box as a container for other report items. Rectangles have functionality that becomes useful when doing paging, as it can add page breaks before or after the rectangle.
- ❏ **List:** Displays a set of report items repeated for each group or row of data.
- ❏ **Image:** Displays an image such as a logo on the report.
- ❏ **Subreport:** Displays an embedded report within a report.
- ❏ **Chart:** Displays data in chart types such as bar, pie, and line graphs.
- ❏ **Gauge:** Displays a value, field, or expression in a linear or radial gauge format.

To create any report, you will use at least one of these items in BIDS, which makes this tool window a very popular one. To enable this tool window, click View ➪ Toolbox or perform the following key combination: Ctrl+Alt+X.

Text Boxes

Text box is one of the most widely used report items. Initially, the name gives the impression that it's only used as a label on a report, but the text box is far more powerful than a regular text box. With the help of expressions, you write your own text in a text box but can also bind it to a field in your dataset using expressions. So when a text box is combined with the powerful expressions of the report, the number of things you can do is limitless.

To add a text box to a report, simply click the text box report item under the Toolbox tool window and drag it into your report. Once the text box is in the report design region, right-click the text box and click its properties to modify the properties of the report, as shown in Figure 4-14. To assign a value to the text box, click the Expression button (fx) located next to the Value section. Once you click the Expression button, you will get the Expression dialog box, which will allow you to bind the text box to the available items in your report, as shown in Figure 4-15. For example, if you wanted to display the Report Name on the text box, you would assign the value [&ReportName] to the text box value. You see that the value in the Text Box dialog box is represented as [&ReportName], as shown in Figure 4-14. When viewed in the Expression dialog box, it is represented as =Globals!ReportName, as shown in Figure 4-15.

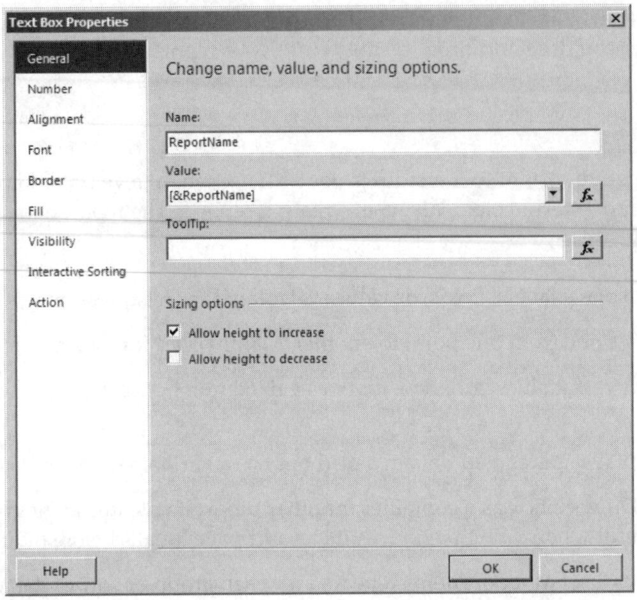

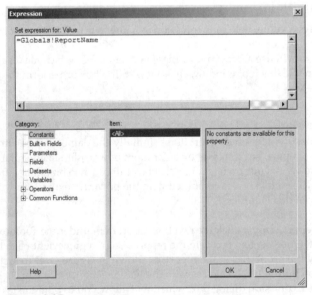

Figure 4-14

Figure 4-15

So what is the term Globals located in front of the ReportName field in the expression? Globals is a built-in collection of information provided by Reporting Services, and there are other collections available when you're creating an expression. The expressions allow you to create very powerful formulas that utilize different collections, as shown in Figure 4-16.

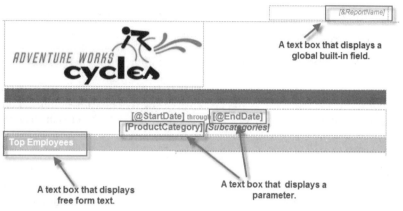

Figure 4-16

The collections available through the expression builder are listed in the table that follows. You can create dynamic text boxes with expressions, but text boxes are not the only types of report items you can use with expressions. As you develop reports, you'll notice that expressions are used widely and are very powerful when creating reports.

Built-in Collection	Category	Example
Globals	Built-in Fields	`=Globals!ReportName`
User	Built-in Fields	`=User!UserID`
Parameters	Parameters	`=Parameters!ProductCategory.Value`
Fields	Fields	`=Fields!Sales.Value`
Datasets	Built-in Fields	`=Sum(Fields!SaleAmount.Value,` `"TopCustomerStores")`
DataSources	Not Shown	`=DataSources("AdventureWorks").Type`
Variables	Variables	`=Fields!YearlyIncome.Value`
ReportItems	Not Shown	`=ReportItems("Textbox1").Value`

Operators and common functions are also available to you when creating expressions. Especially on text boxes, one of the most common groups used is the Text function group, which provides functions such as:

❑ **UCase:** Used as UCase(Fields!Description.Value) and returns the string in uppercase.

❑ **Join:** Used as =Join(Parameters!MultivalueParameter.Value,",") and joins substrings and provides a single string.

❑ **Format Currency:** Used as FormatCurrency(string) and formats the string as currency format.

❑ **Space:** Used as Space(3) and returns the number of spaces provided.

❑ **Trim:** Used as Trim(string) and returns the passed string with no leading and no trailing spaces.

So remember that the Text Box report item is your friend when you're creating a report. The consumer of the report will not know that there are several text boxes being dynamically populated on your report but will appreciate the information being displayed on the report, which helps the user make fast and accurate business decisions.

Rectangles and Lines

Rectangle and Line report items are used mostly for their help in making the report look better and are not data bound. The Line is mostly used for decoration purposes to clearly separate the other report items. You'll see it used as header and footer lines. You can change the properties of a Line by using the Properties pane discussed later in this chapter.

Rectangles are a little bit more than decoration tools; they can also serve as containers for report items. Rectangles are a great way to add page breaks to reports. Although the Line report item doesn't have a GUI for the properties, if you right-click the Rectangle report item and click the rectangle properties, you will get the Rectangle Properties dialog box. In the Rectangle Properties dialog box, you have the ability to customize the following page-break options, as shown in Figure 4-17.

❑ Add a page break before the rectangle.

❑ Add a page break after the rectangle.

❑ Omit border on page break.

❑ Keep the contents together on a single page if possible.

This is one of the most powerful things you can do with rectangles, since not all the reports you'll be developing will fit on one page. In some cases, you might have groupings that you want to start from their own pages because you might be giving each groups' report print out to a different person. With page breaks you can take care of these types of business requirements.

When a Rectangle is used as a container, it can also be used to show and hide parts of the report based on expressions. Say you want to show a bar chart if the product categories are less than three and a pie chart if they are three or more. With a rectangle you can create two rectangles and determine their visibility based on the expression. You can also have a button that allows the user to toggle the rectangle by clicking a report item.

You can also use the Rectangle report item for decoration purposes, as it can have background colors, images, and borders, as shown in Figure 4-18.

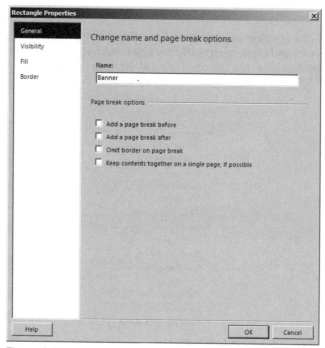

Figure 4-17

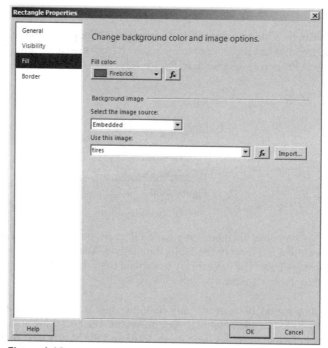

Figure 4-18

Lists

The List report item is the simplest way to display repeating data in a report and is a free-form data region. The Table, Matrix, and Chart report items are also considered data regions, since they display repeating data in different views. The List report item allows you to display data in a basic list format, as shown in Figure 4-19.

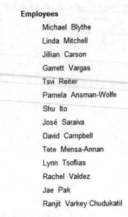

Employees
Michael Blythe
Linda Mitchell
Jillian Carson
Garrett Vargas
Tsvi Reiter
Pamela Ansman-Wolfe
Shu Ito
José Saraiva
David Campbell
Tete Mensa-Annan
Lynn Tsoflias
Rachel Valdez
Jae Pak
Ranjit Varkey Chudukatil

Figure 4-19

The List report item can be added to a report by dragging and dropping it to the report design area. Once you drag and drop the List report item to the report design area and right-click the area, you will see an option for Tablix Properties, as shown in Figure 4-20.

Insert Column
Delete Columns
Add Group
Row Group
Column Visibility...
Tablix Properties...

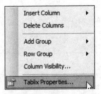

Figure 4-20

You've added a list, so why does the menu only have Tablix properties and not List Properties? This is because the List report item is a form of the Tablix data region. The Tablix data region is a new addition to SQL Reporting Services 2008. The easiest way to explain the Tablix data region is the following representation: Tablix = Table + Matrix.

This is the ultimate data region, because it's fully customizable. You can easily add rows, columns, groups, and report items to it, which makes it very powerful. The best thing about the Tablix is that it comes with no restrictions like the older versions of Table and the Matrix data regions did. With a Tablix data region, you get the best of all worlds. You can have all of the good qualities of the Table and Matrix data regions combined.

The List data region is the simplest form of a Tablix data region. In SQL 2008, the new Table and Matrix data regions are also derived from the Tablix data region. So the Matrix and the Table are now just templates created from a Tablix data region. You can start from a List report item and easily create a Table report item by adding a header and a column or start with a Table data region and create a Matrix data region or have both in one data region.

> Tablix is a data region that displays repeating data that can be organized in rows and columns. Each Tablix cell can include any report item and any number of report items if you use a Rectangle as a container. The Table tablix template displays data in a grid format, the Matrix template groups data in a grid, and the List displays data in a free-form layout.

Tables

The Table report item is the data region that allows you to display data in a tabular or grid format. Unlike the List report item, the Table report item has several columns, as shown in Figure 4-21. In the Table report item, the most important thing to remember is that the columns will not change at runtime. This report will always have three columns: Employee Name, Job Title, and Sales YTD. So if data is displayed in a tabular format and the columns are locked, you have used a Table report item.

Employee Name	Job Title	Sales YTD
Michael Blythe	Sales Representative	$4,557,045.05
Linda Mitchell	Sales Representative	$5,200,475.23
Jillian Carson	Sales Representative	$3,857,163.63
Garrett Vargas	Sales Representative	$1,764,938.99
Tsvi Reiter	Sales Representative	$2,811,012.72
Pamela Ansman-Wolfe	Sales Representative	$0.00
Shu Ito	Sales Representative	$3,018,725.49
José Saraiva	Sales Representative	$3,189,356.25
David Campbell	Sales Representative	$3,587,378.43
Tete Mensa-Annan	Sales Representative	$1,931,620.18
Lynn Tsoflias	Sales Representative	$1,758,385.93
Rachel Valdez	Sales Representative	$2,241,204.04
Jae Pak	Sales Representative	$5,015,682.38
Ranjit Varkey Chudukatil	Sales Representative	$3,827,950.24

Figure 4-21

Matrixes

The Matrix report item is the data region that allows you to display data in a tabular or grid format and allows you to group columns. Unlike the Table report item, the Matrix report item can group columns, as shown in Figure 4-22. With the Matrix report item, the most important thing to remember is that the columns can change at runtime. If there are multiple years, this report will show all of them as columns.

		2002				2003
		Q1	Q2	Q3	Q4	
Accessories12/1/2003		$4,946	$11,639	$45,335	$31,877	$531,597
Bikes 12/1/2003	Mountain Bikes	$2,497,518	$2,416,837	$3,141,467	$2,837,647	$12,235,870
	Road Bikes	$3,171,788	$3,478,964	$4,930,693	$4,189,622	$14,748,072
	Touring Bikes					$6,640,069
Clothing12/1/2003		$11,712	$20,310	$265,585	$192,213	$994,490
Components12/1/2003		$175,044	$376,247	$1,935,906	$1,123,845	$5,489,741

Figure 4-22

So depending on the parameters being passed to your report, you can have one or several columns. If data is displayed in a tabular format, the columns can be grouped, and the number of columns is determined at runtime, you have used a Matrix report item.

Images

The Image report item is mostly used for look and feel purposes for adding backgrounds and logos to your reports but also can be used to display images hosted in the database. A good example of this is the Product Catalog report that is a part of the AdventureWorks2008 report solution. For example, in the Product Catalog sample report shown in Figure 4-23, the images displayed are being pulled from the database.

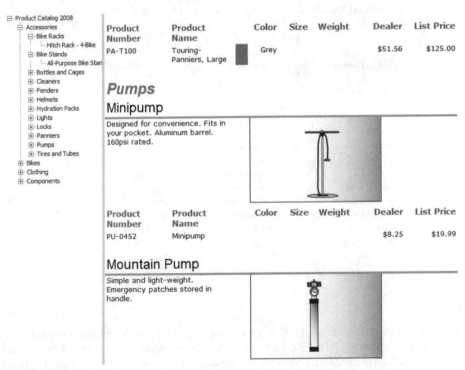

Figure 4-23

One of the other utilizations for images is using an image based on a condition. You can get a Key Performance Indicator (KPI) experience when you show and hide images based on their condition. For example, you can show a red stop light when sales are below a certain number, or you can display a green circle when the product is in stock or a orange exclamation point when a project is not doing so good. So when using expressions, you can customize the look and feel of the report at runtime.

Subreports

The Subreport report item is used to display other reports inside the body a report. You can think of the subreport as a Page Viewer Web Part in SharePoint. Subreports are very useful when you need to create cascading reports, since you can use the data on the parent report and pass it on to the subreport. And now with the addition of Tablix you can even add a subreport in a Table or Matrix and have it repeated in the main report.

To add a subreport to your report, all you have to do is drag and drop the subreport report item from the Toolbox into your report region. When you add the subreport to your report, you will see a gray area on your report, as shown in Figure 4-24. Using the properties of the subreport, you will link a report to this region and when the report is rendered, the subreport, in this case, the Sales Trend 2008, will appear, as shown in Figure 4-24.

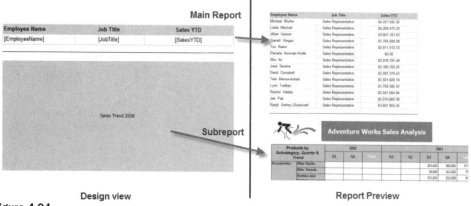

Figure 4-24

You should know that using subreports does have a performance hit on your reports. If you can, try to use the data regions to meet the business requirements. Subreports are typically used when you need to use two different data sources within a single data region. Since you normally cannot add a different data source in a Tablix region when it's associated with another one, the best way to overcome this issue is to add a subreport in the Tablix, and the parent report will pass on a parameter to the subreport. This way you get to use two different data sources without having to custom code.

> **Always remember to refresh the parent report's preview after making changes to your subreports.**

Charts

The Chart data region is used to display charts in your reports. Charts are the graphical representation of your data and one of the most popular data regions.

When you drag and drop the Chart report item to your report region, you will automatically get the Chart wizard, which will ask you to select the Chart type you wish to create. There are 58 different types, so you have a wide variety of options. After you select the type of report you wish to have with SSRS 2008, you have the ability to fully customize your charts.

You can easily change the type of the report by right-clicking the Chart Area, as shown in Figure 4-25, and clicking the Change Chart Type option. When you right-click the Chart Area, you also get the Chart menu, which allows you to add a new title, add a new legend, and add a new Chart Area. You can also get to the Chart properties, Chart Area properties, Value Axis properties, Category Axis properties, Series properties, and Legend properties using the Chart menu.

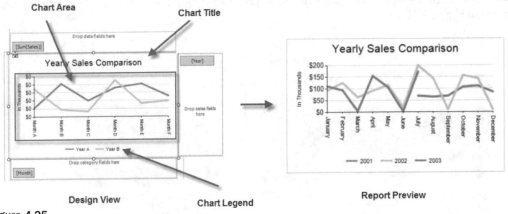

Figure 4-25

Depending on where you right-click, you will get different options. If you click the bars of the graph, you will see a Show Data Values option, which will show the values on top of the bars. Similarly, if you were to right-click the axis, you will get the option to either show or hide the axis, show or hide the axis title, and show or hide major or minor gridlines. Be sure to right-click anything you are looking to modify. When modifying charts, right-clicking is your friend.

To modify the chart properties, click the Chart Properties option, as shown in Figure 4-26. In the Chart Properties dialog box, you can change the dataset the chart uses. You can also make look and feel changes to the chart using the Chart Properties dialog box. There are several color palettes to choose from, as shown in Figure 4-27, and the Color Palette option allows you to quickly change the colors applied to your graph.

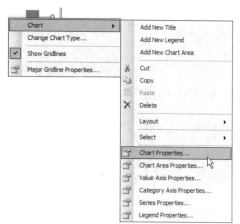

Figure 4-26

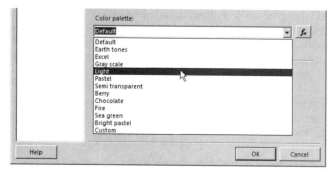

Figure 4-27

Gauges

Gauges are the newest addition to SQL Reporting Services. There are two types of gauges: linear and radial. Gauges are made up of several components, such as the major tick mark, scale label, minor tick mark, pointer, pointer cap, and range, as shown in Figure 4-28.

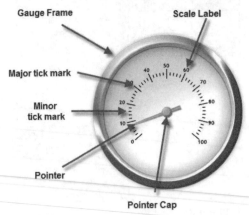

Figure 4-28

To get a better idea of what you can do with gauges, take a look at the sample Gauges project that also comes with the Adventure Works Reporting Services sample reports. The Gauges project is located under the Offline reports solution. You can access this project at [Drive Letter]:\Program Files\ Microsoft SQL Server\100\Samples\Reporting Services\Report Samples\ AdventureWorksOffline Sample Reports.

Similar to charts, when modifying the gauge you can right-click the component you wish to modify to get the menu items for that item. For example, by right-clicking the pointer, you can get to the pointer properties and change the needle style, as shown in Figure 4-29.

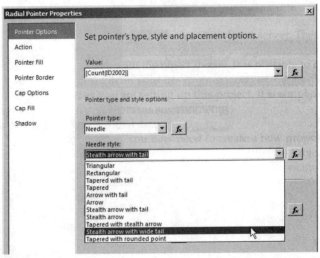

Figure 4-29

The Properties Window

The Properties window lists the properties of an object. This window is used to update or view the properties of an object. One of the most important properties you will update through this tool window is the Properties window for the solution, since this is where you define where in SharePoint the reports will be deployed. This book will cover how to deploy reports to SharePoint in greater detail in the following chapters. To enable the Properties window, click View ⇨ Properties or click F4.

Once you're comfortable creating reports, you'll find yourself using the Properties window more often. The Properties window is a quick way to update a specific setting in an object. It's a little more advanced, since there is no nice interface, but when you know what you want to change, having the Properties window is a time saver. Once you select a report item on the report region, the Properties window will immediately get updated with the properties of that report item. For example, if you click a Tablix report item such as a Table or a Matrix, you will see a Properties window similar to the one shown in Figure 4-30.

You can either see the properties of a report item grouped by the settings it applies to or alphabetically listed using the sort icons on the top of the Properties window. You can also click the Properties dialog box icon, which will launch the Properties dialog box for that object.

The dropdown at the top of the Properties window will allow you to easily switch among the objects you have in your report. If you name your report items intuitively, this menu will be easier to use and will allow you to update any setting through the Properties window much faster.

Figure 4-30

The Report Designer Window

This window is the most used area when designing reports in BIDS. This is where you design your report. You can drag and drop report items from the toolbox to the Report Designer window, as shown in Figure 4-31. This is a WYSIWYG type of report layout tool, since the report will look exactly like what you have in the report designer view. Once you open a report, the report designer view is shown for report design.

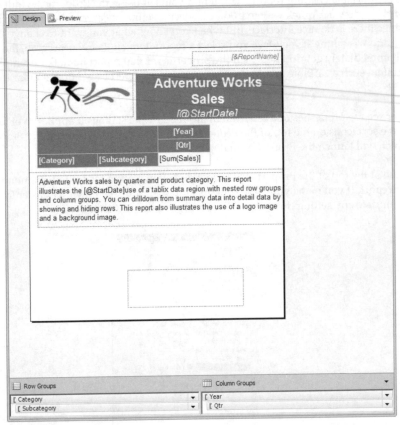

Figure 4-31

When you right-click the report region, you will get the ability to change the properties of the report and add a header and a footer. Once you click the Report Properties option, you will get the Report Properties dialog box, as shown in Figure 4-32. In the Report Properties dialog box, you can change the orientation of the page and the size of the report.

This is also the place where you go to add a variable, a reference to a dll, or custom code to your report. The custom code that will be used by the expressions in your report are methods written in Visual Basic. You can have multiple methods in your custom code, and you can reference your methods in your expressions using the collection named Code. An example of an expression that uses custom code is as follows: =Code.MyCustomMethod(Fields!StandardCost.Value).

> When you load a custom assembly for your report, BIDS will not unload it until you close it. So if you make changes to your custom assembly, make sure you close BIDS to see your changes.

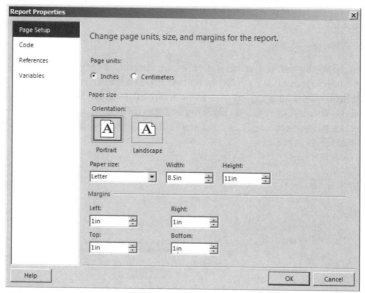

Figure 4-32

The Report Preview

The report preview goes hand in hand with the Report Designer window. The tab for this window is right next to the Report Design view tab. Once you have completed the design of a report, you can quickly view how your report will look and feel by clicking the Report Preview tab. Without having to deploy the report, you can preview your report to see if all of your expressions are being calculated correctly or if the grouping is working the way you designed it. This can be considered the design debugger of a report.

Also note that BIDS will cache the dataset to disk as a .rdl.data file to improve performance when generating the preview, so make sure that when you make changes to the data the report is not being loaded from the cache. Sometimes you might forget that BIDS caches the data it displays, and the totals of your calculations might seem wrong even though they are not. Always make sure that the data being displayed is correct when debugging totals in the report preview.

To get rid of cached data, delete the .rdl.data file. This file is in the same location as your .rdl files. In the Adventure Works Sample Report project, this is located under the `[Drive Letter]:\Program Files\ Microsoft SQL Server\100\Samples\Reporting Services\Report Samples\AdventureWorks Sample Reports` folder, as shown in Figure 4-33.

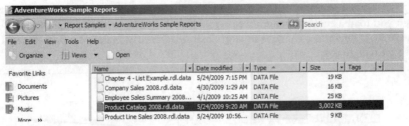

Figure 4-33

Although you can manually delete the .rdl.data files, this becomes very tedious when you're developing a report. But don't worry; there is a free add-in named BIDSHelper that can be found at CodePlex. The BIDSHelper has a little menu item that allows us to delete all .rsl.data files with matter of a click, as shown in Figure 4-34. You can download BIDSHelper from the following location: `http://bidshelper.` `codeplex.com/Wiki/View.aspx?title=Delete%20Dataset%20Cache%20Files`. You can also search for BIDSHelper `www.codeplex.com`.

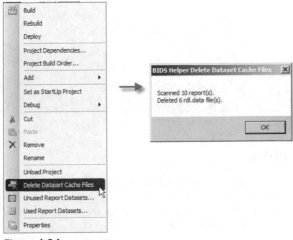

Figure 4-34

The Grouping Window

This window is a new addition with BIDS 2008; report developers can now easily see what kind of grouping is being applied to the data that the report is utilizing. The Grouping window is located right underneath the Report Designer window. An example of a grouping window can be seen in one of the earlier figures, Figure 4-31. This window will show the row and column grouping of the data. For example, the column grouping for the report being displayed in Figure 4-31 is "First group the data by category, then by subcategory."

Using this window, you can modify the grouping by simply right-clicking the columns shown in the Grouping window. You can add a new group before or after the column, delete a group, and also add totals to the report, as shown in Figure 4-35. You can also change the group properties by right clicking the group name, which allows you to change properties such as Page Breaks, Sorting, Visibility, and Filtering. You can also create page breaks between each instance of a group using the Group Properties dialog box.

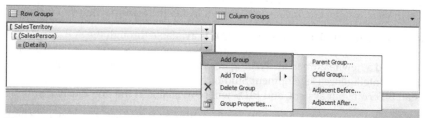

Figure 4-35

The Errors List and Output Windows

The Error List and Output windows are generally used when you are deploying reports to SharePoint. Before a report is deployed to SharePoint, BIDS validates the report, and if there are any errors, it will display it on the Output and Error List windows.

The Output window displays each of the steps when deploying reports to SharePoint, as shown in Figure 4-36. It will notify the developer by letting him know where the report is being deployed and how many errors there are, if any errors arise during deployment. The details of the error can be viewed at the Error List window.

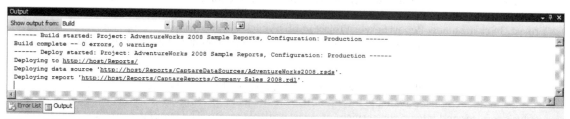

Figure 4-36

Using BIDS 2008 on Your Machine

Now that you've covered the bits and pieces of BIDS at a high level, the next thing is to start the BIDS 2008 application on your development machines so you can go ahead and create a report. But before you start, you need to know how to access BIDS 2008 or, better yet, how to install it if you don't have it on your development machines. Consider the following questions:

❑ **Where can you find BIDS 2008?** To access BIDS, navigate to Start ⇨ All Programs ⇨ Microsoft SQL Server 2008 ⇨ SQL Server Business Intelligence Development Studio. If you do not see BIDS 2008 in your system, that means you did not install the feature when you installed SQL Server.

❑ **How do you install BIDS 2008?** BIDS 2008 is available through the SQL Server install CD. To install BIDS 2008, you must start the SQL installation process and select the option that allows you to add a new feature to an existing instance. On the Feature Selection dialog box, check the Business Intelligence Development Studio check box and continue with the install. This will install BIDS on your system, and BIDS will be available at the previously mentioned path.

❑ **How do you install BIDS 2008 without installing SQL Server?** The above section explained how you can install it if you already have a SQL instance installed on your system, but what if you don't have SQL server installed? Can you install BIDS 2008 without installing SQL Server? The answer is yes.

In SQL Server 2005 there was a Tools folder, but in SQL Server 2008 this was removed. To install BIDS 2008 without installing SQL, you need to run sql_bids.msi, located under the Setup folder (%source%\ x86\Setup) of the SQL install CD.

Creating Report Projects Using BIDS

Now that you know where to find BIDS, let's go through what you can do with it. The next sections of this chapter will walk you through creating a report using BIDS and will allow you to use the tool windows and report items detailed in earlier sections. Please note that in this chapter you will not go into all of the details of creating the report. The goal of this section is to get you prepared for the next chapter, where you will be creating your first report using BIDS. So let's go ahead and start by creating a project. To create a new Report Server Project in BIDS, click the File ⇨ New ⇨ Project menu item. (Depending on your version of the Visual Studio your settings, you might need to click on File ⇨ New Project.)

Once you do this, you will get the New Project dialog box, as shown in Figure 4-37. As you can see from Figure 4-37, the templates available through BIDS are not just reporting-services related. There are also analysis services and integration services projects available to you. The templates used for report projects are:

❑ Report Server Project Wizard

❑ Report Server Project

❑ Report Model Project

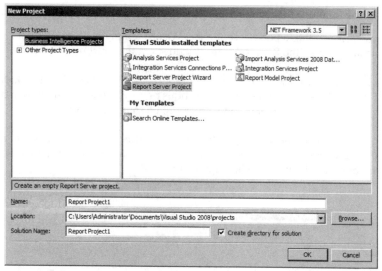

Figure 4-37

Using the Report Server Project Wizard

To get you exposed to BIDS, in this section you will select the Report Server Project Wizard template to create a report project. This template will walk you through the steps in creating a report. The Report Server Project Wizard template will help you greatly if you are creating a report for the first time, and you'll see this in greater detail in the next chapter.

The wizard will allow you to first select a data source or create a new one, which will allow you to get the data that you will report on. In the second step, the wizard will walk you through creating your query, which will allow you to get the data you will report on. The next step is to choose the type of the report; once you select the type of report, the final steps allow you to modify the look and feel of your report.

So let's go through these steps to better understand the capabilities of BIDS. We will start with creating a new project. To create a new project in BIDS using Report Server Project Wizard template, perform the following steps:

1. In the New Project window, click the Report Server Project Wizard template.

2. Once you select the template, you will see that BIDS will automatically name your project Report Project 1. At this point, give your project a name.

3. Then set the location where you wish to save your project files and click OK to continue.

4. Since you selected the Report Server Project Wizard template, BIDS will first create the project files and will pop up the Report Wizard window. On the welcome screen, click Next.

After the project is created, the first step of the Report Server Project Wizard will make you select the data source that you will use in your report. Since at this point you really don't have a data source, in the next steps you will create a new data source that will be shared across the reports.

1. This will bring you to the first step of the process: "Select the Data Source." In this screen, change the Data Source name to something related to your project; in your case, you will name the data source dsChapter4, as shown in Figure 4-38.

Figure 4-38

2. In the Connection String text box area, you can directly paste the connection string you might have, or you can use the connection string wizard to create a new one. To create a connection string, click the "Edit..." button located next to the Connection string text box, as shown in Figure 4-38.

3. Once you click Edit, the Connection Properties dialog box will appear, as shown in Figure 4-39. Select the name of your server and the name of the database, as shown in Figure 4-39. In your case, you will use the AdventureWorks2008 database, which is located on the server localhost.

4. Once you have selected the data source, server, and database name, click Test Connection. If the connection is successful, you will get a dialog box letting you know that the connection was successful as. Once the connection is successful, click OK.

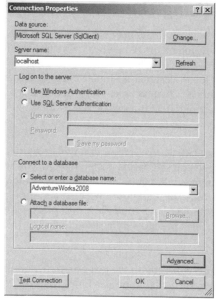

Figure 4-39

5. Once you have selected the data source, server, and database name, click Test Connection. If the connection is successful, you will get a dialog box letting you know that the connection was successful. Once the connection is successful, click OK on the Connection Properties screen.

6. Once you click OK, the wizard will automatically create your connection string, as shown in Figure 4-38.

What Other Data Sources Can You Use?

Please note that on the Connection Properties dialog box, the data source you have selected is Microsoft SQL Server (SqlClient). But this is not the only option when creating a data source. If you click the Change Data Source button, you will see that you can connect to your data hosted in Hyperion Essbase, Microsoft SQL Server Analysis Services, ODBC, OLE DB, Oracle, and SAP NetWeaver BI, as shown in Figure 4-40.

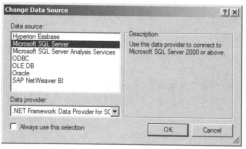

Figure 4-40

Creating the Query Using the Query Designer

At this point, you are ready to move on to the next step: designing the query. In this step, you can paste a query written by one of your developers or create your own query on the fly using the Query Designer.

If you're a SQL developer, the Query Designer is similar to the designer query provided with SQL Management Studio. If you're not a SQL developer, think of this as a powerful and easy to use user interface that will allow you to design data queries on the fly by dragging and dropping tables and selecting the columns you wish to show.

Once you click OK on the Select Data Source screen, you will be redirected to a screen that will ask you for your query. Since the database you selected is hosted in SQL, you will be writing a SQL statement to select data. The result of this query is what you will present in the report. If you're not a SQL Developer, you must always remember to think through your query. At a minimum, make sure that your query does not take too long to run and make sure you follow best practices when creating SQL Queries. You can get a head start on SQL best practices by visiting http://msdn.microsoft.com/en-us/sqlserver/bb671432.aspx.

Although you can paste your query directly in the text box shown in Figure 4-41, in this walkthrough you will create a query that will return all of the Sales Employees for Adventure Works using the Query Builder.

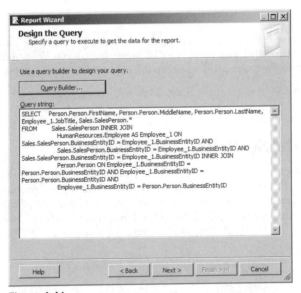

Figure 4-41

1. To start designing your query, click the button named Query Builder. This will open the Query Designer. On the white space, right-click and click the Add Table option on the dropdown menu.

2. This will open the Add Table window. In this window, find the tables named Employee, Person, SalesPerson, and SalesTerritory, using the Add Table window. You can also use the CTRL key when selecting tables. By using CTRL, you can select all the tables by clicking once instead of doing it four times. Once you have selected all of the tables, press the Add button to add these tables to your query.

3. Once the tables are added to the designers relationship view, click Close to close the Add Table window. If you're new to terms such as JOIN, INNER JOIN, LEFT JOIN, and CROSS JOIN, you'll appreciate this step. At this point, you have added all of the tables you are going to collect data from. One of the advantages of the Query Designer is that it automatically understands the relationship between the tables and creates the SQL statement for the relation. It creates your JOINs on the fly, and this is one of the most valuable parts of the Query Designer, as it saves several minutes before coding is applied.

4. Once you add the tables to your designer, your next step is to specify which columns you would like to bring back when you execute the query. To do this, click on the checkboxes next to the fields you want to return in the table definitions shown in the relationship view, as shown in Figure 4-42.

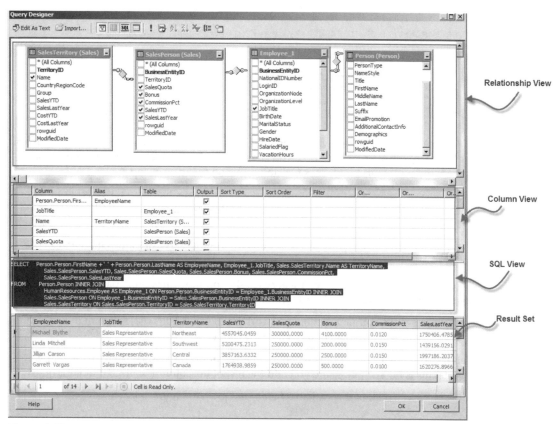

Figure 4-42

5. Make sure you have select the Name column from the SalesTerritory table; the SalesYTD, SalesQuota, Bonus, CommisionPct, and SalesLastYear, columns from the SalesPerson table; the JobTitle column from the Employee table; and the First Name and Last Name columns from the Person table. Once the proper columns are selected, the SQL code will be generated.

At this point, you can customize your query to your needs. For example, you can combine the First Name and LastName into one column and call it EmployeeName and you can also create an alias for the Name column in the Territory table as TerritoryName. The following SQL code creates these aliases:

```
SELECT      Person.Person.FirstName + ' ' +
            Person.Person.LastName AS EmployeeName,
            Employee_1.JobTitle,
            Sales.SalesTerritory.Name AS TerritoryName,
            Sales.SalesPerson.SalesYTD,
            Sales.SalesPerson.SalesQuota,
            Sales.SalesPerson.Bonus,
            Sales.SalesPerson.CommissionPct,
            Sales.SalesPerson.SalesLastYear

FROM        Person.Person
                INNER JOIN HumanResources.Employee AS Employee_1 ON

            Person.Person.BusinessEntityID = Employee_1.BusinessEntityID
                INNER JOIN Sales.SalesPerson ON

            Employee_1.BusinessEntityID = Sales.SalesPerson.BusinessEntityID
                INNER JOIN Sales.SalesTerritory ON

            Sales.SalesPerson.TerritoryID = Sales.SalesTerritory.TerritoryID
```

Paste the above code in your Query Designer and click the Run button at the top of the menu of the designer. Once the query is executed, you should see 14 results returned in the Result Set pane of the window. At this point, click OK and move on to the next step.

6. In this step, you will select the type of report you wish to create. By default, two types of reports come with the Report Wizard: Tabular and Matrix. In this walkthrough, you will select the Tabular type and click Next.

7. On the Design the Table page, you are asked three important pieces of information: Page, Group, and Details.

❑ **Page:** Under the Page section, you will select the column you wish to page the data by. In your case, you will select the TerritoryName column.

❑ **Grouping:** In the Grouping section, you add the columns you wish to group the data by. In your case, you will group all of the data by Job Title.

❑ **Details:** And finally, the Details section will be all of the data you wish to display in your report. This is the section where you add the rest of the columns collected in your query.

Once you have selected all of the available fields, as shown in Figure 4-43, click Next.

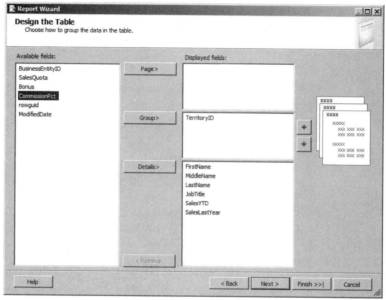

Figure 4-43

8. On the Choose the Table Layout page, you design the table layout. You can either choose Stepped or Block and also have the option to include subtotals and enable drilldown. With the Block option, you don't get drilldown capability, but you get footers that display totals. The totals are displayed at the bottom of the table. With the Stepped option, you don't get footers, but you get drilldown capabilities. You can also include the totals with the Stepped option, but the totals will be shown in the header groupings versus at the footer like the Block option. In your example, select the Stepped option and enable drilldown, as shown in Figure 4-44 and press the Next button to continue.

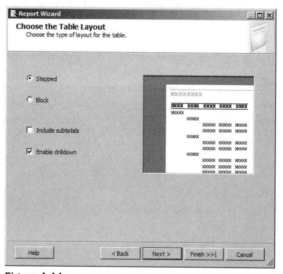

Figure 4-44

9. On the Choose the Table Style page, you select the colors of your report. There are six different types of color combinations you can choose from. In this example, you will select the Corporate look and feel for your report, as shown in Figure 4-45. Once you select the color template you wish to use, click Next.

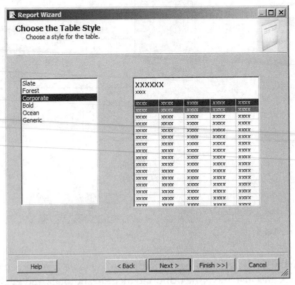

Figure 4-45

10. On the Completing the Wizard page, you name your report and click Finish. In your example, you will name your report Chapter 4 – BIDS Report, as shown in Figure 4-46. Once you name your report, click Finish.

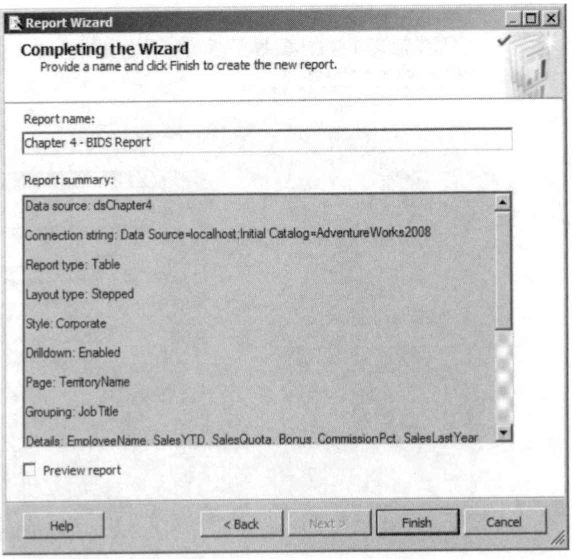

Figure 4-46

11. Once you finish, the Report Wizard BIDS will close the wizard and open the report that you created using the wizard. At the end of this walkthrough, you should see the report shown in Figure 4-47.

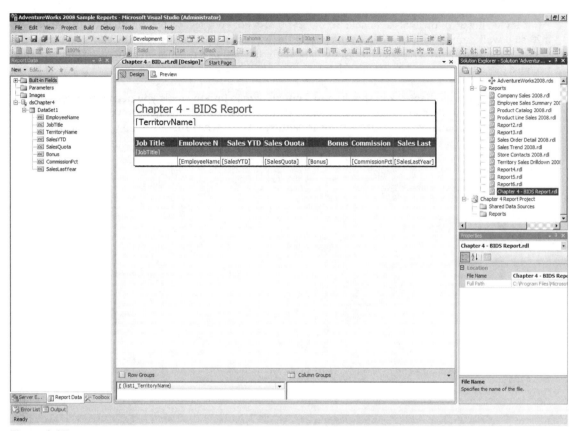

Figure 4-47

Now that the report is created, click Preview to see the report preview.

Summary

In this chapter you were introduced to the powerful report-authoring tool BIDS. The chapter started by going over the tool windows available in Business Intelligence Development Studio. Also, it highlighted the report items used when a report is created. Whether treating a tool window or a report item, each section included a valuable piece of information that will help you in the real world of report developing.

This chapter touched on real-life problems such as the dataset caching on previews. Knowing that BIDS caches the dataset when creating the preview will help you troubleshoot your report issues faster. There are times when the simplest things take the longest amount of time to figure out. And the goal of this chapter was to get you started on the right foot so that you don't lose much time trying to figure out these mysterious BIDS issues.

After reviewing all of the tools available in BIDS, you also got your feet wet using BIDS by running a 20-step walkthrough and creating a report using the wizard. With a matter of a few clicks you created a very informative report. This chapter did not talk about the best practices for creating your first report, because that will be covered in the next chapter.

After completing this chapter, you should now know where to find the tools you need when you're creating reports. As a report author, it's important that you know what you have in your toolbox and how to access it. You know what BIDS stands for and you know what a Tablix is, so you are ready to create reports using BIDS. Have fun creating your first report in the next chapter.

5

Creating Your First Report

When you first picked up this book, you may have thought you were going to learn all about the intricacies of creating a report. However, at this point, you still have not created your first report. You have learned essential things necessary for creating and deploying your reports, such as setting up your server, planning your report, and getting an overview of the tools you will use to create your reports, but you still haven't created a report. It's finally time to do so.

In this chapter, you will get a solid understanding of creating a very basic report. You will be exposed to the Report Wizard that makes creating simple reports a snap. You will learn about the different data types you can use in your report and will see exactly how to utilize SharePoint data in your report.

The next few chapters will go deeper into the report-creation process, but by the end of this chapter, you will have the necessary knowledge to create your own reports in your own environment.

And with that, it's time to get started.

Creating Your Data Backend

The first thing you will need for your reports is a data source. You can use any number of data sources, including the following:

- ❏ Microsoft SQL Server
- ❏ OLE DB
- ❏ Microsoft SQL Server Analysis Services
- ❏ Oracle
- ❏ ODBC

❏ XML

❏ Report Server Model

❏ SAP NetWeaver BI

❏ Hyperion Essbase

❏ TERADATA

Some of these may seem very familiar and some may not. However, one thing you will probably notice is that, with options such as OLE DB, ODBC, and XML, you have a great selection of data repositories at your disposal.

Of this list, probably the two most widely used options are Microsoft SQL Server and XML. SQL is probably fairly intuitive, since this discussion revolves around Microsoft SQL Server Reporting Services, right? It is only logical that the most popular data source to connect to your report would be the parent data backend: SQL Server.

However, the XML data option is at least as important and, depending on your business needs, could be vastly more important than any of the other options. Why is that? Because this allows you to directly connect to any web services rendering XML data. This may not seem like a big deal on the surface but, when you think about it, it really opens up a lot of possibilities. Assume, for example, that you have data that you really need to massage and filter, but it isn't sitting in a typical relational database format. You can create your own web service (using .NET, for example) and do whatever you want to do to data and then just return a dataset or datatable to SSRS with only the data needed for the report.

To add to that, remember that all SharePoint list data is available via web services. So an easy tie-in for SSRS and SharePoint is to access a list's web service and report the information directly in your SSRS report. For example, if you have a task list in your site collection, you can pull up the site list web service and display the task information directly in your SSRS report. And with the tools included in SSRS, this means you can easily export this snapshot of information directly into something like a PDF file to share with others. This gives site administrators a lot of power with the data within SharePoint.

Web services, unfortunately, are a bit tricky to get working, especially if you are using your own custom web service. And since SQL Server is easier to get started with, it makes sense to at least get started with the SQL Server backend to teach you the nuts and bolts of connecting your report to an external data source. Once you have that understanding, it will be time to go deeper into the data backend realm and start working directly with web services.

Don't get discouraged, though. As this book proceeds, you will get to see some of these XML Web Service data sources in action within SSRS. In Chapter 6 you will see how to access SharePoint list items through the SharePoint web services. And then, to take this concept to the next level, in Chapter 7 you will see how to create your own web service in .NET and then access it directly within SSRS. These chapters will show you how this XML data source can open up all kinds of possibilities for getting data from a lot of different sources directly into your reports.

However, before you go that deep in the data sources of SSRS, you need to build your foundation and get a grasp on the basics of SSRS and connecting to data sources to get your reports working.

With that being said, the first report you will create in this chapter will be with a SQL Server data backend. The next section will focus on getting your database set up properly for your reports.

Using the Adventure Works Database

If you have worked with SQL Server as your backend for any application since the 2005 release, you are probably at least familiar with the Adventure Works database project. This freely available sample of databases provides all of the tables, stored procedures, and other objects you need for an online storefront selling outdoor biking equipment. The tables are already populated with data, and the stored procedures are already generated for you. This provides the perfect backend for your first reports, since it is data that you can have readily available that will match the data of the examples in this book.

To get your Adventure Works database, go to the codeplex project located here: `http://msftdbprodsamples.codeplex.com/`.

From that location, you can read about the latest releases of the project and find out a little more about things such as the change history or customer reviews.

To get the databases, click the Downloads link near the top of the page, and you will be presented with several options to download:

- ❏ SQL2008.AdventureWorks_All_Databases.x86.msi

- ❏ SQL2008.AdventureWorks_All_Databases.x64.msi

- ❏ SQL2008.AdventureWorks_All_Databases.ia64.msi

- ❏ SQL2008.AdventureWorks_All_Databases.zip

- ❏ SQL2008.AdventureWorksLT2008_Only_Database.zip

Of these options, choose one of the first three (the *.msi packages). The one you choose will depend on the operating system you are installing on. For example, if you are using a 32-bit server, choose the first one. If you have a 64-bit server, choose one of the other two, depending on whether you are using x64 or ia64 processors.

When you click one of the options, you will be presented with a standard Microsoft Public License message asking that you agree to the terms of the license (see Figure 5-1). You will need to agree to the license in order to download the file. Make sure you read through the license and then press the I Agree button to continue.

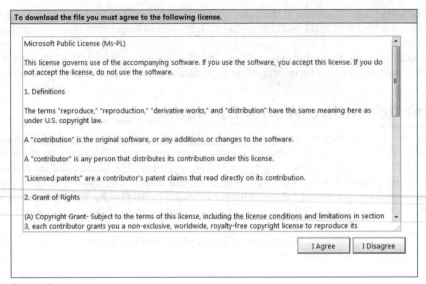

To download the file you must agree to the following license.
Microsoft Public License (Ms-PL)
This license governs use of the accompanying software. If you use the software, you accept this license. If you do not accept the license, do not use the software.
1. Definitions
The terms "reproduce," "reproduction," "derivative works," and "distribution" have the same meaning here as under U.S. copyright law.
A "contribution" is the original software, or any additions or changes to the software.
A "contributor" is any person that distributes its contribution under this license.
"Licensed patents" are a contributor's patent claims that read directly on its contribution.
2. Grant of Rights
(A) Copyright Grant- Subject to the terms of this license, including the license conditions and limitations in section 3, each contributor grants you a non-exclusive, worldwide, royalty-free copyright license to reproduce its
I Agree
I Disagree

Figure 5-1

After accepting the license agreement, you will be given the option to run the file from its current location or to save it on your own computer and run the install locally (see Figure 5-2). This is really a matter of preference, but if you plan to use this file on more than one server or want to keep it for recovery purposes, it might be a good idea to download it to your local system. Also, keep in mind that this installation must be run on the machine that the SQL Server instance is running on. If you are downloading the .msi file from a different machine, you will need to download the file to the machine and then transfer it over to the server when the download completes.

If you would like to save the .msi file, press the Save button and select a location to save your file to continue (you will need to click Run once the file has completed downloading). Otherwise, simply click the Run button.

File Download - Security Warning
Do you want to run or save this file?
Name: SQL2008.AdventureWorks_All_Databases.x86.msi
Type: Windows Installer Package, 60.2MB
From: download.codeplex.com
Run
Save
Cancel
While files from the Internet can be useful, this file type can potentially harm your computer. If you do not trust the source, do not run or save this software. What's the risk?

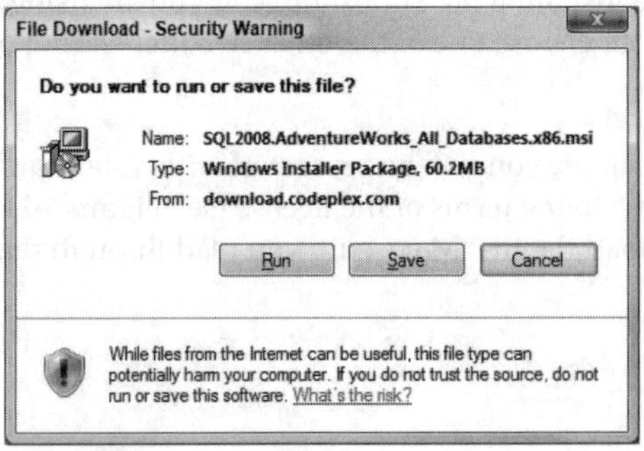

Figure 5-2

Once the setup utility launches, you will be presented with the welcome screen shown in Figure 5-3. Simply click the Next button to continue.

Figure 5-3

Before you can continue your installation, you will be asked to accept the End User License Agreement for Microsoft, as shown in Figure 5-4. The bold text at the top of the agreement sums it up best: "If you use the software, you accept this license. If you do not accept the license, do not use the software." The rest of it is pretty standard verbiage for licensing agreements. To accept the terms of the agreement, click the checkbox control for "I accept the terms in the License Agreement" and press the Next button.

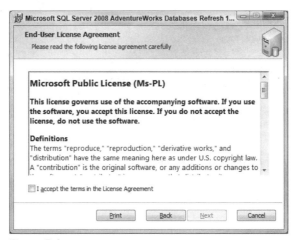

Figure 5-4

The next screen will allow you to (slightly) customize the installation (see Figure 5-5). Honestly, the only thing that isn't getting installed is the "Desktop Shortcuts" options, which is just some shortcut icons installed on your desktop for things like the license agreement. You shouldn't need to customize anything on this screen, so just click the Next button to continue.

Figure 5-5

The next screen allows you to set the only option you really need to set during this installation: the target database (see Figure 5-6). As you can see in the screen depiction, there aren't a lot of customization options on this screen, meaning you can't put in custom credentials to install these databases to a different location. You simply have a single drop-down box that lists all MSSQL Server 2008 database servers found on the current machine. This is why you have to run this installation from the computer running the SQL Server instance you want the Adventure Works databases installed on.

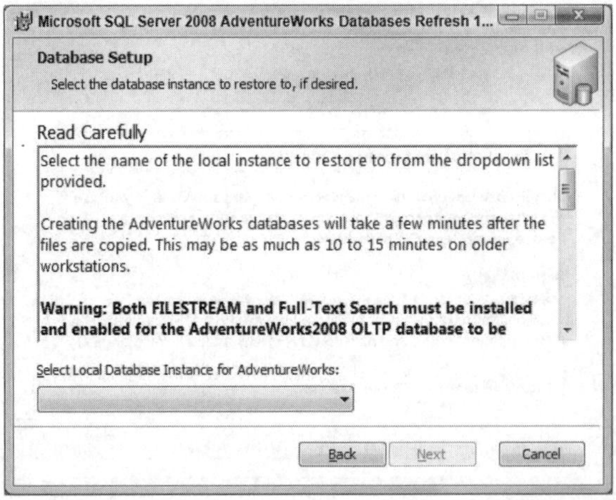

Figure 5-6

So, with that in mind, select your database instance from the drop-down box and press the Next button to continue.

At this point, the installation routine has all of the information it needs to proceed and is ready to install the Adventure Works databases, as shown in Figure 5-7. Press the Install button to get started.

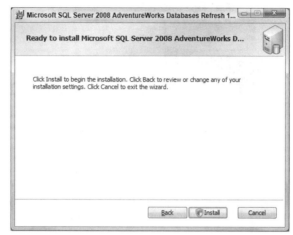

Figure 5-7

At this point, you should see the progress of the installation, as shown in Figure 5-8. When it completes, you'll see the Installation Complete screen, shown in Figure 5-9. You can click the OK button to close out the installation.

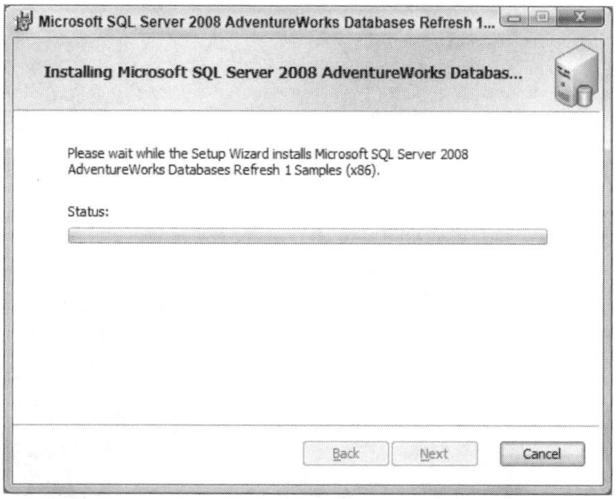

Figure 5-8

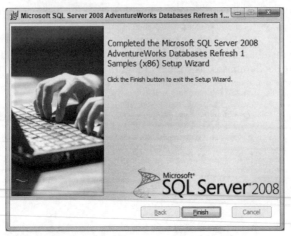

Figure 5-9

If everything has gone smoothly, you should be able to launch Microsoft SQL Server Management studio and see six new Adventure Works databases in your MSSQL Server 2008 instance, as shown in Figure 5-10. These databases will be used throughout the rest of this book, so you need to ensure you have them. And with that being set up, you are now ready to create your first report.

Figure 5-10

Creating Your First Report

Now that you have the database and BIDS (see Chapter 4), you are ready to create your first report. There are two primary ways to create reports: using the Report Wizard or from scratch. You will learn to create a report from scratch in the next chapter. However, in order to introduce you to the concepts involved in creating any report, this chapter will use the wizard. Hopefully, by the end of Chapters 5 and 6, you will have a pretty good idea of the differences between both approaches and be able to decide which method to use for your own reporting needs.

And, with that, it's time to start your report.

Creating the Dataset

A report is essentially a representation of data, right? Well, at least in the world of Reporting Services this is true. You are creating a way of looking at data that will help those using the report to understand it and use it to make business decisions. If they looked at business data sitting in a SQL table, the data wouldn't make much sense. However, with Reporting Services, you are taking raw data and putting it in a form that non-technical people can understand. The key to all of this is the data. You must have a set of data to feed the report, or the report is useless.

As discussed previously in this chapter, these reports all use the Adventure Works databases freely available from Microsoft. However, you will still need to generate a dataset for your report to use. This can be done in several different ways. At the core, this means you will need to write an SQL statement that will return data you can use in the report. However, the decision depends on where these SQL statements reside.

It is possible to write straight T-SQL statements directly in the report design in the wizard or in the custom modes. While this can serve its purpose, it is not really a best practice, at least not when accessing SQL data. A better approach is to have the SQL commands encapsulated within stored procedures within the target database and then executed from the report. This allows you to keep the data manipulation where it belongs: in the data repository. After all, Reporting Services is no different from other applications. You really want to keep your data, design, and logic layers separate. Doing so will afford you a lot of benefits. For example, if you deploy a report and it comes up that one of your calculations is not working properly, you will need to go into the report, fix the SQL commands, and redeploy the report if you encapsulate all the commands within the report itself. This can introduce other problems as you are physically modifying the report and redeploying it. However, if you have the data logic sitting in a stored procedure, you simply go into the stored procedure and make the change. The deployed report will, at that point, automatically use the fix. After all, it's just executing the stored procedure; it doesn't know (or care) what the underlying logic is. Whatever the stored procedure generates, the report will use. So, in this way, you are making data corrections in the data layer, which is the way it should be.

There are also the usual advantages of using stored procedures such as SQL code compilation, faster access times, and security around the data logic. Using stored procedures is just the better way to do it.

Now, with that being said, it is time to create a stored procedure that will feed the first report. The stored procedure will simply return the number of Internet Sales for each mountain bike in the Adventure Works inventory.

So the first step is to open Microsoft SQL Server Management Studio. This should have been installed when you installed SQL Server 2008 and can be located by clicking the Start button and then locating the Microsoft SQL Server 2008 program folder. If you are creating your reports on a different machine than your SQL Server machine, you may not have this installed. In this case, you can download Microsoft SQL Server Management Studio Express directly from Microsoft. You can read about this product and get a link to its download site from this page: `http://msdn.microsoft.com/en-us/library/ms365247.aspx`.

With Management Studio opened, make sure you are connected to the SQL Server 2008 instance containing the Adventure Works databases, and then expand the database AdventureWorks2008 all the way down to the Stored Procedures objects, as seen in Figure 5-11.

Figure 5-11

Right-click Stored Procedures and choose the first option, New Stored Procedure. This should give you a new window in Management Studio with the following code in it:

```
-- ================================================
-- Template generated from Template Explorer using:
-- Create Procedure (New Menu).SQL
--
-- Use the Specify Values for Template Parameters
-- command (Ctrl-Shift-M) to fill in the parameter
-- values below.
--
-- This block of comments will not be included in
-- the definition of the procedure.
-- ================================================
SET ANSI_NULLS ON
GO
```

```
SET QUOTED_IDENTIFIER ON
GO
-- ================================================
-- Author:          <Author,,Name>
-- Create date: <Create Date,,>
-- Description:     <Description,,>
-- ================================================
CREATE PROCEDURE <Procedure_Name, sysname, ProcedureName>
    -- Add the parameters for the stored procedure here
    <@Param1, sysname, @p1> <Datatype_For_Param1, , int> = <
    Default_Value_For_Param1, , 0>,
    <@Param2, sysname, @p2> <Datatype_For_Param2, , int> =
    <Default_Value_For_Param2, , 0>
AS
BEGIN
    -- SET NOCOUNT ON added to prevent extra result sets from
    -- interfering with SELECT statements.
    SET NOCOUNT ON;

    -- Insert statements for procedure here
    SELECT <@Param1, sysname, @p1>, <@Param2, sysname, @p2>
END
GO
```

The first thing you will want to do is make this more readable by deleting out all of the bolded text above. You will also probably want to fill in the Author, Create Date, and Description information for posterity sake. If you have a lot of stored procedures, this will prove very valuable when you are looking at this stored procedure in 6 months with no idea why you created it.

The next step is to add the actual code that will render the dataset for the report. You can just add the bold text in the following code block (notice the procedure name at the top has changed as well):

```
SET ANSI_NULLS ON
GO
SET QUOTED_IDENTIFIER ON
GO
-- ================================================
-- Author:          Jacob J. Sanford
-- Create date:     May 10, 2009
-- Description:     Returns Internet Sales Data
-- ================================================
CREATE PROCEDURE uspGetInternetSalesData
AS
BEGIN
    SET NOCOUNT ON;

    SELECT
        PM.Name, COUNT(*) AS InternetSales
    FROM
        Sales.SalesOrderHeader SOH
    INNER JOIN Sales.SalesOrderDetail SOD
```

```
                ON SOH.SalesOrderID = SOD.SalesOrderID
    INNER JOIN Production.Product PP
            ON SOD.ProductID = PP.ProductID
    INNER JOIN Production.ProductModel PM
            ON PP.ProductModelId = PM.ProductModelID
    WHERE
            (SOH.OnLineOrderFlag = 1 AND PM.Name LIKE ('%Mountain%'))
    GROUP BY PM.Name
    ORDER BY PM.Name
END
GO
```

You now need to execute this query to create this new stored procedure. You can do this by clicking Query and then selecting Execute or by simply pressing the F5 key. Once you have done this, you should get the following message: Command(s) completed successfully.

Now, to test the stored procedure, while you still have the above query window still open, click the New Query button and type the following command in the window that appears:

```
EXEC uspGetInternetSalesData
```

This will execute your newly created stored procedure. If everything goes smoothly, you should get a dataset with the following results:

Name	InternetSales
Fender Set - Mountain	2121
HL Mountain Tire	1396
LL Mountain Tire	862
ML Mountain Tire	1161
Mountain Bottle Cage	2025
Mountain Tire Tube	3095
Mountain-100	396
Mountain-200	3552
Mountain-400-W	543
Mountain-500	479
Women's Mountain Shorts	1019

If you have this dataset, you are ready to create the actual report that will use it.

If you get the error "Could not find stored procedure 'uspGetInternetSalesData'." when you execute the stored procedure, make sure you are accessing the AdventureWorks2008 database. Sometimes, when you open a new query window, the target database is set to the master database. If you look at the toolbars at the top of Management Studio, you should see a drop-down box with the available databases. If it is not set to AdventureWorks2008, change it and run your query again.

Creating a Shared Data Connection

There are two ways to connect your report to your dataset. Perhaps the easiest way is to just create the data connection within the report itself. With Reporting Services, you can actually embed the data connection properties directly in the report. This means that everything for that report will be encapsulated in one file, which can make deployment easier.

However, unless you are creating only one report (or have different data sources for each report), there is a problem with this approach: You are storing the same data connection information in several sources. This means that when you have to change your data connection information, you have to change it in every single report. If you have only one report, this may not be that big of a deal. But if you have 10 or 20 reports, this becomes a maintenance issue. And connection information changes enough in most environments that this will be a problem for developers. For example, in development, you may need to hook your report into a development database, then to a staging database during testing, and finally to a production database when the report goes live. If you have 20 reports, this means you are setting the connection string 60 times in this cycle. And that's just for the normal production lifecycle stuff. Add credentials changing, server names (or IP addresses) changing, or any other changes that could affect your connection string, and this can be a management nightmare.

So, just as in your .NET applications where you typically store your connection string in your web.config so that you maintain all of your connections in one place, Reporting Services has the concept of shared data sources. This allows you to set up a single data connection that can be shared among all reports that need the same connection. Since many of the reports will access the Adventure Works database set up earlier in this chapter, it makes sense to set up the connection to this database one time and then allow as many reports as you need to use it. This way, if something changes, you just adjust the shared data source, and it carries forward to all reports using it.

So the first step is to create your new project in BIDS by clicking File and then New Project, which will bring up the screen shown in Figure 5-12.

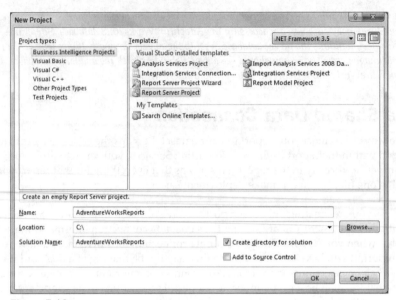

Figure 5-12

As shown in this diagram, you will want to choose the Report Server Project option and then provide the properties of this project. In this example, the name of the project is AdventureWorksReports, and it will be stored on the local C drive. The Solution Name is automatically generated based on the project name and there is no real need to change this. The option for "Create directory for solution" is checked. While you don't have to have the exact same properties for your own project (you might, for example, want to store it in a different location), it is recommended that you use the same name since this is the name that will be referenced throughout this project. If you decide to name your project something different, please remember to substitute your project's name in when AdventureWorksReports is referenced from this point forward.

Press the OK button to create your project.

If you are familiar with development of .NET or Silverlight applications, you will notice that what is actually created for you in your project is pretty simple, as shown in Figure 5-13. You only get two folders (Shared Data Sources and Reports) and no files are created for you. While this might surprise you at first, it's really all you need to create reports.

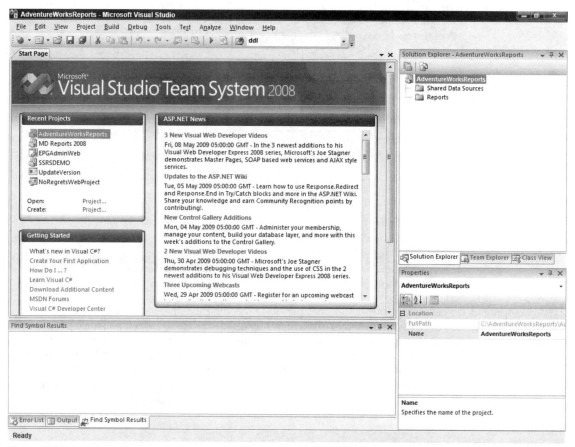

Figure 5-13

So the next thing you need to do is create your shared data source. To do this, right-click the folder Shared Data Sources in the Solution Explorer and select Add New Data Source. This will display the screen shown in Figure 5-14.

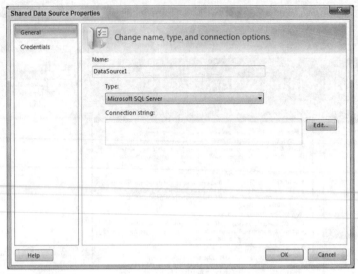

Figure 5-14

While optional, the next thing you should do is provide a meaningful name for the data source. It's possible, and maybe even likely, that you will have multiple shared data sources for a single project. For example, you may have some reports that connect to one database and others that connect to a different database. Or maybe you may have some reports that actually hit a web service or entirely different data source rather than a SQL Server database. If you have multiple shared data sources, and you will by the end of this book, it makes it much easier if you name it something other than DataSource1. So, with that in mind, change the name property to AdventureWorks2008DB, and press the Edit button to set up the connection information to your database, as shown in Figure 5-15.

Figure 5-15

For this example, you can leave the data source property as Microsoft SQL Server (SqlClient), but you will need to change the server name to the server that you installed the Adventure Works database on by using the drop-down box to select it.

Depending on how you set up your server, and depending on whether or not you are running reports from the server itself or from a different machine, you may need to change the logon properties. The default is to use Windows Authentication, which should be fine if you are running BIDS on the same machine as the database. However, if Windows Authentication does not work, you will need to change the option to use SQL Server Authentication and then provide the appropriate credentials.

> *You can read more about advanced installs in Chapter 2. You can also read more about advanced deployments in Chapter 9.*

Finally, you will need to select the AdventureWorks2008 database from the database drop-down box (located under Connect to a database). Make sure you select AdventureWorks2008; there will be several similarly named databases in the list.

Once you have the data source properties set, it is probably a good idea to test your connection information by pressing the Test Connection button. You should receive the message "Test connection succeeded"; then you are ready to proceed. If not, you will need to adjust the connection properties on this screen until you get a successful connection. When your connection is finished, press the OK button to close out of the Connection Properties dialog box. You will notice that the Connection string property of the Shared Data Source Properties dialog box is now filled in for you with the information you just provided. You could have just typed this information if you knew it, but using the wizard is much easier and helps reduce errors that might get introduced from manually providing this information.

You can press the OK button to create this shared data source and close out the dialog box. You should now see a new item called AdventureWorks2008DB.rds in the Shared Data Sources folder of your project. You are now ready to create the report that will use this connection.

Using the Report Wizard

Now it's time to generate your first report. You've created your data repository, generated your data access procedures, and created your shared data source. It's finally time to bring all of that together into your first report.

So, with your AdventureWorksReports project open, right-click the Reports folder in your Solution Explorer and choose Add New Report. This will kick off the Report Wizard, as seen in Figure 5-16.

Figure 5-16

From the Welcome screen, you will press the Next button to continue. This will bring up the data source options shown in Figure 5-17.

Figure 5-17

If you had not set up your shared data source earlier in this chapter, here is where you could create a new data source for this report. However, if you make your data source on this page using the New data source option, you need to make sure you check the Make this a shared data source option at the bottom of the page so that this will be shared out. Failing to make this a shared data source will embed all of the data connectivity information directly in the report and, as such, will not be available to share with other reports. So, if you do choose this option, always check the shared data source option even if you don't think you are going to need it to be shared. It's much easier to set it up now than to go back and change it later.

> *While it is true that you could have waited until this point in the book to create your shared data source, it was determined that it would be more beneficial to have a full discussion about the shared data source option before the report was started. Also, creating the data source independently of the report shows additional functionality of BIDS that might be overlooked if not specifically outlined in this manuscript. Therefore, for the context of this chapter, the data source was explained prior to the report. However, it is perfectly fine to wait until this point in the wizard to create your data source in your own projects.*

Since you already created the AdventureWorks2008DB shared data source earlier in this chapter, it should be available as an option in the Shared Data Source property of this screen. Make sure it is selected and press the Next button. This will bring up the Query Designer screen shown in Figure 5-18.

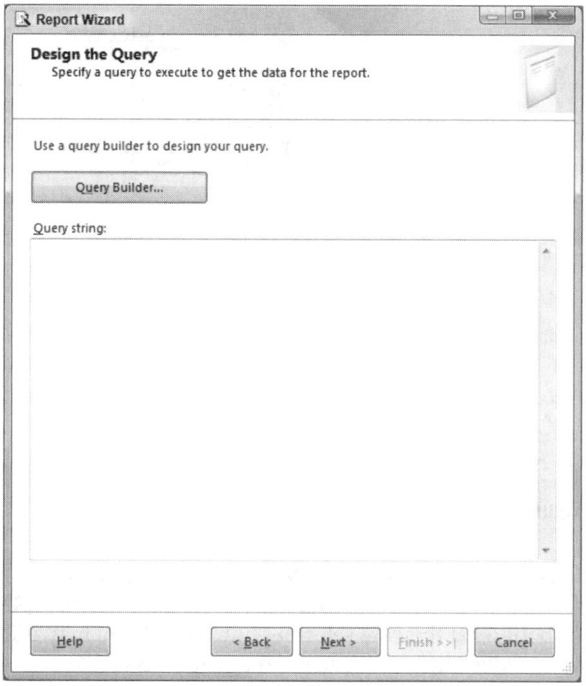

Figure 5-18

This is where you provide your T-SQL commands to retrieve the data from your data source. As discussed earlier in this chapter, you could just type straight SQL commands on this screen to retrieve your data. You could pretty much type out whatever you could type out in a SQL Server Management Studio query window (SELECT, JOIN, UNION, and so on). However, it is a much better practice to keep the data access commands encapsulated within stored procedure logic residing in the SQL database and then just provide the stored procedure execution method in the report.

While not shown in this example, it is possible to provide parameters for your stored procedure that get passed from the report. You will see this in more detail in Chapter 6.

For this screen, you need only provide the stored procedure name (uspGetInternetSalesData) in the query string properties box. Once you have input that into the textbox, press the Next button to continue. This will bring up a screen allowing you to select the report type, as shown in Figure 5-19.

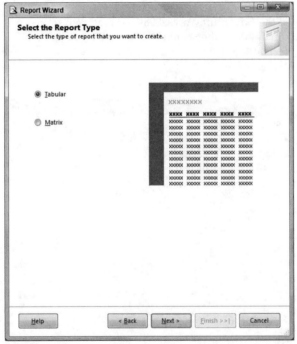

Figure 5-19

There are only two options available: Tabular and Matrix. These report types are not unique to reporting services but that doesn't mean you will know what they both are. Many people just click through this screen without thinking about what they are selecting but, so that you may understand what you are choosing, it is important to understand what each of these options are.

You probably already know what a tabular report is. It is easily the most common report type for data. In fact, you saw a version of it earlier in this chapter when setting up your stored procedure. Essentially, the returned dataset is a tabular report. To refresh your memory, here is the dataset again:

Name	InternetSales
Fender Set - Mountain	2121
HL Mountain Tire	1396
LL Mountain Tire	862
ML Mountain Tire	1161
Mountain Bottle Cage	2025
Mountain Tire Tube	3095
Mountain-100	396
Mountain-200	3552
Mountain-400-W	543
Mountain-500	479
Women's Mountain Shorts	1019

So what defines a tabular report? A tabular report has a series of data columns (in this case, Name and InternetSales) and then any number of rows of data falling under the column headers. So when you ran your stored procedure query in SQL Server Management Studio to test it, you created a tabular report when the data was returned.

So what is a matrix report? A matrix report is a cross-tab report. This means that you have headers for each column but also for each row. While technically the preceding example can be seen as a matrix report, as the first column of data fields can be considered row header fields, typically you see a matrix report that looks more like the following:

	Q1	Q2	Q3	Q4
Northeastern Region	$1,000	$1,100	$900	$450
Southeastern Region	$9,800	$8,900	$9,100	$6,700
Northwestern Region	$4,400	$3,400	$2,400	$1,400
Southwestern Region	$6,700	$8,900	$5,600	$4,500

The default option is to select the tabular report type, and for this report, that will work perfectly. While you probably could make the dataset work in a matrix report type, it isn't really set up to be a cross-tab report, and trying to make it so would just be overkill. And for most reports, tabular is the style you will want to use. It is important to understand the differences among these options.

So, with that in mind, select the Tabular option and press the Next button. This will bring up the table design options shown in Figure 5-20.

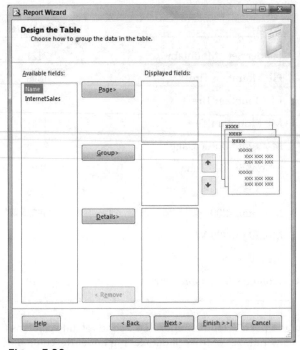

Figure 5-20

One of the interesting things to note on this screen is that the wizard has already figured out what the returned fields are from the query you provided earlier in the wizard. In other words, it knows that if it runs your stored procedure, it will return two fields: Name and InternetSales. It has provided those for you in the "Available fields" area of the screen.

This screen is here to allow you to select what these fields are in respect to this report. In other words, are these just data fields? Or will you use one of them for grouping? Or do you want to generate a new report page for each instance of field?

To help understand what this means, think of the following scenario. You have sales data that you want to report on. In that data, you have all sales information, including the store where the sale took place (StoreName) and the salesperson responsible for the sale (SalesPerson). In this scenario, you might want to create a new page of reports for each store. You would then put the data field StoreName in the Page field. Within each store's report, you want to have a drilldown report grouped by employee. In other words, you want to have a report that shows all employees and their total sales with the option to expand a particular employee's row and see all sales details for that employee. You would drop the SalesPerson data field into the Group field and then put all sales data fields (e.g., date of sale, sales amount, description of sale, and so on) into the Details field.

It is important to realize that the options here are only for the tabular layout of the report. Had you chosen the matrix layout on the previous screen, you would have seen different options, primarily the option to select the data that would be used as the row headers.

For this example, none of this is really necessary. It is such a small set of data and there is nothing really available to group or page by. So you will want to just put both data fields in the Details group. You do this by highlighting both fields (you can press the Shift key while clicking the fields to select them both) and then clicking the Details button. This should move both fields over to the Details fields on the screen. When the fields have been moved, press the Next button to continue. This will bring up the Table Style Options screen, as shown in Figure 5-21.

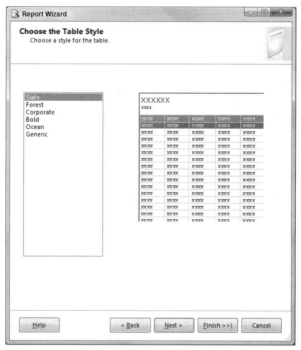

Figure 5-21

The Table Style screen allows you to apply some basic style elements to your returned table. You can click the options on the left side of the screen, and a preview will show up on the right. These styles will control the fonts and colors for your report, including the header row and any grouping rows. One thing to take note of, though, is that none of these options formats an alternating color scheme for your rows of data (i.e., the first row is one color, the second row is a different color, and back and forth through all rows of data). So don't be surprised when you see the final report and there are no alternating colors within your rows of data. There is a way to accomplish this, which you will see in the next section. But for now, just choose one of the options and press the Next button to continue. This will bring up a screen, shown in Figure 5-22, that allows you to provide the name of the report and review the options you selected in the wizard.

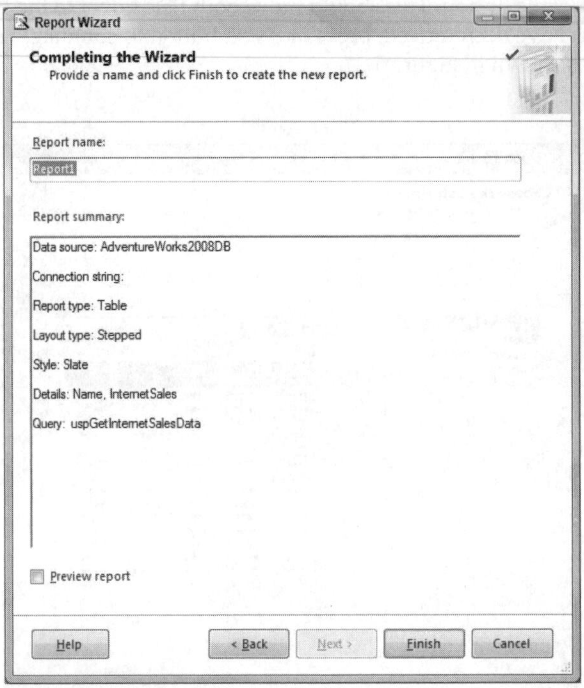

Figure 5-22

Change the name of the report to InternetSalesReport and press the Finish button. This will complete the wizard and create your first report, which will load in design mode after the wizard shuts down. You will also see the report listed under the Reports folder in your Solution Explorer (Figure 5-23).

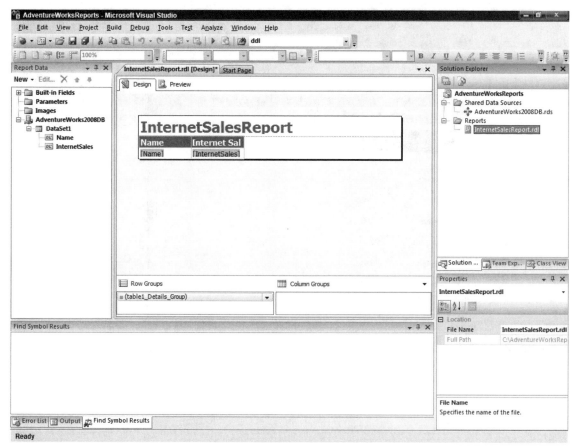

Figure 5-23

Now, if you click the Preview tab within BIDS, the report will actually run and you can see it with its returned dataset, as shown in Figure 5-24.

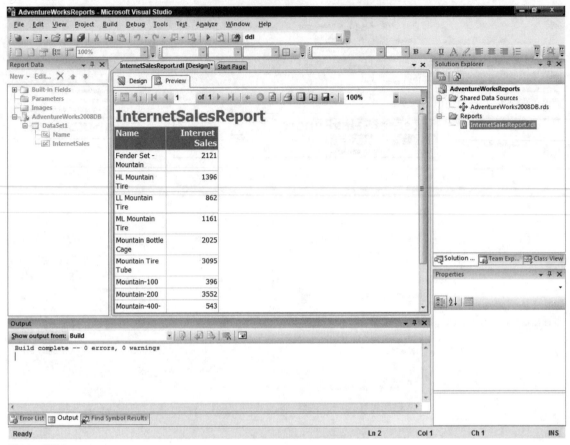

Figure 5-24

At this stage, the report isn't anything spectacular, but it does show how, in just a few steps, you have a usable report.

One nice thing about the Preview tab in BIDS is that, without actually deploying the report anywhere, you can export the rendered report to other formats such as Adobe PDF, Microsoft Word, or a comma-delimited file. So if management just wants a PDF sent to them, you don't even have to deploy the report. You can just load it in your development environment, click over to preview mode, and then export the results to PDF and send the exported file to management. Of course, that takes away from the "cool" factor of having the report deployed somewhere like SharePoint where management can run their own reports without needing developer involvement, but it's still nice to know that this feature is available if you need it. And, in all honesty, it does provide an easy way to send out mock-ups to management for approval. Rather than deploying the entire report, you can just send out the rendered PDF to management for approval and, after approval, deploy the report to the appropriate location.

Cleaning Up the Report

While the report is functional, which is the primary goal of any report, it could certainly use some cleaning up. The header is the name of the report (without the RDL extension), which means it is all crammed together with no spaces. The columns are not wide enough to show the data easily. The rows do not show any alternating color changes. And, finally, the numbers don't look that great (they aren't formatted as currency, for example). So it is time to clean that up. While this may showcase some of the limitations of the wizard, it also gives you a chance to work with formatting options within BIDS, which is pretty easy and can make a huge impact on the overall presentation of the report. So, with that, it's time to get started.

Fixing the Header

Like most things in any Visual Studio IDE, there are several ways to fix the formatting of the header. One way is to look at the Properties pane shown in Figure 5-25. Click the header to display the header properties.

Figure 5-25

As this depiction shows, you can set formatting options such as the color and font of the text. If you scroll through the options, you will see that you can also set positioning properties as well as textbox behaviors (e.g., line wrapping). So if you just want to format what is already there, you can certainly do that here.

However, one thing missing here is a property to set the value of the textbox. In other words, if you scroll through all of the properties, you will not see a single thing set to InternetSalesReport. So how do you change the text?

Well, BIDS is a pretty perfect example of a WYSIWYG (What You See Is What You Get) editor, meaning you can just type in the textbox and change the text directly on the report.

To see how this works, double-click on the header text, which will provide a blinking cursor at the beginning of the text. (If the header text already has focus before you double-click on it, you might see the entire header text get highlighted. Just click anywhere in the text to remove the selection.) At this point, add some spaces in your title to make it read "Internet Sales Report" and press Enter. Your title has now been changed. If you review your report in the Preview tab, you will see the changes have been included.

It is also possible to do your text formatting without using the properties pane. If you look at the top of your IDE, you will notice the Report Formatting toolbar, shown in Figure 5-26.

Figure 5-26

This toolbar will let you adjust things like the font family, color, and weight of the text. To see how this works, use the first drop-down box to set the font to Arial and click the I button to make the text italics. You should immediately see the changes take place as you make changes on the toolbar. When you are finished, preview your report and it should look like Figure 5-27.

If you don't see the changes being made, make sure you are not in text editing mode (which you went into when you double-clicked the textbox to edit the text). If you are in text editing mode, you will need to do one of two things: Get out of text editing mode or highlight all of the text before making formatting changes. You can get out of text editing mode by pressing Enter on your keyboard. You will know you are out of text editing mode when you see the handles around your textbox again.

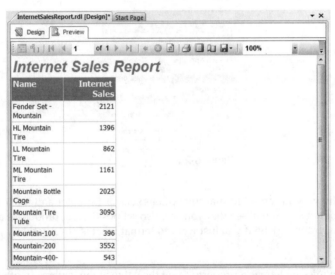

Figure 5-27

Resizing the Columns

The next step in the cleanup process is to resize the columns so that the text is contained in one row of data (no wrapping). This is such a simple (small) report that there is no need to do the wrapping that has been created when the report is run. The report will look a lot cleaner and easier to read if everything is in a single line of text. Fortunately, because of the WYSIWYG nature of BIDS, this is really easy to do.

First, click the data table (you can click anywhere within the table to select it). You will notice previously invisible controls show up around the table, as shown in Figure 5-28. These are the "handles" of the control.

Report
Name
Internet Sal
[Name]
[InternetSales]

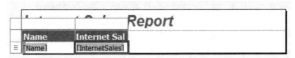

Figure 5-28

You will notice that the little boxes that appear around the table make the table look more like an Excel spreadsheet, if you are familiar with Excel. This means you are in the editing mode of this table and now resizing the columns is exactly as easy as it is in Excel. You simply need to click the edge of one of the columns and drag the column border to the desired width, as seen in Figure 5-29.

Name
Internet Sal
[Name]
[InternetSales]

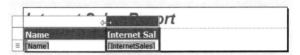

Figure 5-29

Play around with the widths until everything in a row is displayed on a single row of text in the Preview tab, as shown in Figure 5-30.

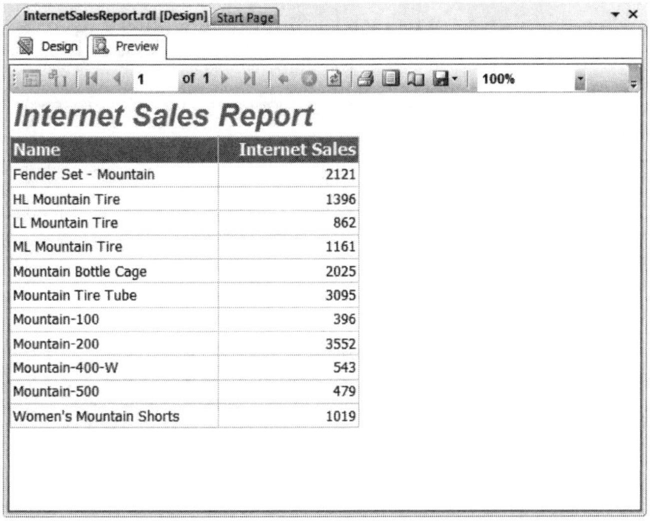

InternetSalesReport.rdl [Design]
Start Page
Design
Preview
1
of 1
100%
Internet Sales Report
Name
Internet Sales
Fender Set - Mountain 2121
HL Mountain Tire 1396
LL Mountain Tire 862
ML Mountain Tire 1161
Mountain Bottle Cage 2025
Mountain Tire Tube 3095
Mountain-100 396
Mountain-200 3552
Mountain-400-W 543
Mountain-500 479
Women's Mountain Shorts 1019

Figure 5-30

Setting up the Alternating Row Color Schema

As stated earlier in this chapter, there is no property you can set to create alternating row background colors in SQL Server Reporting Services. This has been true since SSRS's inception and, unfortunately, has not been changed with the 2008 release. This is particularly frustrating because, especially in large reports, people are used to having alternating row colors to help the eye follow the row of data. This makes things much easier to read and process. And, in web development, it is almost a given that any data grids will have alternating row background colors. In the .NET world, for example, the gridview control has different styling for rows and alternating rows. This is just common practice so it becomes a necessity to make this work in SSRS as well.

So, as with most necessities, a hack is available to help get you around this limitation.

The workaround involves going into the row properties and adding a formula to determine if the data row is odd or even and apply a different background color based on whichever it is. To do this, you first need to select your table on your report by clicking anywhere on it to get the table controls to show up (the Excel-looking cells around the table). When these controls appear, click the cell control for the row of data, as seen in Figure 5-31. This will select the entire row (so that formatting changes will be applied to all cells in that row).

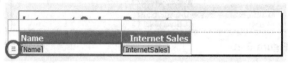

Figure 5-31

Now, with the row selected, go to the Properties pane in BIDS and find the property settings for BackgroundColor, which should be set to No Color. When you click the property (the part that says "No Color"), a drop-down arrow will appear. Click the arrow and select Expression. This will bring up an expression editor, which is SSRS's way of using basic built-in functions (Figure 5-32).

Figure 5-32

You will notice the expression is currently set to Transparent. You will need to replace that text with the following expression:

```
=IIF(RowNumber(Nothing) Mod 2, "Silver", "White")
```

If you are familiar with VBScript, this formula may already make sense to you. However, if you are not familiar with VBScript, you may be curious what is going on. There are a couple of things. The IIF expression is SSRS's version of the IF . . . ELSE statement, which (in SSRS) has three members. The first member is the expression to evaluate, the second is what the value should be if the expression evaluates to true, and the third member is the value to use if the expression evaluates to false. So, in this formula, the true and false values are probably fairly intuitive; if true, set the row background color to Silver; otherwise, set it to White. The expression is the part that might be confusing. However, all it is doing is determining if this is an even or odd row. To do this, the expression must first decide what the current row number is, which it does through RowNumber(Nothing). In this method, "Nothing" is representative of the scope to evaluate. When using "Nothing," it means just use the outermost scope available. If you are using grouping, you will need to include the group name in this expression. The MOD argument means divide the two numbers provided and return the remainder (the second number is the 2 on the other side of MOD). So if this is row #5, it would divide 5 by 2 and return the remainder of 1; for row #12, it would divide by 2 and return the remainder of 0. Using this expression, then, always returns a zero or 1, which are the bit values for true and false (true = 1 and false = 0). So, using this logic, row #5 returns 1, which evaluates to true (which means it will get a background color of Silver) and row #12 returns 0, which evaluates to false (which means it will get a background color of White).

So now that you have your expression entered in the expression editor textbox, press the OK button to add your changes to your report. If you go into the Preview tab at this point, your report should resemble Figure 5-33.

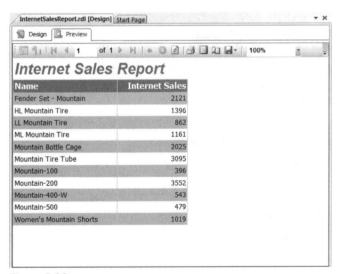

Figure 5-33

Formatting the Numbers

The last thing you need to take care of in the report cleanup phase is formatting the Internet Sales sales numbers. Fortunately, using the knowledge you have acquired in the previous sections, this should be a fairly easy task.

First, select the textbox in the table for the Internet Sales data (the textbox that has [InternetSales] in it) by clicking it with your mouse. After it is selected, right-click the box again to reveal options for that textbox and select Expression . . . to bring up the expression wizard shown previously in Figure 5-32. The expression already there should be the following:

```
=Fields!InternetSales.Value
```

This just means that it is pulling the InternetSales data from the shared data source you created earlier. You need to modify this formula to the following (additions in bold):

```
=FormatNumber(Fields!InternetSales.Value, 0)
```

The `FormatNumber()` function does as the name implies; it formats your number for you. There is only one required parameter, the number to be formatted (in this case, the InternetSales value). There are four optional parameters that can help you more finely tune how the number is formatted. The first one, which is the one provided in the above formula, tells the formatter how many numbers to leave after the decimal. Using zero will force no trailing numbers after the decimal in the formatted number. Press the OK button to make this change to your report, which should now look like Figure 5-34 when viewed in the Preview tab.

> *You can see a full list of the functions under Common Functions in the category list of the expression editor screen.* `FormatNumber()` *is listed under the Text group.*

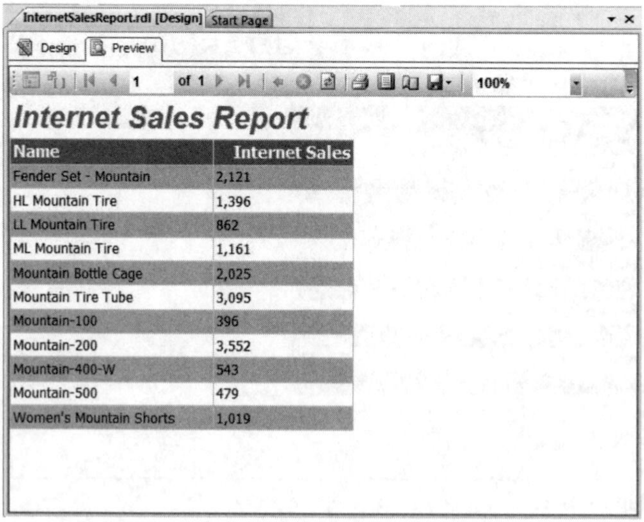

Figure 5-34

One thing you might notice is that the numbers got shifted when you made this change. After setting up the alternating row color schema, they were still aligned to the right. However, after making the textbox a function/expression, the numbers shifted to a left-aligned position. While this isn't necessarily wrong, it looks a little odd to have the header right-aligned and the data row left-aligned. The easy way to fix this is to select the InternetSales data cell in your table by clicking it once with your mouse and then clicking the right alignment button on your Report Formatting toolbar (Figure 5-35). You can do this same trick for header or footer cells, or you can do it for an entire row or column by selecting that row or column. This should make everything look tidier.

Figure 5-35

Adding a Chart

Now that you have a functioning and professional looking report, albeit a very basic one, it might be nice to dress it up a bit with a cool looking chart or graph. They say a picture is worth a thousand words and, in the world of reporting, this seems to be especially true. Decision makers love seeing their data graphed out so that they can very easily see the impacts and transgressions of the underlying data and past performance/decisions. It is often a big hit with management and, fortunately, is fairly easy to accomplish in Reporting Services.

The first thing you need to do is make sure you have room on your report to hold the chart. Using the existing report InternetSalesReport.rdl in the AdventureWorksReports project, find the lower edge of the report (the bottom of the page) in the Design tab and drag it to make room below the current table. You don't need a lot of room for now; just enough space to drag the chart below it. The report will resize it to accommodate the chart, but it makes it easier to drag an object below the table if there is room available.

Now, the next step is to locate the Chart item in the Report Items group of the Toolbox pane of BIDS. If you do not see the ToolBox pane, you may have to make it visible by clicking View and then selecting Toolbox from the options presented as shown in Figure 5-36.

Figure 5-36

Now simply drag the Chart item onto your report directly below the table. This will launch the Select Chart Type screen shown in Figure 5-37.

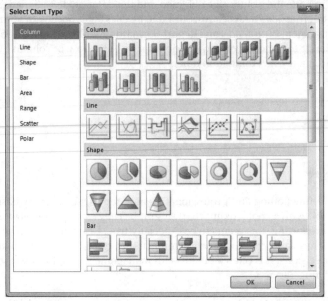

Figure 5-37

As the title of the screen indicates, this is meant to allow you to choose the type of chart you want to use. While you are certainly free to choose whichever style suits you best, for this particular kind of data, a pie chart seems the most logical fit. This is because there is a single relationship between each listed item and an associated graph point. In other words, for each mountain bike item, there is only one sales number associated. So, while you could do a bar chart or something similar to compare these numbers, a pie chart really shows where the most sales are happening in a very easy to see manner.

With this in mind, choose the pie chart, which is the first option shown in the Shape section in Figure 5-37 and press the OK button. You will notice that the report did in fact resize itself to make room for the pie chart and that a generic pie chart has been added to your report. At this point, no data is associated with it, so it doesn't have anything to report. You can move the chart to position it better under the table simply by clicking on the chart and dragging it to its new position before releasing the mouse button. Do this to get the chart even with the left margin of the report, and aligned with the header text and the table already in existence on the report.

It's time to wire the chart up to your data. Much like everything else up to this point in the chapter, this is a fairly easy process.

The first step is to switch over to the Report Data pane (probably hidden by the Toolbox). It should resemble Figure 5-38.

Figure 5-38

You can see in Figure 5-38 that there are two fields in the dataset: Name and InternetSales. With the pie chart, there are two corresponding field types: series and data. The series represents the information you would see in the legend, for example. So, for the AdventureWorks2008DB dataset, this would correlate to the Name field. Similarly, the data fields of the pie chart represent, obviously, the numerical data that is to be charted, which corresponds to the InternetSales field of the dataset.

So how do you databind these dataset fields to the pie chart? Simple. Drag and drop.

Click on the Name field in the Report Data pane and drag it over the chart. When you do, you will see that new areas become visible around the chart as seen in Figure 5-39. Above the chart is an area that reads "Drop data fields here" and to the right of the chart should be an area that reads "Drop series fields here". Since the Name field is a series field, continue dragging the Name field until it is over the area of the chart that reads "Drop series fields here" and then release your mouse. Similarly, drag the InternetSales field to the part of the chart that reads "Drop data fields here" and drop them there. Your chart is now bound to these fields.

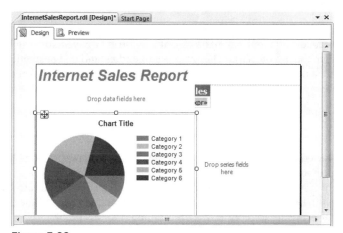

Figure 5-39

You will also find that it is fairly easy to modify things like the report title. If you double-click the text that reads "Chart Title" at the top of the pie chart, that textbox becomes the focus. Double-click it again, and it becomes editable. Do this and give the chart a new name: Internet Sales Pie Chart.

As a final step, you can resize the chart by clicking the chart to select it and then dragging any of the corners outward to increase its size. You might want to do this so that you can see the data a little more clearly when it is rendered.

Once you have finished this step, click the Preview tab, and your report should resemble Figure 5-40.

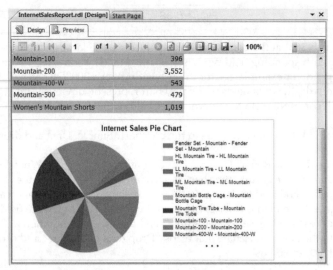

Figure 5-40

And with that, you have added a really professional looking chart to your report, and, hopefully, you found it fairly simple. Many reporting requirements, especially if you ever have to do any kind of dashboard report, will benefit from the use of charts. They are easy to understand and aesthetically pleasing to the reader. And now you have the tools to add them easily to your reports when the need arises.

Summary

When this chapter started, you were probably fairly new to creating reports in SQL Server Reporting services. While the previous chapters had prepared you for generating reports (and, admittedly, there is a lot of preparation necessary to get to the point where you are ready to generate reports), you hadn't really gotten too far into report generation. In fact, other than an overview of the development tools used to create reports, your exposure to reports was pretty limited to this point.

However, this chapter attempted to get you started in report development. The example was a very simple one but allowed you to get exposed to the nuts and bolts of creating reports in SSRS. You learned some best practices, for example. You know that you should keep your data in the data layer and just display it in SSRS. You now know that you should use a shared data source for your reports much in the same way you would use your connection string information in your web.config in a .NET application.

You also saw how to use the Report Wizard to generate a very basic report. In doing so, though, you also learned some reporting concepts like the difference between tabular and matrix reports and how they are used in typical reports. You saw how powerfully simple the wizard is but also saw some of the formatting flaws of its final result and how to fix them.

You saw how easy it was to add a chart to your report and bind it to your report's existing data source. You saw some of the easy ways to modify the report, like resizing it and changing the header for the report.

At the end of this chapter, even though the report itself was a pretty simple one, you learned some very fundamental concepts of report generation and how they are handled in SSRS. You should now have a very solid understanding of how to create reports, and should be able create your own report to meet your own needs.

But the journey isn't over. In the next chapters, you will get deeper into some of the more advanced techniques within SSRS, such as access web services, linking reports, and creating reports without using the wizard. You have the requisite foundation now. So it's time to dive deep.

6

Intermediate Reporting Techniques

At this point in the book, you should feel fairly comfortable using BIDS and creating simple reports. For example, you should know what BIDS is, how to use it to create a new Reporting Project, and how to create a new report using the report wizard. You should have an understanding of basic best practices, like using shared data sources for your report projects and keeping the data manipulation in the data layer. In a pinch, you should be able to prepare and present a simple report to meet your business needs.

You have merely scratched the surface of what you can do with Reporting Services. In this chapter, you will see how to build a more powerful report completely from scratch. You will also see how to create a report that links to another report, passing required parameters from one report to the second. You will even get a glimpse of accessing web service data. More specifically, you will be able to access SharePoint list data in your reports. It's time to step up to the next level.

Creating a Linked Report

One of the really powerful features in Reporting Services is the ability to create two reports and, essentially, hyperlink them together. To understand what this means, take a look at Figure 6-1.

Figure 6-1

This provides a good example of how a linked report might flow and be used in your own environment. In this example, the first report is a pie chart that shows summary sales data information for the year 2003, while the matrix of data is a more detailed listing of sales data for a particular region. The "link" for these reports, then, is the pie segment associated with a particular region (for instance, the Southwest region). For these reports, a user would simply click the pie segment for the Southwest region and be automatically and seamlessly taken to the detail report for the Southwest region. This is a linked report.

In this section, you will see how to create both reports and how to link them together. Linked reports can be a really big piece of any kind of dashboard reports or other aggregate data reports you may need to generate for your own projects. Once you understand how reports are linked, it isn't terribly hard to make linking work.

STEP 1: The Data Backend

As discussed in Chapter 5, it is a good idea to keep all of your data objects in your data layer and merely call them from your reporting layer, much like any other n-tier application you might develop. This typically means that it is a good idea to keep all of your data and manipulation logic in the same area. Since this report will still be using the AdventureWorks 2008 database used in Chapter 5, this translates to keeping the tables and stored procedure objects in the AdventureWorks database and executing only the stored procedure from the report itself.

To create the reports shown in Figure 6-1, you will need a dataset of sales data filtered by year and region. The AdventureWorks database containse multiple years of sales data and, within each year, multiple regions generating the sales. For the pie chart example it will display only information for the year 2003. This means that, as some point, you need to say "Hey, report, only show me 2003 stuff." This could be filtered in the report itself, but that isn't ideal. For one, that means you would be bringing all of the sales data for all years in your initial data load and then working in the report to filter out the data you don't want. This is a pretty big performance consideration. Instead, what makes more sense is to tell the stored procedure that you only want information for year 2003. This means that you will need a year parameter for your stored procedure.

Related to this, you will also need a parameter for the region. This parameter will be used by the second report only. The region parameter provides a necessary data layer filter rather than a filter in the report. For this report, you only want to see data for, the year 2003 for the Southwest region. So why bring back all sales data or, even, all sales data for 2003? Instead you just want to bring back the data that meets the criteria of the report. So you will need a second parameter for the region.

You should also consider the concept of code reuse. Does the pie chart report need the region filter? No, it does not. In fact, if you filtered by region at all, this would entirely corrupt your report. The report is built off of the idea that you want to display summary data for each region. So, if you filtered by any region, you would only get that region and your pie would just have one huge slice. So does that mean you need two stored procedures? Perhaps. But it might be easier, at least from a maintenance perspective, to have all of the code for both reports encapsulated in a single stored procedure. This can be accomplished by creating a stored procedure that has one required parameter for Year and one optional parameter for region. If region is provided, you add an additional filter at the end of the stored procedure to return only that particular region. Otherwise, you return all data for all regions for the year provided in the year parameter.

Here is an example of a stored procedure that returns all sales data from the AdventureWorks 2008 database and filters by year (required) and region (optional):

```
SET ANSI_NULLS ON
GO
SET QUOTED_IDENTIFIER ON
GO
-- =============================================
-- Author:      Jacob J. Sanford
-- Create date: May 15, 2009
-- Description: Returns Sales Detail Data
-- =============================================
CREATE PROCEDURE [dbo].[uspGetSalesDataDetail]
     @YEAR NVARCHAR(4)
     ,@REGION NVARCHAR(50) = NULL
AS
BEGIN
    SET NOCOUNT ON;

    DECLARE @STARTDATE NVARCHAR(25)
        ,@ENDDATE NVARCHAR(25)
    SET @STARTDATE = '1/1/' + @YEAR
    SET @ENDDATE = '12/31/' + @YEAR

    DECLARE @SQL NVARCHAR(1000)
    SET @SQL = 'SELECT
         ST.Name AS [Region]
        ,ISNULL(PER.LastName + '', ''
            + PER.FirstName, ''N/A'') AS [SalesEmployeeName]
        ,SOD.SalesOrderID AS [OrderID]
        ,SOH.OrderDate AS [OrderDate]
        ,SUM(SOH.TotalDue) AS [TotalSale]
    FROM
        Sales.SalesOrderDetail SOD
        LEFT JOIN Sales.SalesOrderHeader SOH
            ON SOD.SalesOrderID = SOH.SalesOrderID
        LEFT JOIN Sales.SalesTerritory ST
            ON SOH.TerritoryID = ST.TerritoryID
        LEFT JOIN Person.Person PER
            ON SOH.SalesPersonID = PER.BusinessEntityID
    WHERE
        SOH.OrderDate >= ''' + @STARTDATE + '''
        AND SOH.OrderDate <= ''' + @ENDDATE + ''''

    IF @REGION IS NOT NULL
        SET @SQL = @SQL + ' AND ST.Name = ''' + @REGION + ''''

    SET @SQL = @SQL + ' GROUP BY ST.Name, PER.LastName,
        PER.FirstName, SOD.SalesOrderID, SOH.OrderDate'

    EXEC(@SQL)

END
```

It is not in the scope of this book to provide a primer on SQL queries or the T-SQL language. If the preceding procedure does not make any sense to you, it might be a good idea to pick up a copy of Beginning T-SQL with Microsoft SQL Server 2005 and 2008 (Wrox) or possibly Professional Microsoft SQL Server 2008 Programming (Wrox) to get up to speed on T-SQL. You can also download this query directly from the Wrox website to avoid typing the entire thing in yourself.

So is that all that you need for these reports to work? Well, yes and no. This certainly could satisfy the requirements set forth to this point. If you run the query and provide '2003' and 'Southwest' for the @YEAR and @REGION parameters respectively, you will get a returned dataset similar to the following (just the first 10 rows are shown here for brevity's sake):

Region	SalesEmployeeName	OrderID	OrderDate	TotalSale
Southwest	N/A	48799	2003-01-01 00:00:00.000	2288.9187
Southwest	N/A	48811	2003-01-02 00:00:00.000	865.204
Southwest	N/A	48818	2003-01-03 00:00:00.000	865.204
Southwest	N/A	48834	2003-01-05 00:00:00.000	2288.9187
Southwest	N/A	48853	2003-01-08 00:00:00.000	865.204
Southwest	N/A	48861	2003-01-09 00:00:00.000	2288.9187
Southwest	N/A	48862	2003-01-09 00:00:00.000	2288.9187
Southwest	N/A	48863	2003-01-09 00:00:00.000	2288.9187
Southwest	N/A	48872	2003-01-10 00:00:00.000	865.204
Southwest	N/A	48880	2003-01-11 00:00:00.000	2699.9018

If you had only provided the year, you would have seen that the exact same columns of data and all rows would have been from the year 2003; the only real difference is that the region would not be limited to the Southwest region and, consequently, there would be significantly more rows returned.

So, it works. The business requirements of these reports are met. But there is still room for improvement.

With the dataset provided, you can get your data but you have to provide your two parameters: @YEAR and @REGION. While it is certainly true that you could just manually enter these values in a textbox control and it would work, how tedious (and not cool) is that? Wouldn't it be much better to have a dropdown box databound to the available years so that the user running the report could ONLY select those values? Wouldn't that be easier, both for the user and for you in regard to training and troubleshooting time at least, to do it this way? Same thing with the region. Is anyone going to remember every region exactly? If they had free text, they could potentially enter something like "SW" to mean "Southwest." Do you want to code for that? Or, worse, do you want the CIO to enter "SW" and then tell you that your reports don't work? Again, it would be easier to just provide the user with the available options in a dropdown control that they can only choose valid options to set for the parameters for your stored procedure. That way, you ensure data returned and valid arguments going in.

So, with a little foreshadowing, SSRS can allow you to do this. You can set up report parameters that can be bound to a dataset of information. As this section continues, you will see exactly how to do that. However, while still in the data layer, it is a good idea to go ahead and create the stored procedures that will generate the data needed for these dropdown controls.

First, you can use the code similar to the following in your own stored procedure to create a dataset for years that have any sales data in the AdventureWorks database:

```
SET ANSI_NULLS ON
GO
SET QUOTED_IDENTIFIER ON
GO
-- ===============================================
-- Author:      Jacob J. Sanford
-- Create date: May 15, 2009
-- Description: Returns all years that had sales
-- ===============================================
CREATE PROCEDURE [dbo].[uspGetSalesYears]
AS
BEGIN
    SET NOCOUNT ON;

    SELECT
        DISTINCT YEAR(SOH.OrderDate) AS [SalesYear]
    FROM
        Sales.SalesOrderHeader SOH
    ORDER BY
        SalesYear ASC
END
```

If you were to execute this stored procedure in your own environment, you should get a dataset similar to the following:

SalesYear
2001
2002
2003
2004

Similarly, the following code will return a dataset with all regions from the AdventureWorks database:

```
SET ANSI_NULLS ON
GO
SET QUOTED_IDENTIFIER ON
GO
-- ===============================================
-- Author:      Jacob J. Sanford
-- Create date: May 15, 2009
-- Description: Returns all Sales Regions
-- ===============================================
CREATE PROCEDURE [dbo].[uspGetSalesRegions]
AS
BEGIN
    SET NOCOUNT ON;

    SELECT
        DISTINCT ST.Name AS [Region]
    FROM
        Sales.SalesTerritory ST
    ORDER BY
        ST.Name
END
```

Executing this stored procedure will result in a dataset similar to the following:

Region
Australia
Canada
Central
France
Germany
Northeast
Northwest
Southeast
Southwest
United Kingdom

At this point in the chapter, you should have the following new data objects in your own data repository:

❑ uspGetSalesDataDetail(@YEAR, @REGION)

❑ uspGetSalesYears

❑ uspGetSalesRegions

With that, you have all of the objects in your data layer and are ready to move into your actual report.

STEP 2: Using the Existing Shared Data Source

If you worked through the examples in Chapter 5, you should already have a project called AdventureWorksReports with a shared data source called AdventureWorks2008DB.rds. If you did work through the examples in Chapter 5 for any reason, you will need to create this project and shared data source just as outlined in that chapter. The rest of this chapter will assume you already have these files in place. If you are unsure how to create either, please return to Chapter 5 to see how they were created.

STEP 3: Creating the Details Report

When creating two reports that you plan to link, you should create the second report first, meaning create the report that is filtered based on a passed parameter first. To put it in terms that make more sense to this specific example, you want to create the report that shows only the details of a particular region for a particular sales year. This is because the pie chart will have to pass some information to this report to create the filter. So it makes sense to set up the filter first so that the pie chart knows what it needs to send and to which report. This will make the linking easier when it is time to link the reports.

STEP 3-A: Adding a New Report

You will need to create a new report in the AdventureWorksReports project. However, unlike the example in Chapter 5, this example will not use the project wizard. While you certainly could use the wizard, doing this manually will give you a better grasp of what is required to create a report and give you additional skills for modifying reports and creating more custom solutions for your own reporting needs.

With the AdventureWorksReports project opened in BIDS, right-click the project name in the Solution Explorer and select Add and then New Item . . . to bring up the Add New Item screen shown in Figure 6-2.

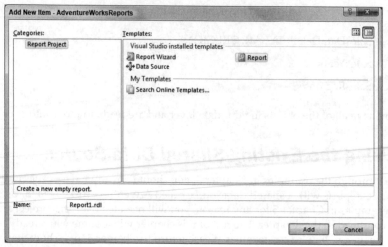

Figure 6-2

Make sure you select the Report option located within the Report Project category in the Visual Studio installed templates options section. Change the name of the report to "SalesDetailReport.rdl." Press the Add button to create a new blank report, as shown in Figure 6-3.

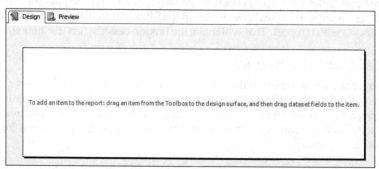

Figure 6-3

STEP 3-B: Adding Your Data Elements

You will notice that there is an essentially empty Report Data pane for your new report, as shown in Figure 6-4.

Figure 6-4

The first step is to provide the report with data, which means that you will need, at a minimum, a new Data Source relationship and associated Dataset. To add these, you can use the dropdown control indicated by New at the top of the Report Data pane. Click on New and select Data Source . . . to get the Data Source Properties box shown in Figure 6-5.

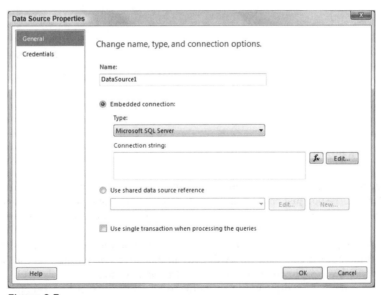

Figure 6-5

You want to tell the report where to get its data from or, at least, one of the sources of data. Since this example will be using the AdventureWorks2008DB shared data source, you are using this screen assocaiate the report with the data.

To associate the data to the form, first change the Data Source's Name to ReportConnection and then change the option from Embedded connection to Use shared data source references. This will enable the shared data source refernce dropdown box and, if you click the dropdown control, you should see the AdventureWorks2008DB option available. The AdventureWorks2008DB data source will probably be the only option unless you have created other data sources on your own. Select the AdventureWorks2008DB shared data source and then press the OK button. Your report now is associated with the AdventureWorks2008DB shared data source. So it is time to create an actual dataset.

To add your report details dataset, click the New dropdown control in the Report Data pane of BIDS again and, this time, select Dataset . . . to get the Dataset Properties box shown in Figure 6-6.

Figure 6-6

You should see that the Data Source dropdown control is already defaulted to the Report-Connection data source you just created. If it is not, go ahead and change it so that it is using the ReportConnection data source. Now set the Name property of the dataset to ReportDetails.

The next step is to create the logic that will return your dataset to the report. As discussed previously in this book, you could embed your data query directly in this screen by typing it in the Query text area control shown in Figure 6-6. However it is a much better practice to keep your data logic in your data logic layer, which can be easily done with the use of stored procedures. Since you have already created your stored procedure to return the detail listing of sales data previously in this chapter, it's time to use it.

To use the uspGetSalesRegions stored procedure, select the Stored Procedure option for the Query type. This will hide the query text editor window and display a new dropdown control with the instructions Select or enter stored procedure name:, as seen in Figure 6-7.

Figure 6-7

Since the report already knows which data store you are connecting to, it will query the database and display all stored procedures available for selection. If you have created the stored procedures discussed earlier in this chapter, you should see a stored procedure called uspGetSalesDataDetail. Select that stored procedure and press the OK button to add this dataset. When you do this, BIDS will recognize that the stored procedure requires two parameters (@YEAR and @REGION) and will prompt you to provide their values, as seen in Figure 6-8. You will need to provide values here so that BIDS can execute the stored procedure and get the returned fields. For this example enter 2003 for the YEAR parameter and Southeast for the REGION parameter (do not actually type the quotes for either parameter when you are entering them in BIDS) and then press the OK button. The dataset should now be added to the report, and if you expand the Parameters folder in the Report Data pane, you should see that both parameters have been added as well. You should also notice that the ReportDetails dataset is listed under the ReportConnection data source and that all available fields are listed below it.

So how are these parameters used at this point? You can get an idea if you take your report into the Preview mode by clicking the Preview tab of your report, the result of which is shown in Figure 6-8.

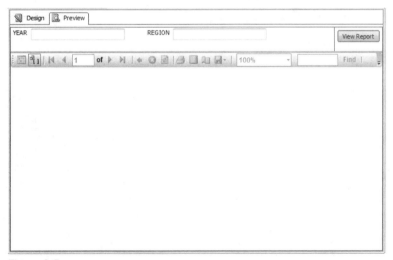

Figure 6-8

You can see that, even though there is nothing to display in the report (you haven't added any actual reporting elements to the report at this point), the report has provided two text boxes at the top of the report for the user to manually enter a YEAR and REGION value to run the report. The report is smart enough to recognize that it needs these two parameters for the stored procedure used by the report and has provided default text-entry fields that allow the end-user to provide this information.

If you have created any kind of application in the past, you probably get a bit nervous allowing end-users to provide free text for these values. After all, they will be compared to existing data in the database to find matches, and, with the slightest unintentionally typographical error, no results would come back. Besides, would anyone expect any user to remember all region names exactly? It would be much easier to provide the allowable options in dropdown box controls.

This is the reason for the two extra stored procedures created earlier in this chapter: uspGetSalesYears and uspGetSalesRegions. These stored procedures will return all allowable fields for the two parameters required for the main data feeding this report.

To associate the two parameters to the stored procedures, make sure you are on the Design tab of your report so that all of the options in the Report Data pane are enabled. (The options in the Report Data pane are disabled in preview mode.) Both stored procedures and their results will need to be added to your report in the same way that you added the ReportDetails dataset previously. Click the New dropdown control in the Report Data pane, repeat the procedures outlined earlier for the ReportDetails dataset and create two new datasets: ReportYears and ReportRegions. You should see both of these new datasets listed in the Report Data pane in BIDS. You should also notice that all returned fields are listed below each.

Once you have done this, double-click the YEAR option listed under Parameters in the Report Data pane to bring up the Report Parameter Properties box shown in Figure 6-9.

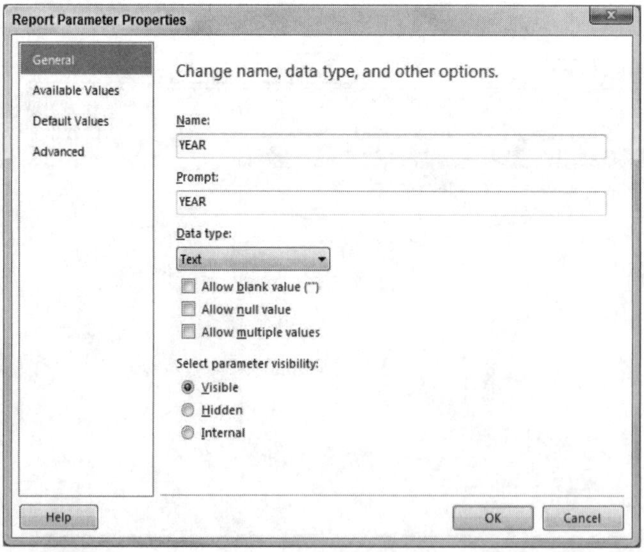

Figure 6-9

One easy cosmetic change you can make is to change the Prompt field. This is the text SSRS will use to precede the parameter selection field on the report. In other words, if you look back at Figure 6-8, you saw that the textbox controls for each parameter were preceded with their parameter name (YEAR and REGION). You can change this to whatever you want by updating the Prompt property. For now, just remove the all-caps nature of the prompt by changing it to read Year.

Now, while you are still in the Report Parameter Properties, click the Available Values tab to see the Report Parameter Properties screen shown in Figure 6-10.

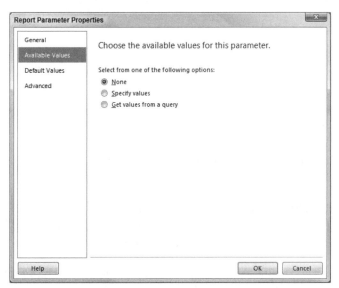

Figure 6-10

The Available Values property defaults to None. SSRS does not provide any predefined values, which means your users will get the free text option shown in Figure 6-8. You want to take advantage of the new ReportYears dataset that you just created to only allow users to select one of the available years from the AdventureWorks2008 database.

The first step is to change the option to Get values from a query, which will provide you a new dropdown control for the dataset. If you click the control, you should see the ReportYears option; select it. This will enable the Value and Label fields. Click each of those and select the only option, SalesYear. Press the OK button to make this change.

Now repeat these steps for the REGION parameter, ensuring that you use the ReportRegions dataset and its Region return value for both the Value and Label fields.

If you have done everything correctly, your report, in Preview mode, should now have dropdown controls for each of the two properties and resemble Figure 6-11.

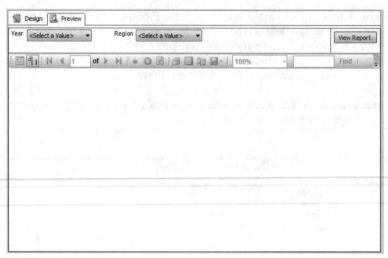

Figure 6-11

At this point, all of the data elements are set up and you are ready to begin creating your reporting elements to display your data.

STEP 3-C: Adding Your Reporting Elements

It is now time to make your report actually display something besides a white page. It is time to take the data elements and drop them into reportable/viewable items on your report.

The first thing you will add to this report is a report title. This title should be informative enough to tell someone seeing a disseminated copy of the report know exactly what the report is telling you. Since this report is showing sales data for a particular region and particular year (defined by the report parameters), an appropriate title might be something like "2003 Sales Data for the Southeast Region."

To begin the process of adding the report title to your report, make sure you are in the design pane of the report and the Report Data pane is in focus and enabled. If the Parameters folder is not expanded, expand it so that you can see the available parameters. Click the YEAR parameter and drag it to an area near the top of the report and drop it there. You should see that a new text box control has been added to your report and that it is populated with "[@YEAR]." Right-click the text box content and choose Expression to bring up the Expression editor shown in Figure 6-12.

Figure 6-12

The expression should be currently set to the following value:

```
=Parameters!YEAR.Value
```

This expression sets the value of the displayed text on your report. One of the nice things is that it is easily modifiable to fit your needs. For example, you can add Sales Data after the year value by modifying your formula to the following:

```
=Parameters!YEAR.Value + " Sales Data"
```

You should also see several categories of available fields listed below the expression editor box, one of which is Parameters. If you click Parameters in the Category list, you should see both parameters, YEAR and REGION, listed in a new Values list. If you double-click any of those values, you will see it get added to your expression where your cursor position was in the expression. To modify your expression to look like the following:

```
=Parameters!YEAR.Value + " Sales Data for the " +
```

With your cursor still at the end of the expression, double-click the REGION value under the Parameters category. Your expression should be modified to resemble the following:

```
=Parameters!YEAR.Value + " Sales Data for the " + Parameters!REGION.Value
```

Finally, add " Region" to the end of your concatenated string value so that your expression now resembles the following:

```
=Parameters!YEAR.Value + " Sales Data for the " + Parameters!REGION.Value + "
Region"
```

179

Now press the OK button to accept your changes.

With the text box selected, you should see draggable handles surrounding the control. If you click one of the handles, you can easily resize the control by dragging it across the report. Do this to your report title text box to make it as wide as your report.

You should also be able to modify the text format by utilizing the Report Formatting toolbar at the top of the BIDS interface. You can set the font size, color, and family. Play around with this until you find a combination that suits you. Once you are done, go to the Preview tab, select 2003 for the Year and Southeast for the region. Next press View Report. Your report should look similar to Figure 6-13.

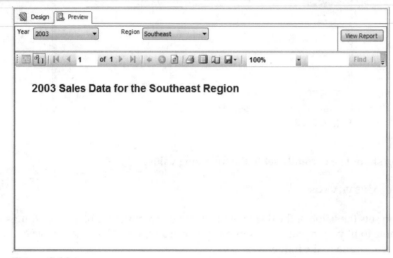

Figure 6-13

This report title is fairly unique in that it is only using static text and parameters provided to the report by the user. For now the dropdowns are selected by the user. Later the parameters will be passed from the main report to the linked report. It is not, then, using any fields from your main dataset.

The meat of this report will come with the data from the ReportDetails dataset. So now it is time to add the ReportDetails data in to your report.

First, make sure you are in the Design tab of your report. Next, instead of the Report Data pane, switch over to the Toolbox pane, shown in Figure 6-14.

Figure 6-14

This gives you all of the reportable elements you can add to your own report. Locate the Table element (Figure 6-15) and use your mouse to drag it onto your report just below your Report Title so that your report resembles Figure 6-16.

Figure 6-15

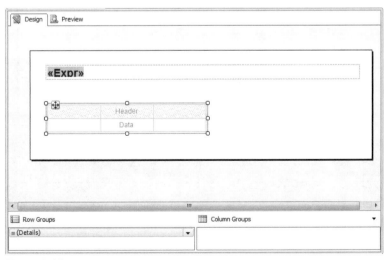

Figure 6-16

Now switch back to the Report Data pane so that you can see all of the available fields for the ReportDetails dataset. At this point it is a good time to think about how the data will be presented. For this report, you want to show all of the sales details for a particular region. However, a nice feature would be to have it grouped. Why not group by employee? That way you can have a report that summarizes how much sales a particular had during a reporting period in a particular region. If you group by the employee, you can hide the detail information on the initial load but allow the user to expand the details below the user if they want to see the total number of sales.

This means you will use the following fields (categorized as either a Group or Detail field):

Group	Detail
SalesEmployeeName	OrderID
	OrderDate
	TotalSale

So the first thing you will want to do is drag each of the three detail fields into one of the data cells in the table shown in Figure 6-16. Fortunately, there are already three cells there so you don't have to add any more cells. If you need more cells, you can right-click one of the cells and choose Insert Column and then choose Left or Right to insert a new column at the appropriate location.

So, once you have dragged all three detail fields to the appropriate cell, your report (in the Design tab) should now resemble Figure 6-17.

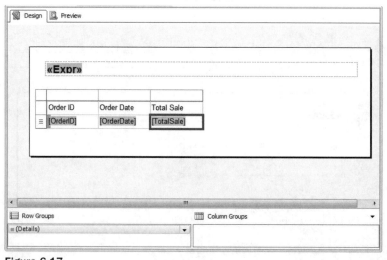

Figure 6-17

If you were to switch to the Preview tab and run the report, you should see that it now contains data based on the parameters you provide. The report isn't pretty and there is no grouping yet, but at least data is returning. Now it's time to add the Employee Name grouping. This is where it gets a little tricky.

Make sure you are in the Design tab of your report and highlight the row by clicking the row handle (the bar next to the data row), shown in Figure 6-18.

Figure 6-18

Once the row is selected, right-click the same bar, and select Add Group and then Parent Group . . . to get the Tablix group screen shown in Figure 6-19.

Figure 6-19

If you click the dropdown control for Group by, you should see all of the fields for the ReportDetails dataset. This is because, since you dragged the other fields from this dataset onto the table, it is already bound to this dataset. So it knows that you will be using data from this dataset. So, click the dropdown control and select [SalesEmployeeName] from the list.

You will also want to check the option for Add group header so that the Employee Name information is sitting on its own row. Press the OK button and your report should now look like Figure 6-20.

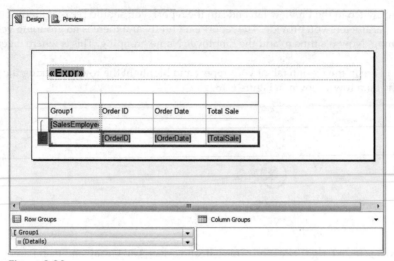

Figure 6-20

One thing that SSRS does by default when you create your grouping this way is to merge the group table cells into a single cell for each grouping. In other words, if you have 10 rows of detail for one employee you will have 10 rows of details on your table but one cell for the grouping field that spans all 10 rows. This is obviously a personal choice, but if you are not happy with this default behavior, it's easy enough to fix.

Click the grouping cell (the tcell in Figure 6-20 that is displaying "[SalesEmployeeName]") and you will see that it is merged between the group header row and the detail row. With the cell selected, right-click the cell and select Split Cells. Now there will be a unique header row and then just an empty cell for that column on each of the detail rows. Aesthetically, this seems more in line with most drilldown reports.

Now, to hide the detail rows on load and to toggle their visibility based on clicking the header row, you need to right-click the bar next to the detail row again (the area shown in Figure 6-18) and select Row Visibility . . . , which will bring up the Row Visibility screen shown in Figure 6-21.

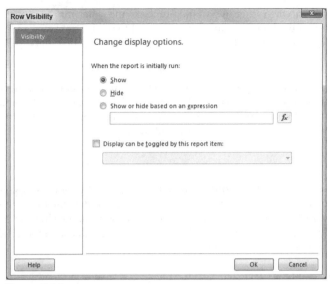

Figure 6-21

The first option sets what the initial state will be for the detail row. By default, it is set to show the row. Change this to Hide so that, when the report first displays, all detail rows are hidden. This means that only the header row will display.

To make the detail toggle on and off when a user clicks the header row, you need to create the toggle. To do this, make sure the checkbox is selected for Display can be toggled by this report item: at the bottom of the form. This will enable the dropdown box control, which you can use to select Group1 (the default name given to your parent group when it was created). Click the OK button to set these changes.

If you were to run the report in the Preview tab right now, you would see that the report works as planned to this point. The report loads with the correct title at the top based on the parameters you pass the report and the data is similarly reflective of those same parameters. You will also see that the table only shows the employee name header row but a new "+" symbol is next to the name that allows you to show or hide the detail rows.

The report could use some tweaking to make it more useful and easier to understand. This mostly just means some cosmetic formatting changes. But these changes can really impact the overall effectiveness of the report so it's smart to go ahead and clean up the report.

The first thing you will want to do is resize some of the columns. You did this in Chapter 5, but if you have forgotten how, you need only use your mouse on the border of any cell, while in design mode, to drag the cell to your desired width. Drag each cell to the appropriate width so columns are wide enough so the text does not wrap. Similarly, you can modify the alignment of a particular column by clicking the bar above any column to select the entire column and then use the Report Formatting toolbar to set the alignment (shown in Chapter 5). Use this approach to set the Order ID and Order Date columns to center aligned and the Total Sale column to right aligned. Also, you can select the header row and change the alignment for all header cells in the same fashion.

The next step is to clean up the formatting of the numbers and dates for the report. While 507391.6008 is not technically wrong for the total sales amount, it is hard to read. The same can be said with 3/1/2003 12:00:00 AM. Making these columns display in a more common format will help decision makers make sense of the report faster.

To make these changes, make sure you are in design mode for your report within BIDS and then right-click the cell containing the data your want to format. First, select the Order Date field. From the options that are presented, select Expression . . . to get the expression editor screen shown earlier in this chapter (Figure 6-12). The formula will look similar to the following:

```
=Fields!OrderDate.Value
```

If you look in the Category list, at the bottom, there is an expandable category called Common Functions. Expand that category item out to see several more options; the first one should be Text. Click the Text subcategory and you will see a number of functions you can use in your expression. Specifically, you will see one called FormatDateTime, which is what you want to use to format this DateTime field. Modify your expression to use this function like so:

```
=FormatDateTime(Fields!OrderDate.Value)
```

Using this same approach, modify your Total Sale field to use the following expression:

```
=FormatCurrency(Fields!TotalSale.Value)
```

If you go into the preview mode of your report, you should now see that both the date and sales numbers are much easier to read and will make more sense to the end users of this report.

One problem with this report, though, is that it is basically useless upon initial load. The only thing it really shows is who works for that region. You don't see any numbers unless you expand each column and that isn't how a drilldown report should work. Instead, you should be able to see a high-level picture of sales figures for this report when the report loads, and then, if you want more detail, you can expand the grouping to get it. So this means two things: you need group-level sales numbers and region-level summary figures.

First, you need to add summary sales information for each group row. While in design mode, right-click the empty cell in the group header row for the Total Sale column and select Expression. In the expression editor, use the following formula:

```
=FormatCurrency(SUM(Fields!TotalSale.Value))
```

The important thing to note about this formula is the addition of the SUM function. This is telling SSRS to sum up all of the TotalSale fields for this grouping. Other than that, this is the same formula used on the detail row for Total Sales.

Now to add a footer, right-click the Group1 cell in the detail row (the only empty cell in the detail row) and select Insert Row and then Outside Group - Below. This will create a new row directly below the detail row that is independent of the Employee Name grouping. In this new row, click the for Total Sale and enter the same formula used in the group header:

```
=FormatCurrency(SUM(Fields!TotalSale.Value))
```

This will create a footer row that gives a total sales amount for the entire region for all employees. Now, if you look at your report in Preview mode, it should resemble Figure 6-22.

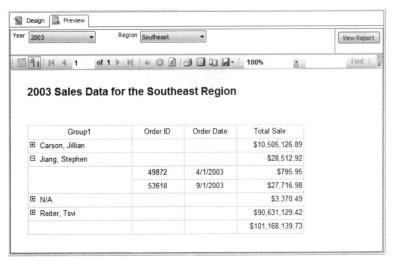

Figure 6-22

This figure uses "2003" for the Year parameter and "Southeast" for the Region and has expanded one employee (Jiang, Stephen) to show the detail rows. So, if you don't make these exact choices, your report will look at least slightly different. But, it should be pretty close to this at this point.

The only thing left at this point is cosmetic/stylistic modifications just to make it look pretty.

One of the easier things to fix is any column headers you may want to modify. For example, you probably don't want the first column to say Group1, since that won't make sense to anyone but you. While in Design mode double-click the cell in the header row that contains the text Group1 to make it editable. Change the header to read Employee. While you're at it, go ahead and fix the grammar for the Total Sale column to read Total Sales. If you don't remember how to do this, you may want to go back and look at Chapter 5.

As you will hopefully remember from Chapter 5, you can also format the entire row of the table at once by selecting the row and then applying formatting changes using, for example, the Report Formatting toolbar. Do this to give the header and footer row one look and the group header rows a different look. You can leave the details row alone for now.

Once you have finished playing with the report look and feel, it should now look more like Figure 6-23.

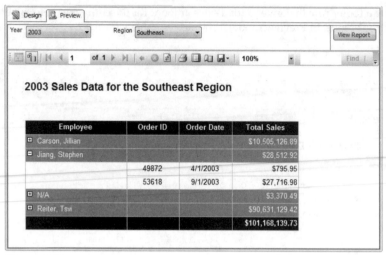

Figure 6-23

And with that, the SalesDetailReport.rdl is completed. You have created a parameterized report complete with grouping and detail visibility toggling from scratch. While this could have also been accomplished using the wizard, now you understand more what goes into making your table work, which will give you greater insight into fixing problems and modifications that will inevitably come along throughout the lifetime of the report. It's like the difference between taking your car to the mechanic and fixing it yourself. With this section, you fixed it yourself.

If you have a particularly strong eye for detail, you may notice that the sales totals for Stephen Jiang do not add up properly in the screenshots. His two sales, $795.95 and $27,716.98 should add up to $28,512.93. However, the group header row shows the total as $28,512.92, a difference of one cent. This may lead you to wonder if the summation is working properly. Well, the short answer is, it is working. The problem is that, as you will recall, the numbers did not come in at 2 digits past the decimal. Instead of $795.95 and $27,716.98, these amounts came through as 795.9481and 27716.975, respectively. These amounts total 28512.9231, which rounds down to $28,512.92. In a real-world scenario, the rounding should have taken place in the stored procedure itself. However, this was intentionally not done in this example so that you could see all of the changes the FormatCurrency() function performs. In your own projects, make sure you look for rounding errors like this so that you can eliminate them or, failing that, explain them.

STEP 4: Creating the Summary Report

Compared to the detail report you just finished, this one is going to be really simple, especially considering that you've already created a pie chart in Chapter 5. This is going to be, more than anything, a brief refresher on the topics presented in Chapter 5 and to some extent earlier in this chapter. This section won't have any new material in it, but if you plan on going to the next section (linking the reports), you need to finish this report so that you can use it to link to the detailed report. So be patient and count the redundancy as reinforcement of these ideas. And, since this section will gloss over a lot of material already covered, maybe even a quiz to gauge where you are as far as your comfort level with report development in BIDS 2008.

The first step is to add a new report to your project. You can name this report SalesSummaryReport.rdl.

Just as with the detail report, you will need to add your data from the uspGetSalesDataDetail stored procedure. To do this, add a new Data Source called ReportConnection and link it to the Shared Data Source, AdventureWorks2008DB.rds. Now add a new dataset called ReportDetails to connect with the ReportConnection report data source and utilize the uspGetSalesDataDetail stored procedure. Remember to use a valid parameter for the year (2003), but this time, unlike in the detail report, leave the region parameter with its default <Null> value. If you remember the stored procedure from earlier in this chapter, if you pass a null value, you will return all data for all regions for a specific year. This is what you need for this particular report.

You will also need to change your parameters. For the Year parameter, create a new dataset called ReportYears that utilizes the ReportConnection report data source and connects to the uspGetSalesYears stored procedure. Use that dataset to provide the available values for the Year parameter. Also, while you're in the parameter properties, change the prompt from YEAR to Year.

With the Region parameter, you need to do something different this time. For this report, you don't want to filter your data by region. Instead, you want to always pass in a null value so that all regions are reported back. After all, if you set up your pie chart to allocate slices of the pie by region sales dollars and only bring back one region, that is going to be a boring pie chart (just one slice).

To do this, double-click the REGION parameter in the Report Data pane of BIDS to get the Report Parameter Properties screen used earlier in this chapter to define your parameters. On the General tab, you need to make two changes. First, you need to allow null values since you only want to pass a null value. Check the Allow null value option. Next, you don't want the user to get prompted for this property. At the bottom of the screen, check the Internal option for the parameter visibility. This will keep the parameter valid, but the user will not be able to see or select it.

Next, click to the Default Values tab of the Report Parameter Properties screen. Since there is no user interaction on this parameter, you need to tell the report what the default value is. In the first section, change the option to Specify values. This will show a new area of the screen that allows you to add new values. Press the Add button and a new value will be added to the list. It should default to (Null); if not, use the dropdown control to select (Null) from the options. Now press the OK button to keep these changes.

Finally, add the chart to the report. From the Toolbox pane in BIDS, drag and drop a Chart control to your new report. For this example, use the simple Pie Chart found under the Shape objects in the Select Chart Type screen. This should be the first option in that section. Play with the size of the chart until you feel comfortable that it will show the level of detail you want. Make sure you don't make it any wider than the default margins so that you don't spread past the horizontal dimensions of a printed page.

Now change the Chart Title to use the expression:

```
=Parameters!YEAR.Value + " AdventureWorks Sales Figures"
```

To do this, you need to go into the Chart Title properties (see Figure 6-24). In your report click the chart title to select it and then right-click the title and select Title Properties . . . . From there, you can set the expression for the text and modify the font using the Font tab. So, while you're in there, make the title a little bigger and change the color to match the colors you set in your details report. Press OK to accept the changes to the chart title.

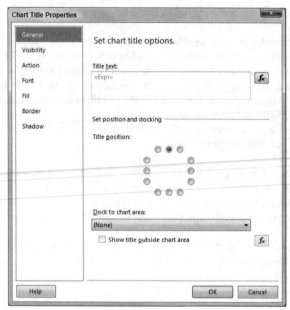

Figure 6-24

The last thing you need to do with your chart is bind it to your data source. Just as in Chapter 5, you need only drag and drop your fields from the Report Data pane of BIDS to the appropriate sections of your pie chart. With that in mind, drag the TotalSale field to the data area of the chart and the Region to the series area.

If you have done everything correctly and you switch over to Preview mode and select 2003 as the report year, your report should resemble Figure 6-25.

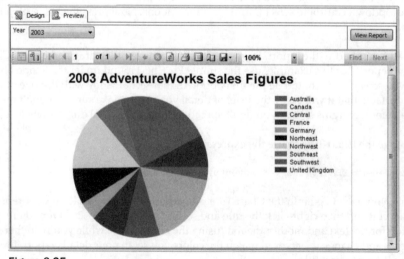

Figure 6-25

STEP 5: Linking the Reports

Linking reports is a pretty cool feature of reports and fortunately is fairly easy to implement. The goal of this step is to display the SalesSummaryReport for a specific year and click one of the pie slices which represents a specific region. Clicking a pie slice will take the reader to the SalesDetailReport with the parameters for YEAR and REGION being already communicated from report to report. The SalesDetailReport does not require the user to select any parameters. To set up the linking, open the SalesSummaryReport in design mode. Right-click anywhere in the chart control and look at the options presented. Depending on where you click, you may see Series Properties in the initial list. Click Series Properties. Otherwise, select Chart and then select Series Properties to get the Series Properties screen shown in Figure 6-26.

Figure 6-26

Click the Action tab to set up hyperlinking for your report. The default is set to None. Change this value to Go to report. This will bring up several new options, the first of which is to select which report you want to link to. Use the dropdown control to select the SalesDetailReport. You will also see that, immediately below this option, there is the ability to add parameters to run the report you are linking to.

Click the Add button to add a new parameter to pass to the linked report. The nice thing about this feature is that it creates a dropdown box populated with the parameters the destination report requires. So, if you click the dropdown box, you will see that you can select YEAR or REGION. For the first one, select REGION. To select the value you click the dropdown control and see all of the fields that are brought back with this report's dataset. In that list, you should see [Region]. Select [Region]. Click the Add button again to add the second parameter. For the Name, choose the YEAR option. This option is a bit different, though. Instead of using the dropdown control to select the value, you need to click on the expression button next to it (see Figure 6-27).

Figure 6-27

This will display the Expression editor. On this screen, select the Parameters item in the Category list and then double-click the YEAR value. This should create the following expression in the expression editor (you could also just type this):

```
=Parameters!YEAR.Value
```

This will pass the YEAR parameter used for the summary report and pass it to the details report. Press the OK button to close the expression editor.

At this point, both parameters for the destination report are set up and the link is defined. Press the OK button to close out the Series Properties window.

If you look at your report now in the review mode and select 2003 as the report year, it should resemble Figure 6-28.

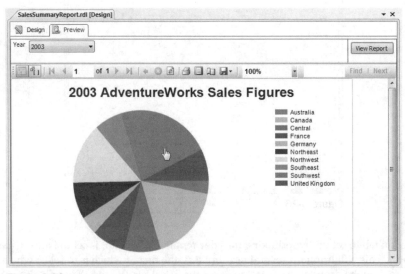

Figure 6-28

It may not be completely clear in the screenshot in this manuscript, but in your own project you should notice that your cursor turns to the pointer icon when you hover over the pie pieces. This means the hyperlink has been established and is working. If you click any of the pie slices, you should be taken to the details report with the YEAR and REGION parameters already passed to the report and the report just loads; no need for user interaction. If you clicked the Southeast region, the report should look like Figure 6-29.

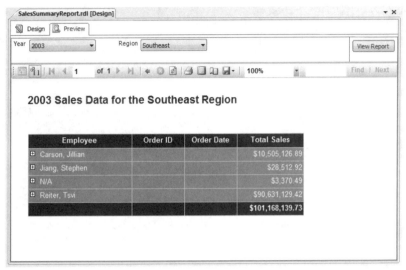

Figure 6-29

One thing that might not be immediately obvious is what report is loaded. If you look at Figures 6-27 and 6-28 (or in your own project), you can look at the tab of BIDS that is showing what report is currently being displayed. Notice anything interesting? They are both showing SalesSummaryReport, even though the second screenshot is obviously SalesDetailReport. This makes the jump from one report to the other seamless. However, it could cause problems (like getting back to the summary report from the detail report). You might consider, in your own projects, creating a text box control somewhere on your report that is essentially a hyperlink back to the original report (you could just create an action on the text box to link back to the SalesSummaryReport pass the YEAR parameter back to it). But for now, you should at least how this linking works and maybe get some ideas how you might use something like this to create your own dashboard reporting applications.

Accessing a SharePoint List

One of the really useful features of SSRS is its ability to populate a dataset through accessing web service methods. And, in the world of SharePoint, that makes an even bigger impact, since all of SharePoint lists are served out through web services. So, for this section, you will see how to make a very basic report that brings a SharePoint list into SSRS and formats the data into a fairly professional looking report.

STEP 1: Getting Prepared

The first thing you will need is a SharePoint list, obviously. For this example, you can use the Tasks list of any SharePoint installation. The list used in this example has five task items mimicking the five steps outlined earlier this chapter in creating a linked server, as you can see in Figure 6-30.

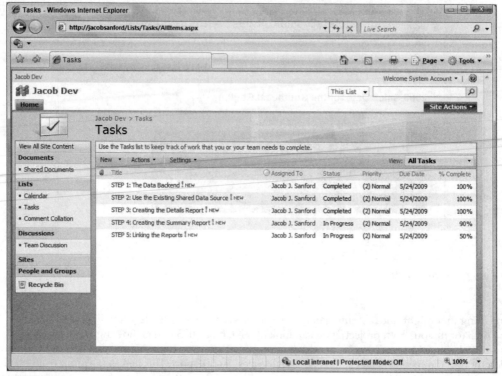

Figure 6-30

In SharePoint, you can access list specific methods using the following URL pattern:

```
http://<server-url>/_vti_bin/lists.asmx
```

Since the task list in Figure 6-29 was located in a site collection using the domain http://jacobsanford, the URL to retrieve list methods would be the following:

```
http://jacobsanford/_vti_bin/lists.asmx
```

In your own project, you will need to use the domain that corresponds to your own server hosting. However, for the remainder of this chapter, the domain http://jacobsanford will be used. Each time you see this in this chapter, please substitute in the domain of your own server.

If you open that URL in your browser, you will see a full list of methods available:

❑   AddAttachment

❑   AddDiscussionBoardItem

❑   AddList

❑   AddListFromFeature

❏ ApplyContentTypeToList

❏ CheckInFile

❏ CheckOutFile

❏ CreateContentType

❏ DeleteAttachment

❏ DeleteContentType

❏ DeleteContentTypeXmlDocument

❏ DeleteList

❏ GetAttachmentCollection

❏ GetList

❏ GetListAndView

❏ GetListCollection

❏ GetListContentType

❏ GetListContentTypes

❏ GetListItemChanges

❏ GetListItemChangesSinceToken

❏ GetListItems

❏ GetVersionCollection

❏ UndoCheckOut

❏ UpdateContentType

❏ UpdateContentTypeXmlDocument

❏ UpdateContentTypesXmlDocument

❏ UpdateList

❏ UpdateListItems

The method that you want to use to return a dataset of list items is GetListItems. This method will bring back all list items from the list you specify. You can even use CAML queries to filter the results at the list level rather than waiting until it gets inside of SSRS to filter it. However, for this example, that is overkill. You just need to note the following two items before you get back into bids:

❏ The URL of your web service (`http://jacobsanford/_vti_bin/lists.asmx` in this example)

❏ The web method (GetListItems)

You can read more about the GetListItems Method by reading the MSDN Library SharePoint SDK Documention on the method, located at `http://msdn.microsoft.com/en-us/library/dd586530(office.11).aspx`.

STEP 2: Creating Your Data Access Elements

With your prep work done, it's time to get back into BIDS and use that information to create your data access methodologies. Just as in all of your previous reports, you will need a shared data source that accesses your list web service URL. You will also need to provide some XML to let SSRS know what list you want to access so that it can create a dataset for you.

To get started add a new data source, right-click the Shared Data Sources folder in the Solution Explorer of BIDS, and choose Add New Data Source to get the Shared Data Source Properties window shown in Figure 6-31.

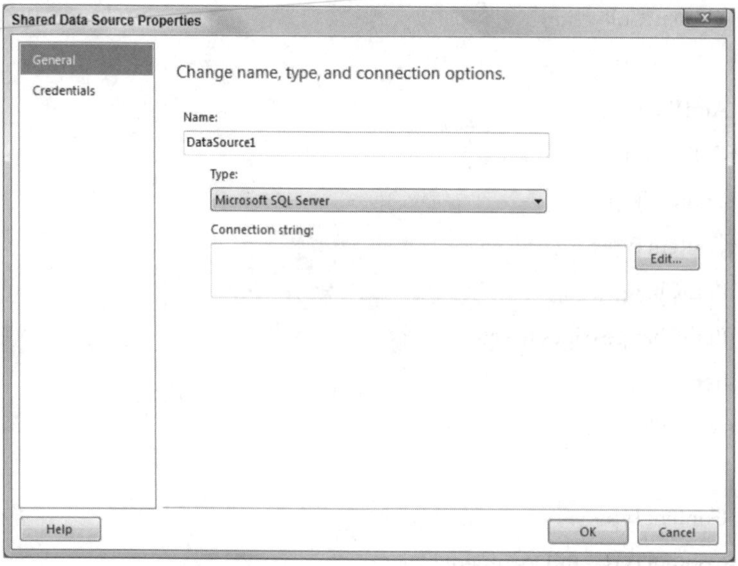

Figure 6-31

Set the name property to a suitable name. You will have two distinct shared data source objects in your project, assuming you have been following along the book to this point. Therefore, you need to be able to easily tell when you open the project in six months to make a change what each one is. For this example change the name property to SharePointListWebService.

In the type dropdown control, you won't see anything referring to a web service, so you might get nervous. However, you need to remember that web services are basically just XML documents sent out over the web. There is an option for XML. For this example select XML. Next enter your list web service URL into the Connection string property. The list web service URL will be specific for your SharePoint environment. Make sure you use your specific URL. (For my server I used http://jacobsanford/_vti_bin/lists.asmx.)

Finally, you should also check the data source's Credentials tab. For web services, you can only use Windows Authentication or No Credentials. The default behavior is Windows Authentication and, hopefully, this will meet your needs in your own project because, in most situations involving

SharePoint, No Credentials will not get you the data you desire. Make sure that one of these two options is selected and then press "OK" to create the shared data source object.

Since datasets are report specific, you need to actually add a new report to your project so you can create your data access methods. To add a new report, right-click the Reports folder in Solution Explorer and choose Add and then New Item . . . . On the Add New Item screen that comes up, choose Report in the Visual Studio templates section and give it the name SharePointTasksReport.rdl. Click the Add button to add a new, blank report to your project.

Now create a new data source for your report. To create a new data source, go to the Report Data pane in BIDS and click the New dropdown control and select Data Source. Just as in the linked reports earlier in this chapter, you will need to add your report data source that links to the shared data source you just created. On the General tab, change the name to TasksList and change your connection type to use the shared data source, SharePointListWebService. Press the OK button to add this data source to your project.

The next and last step is to create the dataset for the report. Creating a dataset from a web service can be challenging. You start this task just like all of the other examples in this chapter. Click the New dropdown control in the Report Data pane and select the Dataset . . . option to bring up the Dataset Properties screen. Just as in the other examples in this chapter, you will want to rename the dataset to something that makes sense when you are looking at this later, especially if you have multiple datasets on a single report. For this example change the name of the dataset to TaskListItems. You also need to make sure your data source property is set to the TasksList data source object you just created.

Now comes the tricky part: the query.

Make sure the query type is Text, which will give you a large text area to write out your query. This is the SOAP command that you will use to access the list:

```
<Query>
<SoapAction>
    http://schemas.microsoft.com/sharepoint/soap/GetListItems
</SoapAction>
<Method Namespace="http://schemas.microsoft.com/sharepoint/soap/"
    Name="GetListItems">
    <Parameters>
        <Parameter Name="listName">
            <DefaultValue>Tasks</DefaultValue>
        </Parameter>
    </Parameters>
</Method>
<ElementPath IgnoreNamespaces="True">*</ElementPath>
</Query>
```

The first two parts in bold, references to GetListItems, tell the web service what method to execute in the web service defined in the data source. The second part in bold, Tasks, tells the GetListItems method which list to access. All of the rest of this query is just standard SOAP to access your web service methods. Notice that nowhere in this code are you referring to your specific installation. In other words, there are no references to your own SharePoint site. This method is pretty generic and easily portable to your own environment.

Click the Refresh Fields button before pressing the OK button. Refreshing the fields will update the dataset with the available fields returned from the web service call. The first sign that you have the query right is that you don't receive an error, which is always a good sign. You can click the Fields tab, and you will see all of the fields coming back with your query. You will probably see quite a few of them. If you are unfamiliar with accessing list data under the hood in this manner, you may be surprised to see a lot of the field names start with ows_, such as ows_AssignedTo. This is normal. If you see the fields, press the OK button to save your dataset in your report.

Assuming you have at least one item in the task list you are trying to access, you should see all of the fields appear under the TaskListItems object in the Report Data pane, as seen in Figure 6-32. If you do, you are done with your data access elements and can now add the reporting elements to display the data. If you do not see the fields, the most likely reason is that the list is empty. You may need to go and add a few list items to your list so that you can see your fields before continuing.

Figure 6-32

STEP 3: Creating Your Reporting Elements

Now that you have your data access elements in place, it's time to put some data on a report so that you can actually display the information to the end-users accessing the report. So, with your report open in BIDS, switch to the Toolbox pane and drag a Table object to your report in the same way you did earlier in this chapter. Just as before, you should notice that the tablix control created has three columns by default. This is not a limitation; it is only a starting point. However, since this is just an example, three will work just fine.

Switch back over to the Report Data pane in BIDS and drag the following fields to your new tablix object:

- ❑ ows_Title
- ❑ ows_AssignedTo
- ❑ ows_Status

And, with that, you will have a functioning report accessing your list data (see Figure 6-33).

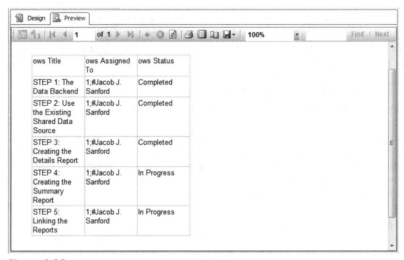

Figure 6-33

Granted, at this point, the report isn't anything spectacular to look at; it definitely needs some aesthetic help and some basic formatting. But it works. You have created a report in SSRS that accesses a list in your SharePoint environment, and that is pretty cool.

STEP 4: Formatting the Report

While completely optional and very subjective, it is probably a good idea to clean up the report to make it friendlier to the eyes. There are a lot of small things that you can do that will make a large impact on the final report. To get started, make sure you are in the design mode of your report.

The first thing you can do is clean up the header titles. Double click on any header title to enter edit mode. Remove the ows text from the header fields. Nobody will know what "ows" is, and it will just confuse people. So, for example, change "ows Title" to just "Title." Do this with all three columns.

Another easy thing to fix is the width of each column. With this limited amount of data, it will be a lot easier to read if the entire row is on a single line of text. So click either side border of a column and drag it to a more appropriate width.

The next formatting item is the only new formatting task for this section and is a slightly complicated part of this process: fixing the display for the Assigned To field. Currently, the value is displaying something like 1;#Jacob J. Sanford. SharePoint does this to track both an ID number and the value of some of its fields. The only real way to address this is to use the expression editor and its included string functions to filter the part of the string you want to display. In this case, that means everything to the right of the pound (#) symbol. Select the data row cell by right clicking the Assign To field and choose Expression to display the expression editor. Enter the following expression in the editor window:

```
=RIGHT(Fields!ows_AssignedTo.Value, LEN(Fields!ows_AssignedTo.Value) -
INSTR(Fields!ows_AssignedTo.Value, "#"))
```

If you are familiar with VBScript or even functions in applications like Microsoft EXCEL, this will probably make some degree of sense to you. However, in case this just looks like jargon to you, here is essentially what is going on. The RIGHT function takes two arguments: the string you want to modify and the number of characters to return. The RIGHT function returns the number of characters starting from the right hand side of the string. For example, if you entered RIGHT("jacob", 2), you would get a new string of "ob." If you modify the formula to RIGHT("jacob", 4), you would get "acob" back. So the first argument of the RIGHT function, Fields!ows_AssignedTo.Value, is pretty straight forward. This is just the Assigned To value of the tasks list, which currently says something like 1;#Jacob J. Sanford.

The rest of the formula is trying to figure out how many characters to return. The first thing you have to determine is how many total characters is the string in the first place. That is where the LEN() function comes into play. This function accepts just one string parameter and returns the number of characters in that string. So you need to include the string being modified again to get its total length. For the example being used to this point (1;#Jacob J. Sanford), the total length is 19.

The final part of the formula figures out at what point in the string the character "#" first appears. You need to know this because you want to return only the characters that occur after the # symbol. So, in this example, this would return a 3, since the # shows up as the third character in the string.

With all of this in mind, the formula you entered above could evaluate to something more like this:

```
RIGHT("1;#Jacob J. Sanford", 19 - 3)
```

When you look at it this way, you can see that the function is bringing back the rightmost 16 characters of this example string, yielding a final result of "Jacob J. Sanford."

With the expression in place, press the OK button to save the changes to your report. Go into the preview mode of your report and verify the Assigned To field displays as expected. If not, you may need to play with your function until it returns the desired string value. However, in this example, this function should work perfectly.

The last thing you may want to do with this report is to bring some color to it. So select the header row and modify the background and font color by using the Report Formatting toolbar as seen in the previous reports in this chapter as well as Chapter 5.

Finally, to create an alternating background color effect for your detail rows, select the details row and then find the Background Color property in the Properties pane of BIDS. If you click in the value part of the property, a dropdown control should appear. Click on the dropdown arrow and select

Expression . . . to get back to the Expression Editor screen. Change the expression to the following, which will alternate the row background color from White to Silver:

```
=IIF(RowNumber(Nothing) Mod 2, "Silver", "White")
```

This was explained in Chapter 5, but what is essentially going on here is that the expression is looking at the current row number and dividing it by 2. If there is a remainder, it sets the background color as White; otherwise, it gets set to Silver.

If you have followed all of these steps, your final report should now resemble Figure 6-34.

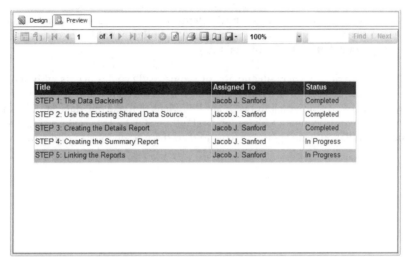

Figure 6-34

While the final report is fairly simplistic, this example demonstrated some pretty lofty concepts. While you may not need to have a report that lists out tasks, you might very well have the need to report other list data in a report. This example showed you exactly how to do that. You saw how to access the SharePoint web service to access the list items and how to get the fields back into a usable dataset. It also showed you how to clean up some of the formatting issues that are common with accessing SharePoint list data in this manner. The final report is fairly elementary but the underlying concepts are anything but.

Summary

Chapter 5 provided you with a good start on your journey to mastering Reporting Services. You learned some best practices and saw a lot of how-to's on formatting and element manipulation. But it could almost be called the cheater's tour because you used a wizard to create your reports. You didn't see or understand anything that was going on under the hood and wouldn't be able to create a custom report from scratch with what you had learned in that chapter. Don't misunderstand; the concepts in that chapter were necessary and valid. But you needed to go to the next level to begin getting a grasp of how SSRS works.

This chapter started taking you to the next level. You got a lot deeper dive into the fundamentals of report design and generation. You saw how to create a new report from scratch. You saw how to create custom data sources and datasets for your project, how to add your reporting elements to your report, and how to connect the two. You saw how to group your report data into logical units and how to toggle the related detail data from merely clicking on the group row header. With this, you should have a better idea of what goes on under the hood when you use the report wizard to create your own reports, and, if you ever have a problem with a report created using the wizard, you should have the understanding to be able to go in and fix it.

Beyond that, you also were exposed to accessing SharePoint information directly in your report via the List web service. After all, this is a book on integrating Reporting Services and SharePoint, so this is a crucial concept to understand. You saw how to create your data source to access your SharePoint list and then make a simple query of that list to get the list items returned in a dataset you could use in your reports. This is a concept that will come into play more and more in your own career as a SharePoint Report Designer (even if that isn't your official title).

You are finally ready to dive deeper still and get into some really cool concepts with Reporting Services. How would you create a merge of two different data sources to create a joined table you can report on in SSRS? For example, how would you join two SharePoint lists to make one dataset you can use in SSRS? Or, even cooler, how would you join a SharePoint list with a SQL table to make a single dataset to use in your SSRS report? Well, you're just going to have to read the next chapter to find out.

7

Advanced Reporting Techniques

At this point in the book, you should have a fairly solid understanding of how to create your report environment, the tools you need to create reports, and how to create some reports. You have either learned that in the previous six chapters or have felt comfortable enough with your skills to skip ahead. Either way, you should be fairly comfortable with creating reports using BIDS, accessing at least some basic SQL or SharePoint data as your data backend.

But what happens when you want to go beyond that? What happens if you have business needs that don't necessarily fit within the confines of SSRS out of the box? Well, you develop your own box. You figure out how to make your project work the way you need it to. If you are a developer, you are probably pretty familiar with this type of development.

So it's time to create your own box. This chapter will help you accomplish this goal.

Creating a Custom Solution

Don't misinterpret the introduction to this chapter. SSRS is a very powerful tool that can do a lot of really cool things that will solve most of your reporting needs. Do you want to create a dashboard of eye-catching gauges or three-dimensional exploding pie charts? You can. Do you want to create drilldown reports that are linked from the pie pieces to a more grid-like display? You can. Do you want to create invoices to ship out to clients? You can. Do you want to create reports on the peer review evaluation cycle your company just went through with individual reports and pie charts for each employee? You can. For probably 95 percent of the reporting needs you will face, SSRS can provide the solution out of the box.

But what happens for that other five percent? Even if that doesn't sound like a huge percentage, when the CIO of your company is demanding something that falls into the five percent category, it is the most important thing in the world. So what do you do? How extensible is SSRS really?

There are a number of ways to address this five percent gap; this chapter will show you one approach that will probably allow you to handle almost all of these types of solutions: go outside of SSRS to fix the problem. This will make more sense as the chapter progresses.

One thing to remember as you are reading this chapter is that, in the world of reporting, regardless of what you are using to generate your reports, the reports are only as good as the dataset feeding them. So, while this chapter is entitled "Advanced Reporting Techniques," you might want to think of it more like "Advanced Data Gathering Techniques." This chapter is not going to teach you much new in the ways of creating the aesthetics of the report. At the risk of foreshadowing, you will learn some of the nuances of handling custom built web services inside of your reports but, other than that, you won't be using SSRS for much of this chapter. Instead, you are going to learn how to think around some of the problems you may come across when you are trying to use SSRS in the real world. You will learn what you can do if, out of the box, SSRS doesn't present your data in a reportable fashion and the data repository (or repositories) can't create a dataset that is usable by SSRS. In that situation, you will need a middle tier to act between the data and the reports, and that is where this chapter will focus. That is the type of advanced thinking this chapter hopes to encourage in you. And, when you think of it like that, maybe this chapter could be more appropriately entitled "Advanced Ways of Thinking About Data in SSRS." So just keep that in mind as you read through this chapter.

The Scenario

To better understand the points of this chapter, it's probably easier to relate things to a real-life situation that you very well might find yourself in one day. So imagine that your boss has come up with what, at face value, seems like a fairly simple request. In your Line of Business data repository, a SQL 2008 database, you have a listing of employees. Additionally, in your SharePoint deployment, you have a listing of phone numbers for each employee. Your boss would simply like a report that links these two data stores to make a listing of all employees and their phone numbers. This should be easy because both the database and the SharePoint list save an ID that can be used to link the information.

Remembering the lessons learned by reading the earlier chapters in this book, you know that SSRS out of the box can support the following data sources:

- ❑ Microsoft SQL Server
- ❑ Microsoft SQL Server Analysis Services
- ❑ OLE DB
- ❑ Oracle
- ❑ ODBC
- ❑ Report Server Model
- ❑ SAP NetWeaver BI
- ❑ Hyperion Essbase
- ❑ Teradata
- ❑ XML

You have seen how to use the SQL 2008 database, which is probably the easiest approach, since SSRS is built on top of SQL Server 2008. You have also seen how you can use the XML data type to access the SharePoint list web services to get a dataset of list data. So now you just have to link them. No problem, right?

Wrong.

There is no way, within SSRS, to combine two different data sources into a single, joined data source that you can use to generate a report. In most situations, you are joining data from a single data repository and doing any joins there. For example, if you need to join two different tables inside of the same database, you would simply create a stored procedure and use JOIN logic to connect these tables. Using linked server relationships, you can even query other databases and create a single dataset in your stored procedure. However, SSRS would just execute the stored procedure and see a single dataset returned. SSRS wouldn't care, in that scenario, how many different data sources actually made up the dataset; data manipulation is taken care of on the data tier.

So how do you create a joined dataset between two disparate data sources such as this example? Or, possibly, how do you create a joined dataset between two data sources of the same source that don't have their own way to join data? (For instance, have you ever tried to join two SharePoint lists?) This chapter will give you a solution to address this and, more important, give you some ideas on how to approach the five percent gap when you encounter it in your own projects.

> *While technically your SharePoint data exists inside of your SQL Server database and, as such, you could just access it directly from the content database, this is a really bad idea. This can violate security polices established within SharePoint, affect performance, and corrupt the integrity of your data as well as create locks and unintended consequences. Any type of direct database access of your SharePoint data is not supported by Microsoft and should not be attempted. It's not that it can't be done; it's that it shouldn't be done.*

The Solution

To borrow from a completely overused expression, it's time to think outside the SSRS box. And that means completely leaving SSRS for a minute or two and making a solution that will work.

Remember from the end of Chapter 6 that SSRS can use its XML data type to access datasets from a web service. In that example, you saw how to take the existing list web services of SharePoint to display the task list from a site. This opens up a whole lot of possibilities if you start examining what this really means. As long as you have a web service that returns a valid dataset, you can use it to be the data source for your report. Sure, this worked really well in the SharePoint example because you already had the web service created and ready for you. But don't limit your options to just existing web services. If you need data and there isn't an easy way to get it within the confines of SSRS, make your own web service to do what you want and send a dataset back to SSRS to use there. That is what you are going to do in this chapter: create a custom web service to join a SQL table and a SharePoint list into a single joined dataset and then return that to SSRS and make a report to display the results.

STEP 1: Create and Setup a New Project

The first step is relatively easy but bears its own step because of a couple of unique considerations. The first is the fact that the examples in this chapter, unlike any other chapter so far, require Visual Studio, and in some capacity you already have a light version from installing BIDS. But if you *only* have BIDS, you just have enough of Visual Studio installed to run SSRS projects. You need the full version so that you can create other projects, such as the web service that will be used for this chapter.

> It is certainly possible to create your web project files in any number of other applications, even something so basic as Notepad. However, you will find it much easier to follow along with the steps of this chapter if you are using one of the full versions of Visual Studio. This chapter uses Visual Studio to create this project and, as such, many of the steps and screenshots are only applicable to Visual Studio. So, while you do not need Visual Studio installed to run the code in this chapter, you will find it much easier to follow along with the example if you have it.

Fortunately, a free version, Microsoft Visual Web Developer 2008 Express Edition, will provide all of the functionality you need for this chapter. You can download Microsoft Visual Web Developer 2008 Express Edition here:

```
http://www.microsoft.com/express/download/
```

If you already have a fully working version of Visual Studio 2008 (any version), you don't need to download this version of Visual Studio and you can proceed to creating your project. However, if you only have BIDS, you will need to download Microsoft Visual Web Developer 2008 Express Edition and install it before proceeding with these examples.

The requirement for Visual Studio 2008 is not the only unique aspect of this project. In the previous report development chapters, you were able to run BIDS on any computer that had access to the data you needed. For example, you could run BIDS on any computer that had access, local or remote, to the data you needed. There was no requirement to run BIDs on the same computer as the SQL database or SharePoint sites.

For this chapter's examples you will need to develop on a SharePoint server. These examples will be accessing the SharePoint object model. It is a generally accepted best practice to develop locally on a SharePoint server instance when working with the object model. It is possible to develop on a remote machine, but it is usually easier to develop on your development server that has WSS or MOSS already installed on it. So keep that in mind as you are setting up this project. It is simply beyond the scope of this book to discuss more advanced development environments.

So, with your version of Visual Studio open, you now need to create a new project. You can click the File option in the toolbar of Visual Studio and select New Project to get the New Project screen shown in Figure 7-1. You will need to navigate to your preferred language (C# in this example) to see the options presented in this screen shot.

This is a good time to point out one additional advantage to going with this approach. In SSRS, you do have access to code blocks. However, these code blocks are limited to VBScript. So, if you are a C# or Visual C++ developer, you may find this cumbersome. Switching over to Visual Studio lets you code in the language you are comfortable with.

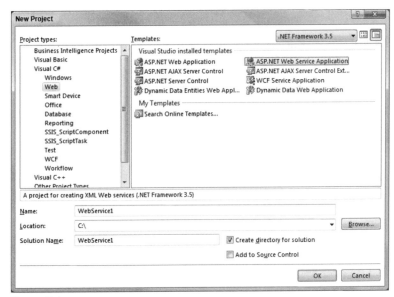

Figure 7-1

As seen in Figure 7-1, make sure you have selected the ASP.NET Web Service Application option under the Visual Studio installed templates section (you may need to select the Web option under your preferred language in the Project Types pane to see the options shown in Figure 7-1). While you can choose whichever language you prefer, this chapter will use C# for its examples. The coding won't be super deep, and, if you are an experienced developer in a different language, you should be able to follow along just fine and convert the code yourself. Otherwise, you may want to use C# for your own project to learn what is going on and then play around with it in your preferred language later on.

For now, select a Name property that describes your project so that you can remember what it is lately. You can use AdventureWorksWebService, for example, since this will be the database you will be accessing for your SQL data. Updating the name will update the Solution Name automatically. You must also choose a location for your files to reside. Visual Studio will provide a default location (for many, this will be the root directory of their machine, usually C:\), which is fine for this example. If this doesn't work for your own environment, select a location that works better for you. If you select the Create directory for solution option and use the name AdventureWorksWebService with a location of C:\, your project will be created in the following location:

```
C:\ AdventureWorksWebService\
```

Press the OK button to continue. This should create a simple web service project with the following web service code set up by default:

```
using System;
using System.Collections.Generic;
using System.Linq;
using System.Web;
using System.Web.Services;

namespace AdventureWorksWebService
{
    /// <summary>
    /// Summary description for Service1
    /// </summary>
    [WebService(Namespace = "http://tempuri.org/")]
    [WebServiceBinding(ConformsTo = WsiProfiles.BasicProfile1_1)]
    [System.ComponentModel.ToolboxItem(false)]
    // To allow this Web Service to be called from script, using ASP.NET AJAX,
    uncomment the following line.
    // [System.Web.Script.Services.ScriptService]
    public class Service1 : System.Web.Services.WebService
    {

        [WebMethod]
        public string HelloWorld()
        {
            return "Hello World";
        }
    }
}
```

Pretty simple, right? If you are familiar with web services, you can see that it has one web method set up: HelloWorld. If you were to run this method, it would return a string value of "Hello World" to the querying application. In the world of web services, this is about as simple as it gets.

The first thing that you may want to change here is the Web Service Namespace, currently set to use http://tempuri.org/, as highlighted below:

```
[WebService(Namespace = "http://tempuri.org/")]
```

While this isn't going to cause anything to crash, it is recommended that you only use this for development and, before making it public, you change it to a more permanent namespace. It is a generally considered best practice to use your own domain name as part of the web service. For example, if your domain is something like http://www.sharepointreports.com, you could use something like http://sharepointreports.com/webservices/ as your namespace. You can read more about namespace recommendations for XML web services here:

```
http://www.w3.org/TR/REC-xml-names/
```

But also remember, this web service probably will not be made public, per se. This is a custom web service that will only be used by your reports. So, for this example, there is no need to change this right now. However, if you run the web service in debug mode, you will see a warning message reiterating what you just read. Be aware of it and make a decision based on your own needs and the intended use of this web service. For this project, however, it is fine to leave the default, `http://tempuri.org/`, alone.

The next thing this project needs is the ability to use the SharePoint object model. Remember from earlier in this chapter that you will use the SharePoint object model to allow you to access list information so that you can get the list data for this exercise.

So, to add a reference to the SharePoint object model to your project, right-click the References folder in your Solution Explorer and select Add Reference. When the Add Reference screen comes up, stay in the .NET tab and scroll to the bottom and find Windows SharePoint Services, as seen in Figure 7-2.

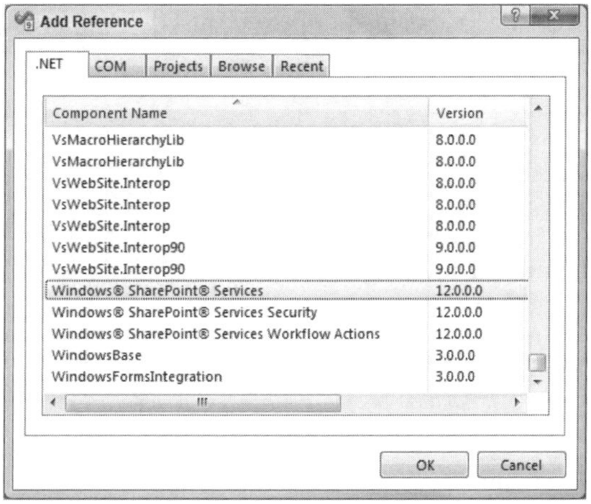

Figure 7-2

Press the OK button and Visual Studio will add a reference to the SharePoint object model allowing you to access SharePoint objects, such as the list you will use for this project.

With the SharePoint assembly referenced in your project you should add a using statement for Microsoft. SharePoint to the list of using statements to the top of the page containing the web service class. Adding the using Microsoft .SharePoint using statement allows you to reference SharePoint classes with the short name as opposed to the fully qualified name. Your web service class should look similar to the example below.

```
using System;
using System.Collections.Generic;
using System.Linq;
using System.Web;
using System.Web.Services;
```

The first thing you will want to add is a reference to the SharePoint object model that you just added. So, to do this, add a new using statement similar to the following:

```
using Microsoft.SharePoint;
```

You should notice that, as you are typing, when you complete Microsoft and type the period, you will see SharePoint in the IntelliSense. If you do not, you may not have added your reference properly before. If this is the case, make sure you can see it listed if you expand the References folder in Solution Explorer.

You will now need to add a reference in your using statements that will allow you to access your ADO objects more easily. Essentially, this will provide a shortcut for typing out database access code later in your project. In other words, you can write out something like SqlConnection rather than System.Data. SqlClient.SqlConnection. Both would work, but, obviously, the first option is a lot faster to write.

So, to do this, add the following two lines to your using statements:

```
using System.Data;
using System.Data.SqlClient;
```

The last step in cleaning up your project to get ready for the real code is to strip out the `HelloWorld` method included in your web service. So, in your project, just delete this entire method:

```
[WebMethod]
public string HelloWorld()
{
    return "Hello World";
}
```

At this point, your code should look like this:

```
using System;
using System.Collections.Generic;
using System.Linq;
using System.Web;
using System.Web.Services;
using Microsoft.SharePoint;
using System.Data;
using System.Data.SqlClient;

namespace AdventureWorksWebService
{
    /// <summary>
    /// Summary description for Service1
    /// </summary>
    [WebService(Namespace = "http://tempuri.org/")]
    [WebServiceBinding(ConformsTo = WsiProfiles.BasicProfile1_1)]
    [System.ComponentModel.ToolboxItem(false)]
    // To allow this Web Service to be called from script, using ASP.NET AJAX,
uncomment the following line.
    // [System.Web.Script.Services.ScriptService]
    public class Service1 : System.Web.Services.WebService
    {


    }
}
```

If yours does, you are ready to go to the next step: adding your code. If not, you should modify whatever code you have in place so that it does resemble the above code before moving on to the next step. Otherwise, you may have some difficulty following along with this example.

STEP 2: Adding Your Custom Code

Before writing any code, it is good to think about exactly what you want this code to do and what you want the return value/type to be. You need to know what your final deliverable, so to speak, will be so that you can work towards that end. It's like reading the last page of a novel so that you know how it ends and you can write the book to get to that point.

So what is the desired result?

In generic terms, you want a single dataset that has the two disparate datasets joined somehow. In .NET terms, this would suggest that you want something like a `DataTable` object returned that is the culmination of joining these two datasets in code. And that is close to what you want, but not all the way there.

In XML web services, which is what you will be creating in this project, you cannot use a `DataTable` as the return type for a web method. In fact, you cannot use anything less than a `DataSet` object as your return type. No `DataRow`, `DataView`, `DataTable`, or `DataViewManager` objects can be used. You must use a `DataSet` object. So, even if you only have a single `DataTable` you want to return, you have to put it in a new blank `DataSet` object and return that object instead. Otherwise, you will receive an error indicating that the return value cannot be serialized. You will do well to remember this in your future projects; if you forget and use the wrong type, you will likely spend hours trying to resolve the problem.

So, then, the end result should be DataSet object containing a single DataTable with the joined data from the SQL Table and the SharePoint list in it. So, with that, you have enough information to stub out your first method, the publicly available web method that will return the dataset to your report. It should look something like this:

```
[WebMethod]
public DataSet GetJoinedTable()
{
    DataSet dsReturn = new DataSet();

    return dsReturn;
}
```

At this point, if an application called this method, it would just receive a blank dataset back. So you need to fill it with information.

At this point, you know you are going to need at least two `DataTables` in a single `DataSet` in order to do the join. Think of this like a database. You have a single database (your `DataSet` object) encapsulating two tables (your `DataTable` objects). You can then, later in your code, provide a relationship between these two tables and perform a join. But first you need your two `DataTables`: one for your SQL data and one for your SharePoint list.

So the first step is to create a code block that will return a `DataTable` containing all of the SQL table information for the following query:

```
SELECT
    CAST(PER.BusinessEntityID AS FLOAT) AS BusinessEntityID
    ,PER.LastName + ', ' + PER.FirstName AS EmployeeName
FROM
    Person.Person PER
```

If you are familiar with T-SQL you may be wondering why you are casting the `BusinessEntityID` field, which is an INT datatype in the database, to a `FLOAT` datatype. At the risk of foreshadowing too much, later in the chapter you will have to join this dataset to your SharePoint list dataset. In that SharePoint list, the `BusinessEntityID` is stored as a number field, which gets converted to a `DOUBLE`. When you are creating the relationship between these two fields in your C# code, the field used to create the relationship (the join field) must be exactly the same datatype. If you use the T-SQL `FLOAT` type, this will match the SharePoint List Number type. This will make more sense as the chapter progresses.

If you were to run the above query in the AdventureWorks2008 database, it would return a dataset similar to the following (only the first 10 rows are shown for brevity):

BusinessEntityID	EmployeeName
285	Abbas, Syed
293	Abel, Catherine
295	Abercrombie, Kim
2170	Abercrombie, Kim
38	Abercrombie, Kim
211	Abolrous, Hazem
2357	Abolrous, Sam
297	Acevedo, Humberto
291	Achong, Gustavo
299	Ackerman, Pilar

So, in order to begin creating your `DataTable` in your web service, you need to stub out a new method that returns a `DataTable`. In this case, it is probably a good idea to keep the method private so that only internal methods can call it since you will be keeping information in this method that you really don't want shared out (database connection information, for example). So, to create the wireframe for your method, add the following code to your web service:

```
private DataTable GetSQLTable()
{
    DataTable SQLTable = new DataTable();

    return SQLTable;
}
```

To fill in the `SQLTable DataTable` object, you need to insert some ADO.NET code into the GetSQLTable method that will access the AdventureWorks2008 database, run the query listed a little earlier, and then populate the `SQLTable DataTable` with the results. Use the following code to fill the DataTable with Employee information:

```
private DataTable GetSQLTable()
{
    DataTable SQLTable = new DataTable();

    string connString = @"Data
        Source=JACOBSANFORD\SQLEXPRESS2008;Initial
        Catalog=AdventureWorks2008;User
        Id=AWReports;Password=AWReports";
    SqlConnection conn = new SqlConnection(connString);
    string strSQLQuery = "SELECT CAST(PER.BusinessEntityID AS FLOAT) AS
        BusinessEntityID, PER.LastName + ', ' + PER.FirstName AS
        EmployeeName FROM Person.Person PER";
    SqlDataAdapter daPerson = new SqlDataAdapter(strSQLQuery, conn);
    daPerson.Fill(SQLTable);

    return SQLTable;
}
```

If you have ever done any web application development in C#, this code will probably be deeply familiar to you. However, if you are new to coding, this might look foreign to you. While it is probably outside the scope of this book to give a hardcore tutorial on data access in C# code, it might help at least to give a brief overview of what is going on here.

The first property, `connString`, is merely storing the connection string the method will need to use to access your SQL data. It provides the server, database, and access credentials needed to get to your data. Obviously, you will need to update this property with the correct server name, database, and credentials to meet your development needs. The next object, `conn` (a `SqlConnection` object), actually creates a connection to your database using the credentials stored in the `connString` property. The next variable, `strSQLQuery`, stores the query from earlier in this section and will be used by SQL Server instance to find the relevant results. The next object, `daPerson` (a `SqlDataAdapater` object) creates a new data adapter in memory using the `strSQLQuery` property and the `conn` object. Finally, the last new line simply fills the `SQLTable DataTable` object with the returned data from the `daPerson` `SqlDataAdapter` object.

Again, this was only meant to provide a brief overview of the code in this section. If all of the above looks like a foreign language to you, you might consider brushing up on your ADO.NET programming by reading a book like *Professional ASP.NET 2.0 Databases*, by Thiru Thangarathinam (ISBN: 978-0-470-04179-6).

The next step, then, is to create a similar method that will return a `DataTable` object containing the SharePoint list data. You can stub out this method like this:

```
private DataTable GetSPList()
{
    DataTable SPListData = new DataTable();

    return SPListData;
}
```

Again, this is a private method only available to other methods in the web service class that will return a `DataTable` object when called.

So what list data should you include? Well, for this example, you can use a list similar to the one shown in Figure 7-3 (a template of this list is available for free download from the Wrox website).

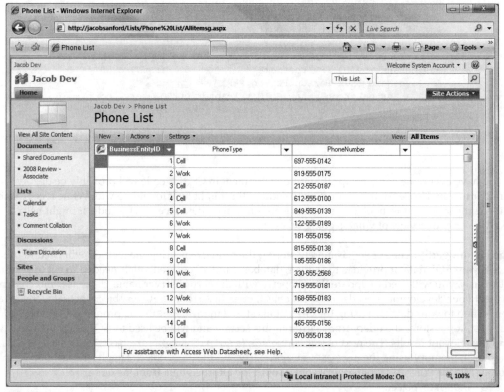

Figure 7-3

If you look closely at this screenshot, you can tell a couple of things:

❑   The URL of this site is `http://jacobsanford/`.

❑   The name of this List is Phone List.

❑   This list contains three fields: `BusinessEntityID`, `PhoneType`, and `PhoneNumber`.

If you can't see this information clearly, just believe that it is true. While this isn't relevant now, it is also important to note that the field types for these values are Number (`BusinessEntityID`) and Multiple Lines of Text (`PhoneType` and `PhoneNumber`). In your own environment, you can verify this by looking at the list settings in SharePoint to find the column definitions of each of these fields.

> *If you are interested, this list was generated from creating a dataset of information from the AdventureWorks2008 database. Basically, this information is already stored in `Person.PersonPhone` and `Person.PhoneNumberType` tables. This information was just ported to SharePoint to create a viable demonstration for this chapter. So, if this information looks familiar, it is. It is just moved to a new medium.*

With the information you have at this point, you have everything you need to hydrate your method to get your SharePoint list data and put it into a `DataTable` object you return when called.

So, first, you need to get access to your SharePoint site. To do this, insert the following code between the two existing lines of code in your method:

```
using (SPSite site = new SPSite("http://jacobsanford"))
{
}
```

This creates a new `SPSite` object, which was enabled when you added your SharePoint references to your project, that essentially allows you to access the SharePoint site collection at `http://jacobsanford`. This code is also incorporating using statements to ensure the SPSite object is properly disposed of. You can read more about disposing of SharePoint objects at `http://msdn.microsoft.com/en-us/library/aa973248.aspx`.

Next, you will need to gain access to the actual Windows SharePoint Services web site. This gets a bit confusing because, with the way this is named, it doesn't make much sense. Think of it this way. If you created a new SharePoint team site, that would be your `SPSite` object. But every time you create a new site within that Team Site using the User Interface, that would be an `SPWeb` object. Hopefully that makes sense.

So, for this site collection, there is only one site, so you can use the following code to open it:

```
using (SPWeb web = site.OpenWeb())
{
}
```

Just insert this code immediately after the `SPSite` line so that you now have access to the site that contains your list. Again, notice the using statement that will properly dispose of this object when your operation completes.

Once you have your SPWeb object, you can get access to your list by using the following line of code:

```
SPList list = web.Lists["Phone List"];
```

This code is saying that from the SPWeb object you just created (web), get the list titled "Phone List". Pretty simple, right?

Now probably the easiest part: getting the list data into your DataTable object. One of the greatest members of the SPList object is the GetDataTable() object, which, as the name implies, actually gets a DataTable object with your list data in it. So, to use this, add the following line of code to your method:

```
SPListData = list.Items.GetDataTable();
```

And that's it for the SharePoint list method! Your final method should look like this:

```
private DataTable GetSPList()
{
    DataTable SPListData = new DataTable();

    using (SPSite site = new SPSite("http://jacobsanford"))
    {
        using (SPWeb web = site.OpenWeb())
        {
            SPList list = web.Lists["Phone List"];
            SPListData = list.Items.GetDataTable();
        }
    }

    return SPListData;
}
```

Now you just have to bring everything back together in your GetJoinedTable() method.

So, the first step is to create a DataSet object that will contain both of the DataTables you just generated in these methods: one each for the SharePoint List data and the SQL table data. Back in your GetJoineTable method, insert the following code after the initial declaration of the dsReturn DataSet object:

```
DataSet SourceTables = new DataSet();
SourceTables.Tables.Add(GetSQLTable());
SourceTables.Tables.Add(GetSPList());
```

This creates a new DataSet called SourceTables that contains a DataTable returned from the GetSQLTable() method and a DataTable from the GetSPList() method.

The next step is to create a parent-child relationship between these two tables. Both tables have a column called BusinessEntityID, and they should both be of the type FLOAT/DOUBLE. This means that you can create a relationship between these two DataTable objects on the BusinessEntityID field by using the following code:

```
DataRelation relationship = new DataRelation("PeoplePhoneJoin",
        SourceTables.Tables[1].Columns["BusinessEntityID"],
        SourceTables.Tables[0].Columns["BusinessEntityID"]);
SourceTables.Relations.Add(relationship);
```

The first line is creating a relationship called "PeoplePhoneJoin" between the two DataTables in the SourceTables DataSet on the BusinessEntityID field, and the second line merely adds the relationship to your DataSet. It needs to be understood that the order in which the two tables are listed in the DataRelation declaration is important. The first listed column will serve as the parent column and the second one will be the child. So, in this example, the SharePoint List data is the parent record and the SQL table is the child record. For this situation, it doesn't really matter which one is the parent and which one is the child. This is because there is a one-to-one relationship between the tables (i.e., for every row in one table, there is one, and only one, corresponding row in the other table). If this were a one-to-many relationship, where one row in one table could be associated with multiple rows in the other table (but not vice versa), you would need to make the first table the parent record and the one with multiple possible matches the child. But, again, since this is just a one-to-one relationship, it doesn't matter which one you put as the parent and which one you put as the child. Just remember which order you applied because it will be relevant later in this section.

The next step is to create a new DataTable object that will be used to store the joined table data. This table will need to have columns for the following fields: BusinessEntityID, EmployeeName, PhoneType, and PhonNumber. You can define your DataTable using the following code:

```
DataTable JoinedTable = new DataTable("JoinedTable");
JoinedTable.Columns.Add("BusinessEntityID", typeof(string));
JoinedTable.Columns.Add("EmployeeName", typeof(string));
JoinedTable.Columns.Add("PhoneType", typeof(string));
JoinedTable.Columns.Add("PhoneNumber", typeof(string));
```

Almost done. The next thing you need to do is iterate through your SourceTables DataSet, using the PeoplePhoneJoin relationship to determine how the tables are related, and add a new row to the JoinedTable DataTable for each joined row in the SourceTables DataSet. You can do this through the following code:

```
{
    DataRow parent = child.GetParentRow("PeoplePhoneJoin");
    DataRow current = JoinedTable.NewRow();

    current["BusinessEntityID"] = child["BusinessEntityID"];
    current["EmployeeName"] = child["EmployeeName"];
    current["PhoneType"] = parent["PhoneType"];
    current["PhoneNumber"] = parent["PhoneNumber"];

    JoinedTable.Rows.Add(current);
}
```

The preceding code will only work if you have a one-to-one relationship between the parent and child tables, meaning for every parent record there is one and only one child record (and vice versa). If there are multiple parent records for each child record in the above scenario, you would need to iterate through each relationship to find each parent record and perform the above steps for each match.

The first line of code, the `foreach` declaration, is creating a new `DataRow` object called child. Pay special attention to which table it is using to iterate through: the SQL data table (remember `SourceTables.Tables[0]` is the SQL table because it was added first and the `SourceTables.Tables[1]` would be the SharePoint list data because it was added second). Why is this important? Because of the relationship. Remember when you created your relationship that you set the SQL table as the child table. This means that the row object is referencing the `DataRow` of a child table. Therefore, in the first line of the loop, you are determining the correlating parent record, aptly called parent, by getting the parent row using the `PeoplePhoneJoin` relationship. In other words, you are using the `BusinessEntityID` field in the child table (SQL Table) to find the matching record in the parent table (SharePoint List).

You are also creating a new row for the JoinedTable `DataTable` object called `"current"`. So, for each column of `JoinedTable`, you have to populate it from one of the two tables: child or parent. While `BusinessEntityID` could be populated from either, you should be able to see why the relationship matters. You can only pull `EmployeeName` from the SQL `DataTable`, which is the child table, and you can only pull the `PhoneType` and `PhoneNumber` fields from the SharePoint List `DataTable`, which is the parent table.

So, while it was fair to say earlier that the order didn't matter as far as who was the parent or the child, you can see that the order you pick is monumentally important when you start using the relationship. For example, you couldn't use the following line of code based on the relationship you have created:

```
current["PhoneNumber"] = child["PhoneNumber"];
```

If you did, everything would compile and look like it worked, but when you tried to actually invoke the web method, it would crash.

So, now that you have the `JoinedTable` populated, it is time to add it to the `dsReturn` dataset so that it can be returned to the application that called the method. You can do this with the following line of code after the loop:

```
dsReturn.Tables.Add(JoinedTable);
```

So, if you have followed everything to this point, your final `GetJoinedTable` method should look like this:

```
[WebMethod]
public DataSet GetJoinedTable()
{
    DataSet dsReturn = new DataSet();

    DataSet SourceTables = new DataSet();
    SourceTables.Tables.Add(GetSQLTable());
    SourceTables.Tables.Add(GetSPList());

    DataRelation relationship = new DataRelation("PeoplePhoneJoin",
            SourceTables.Tables[1].Columns["BusinessEntityID"],
            SourceTables.Tables[0].Columns["BusinessEntityID"]);
    SourceTables.Relations.Add(relationship);

    DataTable JoinedTable = new DataTable("JoinedTable");
    JoinedTable.Columns.Add("BusinessEntityID", typeof(string));
```

```
        JoinedTable.Columns.Add("EmployeeName", typeof(string));
        JoinedTable.Columns.Add("PhoneType", typeof(string));
        JoinedTable.Columns.Add("PhoneNumber", typeof(string));

        foreach (DataRow child in SourceTables.Tables[0].Rows)
        {
            DataRow parent = child.GetParentRow("PeoplePhoneJoin");
            DataRow current = JoinedTable.NewRow();

            current["BusinessEntityID"] = child["BusinessEntityID"];
            current["EmployeeName"] = child["EmployeeName"];
            current["PhoneType"] = parent["PhoneType"];
            current["PhoneNumber"] = parent["PhoneNumber"];

            JoinedTable.Rows.Add(current);
        }

        dsReturn.Tables.Add(JoinedTable);

        return dsReturn;
    }
```

And, as a point of reference, your final code should look like this (including all coding you have done in this section):

```
using System;
using System.Collections.Generic;
using System.Linq;
using System.Web;
using System.Web.Services;
using Microsoft.SharePoint;
using System.Data;
using System.Data.SqlClient;

namespace AdventureWorksWebService
{
    /// <summary>
    /// Summary description for Service1
    /// </summary>
    [WebService(Namespace = "http://tempuri.org/")]
    [WebServiceBinding(ConformsTo = WsiProfiles.BasicProfile1_1)]
    [System.ComponentModel.ToolboxItem(false)]
    // To allow this Web Service to be called from script, using ASP.NET AJAX,
uncomment the following line.
    // [System.Web.Script.Services.ScriptService]
    public class Service1 : System.Web.Services.WebService
    {
        [WebMethod]
        public DataSet GetJoinedTable()
        {
            DataSet dsReturn = new DataSet();

            DataSet SourceTables = new DataSet();
```

```csharp
        SourceTables.Tables.Add(GetSQLTable());
        SourceTables.Tables.Add(GetSPList());

        DataRelation relationship = new
                DataRelation("PeoplePhoneJoin",
                SourceTables.Tables[1].Columns["BusinessEntityID"],
                SourceTables.Tables[0].Columns["BusinessEntityID"]);
        SourceTables.Relations.Add(relationship);

        DataTable JoinedTable = new DataTable("JoinedTable");
        JoinedTable.Columns.Add("BusinessEntityID", typeof(string));
        JoinedTable.Columns.Add("EmployeeName", typeof(string));
        JoinedTable.Columns.Add("PhoneType", typeof(string));
        JoinedTable.Columns.Add("PhoneNumber", typeof(string));

        foreach (DataRow child in SourceTables.Tables[0].Rows)
        {
            DataRow parent = child.GetParentRow("PeoplePhoneJoin");
            DataRow current = JoinedTable.NewRow();

            current["BusinessEntityID"] = child["BusinessEntityID"];
            current["EmployeeName"] = child["EmployeeName"];
            current["PhoneType"] = parent["PhoneType"];
            current["PhoneNumber"] = parent["PhoneNumber"];

            JoinedTable.Rows.Add(current);
        }

        dsReturn.Tables.Add(JoinedTable);

        return dsReturn;
    }

    private DataTable GetSQLTable()
    {
        DataTable SQLTable = new DataTable();

        string connString = @"Data
                Source=JACOBSANFORD\SQLEXPRESS2008;Initial
                Catalog=AdventureWorks2008;User
                Id=AWReports;Password=AWReports";
        SqlConnection conn = new SqlConnection(connString);
        string strSQLQuery = "SELECT CAST(BusinessEntityID AS FLOAT)
                AS BusinessEntityID, LastName + ', ' + FirstName AS
                EmployeeName FROM Person.Person";
        SqlDataAdapter daPerson = new SqlDataAdapter(strSQLQuery,
                conn);
        daPerson.Fill(SQLTable);

        return SQLTable;
    }

    private DataTable GetSPList()
```

```
        {
            DataTable SPListData = new DataTable();

            using (SPSite site = new SPSite("http://jacobsanford"))
            {
                using (SPWeb web = site.OpenWeb())
                {
                    SPList list = web.Lists["Phone List"];
                    SPListData = list.Items.GetDataTable();
                }
            }

            return SPListData;
        }    }
    }
```

With your final code in place, click Debug in the toolbar and select Start Debugging. You will get a prompt asking if you want to modify your web.config file to allow for debugging. Click the OK button and let Visual Studio load the web service. You should get no errors, and, when loaded, you should see something similar to Figure 7-4. If you do get errors, you will need to debug your application to find out where the problem lies and fix it before continuing.

Figure 7-4

Finally, if you click the GetJoinedTable link at the top of that page and, on the page that loads, click the Invoke button, you should get a new window with your full dataset that resembles Figure 7-5.

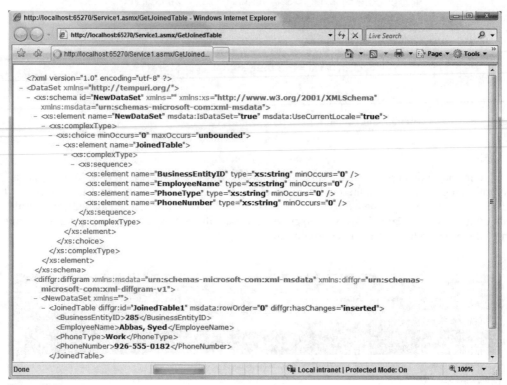

Figure 7-5

It should be noted that there are almost 20,000 records being joined going through a loop and looking at each of the 20,000 records in each table one by one. This will take a while. In fact, it might even freeze up your browser. You might try switching to a different browser to see if you get results. For example, Google Chrome might bring back your dataset faster for a test than Internet Explorer.

Assuming you received the expected results and no errors, you are ready to go to the next step: packaging and deployment. If you did receive errors you should debug your application in Visual Studio to find out where the error lies. This could be any number of things from a connection string issue to not properly referencing one of your objects in code. Whatever the error is, make sure you fix it before proceeding to step 3.

STEP 3: Preparing Your Final Web Service and Deploying It

At this stage, your web service should be working in Visual Studio. This is good but, when you actually deploy the web service, it is not going to work as expected.

Why is that?

This has to do with a problem SharePoint developers deal with on a fairly regular basis: Code Access Security (CAS). CAS allows administrators to set the trust level that your application is running at, thereby determining what it can actually do. In any .NET environment, including Windows SharePoint Services, the following trust levels are defined:

❑ Full

❑ High

❑ Medium

❑ Low

❑ Minimal

Additionally, Windows SharePoint Services defines two additional trust levels:

❑ WSS_Minimal

❑ WSS_Medium

The problem is that in your Visual Studio 2008 environment your code is running at the Full Trust mode, essentially allowing unrestricted permissions to the assemblies of the project.

However, when the assembly gets moved to an application folder under SharePoint, which is where this web service will get deployed so that it has access to the SharePoint site collection, it inherits the SharePoint CAS settings of the Web Application, which is WSS_ Minimal by default. This trust level will not allow the code of the web service to execute and you will get errors as soon as you try to invoke the `GetJoinedTables` web method.

To change the CAS policies to allow the web service to run as expected, you have three basic options:

❑ Increase the trust level of the entire web application.

❑ Create a custom security policy for your assembly (elevate the trust level for just your assembly).

❑ Install your assembly in the Global Assembly Cache (GAC).

The recommended approach by Microsoft is to create a custom policy file for your assembly. This is the most secure option but also requires the most configuration of all three options. This level of configuration is probably overkill for this project, but if you want to read how to do it, Microsoft has provided a really strong step-by-step tutorial on exactly how to do this:

```
http://msdn.microsoft.com/en-us/library/dd583158.aspx
```

For this project, it is enough to just deploy your assembly to the GAC and modify your project to use the GAC assembly instead. This is an easier approach and provides a much higher level of security than increasing the trust level of your entire application or site collection. The application code is running in a protected environment, and, when in the GAC, the assemblies automatically run at full trust.

For many solutions, this might not be the best option. However, for this project, it is a perfect fit. You will be well served to get deep into CAS on your own and make informed decisions on how to deploy your assemblies in SharePoint for your own projects.

Additionally, there are plenty of articles on the web that show you how to modify your SharePoint environment to add custom CAS security profiles for your assemblies. This is a pretty hot topic. However, there are fewer articles showing what you need to do to put your web service assembly in the cache so that it will run in your SharePoint environment.

So, with that being said, it is time to prepare your project to be deployed to the GAC.

The only real requirement to putting your assembly in the cache that you are not meeting at this point in the project is that it must be strongly named. This just means that you need to sign your assembly with a digital key. Fortunately, this is fairly easy to do in Visual Studio.

In Visual Studio 2008, right-click on project name in your Solution Explorer and select Properties. When the properties screen comes up, click the Signing tab so that it looks like Figure 7-6.

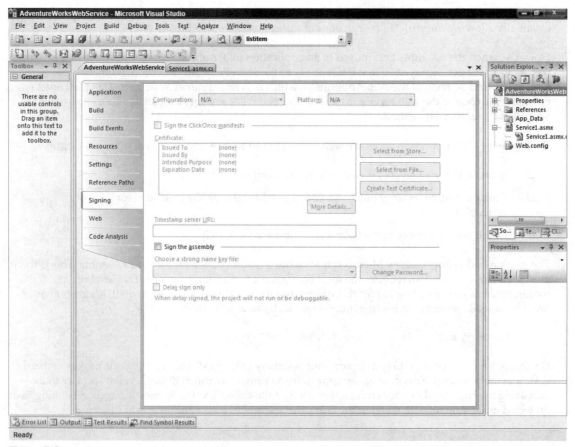

Figure 7-6

At the bottom of this screen, you will see an option to Sign the assembly. Check this box, which will enable the Choose a strong name key file dropdown control. Click the dropdown control and select <New . . . >, which will bring up the Create Strong Name Key dialog box shown in Figure 7-7.

Figure 7-7

Type a key file name such as AdventureWorksWebService, uncheck the "Protect my key file with a password" checkbox control. In this example you don't need to protect your key with a password, and press the OK button. You should see that the dropdown control on the properties screen is now populated with AdventureWorksWebService.snk and that a new file named AdventureWorksWebService has been added to your project in your Solution Explorer pane. You can save your project and then close this tab; this is the only change you need to make.

Now you need to build your project to compile your assembly so that you can deploy it to the GAC. To do this, click the Build option on the Visual Studio toolbar and select Build AdventureWorksWebService. Hopefully you did not get any errors. If you did, fix all errors until you get a clean build.

Building your project will create a new signed assembly into your project's bin. For this example the directory is located at:

```
C:\AdventureWorksWebService\AdventureWorksWebService\bin
```

You will need this to install the assembly to the GAC. If you open that directory, you will see that the assembly has been named the same as the project name. So, with that, the fully qualified path to your assembly will be the following:

```
C:\AdventureWorksWebService\AdventureWorksWebService\bin\AdventureWorks
WebService.dll
```

Now you are ready to install your assembly to the GAC. There are two ways in which you can accomplish this. Theoretically, you can drag your assembly from your folder in Windows Explorer from its current location to a new Windows Explorer instance opened to the following directory:

C:\<<WINDOWSDIR>>\Assembly

However, this doesn't always work, and you may end up with security errors when you try it. The more reliable approach is to use the Global Assembly Cache Tool, gacutil.exe, that you should already have installed on your system. It is packaged as part of the .NET Software Development Kid (SDK), which should get installed when you install Visual Studio 2008, usually in the following location:

```
C:\Program Files\Microsoft SDKs\Windows\v6.0A\bin
```

If you cannot locate gacutil.exe, then you may need to reinstall the .NET SDKs. The .NET SDKs downloads are located at:

```
http://tinyurl.com/dotnetsdk
```

Once you are sure you have it installed, open your Visual Studio 2008 Command Prompt (Start ⇨ All Programs ⇨ Visual Studio 2008 ⇨ Visual Studio Tools ⇨ Visual Studio 2008 Command Prompt).

If you are running your WSS development environment on a Windows Vista Machine, make sure you run your command prompt as an administrator.

Now, when the command prompt opens, type the following command:

```
gacutil.exe /i "C:\AdventureWorksWebService\AdventureWorksWebService\bin\
AdventureWorksWebService.dll"
```

The i switch tells the gacutil.exe application to install the assembly with the path you provide next, in this case the fully qualified path to your assembly. If everything went smoothly, you should get the success message "Assembly successfully added to the cache." If you now go to Windows Explorer to your GAC location (C:\\<<WINDOWSDIR>>\Assembly), you should see that the assembly has, in fact, been added to your machine, as seen in Figure 7-8.

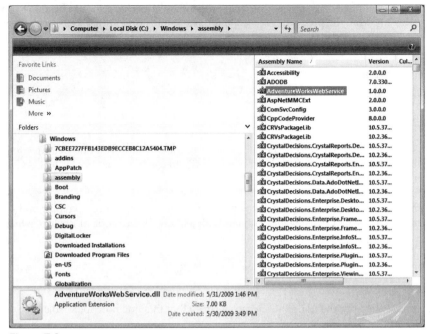

Figure 7-8

If you right click the assembly in the GAC and select Properties, you should see a screen similar to Figure 7-9.

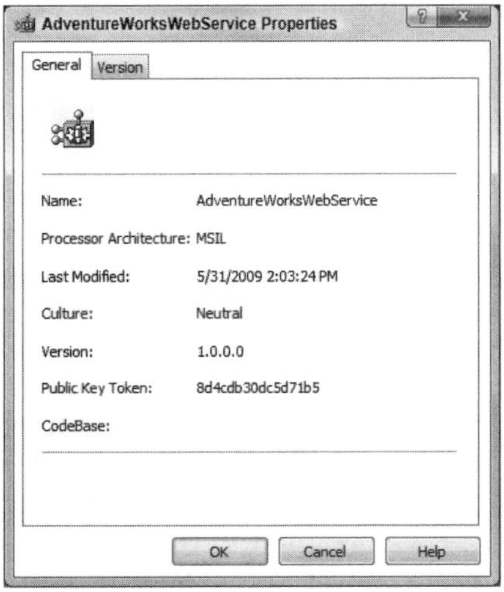

Figure 7-9

To reference the assembly, you will need the following information (you should be able to copy the information directly from the properties screen and paste it into something like Notepad for later use):

- ❏ Name (AdventureWorksWebService)
- ❏ Culture (Neutral)
- ❏ Version (1.0.0.0)
- ❏ Public Key Token (8d4cdb30dc5d71b5)

You can close out the property screen once you have recorded this information. It's time to go back into Visual Studio 2008 and modify your web service code file to use the assembly in the GAC instead of the one it has in its own BIN directory.

So, once you are in Visual Studio, right click Service1.asmx in your Solution Explorer and select View Markup. This should bring up a single document with just one line of code at the top, which should look very similar to this:

```
<%@ WebService Language="C#" CodeBehind="Service1.asmx.cs" Class="AdventureWorksWeb
Service.Service1" %>
```

The first step is to strip out the CodeBehind property so that this line now looks like this:

```
<%@ WebService Language="C#" Class="AdventureWorksWebService.Service1" %>
```

Next, you need to modify the Class property to include the reference to the GAC assembly you just added. This new reference should look like this:

```
<%@ WebService Language="C#" Class="AdventureWorksWebService.Service1,
AdventureWorksWebService, Culture=Neutral, Version=1.0.0.0, PublicKeyToken=8d4cdb30
dc5d71b5" %>
```

This is just adding the information you just copied from the properties of the assembly to your class reference. You should take special care in the typing this in. It must be typed in using this exact format or you risk generating difficult-to-troubleshoot errors. If, for example, you forgot one of the commas delimiting the different properties, you could easily spend an hour trying to figure out why your application keeps crashing.

Once you save this change, your web service will use the GAC assembly instead of any compiled code you have in your BIN directory. More important, the code will run with full trust, since it is stored in the GAC rather than the BIN.

You should remember that the web service is no longer using your BIN assembly in future development, since if you make any changes to your web service and debug it, the changes will not show up. This is because the compiled code that includes the changes will be encapsulated in the BIN directory and will not carry forward to the GAC.

So the last step is to set up your IIS to recognize your directory an application under your SharePoint installation. The first thing you will need to do is open up the IIS Manager. You can do this by going to the Run dialog box (Start ⇨ All Programs ⇨ Accessories ⇨ Run), typing inetmgr, and pressing the OK button. This should bring up the Internet Information Services (IIS) Manager shown in Figure 7-10.

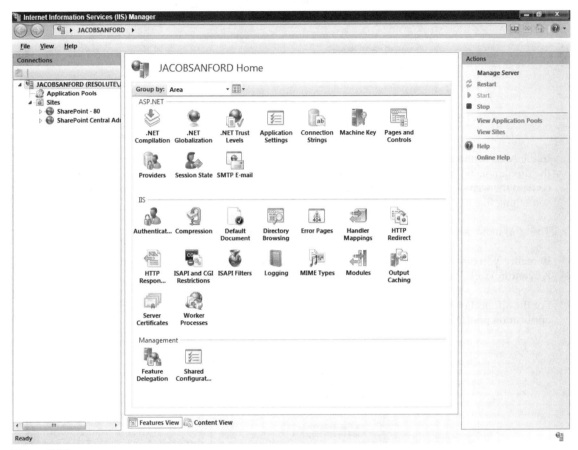

Figure 7-10

Figure 7-10 is from Internet Information Services Manager 7.0. If you are using a different version, you may have a different screenshot and the tutorial that follows may differ slightly in your own environment.

In your Connections pane, right- click your SharePoint directory (named SharePoint – 80, in this example) and select Add Application . . . , which will bring up the Add Application dialog box shown in Figure 7-11.

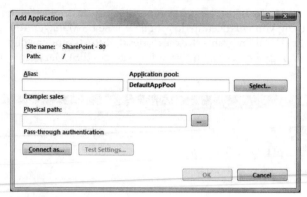

Figure 7-11

In the Alias textbox, enter AWWS. In the URL you type in to reference your webservice, you will have the domain name that is hosting the service, a subdirectory/folder off of the domain that will actual contain the web service, and then the web service itself. In other words, your URL reference will look something like this: `http://domainname/subdirectory/webservice.asmx`.

The alias name will be used as the subdirectory reference in this example.

In reality, you can give your new application any alias you want but, when typing the URL, AdventureWorksWebService is a really long URL to type; AWWS is much shorter.

For the application pool, click the Select . . . button, which will bring up options for selecting the application pool (as seen in Figure 7-12).

Figure 7-12

Use the dropdown control to select the same application pool as your SharePoint installation (it should be named similar to the name of the application, something like SharePoint – 80). Using the same application pool will allow for pass through authentication to work for your SharePoint list access. Press the OK button to make this your application pool.

*If you are unsure which application pool your SharePoint installation is using, go back to the main page
of the IIS manager and click on the web application in the Connections pane. When you do so, you
should see a link to Advanced Settings in the Actions pane on the right-hand side of the screen (under
Manage Web Site). Click on that link and a new Advanced Settings dialog box will appear. The first
property listed will be the Application Pool that the site is currently using.*

For the physical path, press the Ellipse button to look up the directory for your web service. If you have
been following the example in this chapter exactly, this should be at the following location:

```
C:\AdventureWorksWebService\AdventureWorksWebService
```

Once you have all of the properties set, click the Test Settings . . . button to make sure you can connect.
You should get a message similar to Figure 7-13.

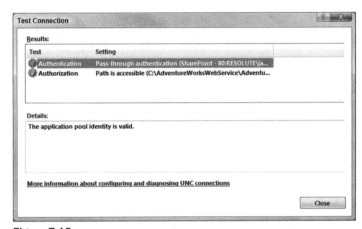

Figure 7-13

If you did not pass any of the tests, you will need to tweak your settings until you pass. For example,
you may need to connect as a different user. Once you have passed your connection tests, press the OK
button to create your new application.

If you have done everything correctly, you should be able to access your new web service by accessing
the AWWS subdirectory off of your SharePoint installation (something like `http://localhost/AWWS/
Service1.asmx`). When you load this URL, you should get the web service opening page, as shown in
Figure 7-14.

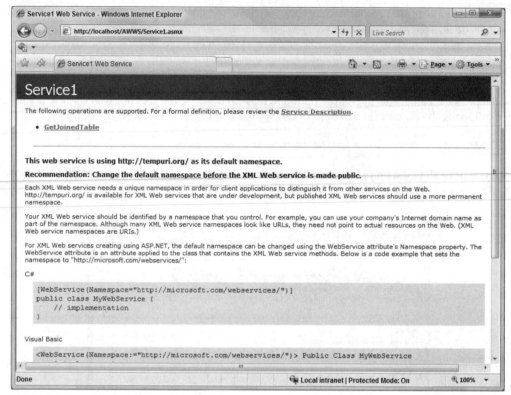

Figure 7-14

At this point, you should have a functioning web service that takes a SQL table and a SharePoint list, joins them in memory, and returns them to the caller. You can now access this web service inside of SSRS to report on this dataset, which is the next step.

You can now close your AdventureWorksWebService project; you shouldn't need it again during this chapter.

STEP 4: Accessing Your Web Service in SSRS

Most of this section will merely be a review of things you should have seen in the previous two chapters and, as such, will go much faster. If you are having trouble following along, you may need to review Chapters 5 and 6 again to get comfortable with the steps in this section.

Open up your AdventureWorksReports project in BIDS and right- click the Shared Data Sources folder in Solution Explorer pane and select Add New Data Source to get the Shared Data Source Properties dialog box. Give the new data source a name of CustomWebService and select XML from the type dropdown box. In the connection string text box, add a reference to the URL of your web service (e.g., `http://localhost/AWWS/Service1.asmx`). Press the OK button to add the new data source to your project.

Now you need to add your report. So, in your Solution Explorer, right-click the Reports folder and select Add and then New Item . . . . Make sure the Report installed template is selected and give the new report the name JoinedTableReport. Press the Add button to add the report to your project.

Once your new report has loaded, click the New button in the Report Data pane and select Data Source . . . to get the Data Source Properties dialog box. Provide the name JoinedReportDataSourceand link to the CustomWebService Shared Data Source just created. Press the OK button to add this data source to your report.

Click the New button in the Report Data pane again and this time select Dataset . . . to get the Dataset Properties screen. Give the dataset the name JoinedData.

Now here is where it gets a little trickier. You can't use the same XML schema you used at the end of Chapter 6 to access this data, since you are querying a different custom web service that is expecting a different structure. Instead, you need to provide the following information in the query textbox:

```
<Query>
    <SoapAction>
        http://tempuri.org/GetJoinedTable
    </SoapAction>
    <Method Namespace="http://tempuri.org/" Name="GetJoinedTable">
    </Method>
    <ElementPath IgnoreNamespaces="True">
        GetJoinedTableResponse{}/GetJoinedTableResult{}/diffgram{}/
        NewDataSet{}/JoinedTable{EmployeeName, PhoneType, PhoneNumber}
    </ElementPath>
</Query>
```

The `<Query></Query>` tags are probably intuitive, especially if you did the SharePoint Task List example in Chapter 6. This just encapsulates the query that you want to run to get your data.

The next section, shown below, isn't that hard to understand either. This is just a reference to your web service namespace, discussed earlier in this chapter. Remember in that discussion that it was decided to just go ahead and use the `http://tempuri.org/` namespace. So the `SoapAction` element just wants the namespace with the web method, `GetJoinedTable`, appended at the end. If your namespace was, for example, `http://www.microsoft.com/webservices`, and your method was `GetData`, your `SoapAction` would be `http://www.microsoft.com/webservices/GetData`.

```
<SoapAction>
    http://tempuri.org/GetJoinedTable
</SoapAction>
```

The next section, shown below, is very similar to the last section. You are just providing a different way of providing the same information. You provide the namespace (`http://tempuri.org`) and the web method (`GetJoinedTable`) in the properties of the `Method` element. If you had parameters that you were using for this web service, you would insert them between the opening and closing tags for this element. However, this web service runs without any parameters so there is nothing there.

```
<Method Namespace="http://tempuri.org/" Name="GetJoinedTable">
</Method>
```

The next section is where the real magic happens. The `ElementPath` element is telling the application how to navigate to the dataset you are trying to retrieve and, in this case, which fields you want to return:

```
<ElementPath IgnoreNamespaces="True">
    GetJoinedTableResponse{}/GetJoinedTableResult{}/diffgram{}/
    NewDataSet{}/JoinedTable{EmployeeName, PhoneType, PhoneNumber}
</ElementPath>
```

This might look completely unfamiliar to you at first but, if you have been looking at your web service when you tested it, you might have seen some of these names around. For example, look at Figure 7-15.

Figure 7-15 shows the references to `GetJoinedTableResponse` and `GetJoinedTableResult`, the first two items in the path to your data.

Figure 7-15

The next path is just a standard element: `diffgram`. It should always be there, so, after the `GetJoinedTableResult` path, just insert `diffgram` before going into the specific data elements of your web service.

> *A DiffGram is a format that is used for sending a DataSet object from an XML Web Service. You can read more about DiffGrams at* `http://msdn.microsoft.com/en-us/library/ms172088 .aspx`.

The next part of the path you might have seen also. If you remember earlier in this chapter, Figure 7-5 showed the rendered XML of the web service. Take a look at it again in Figure 7-16, marked up to highlight a few elements.

```
<?xml version="1.0" encoding="utf-8" ?>
<DataSet xmlns="http://tempuri.org/">
  <xs:schema id="NewDataSet" xmlns="" xmlns:xs="http://www.w3.org/2001/XMLSchema"
    xmlns:msdata="urn:schemas-microsoft-com:xml-msdata">
    <xs:element name="NewDataSet" msdata:IsDataSet="true" msdata:UseCurrentLocale="true">
      <xs:complexType>
        <xs:choice minOccurs="0" maxOccurs="unbounded">
          <xs:element name="JoinedTable">
            <xs:complexType>
              <xs:sequence>
                <xs:element name="BusinessEntityID" type="xs:string" minOccurs="0" />
                <xs:element name="EmployeeName" type="xs:string" minOccurs="0" />
                <xs:element name="PhoneType" type="xs:string" minOccurs="0" />
                <xs:element name="PhoneNumber" type="xs:string" minOccurs="0" />
              </xs:sequence>
            </xs:complexType>
          </xs:element>
        </xs:choice>
      </xs:complexType>
    </xs:element>
  </xs:schema>
```

Figure 7-16

This tells your web application how to navigate through the web service to get to your data elements (EmployeeName, PhoneType, and PhoneNumber). In this example, your web application must go through the NewDataSet element to get to the JoinedTable element, which contains your data elements. You will notice that this query is not bringing back BusinessEntityID. It is certainly an available field, but that doesn't mean that you have to use it. So, in the query, you need only list the fields you actually want to return.

So, with all of this in mind, you are essentially setting this order as the path to the data you want:

```
GetJoinedTableResponse --> GetJoinedTableResult --> diffgram  --> NewDataSet -->
JoinedTable --> Data Elements (EmployeeName, PhoneType, PhoneNumber)
```

However, in the world of XML web service requests, this is represented by the following:

```
GetJoinedTableResponse{}/GetJoinedTableResult{}/diffgram{}/NewDataSet{}/JoinedTab
le{EmployeeName, PhoneType, PhoneNumber}
```

So this is how you get your ElementPath element. Hopefully, this makes enough sense so that, in your own project, you can translate this path to your own data to make your report work correctly.

Now that you have the correct information in your query, press the OK button to add the dataset to your project. You should see that, in the Report Data pane, you will have a new dataset (JoinedData) and, under it, three new fields: EmployeeName, PhoneType, and PhoneNumber.

At this point, you have all you need to create your report. You have a data source, a dataset, and fields you can use on your report. This is just like any other report at stage.

So, to prove this, switch to the Toolbox pane of your report and drag the Table icon onto your report to add a new tablix control. Now switch back over to the Report Data pane and drag your three data fields into the three available spots on your tablix (see Figure 7-17).

Figure 7-17

To test your report, switch over to the Preview tab. Remember, this is accessing around 20,000 records from two different sources, joining them in memory, and then sending back to SSRS. So this might take a bit. But when the report finishes loading, it should look like Figure 7-18.

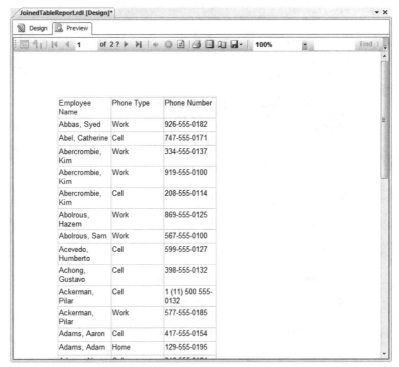

Figure 7-18

And, with that, you have a fully functioning report that meets the requirements of this project. If you click through, you will see that you have somewhere in the neighborhood of 455 pages of results, some of the data coming from SQL Server and some data coming from SharePoint. It isn't dazzling to look at, but the power of what is running under the hood is pretty impressive.

STEP 5: Cleaning Up the Report (Optional)

Since you have seen formatting rows and headers a lot already in this book, it probably doesn't add any value to go line by line on how to clean up the report. However, once you have the report running, you should test yourself by formatting the report to include much of what you learned in Chapters 5 and 6. This is an optional step, but try to make your report look like Figure 7-19. If you can, you have truly gotten to be a skilled report designer using SSRS.

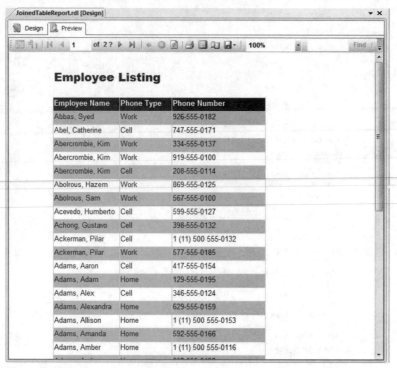

Figure 7-19

Summary

So what have you learned to this point? You learned in Chapters 5 and 6 some of the awesome power that SSRS has right out of the box. You saw how to create simple reports using the wizard and then how to take it to the next step by creating similar reports from scratch. You saw how to access simple SQL data by using stored procedure calls and, later, how to access SharePoint list data through using the included web services for those lists and the XML data source in SSRS. You saw how to customize the look and feel of these reports with drag-and-drop ease and how to go a little deeper and do formatting through the expressions editor. You have learned a lot.

So what did you learn in this chapter that makes it advanced? You learned that there are some limitations to SSRS, and, if you work in reporting long enough, you are likely to run into them. More important, you saw how to get around them. Sure, there are plenty of ways to address problems; unique solutions for unique circumstances. But with the approach you learned in this chapter, you can probably overcome most road bumps you encounter.

With the web service approach you learned in this chapter, you can take any problem and relegate it to your C# (or whatever your language preference) know-how. Whatever your data needs are, however, you need to manipulate that data, and you can do it in C#. You saw how to access two data sources that you had accessed in earlier chapters but in a new way. You directly connected to both a SQL database and a SharePoint list to get the data you needed and stored that data in .NET objects. You then took those objects, joined them together, and returned a single dataset that you could use in SSRS.

You learned some of the nuances of doing it this way, like the requirement to return a full `DataSet` object instead of just a `DataTable`, even if you just need a single table's worth of data. You learned about the security issues surrounding this approach and how to work with them. And you learned how to get your web service up and running once you are finished developing it.

If it's data-related, you can do it in your web service. And, with that being true, you can report on it in SSRS. The possibilities are endless.

If you are comfortable performing all of the tasks in Chapters 5, 6, and, now, 7, you are leaps and bounds above most report developers out there. And you are ready to move on to deploying and displaying your reports in SharePoint.

8

Deploying Reports to SharePoint

Before you dive into deploying reports to SharePoint, consider why you want to deploy them to SharePoint in the first place. The top two reasons why organizations choose to deploy reports to SharePoint are integrated storage and integrated security.

Centrally storing reports with the other content that a business uses is one of the best features of SharePoint integrated mode. When a report is deployed to SharePoint, it becomes a part of SharePoint, just like any other content stored on a SharePoint site. With integrated storage, organizations get:

- ❑ **Ease of Use:** No training is required. Users already know how to access SharePoint, as that is how they get their documents.

- ❑ **Inherited Governance:** As reports are deployed to SharePoint, you instantly get to share the infrastructure that is in place for SharePoint. If you already have a SharePoint governance in place that takes care of disaster recovery (SLAs, support, backups, and so on), you're golden, as you automatically get to push these policies and procedures to your reports.

- ❑ **Inherited Security:** Also with deploying reports to SharePoint, organizations immediately can start utilizing the strong SharePoint security features such as SharePoint security groups, Active Directory security groups, the document library, and folder and item-level security.

This chapter addresses different ways that users and developers can deploy reports to SharePoint. The chapter first goes through the steps to create a SharePoint environment that will host the reports. Then it provides a walkthrough that shows how reports and data sources can be deployed to SharePoint using Business Intelligence Development Studio (BIDS) and Report Builder. Finally, the chapter goes over the Reporting Services features provided via the SharePoint interface that allows you to manage reports deployed on SharePoint sites.

Preparing Your SharePoint Environment

Reports can be deployed to SharePoint using Business Intelligence Development Studio (BIDS) and Report Builder. BIDS is mostly used by developers, since BIDS is a shell version of Visual Studio as explained in Chapter 4, "Overview of Business Intelligence Design Studio (BIDS) 2008." BIDS is more of a developer-oriented tool since it allows developers to create advance reports using code. Report Builder is mostly used by end-users to create ad-hoc reports on the fly and has a much simpler approach to deploying reports to SharePoint.

Typically, the development process happens in two stages. First the reports will be developed by developers and published to SharePoint using BIDS. Then, if needed, organizations can empower their power users to update the published reports using Report Builder. Report Builder can also be used by power users to create reports that do not require any development.

For example, if the user wanted to change the company logo or the title of the report and save it with a different name, they could easily accomplish this with Report Builder without having the need to request for developer hours. Later in this chapter you will see how developers can deploy reports to SharePoint using BIDS and how end users can make changes and save their changes to SharePoint without having a report development environment by simply using their workstations.

Before you start deploying reports to SharePoint, it is a good idea to prepare your SharePoint environment. This section guides you through the approaches you can take with your SharePoint environment that will host reports.

Activating the Report Server Integration Feature

Before you can publish reports to a site, you need to enable the Report Server Integration feature on the site collection where the reports will be deployed. If you do not activate this feature, you will not get any of the report server integration benefits such as subscriptions, snapshots, and so on. For example, if the Report Server Integration feature is not activated, SharePoint does not recognize the RDL file as a report, and the Default Item Context Menu is shown. If the feature is activated, however, the Item Context Menu will display several report server functions on the Item Context Menu, as shown in Figure 8-1.

Default Item Context Menu

**Item Context Menu when
Report Server Integration
feature active**

Figure 8-1

You can see from Figure 8-1 that a lot of functionality gets added to the site when the Report Server Integration feature is enabled on the site collection. You will review each of these functions later in this chapter, but first go through the steps that allow you to enable this feature on your site collection.

Follow these steps to enable the Report Server Integration feature:

1. Navigate to your Site settings page by clicking Site Actions ⇨ Site Settings, which will take you to `http://yoursite/_layouts/settings.aspx`.

2. On the Site settings page under the Site Collection Administration section, click the "Site collection features" link, which will take you to `http://yoursite/_layouts/ManageFeatures.aspx?Scope=Site`.

3. On the Site collection features page, scroll down, find the feature named "Report Server Integration Feature," and click the Activate button located next to it.

4. Finally, verify that the Status for the Report Server Integration Feature is now marked as Active.

Once the feature is activated, the Report Server Integration functionality is now available to all sites that are housed under that site collection.

> **If you don't see the Site collection features link when you go to your site settings, you might not have site collection administrator rights. This feature can only be enabled at the site-collection level, so you must request this from your Site Collection Administrator.**

Creating Libraries for Reports and Data Sources

Once you have activated the report server integration feature, you have technically enabled your site to host reports, but there are still some things you can do to make your site more report-friendly. For one thing, consider creating new libraries that will host report-related items.

You can easily use the existing document libraries on your site or even create a library on the fly using BIDS, but the best approach is to plan for where your report-related items will be stored and set up security accordingly.

As a site owner, you should prepare the libraries before allowing your site users to deploy reports to your site. Before you create new libraries to store report-related items on your site, you must answer the following questions: How many libraries do you need, and what kind of security do you need to set up for these libraries?

Organizing the Libraries

Start by addressing the number of libraries you need. At a minimum, creating one new library is recommended to store all report-related items. Creating a new library for reports will give the users of your site a central location to get the reports. Also, as the site owner, you can create custom permissions for the new library without having to change the permissions of your existing document libraries.

> *The new library should have a name that your site users can remember easily, like Reports or Report Library.*

Note also that these reports should be logically grouped, either by folders in your library or by creating a new library for each business need. For example, you can easily create one library for Budget Reports and another for Project Reports. If your site is a central location for all reports in your organization, you can end up creating one library for Financial Reports and another for Sales Reports, since it's always best practice to group items based on how the business accesses them. There is no point in putting all reports in one location and confusing a user who needs to see only a particular report.

Creating separate document libraries based on the business takes care of the reports, but you also need to determine where your data sources will be stored. The best practice would be to create a central document library that houses your shared data sources. This approach gives you a central location for all of your data sources when you have more than one document library for reports. In most cases, reports grouped by different needs use the same data source. So if reports are stored in different document libraries that use the same data source, it makes no sense to deploy the same data source multiple times to different document libraries, as this would make it hard to maintain the data sources going forward. By having a library for data sources, you can then share these data sources amongst all reports on your site, as shown in Figure 8-2.

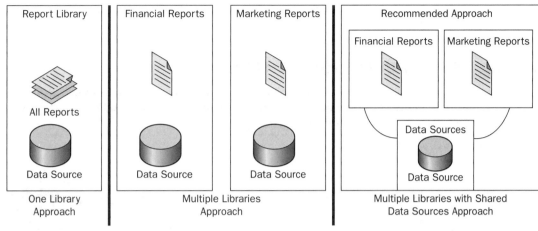

Figure 8-2

Defining Security for Report and Data Source Libraries

After you determine the number of libraries you need for your site, the next thing to define is the security for these libraries. Defining security is an important part of preparing your site for reports. By default, all report server functionality is shown to all contributors on your site, but in most cases you wouldn't want your contributors modifying the settings of your reports using report server integration functionality.

The best way to define security is to create SharePoint groups that map to how your users will interact with the reports on your site. Typically, you will have three different types of users: Report Readers, Report Authors, and Report Developers.

❑ **Report Readers:** These users will only need to view and print reports.

❑ **Report Authors:** These power users will be using Report Builder to create their own reports. They can create reports, but they will not be able to create data sources.

❑ **Report Developers:** These developers will be using BIDS to develop reports and the data sources for these reports.

Once you have defined the groups, the next task is to determine how you will define security to the libraries. The following table is a good starting point when defining security for these libraries.

	Marketing Reports	**Financial Reports**	**Data Sources**
Report Reader	Reader	Reader	Reader
Report Author	Contributor	Contributor	Reader
Report Developer	Contributor	Contributor	Contributor

Please note that the reader must have reader rights to the data source and the report to see the report properly.

Housing Reports in the Report Center

Another approach for housing reports in SharePoint is to use a Report Center site, as shown in Figure 8-3. Microsoft Office SharePoint Server 2007 includes a site template named Report Center, which allows organizations to create a site for managing reports.

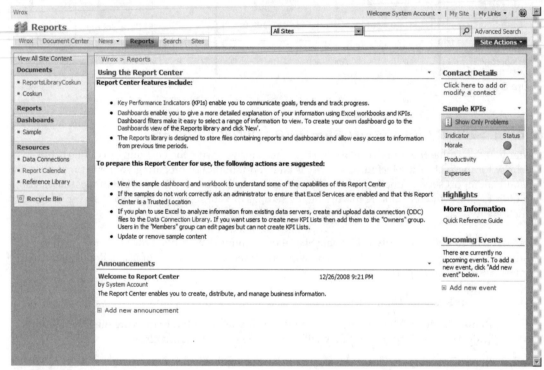

Figure 8-3

The Report Center site allows organizations not only to consolidate reports in a centralized location but also provides the following features:

- ❏ The ability to create dashboard pages
- ❏ The Report Library's custom report content type, which provides additional columns for metadata
- ❏ The Report Library's history functionality
- ❏ The Data Connections Library to store data sources

Based on your business requirements, you can either use one Report Center site to store all of your organization's reports and deliver it to all employees, or you can create specific Report Center sites per team to allow them to see business data securely.

Dashboard Pages

Using a Report Center site to house your reports gives you the benefit of dashboard pages. Dashboard pages are web-part pages designed to display information to users in need of the latest and greatest information to make fast business decisions. A dashboard page is great to use when displaying reports in SharePoint.

To create a dashboard page in your Report Center site, click the Site Actions ⇨ Create Dashboard link, as shown in Figure 8-4.

Figure 8-4

On the Create Dashboard page, you will find several options, as shown in Figure 8-5.

❑   **File Name:** This will be the URL of the page. When naming your dashboard page, try not to leave any spaces. Eliminating spaces makes the URL more user friendly.

❑   **Page Title:** This will appear on the top left of the browser; it is okay to use spaces in this field.

❑   **Description:** This is the description of the dashboard page.

❑   **Location:** You cannot modify this property; all dashboard pages will be stored in the Reports Library.

❑   **Navigation Bar:** You can select where you wish show the link on the Quick Launch. You can also *not* show the link on the Quick Launch menu, based on your needs.

❑   **Dashboard Layout:** There are three different types of dashboard page layouts; choose the one that makes sense for your needs. Oftentimes, the "two column vertical layout" is used to display reports.

❑   **Key Performance Indicators (KPIs):** With report dashboard pages, you have the ability to create KPIs that accompany the dashboard. You can either select the option to automatically create KPIs or select an existing KPI list. In Figure 8-5 the "Create a KPI list for me automatically" is selected.

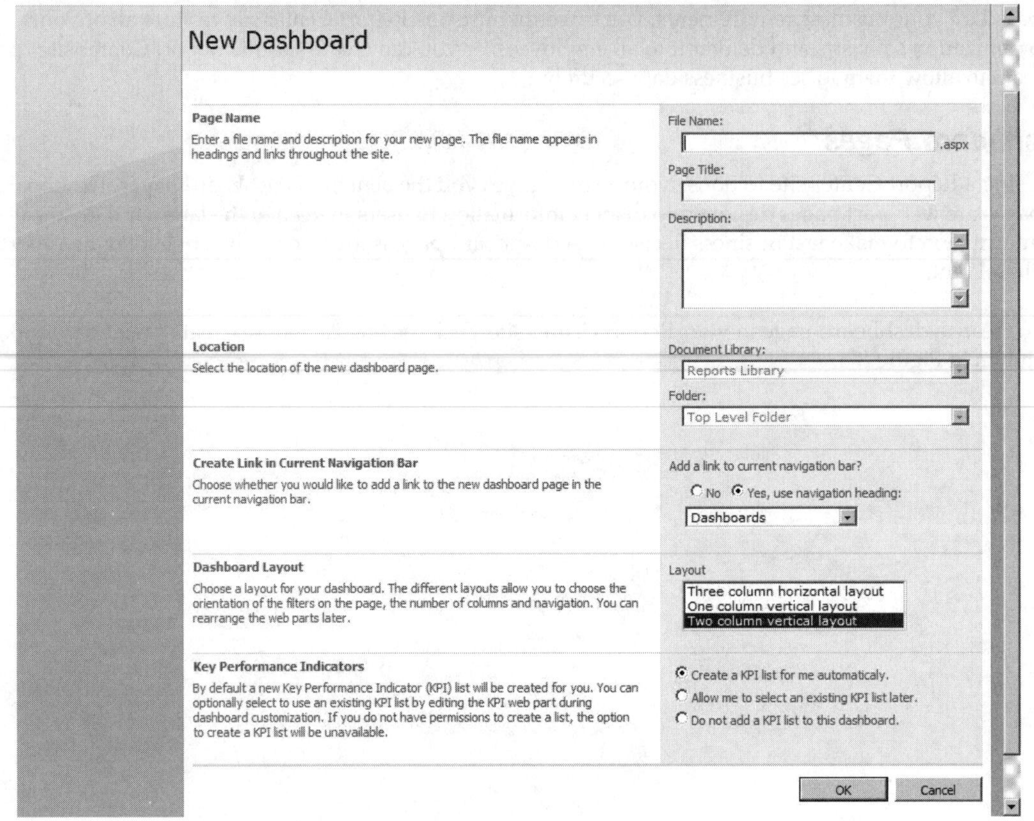

Figure 8-5

Once you have created the dashboard page, you can edit it by simply clicking Site Actions ⇨ Edit Page. When the page is in edit mode, as shown in Figure 8-6, you will see that several web-part zones can be used to add the web parts needed. The Filter web part, in particular, is most widely used with your dashboard pages.

This chapter will not walk through the steps that show you how to display reports in SharePoint, as how a report can be displayed to a SharePoint page is covered in greater detail in Chapter 10, "Displaying your Reports in SharePoint Integrated Mode."

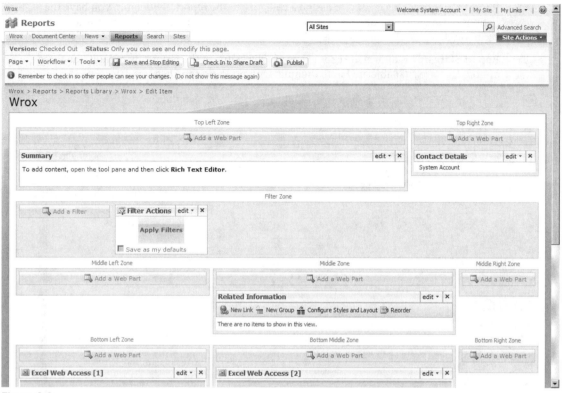

Figure 8-6

The Reports Library

The reports library hosts reports and dashboard pages. This document library has two custom content types that are enabled with this type of a document library: Report and Dashboard. The Dashboard content type is a web part page and is used when dashboard pages are created using the Site Actions ⇨ Create Dashboard link. This content type allows you to create web part pages very quickly and saves them directly to the reports document library.

Although the ability to create dashboard pages on the fly is very useful and helps you display reports intuitively, the Report content type is the main reason why you should choose to deploy SSRS reports to a Report Center site. The Report content type has custom columns that help house your reports, as shown in Figure 8-7. The custom fields for the Report content type are as follows:

❑ **Name, Title, Report Description:** These are the basics of the report file.

❑ **Save to Report History:** If this check box is selected, a copy of the report is saved each time a new version of the report is saved.

❑ **Owner:** This is a very important field. By knowing who owns the report, you can make changes a lot faster.

❑ **Report Category:** This is used to assign a category to the report. By default, you have the options of Category 1, Category 2, and Category 3. You can modify these options to accommodate your business needs.

❑ **Report Status:** This allows the user to specify the status of the report. By default, the three options that are available are Final, Preliminary, and Period to Date.

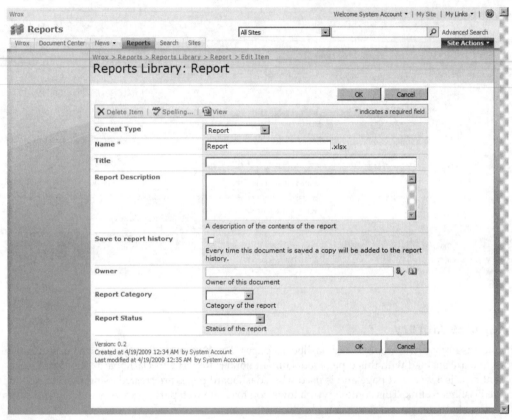

Figure 8-7

When "Save to report history" is checked, the history functionality is enabled. Once this is enabled, a link named View History will appear in the document library. Once you click that link, the history of the report is displayed, as shown in Figure 8-8.

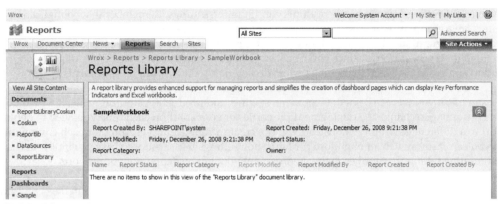

Figure 8-8

The Data Connections Library

The data connections library is a central location to house all of the data connections used by the reports. In this library two custom content types are added by default: office data connection file and universal data connection file. This document library can be used to house the report data sources, but it is not necessary, as it does not provide additional functionality over a regular document library.

Deploying Reports with Business Intelligence Design Studio (BIDS)

After you have prepared your SharePoint environment, you are ready to deploy reports to SharePoint 2007. In Business Intelligence Design Studio (BIDS), publishing reports from BIDS to a SharePoint site is known as deploying reports to SharePoint. The most common way to deploy a report to SharePoint is to use BIDS. In this section, you will walk through the steps involved in deploying a report to SharePoint 2007.

Setting up the Deployment Properties

To deploy a report using BIDS, you must specify the URL of the report server, the location where you wish to deploy reports, the location of the data source folder and whether you will allow the data source to be overwritten. These are the deployment properties of a report project or solution. Setting up these deployment properties is the first step when deploying reports to SharePoint 2007 using BIDS.

The deployment properties of all reports are controlled by the solution's configuration settings. The configuration settings define the properties of the solution, such as the build and deployment properties. One thing to know about the configuration settings in BIDS is that you can only apply one configuration setting at a time to your solution, which means you cannot have different deployment properties for each individual report. Once you configure the configuration settings of a solution or project, which contains the deployment properties for a solution, all reports will inherit those settings when they are deployed.

However, BIDS allows you to create multiple configuration settings. Remember that configuration settings are a group of settings and by creating multiple configuration settings you can easily create a separate configuration setting for each of the environments you have in your organization. This functionality is very powerful since you can always create different configuration settings for your solution and switch between the settings when deploying reports to your environments.

For example, if you were to have development, staging, and production environments, it would be very time-consuming to change the deployment properties of your solution each time you need to deploy a report to a different environment. Instead you can create a configuration setting for each environment and you can easily switch among those configuration settings in the property pages window and use the configuration setting that applies to the environment you will be deploying your reports.

In the following sections you will walk through defining the deployment properties in the configuration settings and will create different configuration settings using BIDS. To demonstrate the deployment properties setup, this section uses the project solution provided by the Adventure Works Sample Reports.

To open this solution, open BIDS by going to Start ⇨ All Programs ⇨ Microsoft SQL Server 2008 ⇨ SQL Server Business Intelligence Development Studio. Once BIDS is open, click File ⇨ Open ⇨ Project/ Solution to open a solution. Then navigate to the following path to open the Adventure Works 2008 Sample Reports solution: [Drive Letter]:\Program Files\Microsoft SQL Server\100\Samples\Reporting Services\Report Samples\AdventureWorks Sample Reports. Once you have opened the solution, you should see it in BIDS, as shown in Figure 8-9. The solution will have a shared data source named AdventureWorks2008.rds and eight examples of SSRS reports.

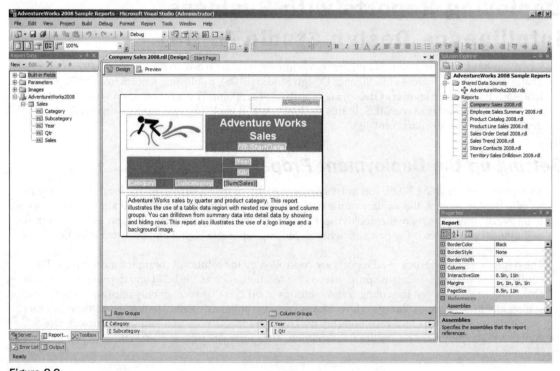

Figure 8-9

To configure the deployment settings, right-click the solution name and click Properties. The Adventure Works 2008 Sample Reports Property Pages dialog will appear, as shown in Figure 8-10.

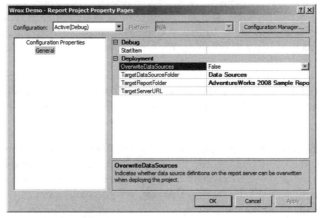

Figure 8-10

There are four deployment properties that you need to fill out in order to deploy your reports to SharePoint: OverwriteDataSources, TargetDataSourceFolder, TargetReportFolder, and TargetServerURL, as seen in Figure 8-10. You will now walk through each of these properties to understand what they are for and what you need to type in them to deploy reports to SharePoint.

The OverwriteDataSources Property

This is the property that allows you to specify how you would like to deploy your data sources. When a report is deployed to SharePoint, the data source associated with that report also can be deployed automatically based on this property. If this property is set to True, as shown in Figure 8-11, it will overwrite the existing data source in the location specified in the TargetDataSourceFolder property. This property is very useful when you make several updates to your data source. When you just need to deploy the report and not the data source, you will set this property to False, and since there is an existing data source, it will not be overwritten.

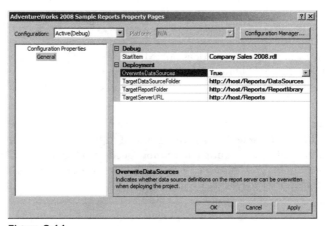

Figure 8-11

One of the most common scenarios in these types of multi-environment report development projects is deploying a report that is ready for user acceptance testing to the staging environment. In most cases, your connection string is going to be different for your development, staging, and production environments. So you will need to have different data sources for each environment, but your reports will be the same and will use the same data source. So instead of updating the data source each time you need to deploy reports to another environment, you will set this property to false and this will only deploy the reports. This way you will not overwrite the data source that is in staging.

Assuming that you are developing against the development database and your project has the development connection string on the data source, you need to update your data source so that it is pointing to your staging environment in order for you to deploy your report to your staging environment.

Instead of changing the connection string on the data source every time you want to deploy a report to another environment, you could quickly turn the OverwriteDataSources property to False and deploy the report to your staging or production environment, assuming the data source with the correct connection string was published at least once. This way you can easily deploy the report for testing and continue to develop without losing much time.

The TargetDataSourceFolder Property

As mentioned in the "The OverwriteDataSources Property" section, when a report is deployed, the data sources associated with that report will also get deployed. But where? You guessed it; this property allows you to specify where you would like to deploy your data sources.

As discussed earlier in this chapter, the location where you wish to store your data source is really determined by your business requirements. Let's assume that you've determined that you would like to store your data sources centrally under a document library named DataSources under the Report Central site of your portal. Once you've determined that, all you have to do is enter the URL to this location in this property. In this example, you will deploy your data sources to `http://host/Reports/DataSources` as shown in Figure 8-11.

The TargetReportFolder Property

This is the property that allows you to specify where you would like to deploy your reports. In this property, you will type the URL of the document library or a folder within a library. In this example, you will publish your reports to `http://Host/Reports/Reportlibrary`, as shown in Figure 8-11.

If the document library you're referring to does not exist under that SharePoint site, BIDS will automatically create the document library for you and deploy the reports under that document library. So when you're deploying for the first time, you don't need to create document libraries in advance.

> **If you are used to working with the native mode of SSRS, one thing to remember is that in SharePoint integrated mode you cannot specify a relative folder. When you specify the location for your report or your data source, SharePoint will assume that this location comes after the target URL.**

The TargetServerURL Property

Even though this property is listed last, it's the most important one. Without this property, you would not be able to deploy reports to SharePoint, as the TargetServerURL property tells BIDS where to deploy the report.

If you try to deploy this solution with its default settings by leaving the TargetServerURL empty, you will quickly get an error dialog letting you know that you need to specify a valid URL for TargetServerURL, as shown in Figure 8-12.

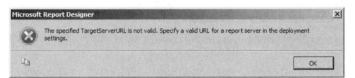

Figure 8-12

In SharePoint integrated mode, TargetServerURL is the URL of the site where you wish to deploy your reports. In this example, this is `http://host/Reports`, as shown earlier in Figure 8-11, since this is the URL to your Report Center. You can use a top-level site or a subsite when deploying reports. In your case, you are deploying reports to the reports subsite, but you can always publish reports to the top-level site by using the URL `http://host` or even to a subsite's subsite by using the URL `http://host/Reports/Subsite`.

Configuration Manager in the Project's Property Pages Dialog Box

In multi-environment deployment scenarios, the configuration manager comes in quite handy. With the configuration manager, you can manage the configuration of the entire solution, and the deployment properties are a part of the configuration of the solution. You can edit existing configurations, but, more importantly, using the configuration manager, you can add new configurations.

Adding new configurations is what makes the configuration manager useful when deploying reports across environments, since you can create a separate configuration setup for each of your environments. This way, you don't have to update the deployment properties when you're deploying reports to SharePoint. By having a separate configuration for each environment, you avoid having to change the URLs for reports, data sources, and the target server each time you deploy across environments.

To create a new configuration using the configuration manager, click the Configuration Manager button located on the top right of the project's Property Pages dialog box, as shown earlier in Figure 8-11. Once you have the Configuration Manager window open, click the drop-down control that is under the Active solution configuration, and click the <New . . . > option, as shown in Figure 8-13.

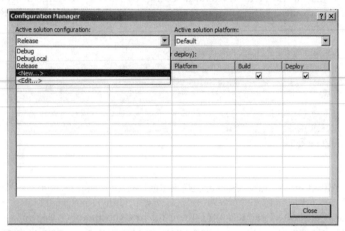

Figure 8-13

Next a pop-up window asks for a name for the new solution configuration. In this section, name your configuration intuitively to something like Development Environment or DEV Configuration. For this example, use the name Development, as shown in Figure 8-14.

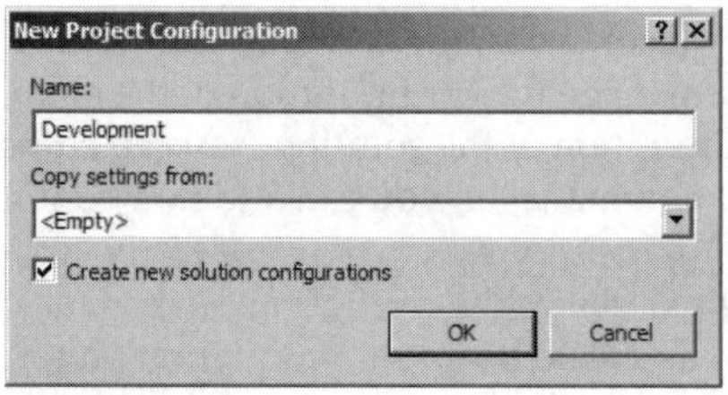

Figure 8-14

With this approach you can create a configuration for all of your environments. Once you've created your configurations, you can select the configuration you want to apply to your solution by using the configuration manager. Under the Configuration column of the project configuration, click the drop-down box and select the configuration you wish to use. In this example, select the Development configuration to be active, as shown in Figure 8-15.

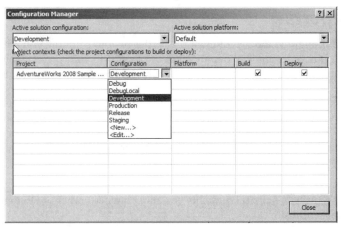

Figure 8-15

Once a configuration is selected and applied, it will become the active configuration. The active configuration can be identified by looking at the Configuration section of the project's Property Pages dialog box. When a configuration is active, it will be noted in the configuration as Active (Configuration Name). In this example, the active configuration is Development, as shown in the Configuration field in Figure 8-16.

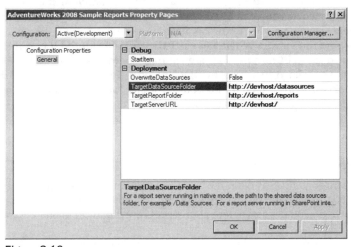

Figure 8-16

Deploying Reports

Now that you have configured the deployment properties of your solution, you are ready to deploy them to SharePoint. It is very simple to deploy all of the reports in your project/solution. To deploy your reports to SharePoint, all you have to do is right-click the solution/project name and click Deploy.

When you click the Deploy option under the Solution context menu, BIDS will deploy all reports and data sources listed in your project/solution. So with one click you deploy your solution to SharePoint. Although this makes it very easy to deploy reports, always make sure you're extra careful when deploying the whole solution/project, as your existing reports will be overwritten.

> **To deploy reports to a SharePoint site, you must have Member or Owner permission on the SharePoint site.**

You can also deploy reports one at a time using BIDS. To deploy one report, right-click the report itself and click Deploy. Please note that when you deploy your report through BIDS, it will automatically deploy the data source associated with the report as well. So make sure you set the OverwriteDataSources property to False if you're not working on the data source before you deploy your reports.

> **You can also upload files the SharePoint way to your SharePoint site. When you upload a report or a data source to SharePoint, there is no validation happening on the upload event. So you will not know if your reports are working until you actually click the report and view it. When you use BIDS or Report Builder to publish reports and related files to a library, the files are validated before they are added. If you upload reports and related files by using the Upload action on a SharePoint library, no validation check occurs. You will not know whether the file is valid until you access the report by managing, editing, or running it.**

Common Deployment Errors

Deploying reports through BIDS also has the benefit of validating the reports on the fly before they are deployed to your SharePoint site. When deploying reports, you can get several errors and warnings that will help you resolve potential issues before your reports are deployed to SharePoint.

Using the Output and Error List windows in BIDS, you can determine the error and work on potential fixes to resolve the problem. In a successful deployment of one report, you will see a report in the Output window similar to the following code, also shown in Figure 8-17.

```
------ Build started: Project: AdventureWorks 2008 Sample Reports,
       Configuration: Production ------
Build complete -- 0 errors, 0 warnings
------ Deploy started: Project: AdventureWorks 2008 Sample Reports,
       Configuration: Production ------
Deploying to http://host/
Deploying data source 'http://host/Reports/DataSources/AdventureWorks2008.rsds'.
Deploying report 'http://host/Reports/ReportLibrary/Company Sales 2008.rdl'.
Deploy complete -- 0 errors, 0 warnings
========== Build: 1 succeeded or up-to-date, 0 failed, 0 skipped ==========
========== Deploy: 1 succeeded, 0 failed, 0 skipped ==========
```

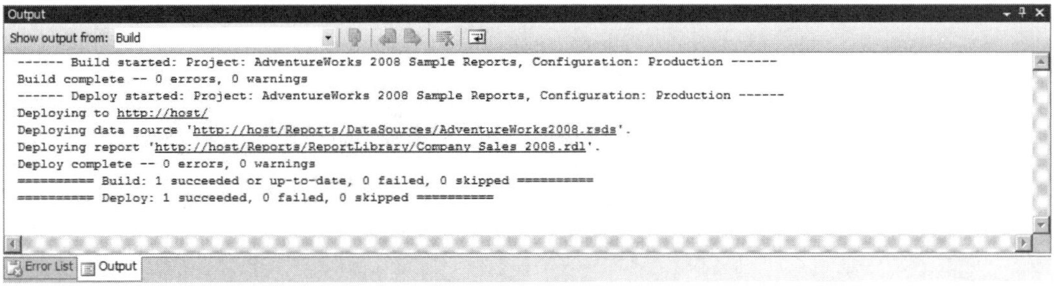

Figure 8-17

In this section, you will review some of the more common errors you might get when working with BIDS and deploying reports to SharePoint.

The Permissions/Login Error

As mentioned earlier, to be able to deploy a report to a SharePoint site, you must have Member or Owner permissions on the site. When deploying reports to SharePoint using BIDS, BIDS will use windows authentication and will pass on your existing credentials to SharePoint. If you are not a Member or the Owner of the SharePoint site, you will get a window asking you to log in, as shown in Figure 8-18.

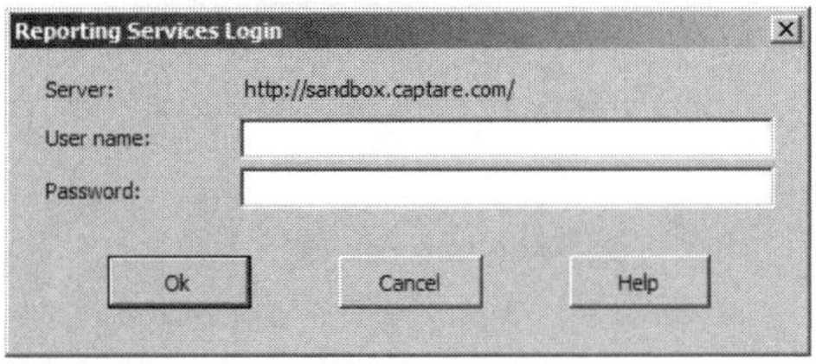

Figure 8-18

Even if you provide the login prompt with the correct credentials to your SharePoint site (in this example `http://sandbox.captare.com`,) you will not be authenticated to SharePoint. And the dialog will keep on asking you for your credentials.

If you find yourself in this situation, the workaround is pretty simple; all you have to do is run BIDS as a user that has Member or Owner rights to the SharePoint site you wish to deploy your report to. The best way to do this is to create a shortcut on your desktop that, when clicked, allows you to run BIDS as another user.

The first thing is to have an account that can be used to deploy reports. You can see the accounts that have owner rights to the Report Center site by navigating to Site Actions ⇨ Site Settings ⇨ People and Groups. There, click the Owners groups to see who is in that group. In your case, you will use the Report Admin (CHICAGO\ReportAdmin) account, shown in Figure 8-19. Note that when added to the SharePoint security group, the user CHICAGO\ReportAdmin is displayed as Report Admin (firstname lastname).

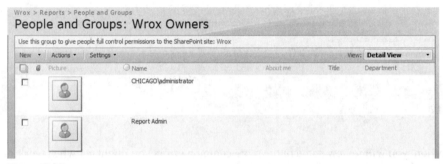

Figure 8-19

Typically, the best practice is to create a domain account such as "ReportAdmin" and add that user as an Owner to the site. This way, you do not have developers deploying reports directly to the site using their account. When a report is ready to be deployed to staging or production, the "ReportAdmin" account will be used, using the preceding method.

Once you have determined the account you will use to deploy the reports, the next step is to create the shortcut that will run BIDS under this account. To run BIDS as the ReportAdmin account, you will use the `runas` command. The command should be as follows:

```
runas.exe /user:DOMAIN\USERACCOUNT "C:\Program Files\Microsoft Visual Studio
9.0\Common7\IDE\devenv.exe"
```

Go to your desktop and create a new shortcut by typing the preceding statement into your Create Shortcut window, as shown in Figure 8-20.

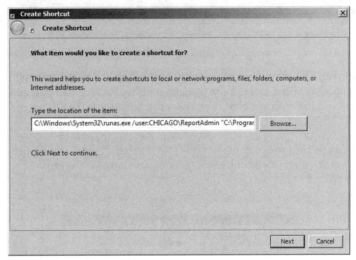

Figure 8-20

Click Next to continue, and the Name screen will appear. Name your shortcut and click Finish. Once you do this, you have successfully created the shortcut for BIDS that will run under the account you have entered in your statement.

When you click the shortcut, a Command Prompt will appear, asking you to log in with the account you have used in the statement, as shown in Figure 8-21.

Figure 8-21

Type your password and hit the Enter key to log in. At this point, Visual Studio will start up and will be running as the account specified in the shortcut statement. This way, when you deploy reports using BIDS, BIDS will pass on the authenticated user, and since this user is the Owner of the site, the reports will be deployed.

Another tool that can be used to accomplish this is ShellRunas. This is similar to runas; the difference is that it provides a convenient shell context-menu entry, as shown in Figure 8-22.

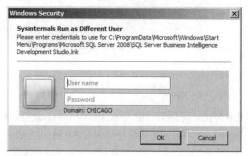

Figure 8-22

To install ShellRunas, you must download the file from http://technet.microsoft.com/en-us/sysinternals/cc300361.aspx.

Once you download the file, register ShellRunas.exe by using the following command-line statement:

```
ShellRunas.exe /reg
```

You will then get a dialog box letting you know that you have successfully registered it. By clicking OK, you have registered ShellRunas, and you can use this to log in to all of your applications as another user by just right-clicking on the application shortcut, as shown in Figure 8-23.

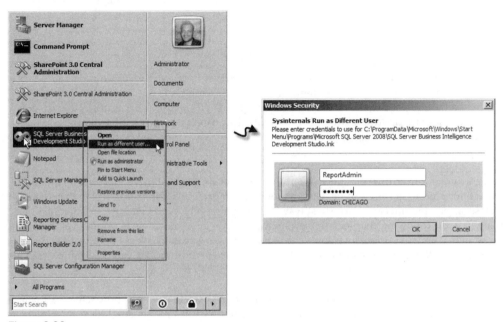

Figure 8-23

The "User cannot be found" Error

This error happens when a SharePoint site has moved across domains. In order to explain this error, this section will use a hypothetical example. For example, say you are developing in your dev domain DEVHOST.COM and your SharePoint site is a member of that domain. Now that you're ready for QA, you wish to bring the site over to staging servers, and the staging servers are hosted under QAHOST.COM.

When you back up the site and bring it over to staging, you will get the "User cannot be found" error. Why? Because when a SharePoint site is backed up, the users of the old domain get carried over to the new location, since it's a part of the site's content database.

So when you have users with DEVHOST domains in the site database and the new environment's report server is going through the users, it sees users from another domain and can't validate them. Thus, it throws the following error:

```
Report Server has encountered a SharePoint error. (rsSharePointError) Get Online
Help

User cannot be found.
```

> **The best way to avoid this situation is not to develop in a different domain and bring the site to the environment, since the following fix is not a best practice and should only be used as a final resort. Doing this will result in breaking your support agreement with Microsoft, as they do not allow direct updates to SharePoint databases.**

If you encounter this error, there is a workaround, but be advised that this is not a recommended approach for production environments since you will have to make direct updates to the SharePoint database, as pointed out earlier. The best way to deploy reports would be to use solution files, as explained in the following chapters. But assuming that you have this issue in your development environment, you will explore an example to explain the workaround. Please note that the results you will see in the following figures will not be the same in your environment. But the example will give you a high-level understanding of the way you will go about when trying to resolve this issue.

So for argument's sake let's say you have determined that you will use this approach to fix the issue. To fix the "User cannot be found" error, you need to find out what user is causing this error, which is where SQL Profiler comes in handy. SQL Profiler allows you to trace all requests that are made to your SQL database. How does this help? Well it's actually pretty slick. You will use SQL Profiler to trace all requests to the SharePoint database. This way when you go to the site that is giving you the error, you will have logged the call that SharePoint made to the database. Once you get the error, you will stop the trace, in the log find the user that is causing the error, and update that entry in the database to fix the issue.

To find the user causing the error and fix the issue, you start by opening SQL Profiler. To open the SQL Server Profiler, go to Start ⇨ All programs ⇨ SQL Server 2008 ⇨ Performance Tools. SQL Server Profiler will open, as shown in Figure 8-24.

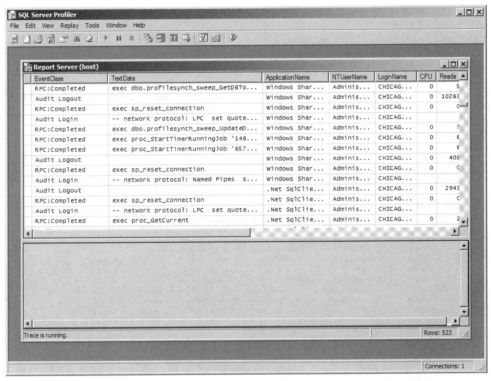

Figure 8-24

Go ahead and start a trace. Once you start the trace, SQL profiler will start logging all calls to the database server. So now that you have the logging started, you will go to the site where you're getting this error so that SQL Profiler can log the request made when you try to access your site. Once you get the error, switch back to the SQL Profiler and stop the trace by using the Stop button located at the top of the SQL Server Profiler.

At this point you have logged the request that SharePoint has made when it was trying to validate the user. SharePoint uses the proc_SecFetPrincipalById stored procedure when trying the validate accounts, so knowing this you will search for all of the calls that are made to the database by this stored procedure. This stored procedure accepts four parameters. The first parameter is a GUID and the other three are integers. The following is a representation of how the call would look like in your SQL Profiler log:

```
proc_SecGetPrincipalById <GUID>, <INT_1>, <INT_2>, <INT_3>
```

Here, the GUID is the ID of the SharePoint site, and <INT_1> is the user ID causing the error.

Now that you have the log, you need to find all calls that are made by the proc_SecGetPrincipalById, since this will be called for all users in the site. You need to find which one of the users is really causing the error, since not all of them are going to be the problem. You need to find the ID of the user that causes this issue. So let's assume that you search for the proc_SecGetPrincipalById call and the following entry is the first call that is made to your database, as shown in Figure 8-25:

```
exec proc_SecGetPrincipalById '6EB39743-A376-430E-A788-8E51810793B6',1073741823,0,0
```

In this case, the GUID of the site is 6EB39743-A376-430E-A788-8E51810793B6, and the User ID is 1073741823.

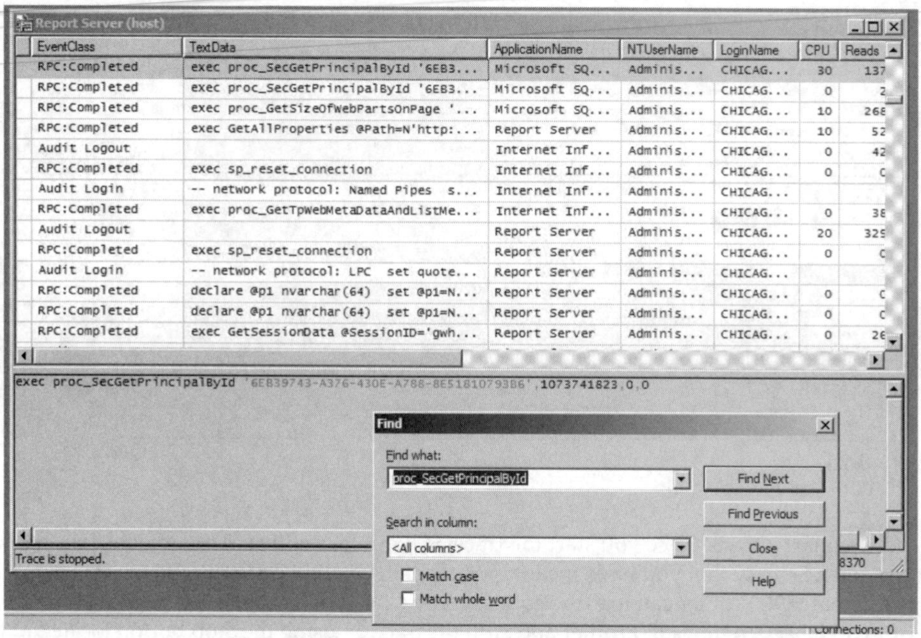

Figure 8-25

So far, you have identified the Site ID and the User ID causing the error. Now that you have found an entry called by the proc_SecGetPrincipalById stored procedure, you need to determine if this is one of the users causing the error. The next step is going to be done on the content database of the SharePoint site giving the error. Before you continue, please make sure you have made backups of your database and are absolutely sure you want to move forward with this approach (because, as mentioned at the beginning of this section, doing so will break your support agreement with Microsoft).

To determine if the user is causing the error, you will need to query the UserInfo table and review the user entry in the UserInfo database table. The UserInfo table of the SharePoint database stores all of the users that are located in the SharePoint site and also gives you more information on the user such as whether the user is deleted from the site.

Using the GUID and ID you found in the SQL Profiler, you will run the following statement:

```
SELECT * FROM UserInfo WHERE tp_SiteID = <GUID> AND tp_ID = <INT_1>
```

In this example, you will replace the GUID and User ID with the values you found in your search.

```
SELECT * FROM UserInfo WHERE tp_SiteID = '6EB39743-A376-430E-A788-8E51810793B6'
    and tp_ID ='1073741823'
```

After running this statement you need to pay attention to the tp_Deleted column. This will tell you whether the user is deleted. You need to look at this column because it needs to be 0 (false) for those users that were brought over from your original domain (DEVHOST). If the value is already zero, you don't need to worry about that user, and you need to go back to the SQL profiler to get the next ID that was called by the proc_SecGetPrincipalById stored procedure. In this case, when you run the SQL command, you get the result shown in Figure 8-26.

As you can see from Figure 8-26, the `tp_Deleted` value is 0, so this is not the user that is causing the error. Now that you have determined that this is not the user ID causing the error, you will need to go back to the SQL Server Profiler and search for `proc_SecGetPrincipalById` again and find the next user ID that is called by the stored procedure.

So say you go through this process a few times and finally you find another User ID, which is 16. And let's assume that when you run the following command, you see that the tp_Deleted column is set to 1, as shown in Figure 8-27.

```
SELECT * FROM UserInfo WHERE tp_SiteID = '6EB39743-A376-430E-A788-8E51810793B6'
    and tp_ID ='16'
```

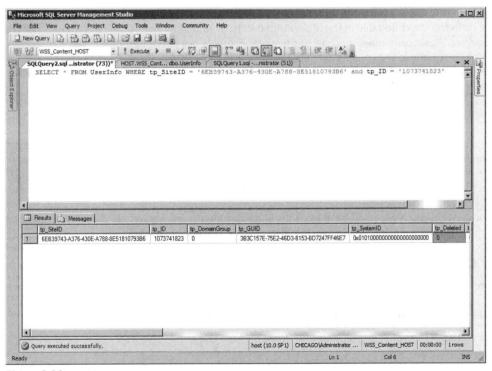

Figure 8-26

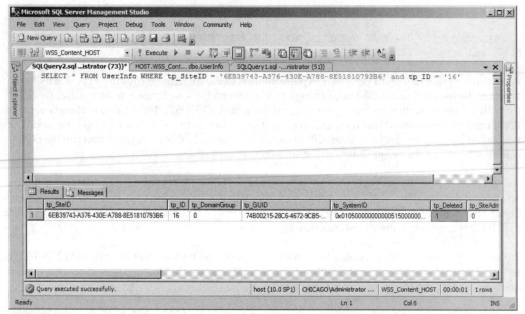

Figure 8-27

So now that you have determined that 16 is the User ID that is causing the error, you need to update this User ID in the UserInfo table of the SharePoint database so that its `tp_Deleted` column is not true but is set to false. Again remember this part of the workaround is not supported by Microsoft, because you are making an update to the content database directly using a SQL statement. Also, please be extra careful when making this update and make sure everything is backed up. Now, you will use the following SQL command to update the `tp_Deleted` field for user id 16.

```
UPDATE UserInfo SET tp_Deleted = 0 where TP_Id = <INT_1> AND tp_SiteID = <GUID>
```

In this case, you will replace the `tp_ID` with 16, which is the ID you found earlier. Once you run the command, you will update the user data in the SharePoint database to `Deleted=0`. Since the User ID 16 is the ID stored in the report server database and the SharePoint database is updated to say that User ID 16 is not deleted, the report server will render the report and not throw an error. If the error happens again, that means that there are other users that the report server needs and they are marked as deleted. At this point you will have to go through the above steps again to find the other users that are causing the error and update them so that they are not marked as deleted.

Other Common Problems

There is also a good section on MSDN that goes over some of the most common problems, such as

❑   Being unable to create a connection to the data source 'datasourcename'

❑   Report server errors on Windows Vista

❑   The RPC server is not listening

You can access the MSDN section at `http://msdn.microsoft.com/en-us/library/ms156468.aspx`.

Deploying Reports with Report Builder 2.0

Another report-authoring tool that can be used to deploy reports to SharePoint is Report Builder. With Report Builder 2.0, you can allow your power users to create reports and deploy them directly to SharePoint.

Once a report is created or opened in Report Builder, deploying the report to SharePoint is no different from saving a Word document to SharePoint. To deploy a report, click the Save As button on Report Builder, as shown in Figure 8-28. In the Save dialog, type the URL of the SharePoint site you wish to save the report to and click OK.

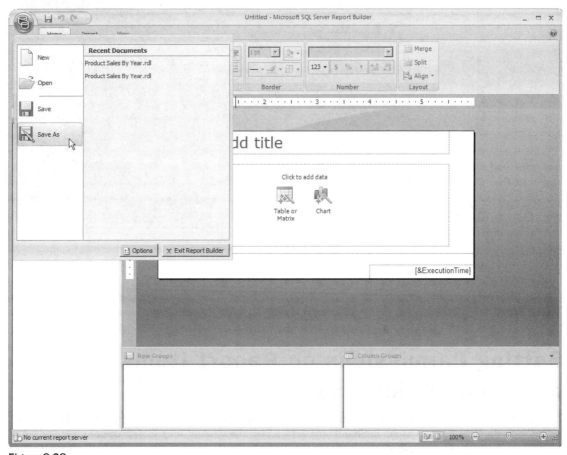

Figure 8-28

Also, in the Report Builder Options, you can specify the default SharePoint site by clicking the Office button and clicking Options. On the Options screen, add the URL of your default site, as shown in Figure 8-29. Once you do this, Report Builder will always start from this location when you are saving a report.

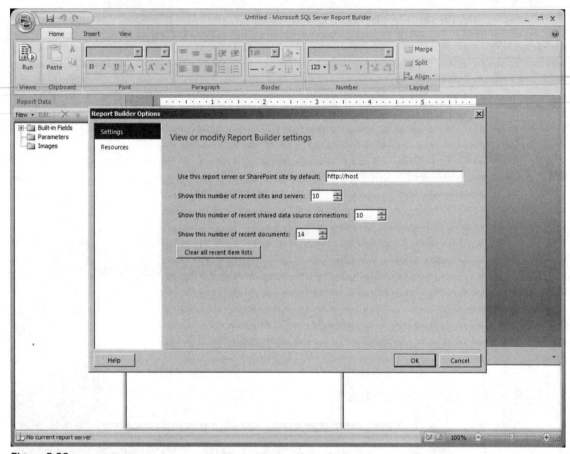

Figure 8-29

Setting Permissions on Report Items on a SharePoint Site

With the reports deployed to SharePoint, you now have several options for managing them. When you click on the Item Context Menu in SharePoint, on a report file you get several new options. One of the options is Manage Permissions, as highlighted in Figure 8-30.

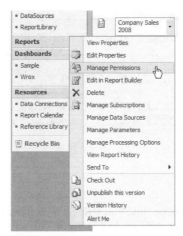

Figure 8-30

The Manage Permissions option, when clicked, will take you to the Permissions page. This is the Item Level Security Settings page. So when deploying a report to SharePoint, you can manage who can see the report and who can modify it.

This is a major benefit when reports are deployed to a SharePoint environment, because the same security groups created for sites in SharePoint can be reused for the reports. For example, if you already have a SharePoint security group called Finance Users that holds all of the users that are a member of the finance department and you want this department's staff to see this report, with item-level security you can easily reuse the Financial Users security group and modify the permissions of the report so that only these users will see that report.

If you don't have an existing security group, you can create a new one. If you have the proper permissions, you can also create new permission levels. But you must remember when you create a new permission level that it is shared across your site collection.

By default, the reports will inherit the security settings of the document library, and the document library will inherit the settings of the site. You can break the inheritance at two levels: first at the document library and second at the item level. Remember that when you do break inheritance, you are adding the work of maintaining the security at the item level. It is not recommended to do item-level security when you have hundreds of items; instead the best way is to logically group them and secure them that way.

How to Break Security Inheritance

To break inheritance, hover over the report item you wish to secure, and under the Context menu click Manage Permissions, as shown in Figure 8-30. Once the Permissions page loads, click the Actions menu and click Edit Permissions, as shown in Figure 8-31.

Figure 8-31

Once you click on the Edit Permissions link, you will get a warning letting you know that you are breaking inheritance; click OK and continue. At this point, you will have the security settings editable, as shown in Figure 8-32. You will have check boxes next to your security groups and/or users who have access to this item. You can select the group and change its security level, or you can just delete the group entirely. Deleting the group will take away access from that group.

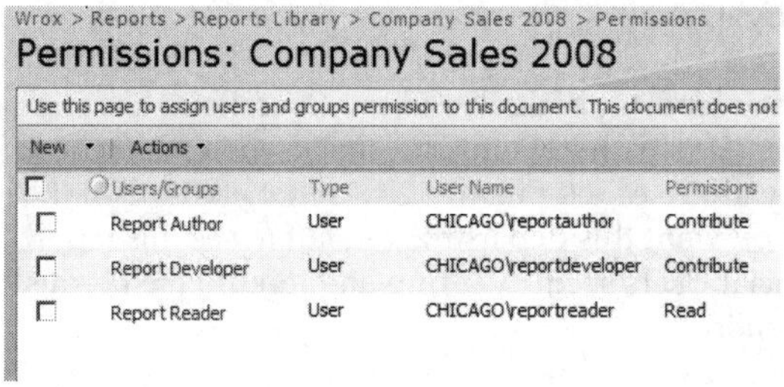

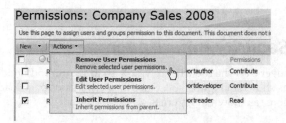

Figure 8-32

For example, to take out the Report Reader group, click the check box and click Actions ⇨ Remove User Permissions, as shown in Figure 8-33. At this point, you will get a warning message asking you to confirm that you are deleting the permission for the item; go ahead and click OK to this warning. With that final step, you will have successfully removed the Report Reader group from the item.

Figure 8-33

After breaking inheritance, if you choose to revert your changes, you can do this by going to the Actions menu and clicking the Inherit Permissions option. Once you click Inherit Permissions, your report item will immediately return to its original state and inherit from the document library that inherits from the site.

Summary

Typically, deploying the report is the last step of the process, but with SharePoint integrated mode, this is only the beginning. In this chapter, you walked through the steps that allowed you to deploy reports to SharePoint. You explored the dos and don'ts when preparing your SharePoint environment. And you learned some quick tips when deploying reports with BIDS and Report Builder 2.0.

Having read this chapter, you have a high-level understating of deploying reports to SharePoint. This chapter is a very good base for the following chapters in this book. Now that you have a good understanding of the basics in deploying reports to SharePoint, you are ready to go through the chapters that discuss advanced techniques when deploying reports and also the managing-reports chapter that talks about the steps after deployment.

9

Advanced Deployment Techniques

Once a report has been created, it must be published to SharePoint so that it can be viewed by end users. In previous chapters, you learned how you can use Business Intelligence Development Studio (BIDS) or Report Builder to publish your reports and other content to a report server instance configured in SharePoint integrated mode. Truthfully, there are more proper ways to publish and deploy your reports. Publishing and deploying a report doesn't have to be done from within Visual Studio! This leads to a question: What is proper and improper in publishing reports using BIDS?

First of all, BIDS is a development tool that's familiar to most report developers, but people who deploy reports and other content are not necessarily report developers; commonly, they are infrastructure people. Second, a lot of customers do not allow BIDS to be installed on their production infrastructure. Third, BIDS doesn't offer any automation capability, and this inflexibility poses particular challenges during the application's life cycle for report developers and IT administrators.

> This chapter uses the term *solution* to refer to the solution package mechanism specific to installation and deployment in SharePoint. The term *feature* refers to a new addition to the SharePoint product that facilitates adding or updating functionalities into existing SharePoint sites. The term *SharePoint web application* refers specifically to a web application based in Internet Information Services (IIS) and provisioned by the Windows SharePoint Services engine. The term *application* is used generally to describe the set of functionality under development to solve a particular business problem.

Thankfully, in the latest SharePoint release, Microsoft introduced a feature and solution framework that provides report developers with an easy way to move reports among development, test, and production environments. This also empowers site owners and administrators to move reports and other content across multiple servers without developer involvement. In addition to the SharePoint's native deployment mechanism, many repetitive tasks of reporting server administration and management such as deployment can be automated using script files. This chapter explores details of some of the more advanced deployment techniques and provides guidance and ideas to ensure that your Business Intelligence applications are successfully migrated among development, test, and production environments.

Understanding the Publishing Process

Before you move on to creating custom deployment solutions, you should understand what happens under the cover when a report and the related files are deployed in Business Intelligence Development Studio (BIDS) or Report Builder. After you have designed and tested your reports, you can use Report Designer in BIDS to publish or deploy them to a report server instance.

In Reporting Services, the terms publish and deploy are interchangeable.

Just Publish It!

One of the first steps you need to take to publish a report is to set the TargetDataSourceFolder, TargetReportFolder, and TargetServerURL properties in a business intelligence project. As discussed earlier in this book, these properties point to fully qualified URLs of a SharePoint site and document libraries that contain the reports and related files. Although the publishing process may seem simple at first glance, there is more to it than just moving the content.

First, the authoring tool validates reports and related files before they are added to the destination document libraries. If you bypass this process by uploading the reports and related files directly (via browser or Explorer views) to a SharePoint library, the validation check never occurs. This means you never know if your reporting files are valid until either you manually access them or a background process such as snapshots, subscriptions, or a caching facility references them. Second, when you publish a shared data source to a SharePoint document library, the .rds file extension is converted to an .rsds file name extension, as shown in Figure 9-1.

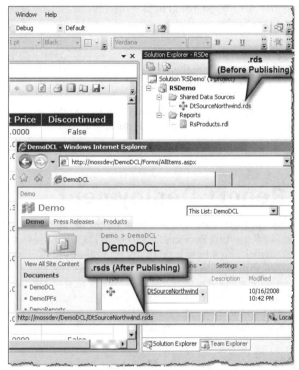

Figure 9-1

Both .rds and .rsds files have the same content but different schemas. The .rsds file cannot be saved locally from a SharePoint site and imported into an existing Reporting Services project or vice versa.

The .rsds file extension is only recognizable by SharePoint by the file extension mapping the insertion into the `Docicon.xml` file when the Reporting Services add-in for SharePoint is installed on SharePoint web front end servers. Start Windows Explorer and then browse to `Drive:\Program Files\Common Files\Microsoft Shared\Web Server Extensions\12\Template\XML`. Open the `Docicon.xml` file and locate the `.rsds` extension, as shown in Figure 9-2.

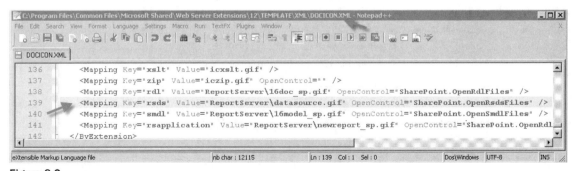

Figure 9-2

The process of converting the .rds file extension to .rsds involves a call, by an authoring tool, to the `CreateDataSource()` web method located at the `ReportService2006.asmx` endpoint.

Finally, there is one more thing that the publishing process does for you. If you happen to publish a report that already exists in the destination document library, the report will be checked out, updated as a new version, and then checked back in for you.

The next section covers building your custom solutions that follow the same publishing behavior as the authoring tool with the exception of having more programmatic control over the publishing process, so keep reading!

Automating Report Deployment

At times it can be quite challenging to satisfy customers' reporting needs using the out-of-the-box functionality that SQL Server Reporting Services 2008 offers. The main focus of Reporting Services is to provide an extensible framework and a new level of interoperability that enables developers to build custom Business Intelligence applications more easily than before. Developers can use any developer tool or platform to interact with a report server instance and its hosted reports, as long as those tools or platforms work with SOAP, WSDL, and UDDI capabilities. This makes it easier to create reports that leverage packaged or custom applications in almost any environment. It's all about making developers' tasks more seamless and their life much easier, right? If it's easy to use, more people will use it!

Anatomy of the ReportServer Folder

As part of the installation of the Reporting Services Add-in, a bunch of proxy endpoints are created in the `12/ISAPI/ReportServer` folder, as shown in Figure 9-3. These SOAP APIs provide several web service endpoints that developers can use to manage a report server instance configured in SharePoint integrated mode or simply interact with reports in their custom reporting solutions.

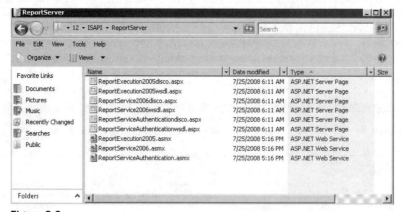

Figure 9-3

> The SQL Server 2000 report server proxy endpoint, which was deprecated in SQL Server Reporting Services 2005, is discontinued in Server Reporting Services 2008. If you have custom solutions built against that endpoint, you should point them to the new endpoints.

The SQL Server Reporting Services proxy endpoints installed by SQL Server Reporting Services Add-in for SharePoint fall into two main categories:

❑ Management

❑ Execution

The management functionality of a SharePoint-integrated report server is exposed through the ReportService2006 proxy endpoint (`ReportService2006.asmx`). The execution and navigation functionality of reports are exposed through the ReportExecution2005proxy endpoint (`ReportExecution2005.asmx`). This endpoint will continue to work in both native and SharePoint integrated modes, while the ReportService2006 proxy endpoint is exclusive to SharePoint integrated mode.

If you look at Figure 9-3, you will see that there is another proxy endpoint called `ReportServiceAuthentication.asmx`. This endpoint is primarily responsible for authenticating users against a report server when the SharePoint web application is configured for Forms Authentication when Integration Authentication mode is set to Trusted Account, as shown in Figure 9-4.

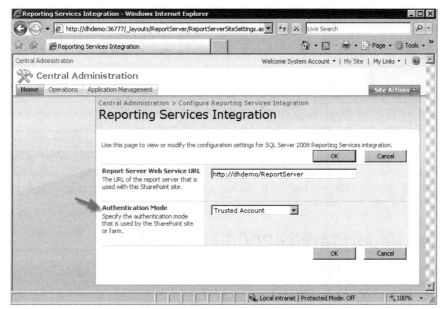

Figure 9-4

The beauty of setting the authentication mode to Trusted Account is that when developing against the proxy endpoints, Reporting Services Add-in handles the exchange of credentials between the SharePoint server and the report server, and that is the security context under which the SharePoint web application is set to.

> Reporting Services proxy endpoints are SharePoint context aware. The Reporting Services Add-in installs its proxy endpoints in a subfolder called ReportServer in the ISAPI folder. The ISAPI folder is a perfect place to share these proxy endpoints among all SharePoint web applications and get them to run within the SharePoint context.

To make a web service SharePoint aware, all you need to do is place it in the ISAPI folder. Thankfully, the Reporting Services team did not stop there and leave developers with only a bunch of web services. They virtualized all of the exposed endpoints by providing a `.disco` and a `.wsdl` ASPX pages for each endpoint, which makes them discoverable (that is, when adding a web service reference in VS.NET IDE), no matter how deeply they are referenced in the overall SharePoint site hierarchy. For example, `http://MyServer/_vti_bin/ReportServer/ReportService2006.asmx` or `http://MyServer/Subsite1/_vti_bin/ReportServer/ReportService2006.asmx` will be resolved to the same endpoint. This redirection and virtualization technique is covered in great detail on MSDN (`http://www.devhorizon.com/go/3`).

Creating a PowerShell Script

Many repetitive tasks of report server administration and management can be automated using familiar scripting languages. Additionally, there are a lot of things you can do with PowerShell on SharePoint server, either interactively to control SharePoint via its Object Model or to create scripts that can be run in a batch to automate certain tasks. PowerShell plays very well with many Microsoft products and is built entirely on top of the .NET platform. PowerShell is an object-based shell, and its tight integration with .NET brings the consistency and ease of use of .NET to IT professionals without requiring them to be experts in programming languages such as C# or VB.NET. That being said, the preferred scripting language for this section is the powerful Windows PowerShell, but nothing prevents you from rewriting the script demonstrated in this section using the scripting language of your choice, such as VB Script.

In this section, you will create a PowerShell script that publishes reports and related data sources to an instance of report server configured in SharePoint integrated mode. The example provided in this section can be extended to cover scenarios such as copying reports from one server to another or even tweaking the permission sets once the reports and data sources have been published. Finally, you can schedule the script to run when traffic is low without affecting the responsiveness of your SharePoint sites. PowerShell scripts can be created using any text editors, but ideally you should use an environment that has support for syntax highlighting, code completion, and IntelliSense. One option is an open-source extensible administrative console based on Windows PowerShell called PowerShell GUI. This tool can be found at `http://www.devhorizon.com/go/7`.

Compiling ReportService2006 Endpoint

As you may know, in PowerShell you cannot reference an assembly, nor can you reference a web service as you do in Visual Studio IDE. You need to compile the `ReportService2006.asmx` endpoint and generate the assembly first and then load it up in your script. There are a few ways to accomplish this, but most likely the easiest way is just by using the `wsdl.exe` command and C# compiler. You have some preparatory steps to perform before you dive into coding the script file.

Browse to the Visual Studio command line and run the following command:

```
wsdl http://Server_URL/_vti_bin/ReportServer/ReportService.asmx
```

`wsdl.exe` parses the `ReportService2006.asmx` schema and its WSDL file and generates a .NET class named `ReportService2006.cs`. If the .NET framework SDK path is not present in the `PATH` system variable, simply browse to `Drive:\Program Files\Microsoft.NET\FrameworkSDK\Bin\` `directory` to run `wsdl.exe`. At this point, you should have `ReportService2006.cs` in the current folder. Next, invoke and point the C# compiler (`csc.exe`) to the generated class and create the `dll` using the following command:

```
csc /t:library ReportService2006.cs
```

This command will generate an assembly named `ReportService2006.dll` that you need to load in your script. Place the `dll` in the folder in which you will create the script. Most likely, at this point your folder structure looks similar to the folder structure shown in Figure 9-5. For this example, you now place all the reports and related files that you want to publish in a folder called Artifacts. All right, the steps for your script to function properly are complete, and you can start coding the actual script file.

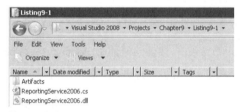

Figure 9-5

A Sample Deployment PowerShell Script

Here is an example of a PowerShell script used to publish reports and data sources to an instance of Reporting Services configured in integrated mode. The main part of the script is the entry point into the application. As shown in the code snippet below, the deployment script begins with parsing the parameters and setting up four variables to hold destination values for the source folder, which contains reports and data sources to be published, target data source and report document libraries, and finally the URL that points to the `ReportService2006.asmx` proxy endpoint. Typically, these variables are needed for the deployment script to work properly, and they may vary from one environment to another.

```
param
(
[string] $sourceFolder   =$(throw 'Parameter -sourceFolder is missing!'),
[string] $targetRptLib    =$(throw 'Parameter -targetRptLib is missing!'),
[string] $targetDCL      =$(throw 'Parameter -targetDCL is missing!'),
[string] $rsProxyEndpt    =$(throw 'Parameter -rsProxyEndpt is missing!')
)
```

Once the local variables are initialized, the tricky step you need to take is to load the `ReportService2006.dll` into PowerShell. From then on, it's much like typical C# programming, with slightly different syntax for object constructors.

```
$void=[Reflection.Assembly]::LoadFrom("ReportingService2006.dll")
```

First, you create a new object from `ReportingService2006` class using the `New-Object` cmdlet (pronounced "commandlet") and store it in the `$rs06` variable. Next, set the URL of the instance (`$rs06`) based on the value of the `$rsProxyEndpt` parameter. Then, the credentials for the current user are passed to the proxy to provide a security context.

```
$rs06 = New-Object ReportingService2006
$rs06.Url = $rsProxyEndpt;
$rs06.Credentials=[System.Net.CredentialCache]::DefaultCredentials
```

Next, the code goes to the source folder (`$sourceFolder` parameter), loops through all the files, and stores the names of files in the respective object array. This is done via a call to the `GetFiles()` method of the `System.IO.Directory` class, which returns the names of files in the source directory that match the specified search pattern (*.rds or *.rdl). Finally, the code loops through each `Object` array and hands each array item over to the respective helper function for further processing. Each data source is passed to `publish-DataSource()` function, and each report is passed to the `publish-Report()` function.

```
#Publish Data sources
[Object[]] $dataSourcesToPublish = [System.IO.Directory]::GetFiles($sourceFolder,
"*.rds");
$dataSourcesToPublish | % { publish-DataSource $_ };
#Publish Data sources
[Object[]] $reportsToPublish = [System.IO.Directory]::GetFiles($sourceFolder,
"*.rdl");
$reportsToPublish | % { publish-Report $_ };
```

Now let's take a look at `publish-DataSource()` as shown in the code snippet below. In the `publish-DataSource()` function, the `Get-Content()` cmdlet gets the content of the data source at the location specified by the path and stores it in the `$DSXml` variable of type `[xml]`. In the next line, an object of type `[DataSourceDefinition]` is instantiated that describes the connection properties for the new data source that will be published to the destination data source document library later in this function.

Next, a new `[DataSource]` object is created, and its `Item` property is set to the data source definition created above. The next lines simply read the data source settings from the returned XML content and populate related properties of the `$dsDefinition` object. As you can tell, the code keeps to the smallest data source settings to make the example as simple as possible, so feel free to make it as complicated as you want.

```
    function publish-DataSource ([string] $dsReference)
{
    #Load the data source Xml
    [xml] $DSXml = Get-Content ($dsReference);
    #Initialize a DataSourceDefinition object
    [DataSourceDefinition] $dsDefinition = New-Object DataSourceDefinition
    #Initialize a DataSource object
    [DataSource] $dSource = New-Object DataSource
    $dSource.Item = $dsDefinition
    #Read the settings from XML and populate related props
    $dsDefinition.Extension = $DSXml.RptDataSource.ConnectionProperties.Extension
    $dsDefinition.ConnectString =
    $DSXml.RptDataSource.ConnectionProperties.ConnectString
```

```
    $dsDefinition.ImpersonateUserSpecified = $true
    $dsDefinition.Prompt = $null
    $dsDefinition.WindowsCredentials = $true
    $dsDefinition.CredentialRetrieval = [CredentialRetrievalEnum]::Integrated
    $dSource.Name = $DSXml.RptDataSource.Name
    $dsFileName = [String]::Concat($DSXml.RptDataSource.Name.Trim(),".rsds")
    $rsdsAbsoluteUrl = [string]::Concat($targetDCL.TrimEnd("/"),"/",$dsFileName)
    # Code omitted for brevity
}
```

> Shared data sources give you the ability to configure and manage a single entry to the underlying data structure for use by multiple reports and subscriptions. If you use shared data sources and have a few of them in the final deployment package, in your deployment script, setting up connection properties exactly as what they should be on the server is not really that important. You can programmatically publish a dummy data source and reference it in all reports. When everything is out on the server, go to the data connection library and fix up the data source to point to the right connection settings. Remember, one of the features that Reporting Services 2008 in integrated mode offers is the ability to configure data source properties from within SharePoint UI.

Once all the properties are set, you can publish the new data source.

```
function publish-DataSource ([string] $dsReference)
{
  #Omitted code for brevity
  #Publish the data source to the data connection library
  $void = $rs06.CreateDataSource($dsFileName, $targetDCL, $true, $dsDefinition,
  $null)
  WRITE-HOST -FOREGROUND Yellow 'Successfully converetd data source:' $dsFileName
}
```

The actual data source publishing process is done via a call into the `CreateDataSource()` method of the `$rs06` object. This method takes five parameters:

❑ **Data Source:** The name of the data source. This is just the name without a path and including the .rds extension.

❑ **Parent Document Library:** The full path to the document library that will host the data source.

❑ **Overwrite:** A Boolean expression that indicates whether an existing data source with the same name in the target data source document library should be overwritten.

❑ **Definition:** An object of type `[DataSourceDefinition]`.

❑ **Properties:** An array of `Property[]` objects that defines the property names and values to set for the data source. In this example, this is set to `$null`.

With the data source publishing process completed, next you need to publish your reports. To do so, you use the `publish-Report()` function. Let's discuss the first part of the `publish-Report()` function shown below.

```
function publish-Report ([string] $rptReference)
{
    [Warning[]]$warnings = $null
    #Get the RDL Item
    $rptFileInfo = Get-Item ($rptReference);
    $rptName = $rptFileInfo.Name;
    #Load the RDL Xml
    [xml] $rptXml = Get-Content ($rptReference);
    #Extract the data source used by report
    $localDSName = $rptXml.Report.DataSources.DataSource.Name
    #Load the RDL Binary
    [Byte[]]$rptContent = Get-Content $rptReference -Encoding byte
    #Publish the report to the Report library
    [CatalogItem] $item = $rs06.CreateReport
    ($rptName,$targetRptLib,$true,$rptContent,$null,[ref] $warnings )
    WRITE-HOST -FOREGROUND GREEN 'Successfully published report:' $rptName

    # --Omitted Code for Brevity--
}
```

First, the `Get-Item()` cmdlet retrieves the report item at the specified location and stores its name in the `$rptName` variable. This doesn't return "content." The first `Get-Content()` cmdlet gets the content of the report at the location specified by the path.

Next, the data source name used by the report is extracted and stored in the `$localDSName` variable. The second `Get-Content()` cmdlet simply loads the binary representation of the report file into an array of type `Byte[]`. Finally, the `CreateReport()` method of the `$rs06` object is called, and appropriate parameters are passed to the method. The `CreateReport()` method would return an object of type `[CatalogItem]`, which represents an item in the report server database that will be used later to fix up the data source pointer in the published report.

The `CreateReport()` method takes six parameters: the first parameter points to the report name; the second parameter is the target report library; the third parameter indicates whether to overwrite an existing report or not; the fourth parameter is the report binary content; the fifth parameter is similar to the `Properties` parameter in the `CreateDataSource()` method; the sixth parameter is an array of `[Warning[]]` objects that describes any warnings that occurred when the report definition was validated. Recall from an earlier discussion that I pointed to a validation process that takes place during the publishing process.

The second part of the `publish-Report()` function is pretty self-explanatory. An absolute path to the newly published report is passed to the `GetItemDataSources()` method, and the data source used in the report is retrieved into the `$catalogItemDtSrcs` array. In this example, it is assumed that the report only used one data source. Next, a new `[DataSource]` object is created, and by calling the `SetItemDataSources()` method, the data source of the report is fixed and points to the right data source, which was published in the first helper method. That's basically it!

```
function publish-Report ([string] $rptReference)
{

    # --Omitted Code for Brevity--

    #Fix up the data source
    $rptAbsoluteUrl = [string]::Concat($targetRptLib.TrimEnd("/"),"/",$rptName)
```

```
    $rsdsAbsoluteUrl = [string]::Concat($targetDCL.TrimEnd
    ("/"),"/",$localDSName,".rsds")
    [DataSource[]] $catalogItemDtSrcs = $rs06.GetItemDataSources($rptAbsoluteUrl)
    [DataSourceReference] $reference = New-Object DataSourceReference
    [DataSource] $dsNew = New-Object DataSource
    $reference.Reference = $rsdsAbsoluteUrl
    $dsNew = $catalogItemDtSrcs[0]
    $dsNew.Item = $reference
    $void = $rs06.SetItemDataSources($rptAbsoluteUrl,$catalogItemDtSrcs)
}
```

The complete code for the script can be found in the code download for this book.

Now let's look at the entire script put together in Listing 9-1.

Listing 9-1: A sample deployment PowerShell Script

```
param (
    [string] $sourceFolder =$(throw 'Parameter -sourceFolder is missing!'),
    [string] $targetRptLib =$(throw 'Parameter -targetRptLib is   missing!'),
    [string] $targetDCL    =$(throw 'Parameter -targetDCL is missing!'),
    [string] $rsProxyEndpt =$(throw 'Parameter -rsProxyEndpt is missing!')
    )
function publish-DataSource ([string] $dsReference)
{
    #Load the data source Xml
    [xml] $DSXml = Get-Content ($dsReference);
    #Initialize a DataSourceDefinition object
     [DataSourceDefinition] $dsDefinition = New-Object DataSourceDefinition
    #Initialize a DataSource object
     [DataSource] $dSource = New-Object DataSource
    $dSource.Item = $dsDefinition
    #Read the settings from XML and populate related props
    $dsDefinition.Extension = $DSXml.RptDataSource.ConnectionProperties.Extension

    $dsDefinition.ConnectString =
    $DSXml.RptDataSource.ConnectionProperties.ConnectString
    $dsDefinition.ImpersonateUserSpecified = $true
    $dsDefinition.Prompt = $null
    $dsDefinition.WindowsCredentials = $true
    $dsDefinition.CredentialRetrieval = [CredentialRetrievalEnum]::Integrated
    $dSource.Name = $DSXml.RptDataSource.Name
    $dsFileName = [String]::Concat($DSXml.RptDataSource.Name.Trim(),".rsds")
    $rsdsAbsoluteUrl = [string]::Concat($targetDCL.TrimEnd("/"),"/",$dsFileName)
    #Publish the data source to the data connection library
    $void = $rs06.CreateDataSource($dsFileName, $targetDCL, $true, $dsDefinition,
    $null)
    WRITE-HOST -FOREGROUND Yellow 'Successfully converetd data source:' $dsFileName
}

function publish-Report ([string] $rptReference)
{
    [Warning[]]$warnings = $null
```

(continued)

Listing 9-1: (Continued)

```
#Get the RDL Item
$rptFileInfo = Get-Item ($rptReference);
$rptName = $rptFileInfo.Name;
#Load the RDL Xml
  [xml] $rptXml = Get-Content ($rptReference);
#Extract the data source used by report
$localDSName = $rptXml.Report.DataSources.DataSource.Name
#Load the RDL Binary
  [Byte[]]$rptContent = Get-Content $rptReference -Encoding byte
#Publish the report to the Report library
  [CatalogItem] $item =
$rs06.CreateReport($rptName,$targetRptLib,$true,$rptContent,$null,[ref]
  $warnings )
WRITE-HOST -FOREGROUND GREEN 'Successfully published report:' $rptName

#Fix up the data source
$rptAbsoluteUrl = [string]::Concat($targetRptLib.TrimEnd("/"),"/",$rptName)
$rsdsAbsoluteUrl =
[string]::Concat($targetDCL.TrimEnd("/"),"/",$localDSName,".rsds")
[DataSource[]] $catalogItemDtSrcs =

$rs06.GetItemDataSources($rptAbsoluteUrl)
[DataSourceReference] $reference = New-Object DataSourceReference
[DataSource] $dsNew = New-Object DataSource
$reference.Reference = $rsdsAbsoluteUrl
$dsNew = $catalogItemDtSrcs[0]
$dsNew.Item = $reference
$void = $rs06.SetItemDataSources($rptAbsoluteUrl,$catalogItemDtSrcs)
}

$void=[Reflection.Assembly]::LoadFrom("ReportingService2006.dll")
$rs06 = New-Object ReportingService2006
$rs06.Url = $rsProxyEndpt;
$rs06.Credentials=[System.Net.CredentialCache]::DefaultCredentials

#Publish Data sources
[Object[]] $dataSourcesToPublish = [System.IO.Directory]::GetFiles($sourceFolder,
"*.rds");
$dataSourcesToPublish | % { publish-DataSource $_ };

#Publish Data sources
[Object[]] $reportsToPublish = [System.IO.Directory]::GetFiles($sourceFolder,
"*.rdl");
$reportsToPublish | % { publish-Report $_ };
```

The full PowerShell source used in Listing 9-1 can be found in the associated code download for this book.

Start Windows PowerShell either by clicking the Windows PowerShell shortcut link or by typing **PowerShell** in the run dialog box. Browse to where you have all the files and type the command line shown in Figure 9-6. Note that if you want to deploy to folders in the destination document libraries, those folders must have been created in advance or your deployment code should create those folders by calling into SharePoint object model. In the PowerShell source used in Listing 9-1, it is assumed a folder called POSH already exists in the destination libraries, but the sample deployment script works fine with whatever destination folder you provide as the `targetRptLib` parameter when executing it via a command line.

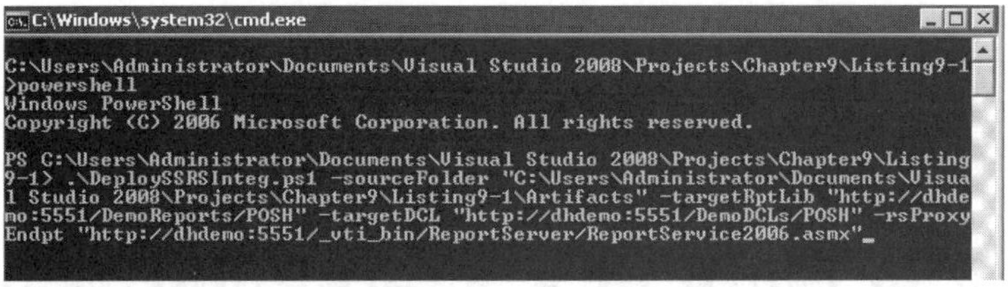

Figure 9-6

As you can see in Figure 9-7, PowerShell script publishes all reports and data sources placed in Artifacts folder.

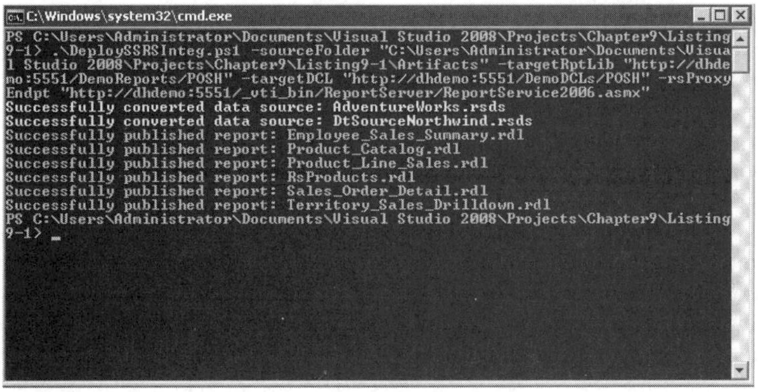

Figure 9-7

At this point, you should be able to see reports and their shared data source available in the POSH folder in both target document libraries, as shown in Figures 9-8 and 9-9.

Figure 9-8

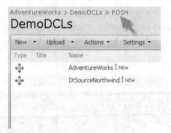

Figure 9-9

Deploying in More of a SharePoint Way

As alluded to earlier in this chapter, in the latest Windows SharePoint Services 3.0 release, Microsoft has introduced a new unified infrastructure to make deployment in SharePoint a lot easier than it used to be by offering feature and solution frameworks. The feature framework not only makes it a cinch to introduce new functionality or apply changes to the existing site functionality at specific scopes; it also empowers administrators with the ability to do their daily deployment tasks.

Recall from the introduction of this chapter that administrators are not necessarily developers, so it's quite reasonable not to expect them to be familiar with tools that developers use on a daily basis. The beauty of the solution framework is that it enables administrators to easily install files on the front-end web servers in a server farm or move them from one farm to another farm across the enterprise without requiring developer support.

In this section, you will use the solution and feature capabilities of Windows SharePoint Services 3.0 to package all of your reports and related files as one single file, add the file to the solution store, and deploy it to the front-end web servers. Once the solution package is deployed and the related feature has been created, you will then activate the feature. When the feature is activated, SharePoint performs the work defined in the feature receiver as follows:

❑ Programmatically creates an instance of the data connection library template.

❑ Programmatically creates an instance of the report library template.

❑ Publishes reports and data sources to the newly created data connection and report library.

Predeployment Configuration Settings

Before you move on to the coding of the main feature and because the entire chapter is focused on making your report deployment as automated as possible, let's put together a proper predeployment configuration management plan. In this section, you will parameterize the name of the Report and Data Connection libraries that will be created before the main feature is activated.

The final component is yet another custom feature responsible for creating two web application property bags (SPWebApplication.Properties) that contain the name of the Report and Data Connection libraries. The main feature will then use these configuration settings for creating the required document libraries and publishing reports and other related files to them.

The markup in Listing 9-2 shows the feature definition file that contains information needed to define the characteristics of the feature. The first thing to note is that feature is scoped to `WebApplication`. In addition, there is a `ReceiverAssembly` attribute that contains the assembly's strong name and the `ReceiverClass` that contains a fully qualified name to the feature receiver class that gets called when the feature's state is changed.

Listing 9-2: Feature Definition with a Feature Receiver

```xml
<?xml version="1.0" encoding="utf-8"?>
<Feature   Id="d2bf5d44-ff9d-46e0-8c34-81a2aefa52b1"
    Title="PersistSSRSDepSettings"
    Description="Creates two property bags that contain the name of the Report and
    Data Connection libraries used in the example provided in Chapter 9"
    Version="12.0.0.0"
    Hidden="FALSE"
    Scope="WebApplication"
    DefaultResourceFile="core"
    ReceiverAssembly="FeaturizedDeployment, Version=1.0.0.0, Culture=neutral,
    PublicKeyToken=4f832458f52648b8"
    ReceiverClass="FeaturizedDeployment.PersistSSRSDepSettings"
    xmlns="http://schemas.microsoft.com/sharepoint/">
</Feature>
```

At this point, you need to code the feature receiver and override the desired event handlers. The code in Listing 9-3 demonstrates how to add two property bags in a feature receiver that implements two events: `FeatureActivated` and `FeatureDeactivating`. When the feature gets activated, property bags are added, and once the feature is deactivated they are deleted. This class needs to be compiled into a signed assembly and deployed to Global Assembly Cache (GAC).

Listing 9-3: Persisting Deployment Configuration Settings Using the Feature Receiver

```csharp
using System;
using Microsoft.SharePoint;
using Microsoft.SharePoint.Administration;

namespace FeaturizedDeployment
{
    public class PersistSSRSDepSettings : SPFeatureReceiver
    {
        public const string ReportLibraryKey = "ReportLibraryKey";
        public const string DataConnectionLibraryKey =
        "DataConnectionLibraryKey";

        public override void FeatureActivated(SPFeatureReceiverProperties
        properties)
        {
            SPWebApplication wepApp = properties.Feature.Parent as
            SPWebApplication;

            if (wepApp != null)
            {
```

(continued)

Listing 9-3: (Continued)

```
            wepApp.Properties.Add(ReportLibraryKey, "ReportsDemo");
            wepApp.Properties.Add(DataConnectionLibraryKey, "DCLsDemo");
            wepApp.Update();
        }
    }
    public override void FeatureDeactivating(SPFeatureReceiverProperties
    properties)
    {
        SPWebApplication wepApp = properties.Feature.Parent as
        SPWebApplication;
        if (wepApp != null)
        {
            if (wepApp.Properties.ContainsKey(ReportLibraryKey))
                wepApp.Properties.Remove(ReportLibraryKey);
            if(wepApp.Properties.ContainsKey(DataConnectionLibraryKey))
                wepApp.Properties.Remove(DataConnectionLibraryKey);
            wepApp.Update();
        }
    }

    public override void FeatureInstalled(SPFeatureReceiverProperties
    properties) {/*No Op*/}
    public override void FeatureUninstalling(SPFeatureReceiverProperties
    properties) { /*No Op*/}
    }
}
```

To maintain complete control over how end users will manage configuration settings and to provide an elegant experience, you need to allow them to override these settings in the appSettings element of the web.config file. This comes in very handy if your solution is deployed to an environment where activating web application-scoped features is not allowed. And yes, those environments do exist in real life, especially in hosting providers!

At this point, you need to create a helper class that retrieves the configuration setting values from the web application's property bags. In case the property bags don't exist (meaning the web application-scoped feature is not activated), the helper class should retrieve the values from appSettings element of web.config file, as shown in Listing 9-4.

Listing 9-4: Helper Class to Retrieve Deployment Settings

```
using System;
using Microsoft.SharePoint;
using System.Configuration;
using Microsoft.SharePoint.Administration;

namespace FeaturizedDeployment
{
    public class SettingLocator
    {
        private const string ReportLibraryKey = "ReportLibraryKey";
```

```
        private const string DataConnectionLibraryKey =
        "DataConnectionLibraryKey";

        public static string ReportLibraryName
        {
            get
            {
                string reportLibName =
                ConfigurationManager.AppSettings[ReportLibraryKey];
                if (string.IsNullOrEmpty(reportLibName) && SPContext.Current !=
                null)
                {
                    SPWebApplication app = null;
                    if (SPContext.Current != null)
                        app = SPContext.Current.Site.WebApplication;
                    if (app != null &&
                        app.Properties.ContainsKey(ReportLibraryKey))
                         reportLibName = (string)app.Properties[ReportLibraryKey];
                }
                return reportLibName;
            }
        }

        public static string DataConnectionLibraryName
        {
            get
            {
                string dclLibName =
                ConfigurationManager.AppSettings[DataConnectionLibraryKey];

                if (string.IsNullOrEmpty(dclLibName) && SPContext.Current
                != null)
                {
                    SPWebApplication app = null;
                    if (SPContext.Current != null)
                        app = SPContext.Current.Site.WebApplication;
                    if (app != null &&
                        app.Properties.ContainsKey(DataConnectionLibraryKey))
                        dclLibName =
                        (string)app.Properties[DataConnectionLibraryKey];
                }

                return dclLibName;
            }
        }
    }
}
```

Creating Document Library Instances via Code

Although SharePoint creates some document libraries for every SharePoint site (varying based on the type of site created), it also enables document libraries to be created by developers, administrators, and end users. As with many other things within SharePoint, there are various ways to create document libraries, and each option has advantages and disadvantages.

In this section, you will start working on the main feature by creating its definition file and related feature receiver. In the feature receiver class, you will override `FeatureActivated` event handler and write some custom code to accomplish a couple of things. First, you check to see if the libraries already exist. Then you create destination document libraries and finally publish the reports and related file. In this section, you look at the part that creates the document libraries. In the next section, you will code the rest of code that deals with publishing process.

In addition to basic information about the feature, note three things from the CAML in Listing 9-5. First, the `<ActivationDependencies>` element specifies that activation of the current feature depends on the enterprise feature and that's because of the data connection library functionality that the main feature relies on.

Second, the `ReceiverAssembly` and `ReceiverClass` attributes in the feature schema point to the `PublishSSRSReports` class shown in Listing 9-6.

> **A well-implemented feature is one that not only does cool stuff but also cleans up after itself if required. You need to complete the feature receiver shown in Listing 9-6, so when the feature is deactivating, the code cleans up the document libraries. Clean up action in features always must be done with extra caution so they do not break other functionalities that may depend on resources that might be wiped out. Due to space constraints and readability, not all the code required to complete this solution is included in this book.**

Third, the report and the shared data source files have been referenced in the `<ElementFile>` element. This will ensure that when the feature is installed, all the unpublished reporting artifacts are copied over to the feature folder in WSS system directory. In the next section, you will learn why you need these files in the feature folder.

Listing 9-5: Publish Reports Feature Definition

```xml
<?xml version="1.0" encoding="utf-8"?>
<Feature Id="adaf815a-4523-425b-a5dc-c4de8ce1a282"
    Title="PublishSSRSReports"
    Description="Publishes reports and related files to a Report library and Data
    Connection library. There is an activation dependency to ensure that
    enterprise feature is already turned on. "
    Version="12.0.0.0"
    Hidden="FALSE"
    Scope="Web"
    DefaultResourceFile="core"
    ReceiverAssembly="FeaturizedDeployment, Version=1.0.0.0, Culture=neutral,
    PublicKeyToken=4f832458f52648b8"
    ReceiverClass="FeaturizedDeployment.PublishSSRSReports"
    xmlns="http://schemas.microsoft.com/sharepoint/">

    <ActivationDependencies>
        <ActivationDependency FeatureId="C88C4FF1-DBF5-4649-AD9F-C6C426EBCBF5"/>
    </ActivationDependencies>

    <ElementManifests>
```

```
        <ElementFile Location="AdventureWorks.rds" />
        <ElementFile Location="Product_Catalog.rdl" />
    </ElementManifests>
</Feature>
```

Listing 9-6 demonstrates the code in `FeatureActivated` event handler, which is quite straight forward. The code simply checks to see if document libraries are already created, and if not, those are programmatically created. The statements used to create these document libraries are pretty standard SharePoint code used for creating any type of lists using SharePoint object model. Also notice that the names are extracted by calling into the helper class you created in Listing 9-4.

Listing 9-6: Publish Reports Feature Receiver to Create Document Libraries

```csharp
public class PublishSSRSReports : SPFeatureReceiver
{
    public override void FeatureActivated(SPFeatureReceiverProperties
    properties)
    {
        SPWeb web = properties.Feature.Parent as SPWeb;
        CreateLibraries(web);
        Publish(web);
    }
public override void
FeatureDeactivating(SPFeatureReceiverProperties properties)
{/*No Op*/}

public override void FeatureInstalled(SPFeatureReceiverProperties properties)
{/*No Op*/}

public override void    FeatureUninstalling(SPFeatureReceiverProperties
properties) {/*No Op*/}

private void Publish(SPWeb web){//Omitted code for brevity}

    private void CreateLibraries(SPWeb web)
    {
        try
        {
            // Check if the Report Library exists
            SPList tList = web.Lists[SettingLocator.ReportLibraryName];
        }
        catch
        {
            // Report Library does not exist - create it
            SPListTemplate template = web.ListTemplates["Report Library"];
            Guid gid = Guid.Empty;
            // Attempt to create the Report Library
            gid = web.Lists.Add(SettingLocator.ReportLibraryName, "Reports
            storage for the sample provided in Chapter 9", template);
            web.Update();
        }
```

(continued)

Listing 9-6: (Continued)

```
        try
        {
            // Check if the Data Connection Library exists
            SPList tList = web.Lists[SettingLocator.DataConnectionLibraryName];
        }
        catch
        {
            // Data Connection Library does not exist - create it
            SPListTemplate template = web.ListTemplates["Data   Connection
            Library"];
            Guid gid = Guid.Empty;
            // Attempt to create the Data Connection Library
            gid =
            web.Lists.Add(SettingLocator.DataConnectionLibraryName, "Data
            soucess storage for the sample provided in Chapter 9", template);
            web.Update();
        }
    }
}
```

Publishing Reports and Data Sources

All the important work of the `PublishSSRSReports` class happen in `Publish()` method, which is not included in Listing 9-6. This method is pretty similar to the `publish-Report()` and `publish-DataSource()` functions in the PowerShell script demonstrated in Listing 9-1 but uses managed code. There is one difference that needs to be highlighted here. As you can see in the highlighted section of Listing 9-7, instead of directly accessing the content of `*.rds` files, a cinch in PowerShell (using `Get-Content()` cmdlet and `[xml]` variable), you need to load the file into an `XMLDocument` object and use an XPath query to extract what you need to find out about the data source properties. Remember, `*.rds` and `*.rdl` are specialized XML files, so all the .NET XML luxury is available to developers when interacting with these files.

To keep things as simple as possible, unlike the PowerShell script discussed earlier in this chapter, the example demonstrated in this section is only limited to one shared data source per feature pack. Feel free to extend this solution to support publishing of more data sources or implementing more complicated requirements.

Listing 9-7: Publish Method

```
private void Publish(SPWeb web)
{
    FileStream stream = null;
    string fileName = string.Empty;
    try
    {
        ReportingService2006 rs06 = new ReportingService2006();
        rs06.Url = web.Url +
        "/_vti_bin/ReportServer/ReportService2006.asmx";
        rs06.Credentials = System.Net.CredentialCache.DefaultCredentials;
        string featurePath = string.Format(@"{0}\FEATURES\{1}\",
```

```
SPUtility.GetGenericSetupPath("Template"), @"PublishSSRSReports");
string[] reportPaths = Directory.GetFiles(featurePath, "*.rdl");
string[] dataSourcePath = Directory.GetFiles(featurePath, "*.rds");
if (dataSourcePath.Length != 1)
throw new Exception("Oops!Only one shared datasource per feature pack
or there is no datasource");

#region Simple rds to rsds conversion
XmlNode extensionNode = null;
XmlNode connectStringNode = null;
XmlNode rptDataSourceNameNode = null;

fileName = Path.GetFileName(dataSourcePath[0]).Replace("rds","rsds");
stream = File.OpenRead(dataSourcePath[0]);
XmlDocument dsDOM = new XmlDocument();
dsDOM.Load(stream);
stream.Close();
rptDataSourceNameNode = dsDOM.SelectSingleNode("RptDataSource/Name");
XmlNodeList connectionPropertiesNodes =
dsDOM.SelectNodes("RptDataSource/ConnectionProperties");
foreach (XmlNode node in connectionPropertiesNodes)
{
    extensionNode = node.SelectSingleNode("Extension");
    connectStringNode = node.SelectSingleNode("ConnectString");
}
DataSourceDefinition dsDefinition = new DataSourceDefinition();
DataSource dSource = new DataSource();

dSource.Item = dsDefinition;
dsDefinition.Extension = extensionNode.InnerText;
dsDefinition.ConnectString = connectStringNode.InnerText;
dsDefinition.ImpersonateUserSpecified = true;
dsDefinition.Prompt = null;
dsDefinition.WindowsCredentials = true;
dsDefinition.CredentialRetrieval =
CredentialRetrievalEnum.Integrated;
dSource.Name = rptDataSourceNameNode.InnerText;
string parentDataSourceLibrary =
string.Concat(web.Url,"/",SettingLocator.DataConnectionLibraryName);
string fullDSUrl = string.Concat(parentDataSourceLibrary, "/", fileName);
rs06.CreateDataSource(fileName, parentDataSourceLibrary, true,
dsDefinition, null);
#endregion
#region Publish rdl files
Warning[] warnings = null;

foreach (string rptPath in reportPaths)
{
    fileName = Path.GetFileName(rptPath);
    stream = File.OpenRead(rptPath);
    Byte[] definition = new Byte[stream.Length];
    stream.Read(definition, 0, (int)stream.Length);
```

(continued)

295

Listing 9-7: (Continued)

```
        stream.Close();
        string parentReportLibrary =  string.Concat(web.Url,"/",
                SettingLocator.ReportLibraryName);
        string fullReportURL = string.Concat(parentReportLibrary, "/",
        fileName);
        CatalogItem item = rs06.CreateReport(fileName, parentReportLibrary,
        true, definition, null, out warnings);
        foreach (Warning warning in warnings)
        {
            //Proceed with logging the warnings
        }

        #region Fix up Data source
        DataSource[] catalogItemDtSrcs =
        rs06.GetItemDataSources(fullReportURL);
        DataSourceReference reference = new DataSourceReference();
            DataSource dsNew = new DataSource();

        reference.Reference = fullDSUrl;
        dsNew = catalogItemDtSrcs[0];
        dsNew.Item = reference;
        rs06.SetItemDataSources(fullReportURL, catalogItemDtSrcs);
        #endregion

    }
        #endregion
    }
    Catch { // Code to handle the exceptions}
}
```

That's it! All of your deployment package files are fully coded and ready to be built into a SharePoint solution package (*.WSP file). Once you create and deploy that package, there should be two features scoped to SPWebApplication and SPWeb, as shown in Figures 9-10 and 9-11.

Figure 9-10

When you activate the feature shown in Figure 9-10, both property bags are persisted and become available to the code with enough permission to access the web application's property bags (`SPWebApplication.Properties`).

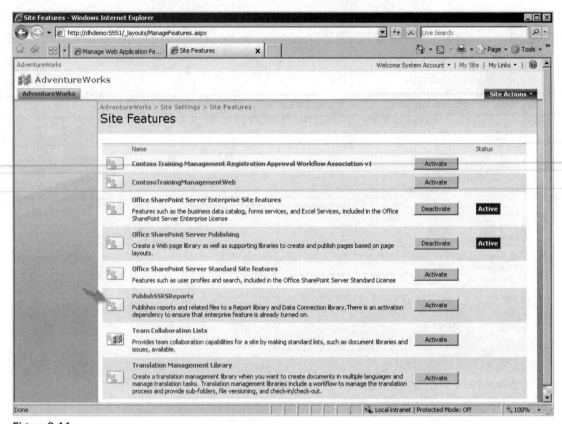

Figure 9-11

When you activate the feature shown in Figure 9-11, document libraries are created, and the report and its data source are published, as shown in Figures 9-12 and Figure 9-13.

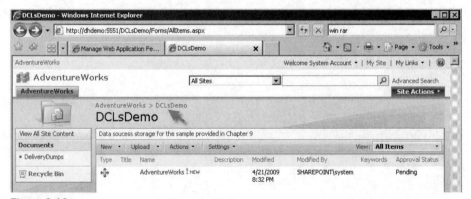

Figure 9-12

Figure 9-13

As stated before, part of the code is responsible for fixing up the data source once everything is up there and published (see Figure 9-14). When the feature is activated, there shouldn't be any orphaned reports, and if the data source is coded, it should be immediately available to be executed.

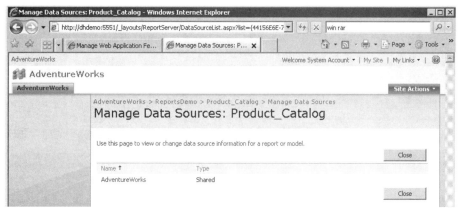

Figure 9-14

The full source, including both features and the sample report and data source used in this section, can be found in the associated code download for this book.

Summary

When you read SQL Server Reporting Services 2008 documentation and books online, it's recommended to use Business Intelligence Development Studio to deploy your reporting files. The issue is that people who are responsible for deployment are not necessarily developers and may not know how to use Visual Studio IDE. One might argue that they can be educated, but the second issue is that a lot of customers do not allow the installation of Visual Studio on their production environments. Directly uploading reports and data sources is not proper publishing, and in the case of data sources, it is not going to work.

To provide a custom deployment experience, this chapter demonstrated two options for automating the deployment of your reports and data sources to an instance of report server configured in SharePoint integrated mode. One option was by leveraging PowerShell scripting language, and the other option was to utilize Windows SharePoint Services 3.0 built-in packaging and deployment capability via solution and feature frameworks. In addition, this chapter demonstrated how developers can consume Reporting Services APIs via proxy endpoints installed as part of the integration Add-in.

10

Displaying Your Reports in SharePoint Integrated Mode

As discussed earlier, Microsoft SQL Server Reporting Services is a platform for building reporting solutions. Besides providing a wonderful report-processing engine and variety of development tools, this platform offers mechanisms for displaying reports to end users. When installed in SharePoint integrated mode, Reporting Services can integrate very well with SharePoint in the same way it integrates with any standard web application.

This chapter contains procedures for viewing reports from a SharePoint site. You will start with some of the out-of-the box functionalities such as the Report Viewer Web Part and out-of-the-box pages. Next, you will look at how to take things to the next level by combining SharePoint Web Parts and the Report Viewer Web Part. Later, toward the end of the chapter, you will dive into how you can extend out-of-the-box functionality to meet your report-delivery needs by displaying your reports the way you want. Remember, it's all about getting the best out of your investments in these two great products.

The Out-of-the-Box UI Experience

The out-of-the-box UI experience in Microsoft SQL Server Reporting Services is rich enough that some organizations do not even need to apply any customizations to the core platform. Unfortunately, many report developers overlook this platform and its capabilities, so this section focuses on the out-of-the-box experience and how to build BI solutions on top of it.

In this section, you will explore some of the key aspects of displaying your reports using what is already shipped with Reporting Services configured in SharePoint integrated mode. In particular, you will learn practical solutions using real-world examples to illustrate the possibilities of combining SharePoint and Reporting Services functionality to provide a better user experience for the BI solutions you build and deploy to your SharePoint sites.

Redirecting to the RSViewerPage.aspx Page

When you publish report definitions (.rdl) to a SharePoint library and select a report, it automatically opens a page (RSViewerPage.aspx) in the ReportServer folder in the _layouts system directory, so reports can be viewed within a Report Viewer Web Part embedded in that page. This redirection behavior is due to the fact that after you configure Reporting Services to operate in integrated mode, the appropriate .rdl extension association is defined at the SharePoint farm level. This gives the WSS runtime engine an understanding of how to treat files with the .rdl extension.

Go ahead and open the RSViewerPage.aspx page in a text editor or Visual Studio IDE and examine the content. Browse all the way down to the bottom of the page. The code snippet shown in Figure 10-1 illustrates how the Report Viewer Web Part is referenced in the RSViewerPage.aspx page.

```
1  <%@ Register TagPrefix="RSWP" Namespace="Microsoft.ReportingServices.SharePoint.UI.WebParts"
2  Assembly="Microsoft.ReportingServices.SharePoint.UI.WebParts,Version=10.0.0.0,Culture=neutral,PublicKeyToken=89845dcd8080cc91" %>
3  <!-- Code omitted for brevity -->
4                  <td style="height:100%" valign="top">
5                      <RSWP:ReportViewerWebPart id="m_sqlRsWebPart" runat="server" ChromeType="None" Height="100%" Width="100%" />
6                      <asp:PlaceHolder runat="server" ID="m_errorPlaceHolder"></asp:PlaceHolder>
7                  </td>
8  <!-- Code omitted for brevity -->
```

Figure 10-1

After a report is rendered, it opens in the RSViewerPage.aspx page, as indicated by the right arrow in Figure 10-2. At this point, you can use the report toolbar on the top of the Web Part to navigate pages, search, zoom, export, and print the report. Although the new Report Viewer Web Part installed by the Microsoft SQL Server Reporting Services 2008 Add-in has the same name as its predecessors, it is totally revamped to suit functionalities and enhancements made in the new version of Microsoft SQL Server Reporting Services 2008. One obvious difference is that the new Report Viewer Web Part has an Actions menu on the toolbar (see the left arrow in Figure 10-2).

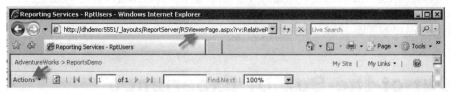

Figure 10-2

The Report Viewer Web Part

In addition to the out-of-the-box redirection to the `RSViewerPage.aspx`, there is another way of incorporating reports into your SharePoint sites through the use of the standalone Report Viewer Web Part. When is the Report Viewer Web Part useful? Consider a dashboard page on which there should be different reports making up multiple views into the underlying data or just as another example, when the out-of-the-box branding of the `RSViewerPage.aspx` page doesn't meet your look and feel requirements. The Report Viewer Web Part is ideal for such requirements.

Adding a Report Viewer Web Part to a page is as easy as dragging and dropping it into a Web Part zone and then setting some simple properties, but wait a minute! Where is this Web Part? This is one of the challenges that tips some people over the edge. Essentially, what happens is that administrators often forget that in addition to activating the Report Server Integration Feature at the farm level (in the Central Administration Site), it should also be activated on each site collection where integration is required. Yes, like many other things in SharePoint, SQL Server Reporting Services integration with SharePoint cannot cross the boundary of a site collection.

This feature can be activated on the Site Settings under Site collection features. When the feature is activated, browse to Site Settings, click the Web Parts link, and make sure you see ReportViewer.dwp, which is basically the descriptor of the Report Viewer Web Part and is physically located in the *Program Files\Common Files\Microsoft Shared\web server extensions\12\template\features\reportserver* folder. Figure 10-3 demonstrates the Report Viewer Web Part in the Web Part gallery of a site collection.

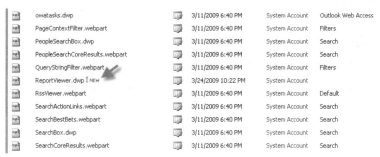

Figure 10-3

Now it's just about time to land an instance of the Report Viewer Web Part onto a SharePoint page.

1. Browse to Site Actions ⇨ Create Page.

2. In the Title text box, enter Dashboard.

3. Choose (Welcome Page) Blank Web Part Page from the available page layouts (see Figure 10-4).

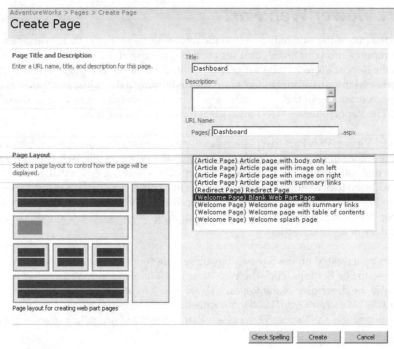

Figure 10-4

4.   Click the Create button.

5.   Go ahead and add an instance of the Report Viewer Web Part to the Right Web Part Zone; then click the Web Part menu and select Modify Shared Web Part to open the tool pane. Notice three extra tabs in the tool pane, which provide custom properties specific to the Report Viewer Web Part, as illustrated in Figure 10-5.

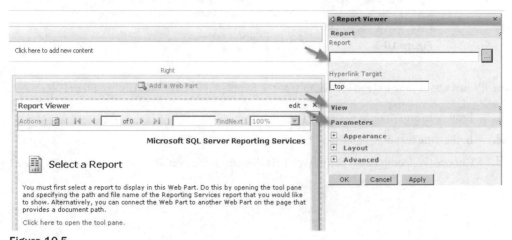

Figure 10-5

6. In the Report text box, specify the path and file name of your report. This URL must be a fully qualified path that points to a report in the current site collection, or in a site within the same web application or farm. See the "Report Viewer Web Part Limitations" section, later in this chapter, for more information. Figure 10-6 shows a rendered report in a Web Part page.

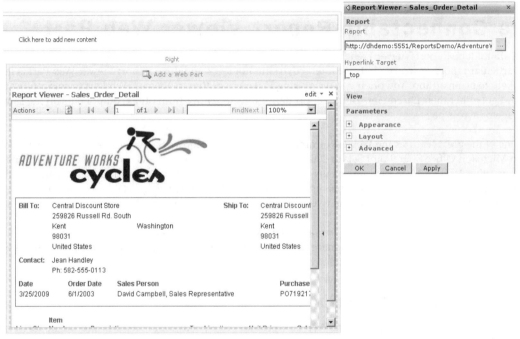

Figure 10-6

7. Leave the default View settings. For more information on customizing the Report Viewer Web Part, refer to the official documentation at `http://www.devhorizon.com/go/0`.

8. The Parameters tab appears only if the report you specified in step 6 accepts user input for parameters defined in the report. You can leave the report to use its default value, or you can override the report to render with another default value of your choice. (See Figure 10-7.)

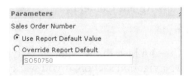

Figure 10-7

9. Click Apply at the bottom of the tool pane, and then click OK to close the pane.

In the preceding procedures, you set the report to run pretty much static with a default value for its parameter. Alternatively, you can connect the Web Part to another Web Part on the page that provides a document path and build more interactive report rendition scenarios. Connecting the Report Viewer Web Part to other Web Parts on the same page or across two pages is covered in greater detail later in this chapter.

The Connectable Report Viewer Web Part

A standalone Report Viewer Web Part is useful when page visitors are likely to be interested in a particular report. However, in more interactive situations, a standalone Report Viewer Web Part is less likely to be an option. You often end up making instances of Report Viewer Web Part to communicate and get either their parameters or the report definitions to render from other components on the same page or across pages.

One of the great features the Web Part framework offers in Windows SharePoint Services (also available in Microsoft Office SharePoint Server 2007) is that you can develop a Web Part to accept connections from other Web Parts on the same page or across pages. The Web Part Connection is a powerful feature that allows users to find new and meaningful views into their underlying data. In a nutshell, a connection is an association between two Web Parts that enables them to share data.

Thankfully, the Report Viewer Web Part acts as a subscriber and implements the interface used for the Web Part connection. The ability to share data allows the Report Viewer Web Part to be used in many ways that exceed the functionality offered by a standalone Report Viewer Web Part.

Passing Report Definitions

Suppose that on a Web Part page one Web Part provides a list of available reports and the Report Viewer Web Part renders each upon selection of a report definition. It's cool, isn't it? You can easily set this up by utilizing the Web Part connection technique.

First, just go ahead and create a Report Library called DemoReports, which essentially is a container for a couple of Adventure Works reports. There's no need to walk through the publishing process of the Adventure Works reports, because it has been covered in previous chapters.

You will then use a List View Web Part representing a DemoReports library and connect it to the Report Viewer Web Part already on the page. This way, you can provide the report's definition via a Web Part connection link.

1. Browse to Site Actions ⇨ View All Site Content.

2. In the top link bar, click Create.

3. On the Create page, click Custom List. In the Name box, type DemoReports as the name for the new Report Library. In the Navigation section, if you want this list to appear on the Quick Launch bar, click Yes.

4. In the Document Template section, chose None, Click Create.

5. Go ahead and use Business Intelligence Development Studio (BIDS) to deploy sample Adventure Works Reports to the DemoReports library. Figure 10-8 illustrates this library after reports are deployed.

Figure 10-8

6. Browse to the `Dashboard.aspx` page you created in the previous section, and add an instance of the DemoReports list to the top of the Report Viewer Web in the right zone.

7. Make sure the current Report Viewer Web Part doesn't point to any reports. You may need to clear the Report Path in the Web Part's property tool pane or simply delete the current Report Viewer Web Part instance and add a new one, as shown in Figure 10-9.

Figure 10-9

8. Click the Web Part Edit Menu for the DemoReports List View Web Part, point to Connections, point to Provide Row To, and then choose the Report Viewer Web Part to which you want to link (see Figure 10-10).

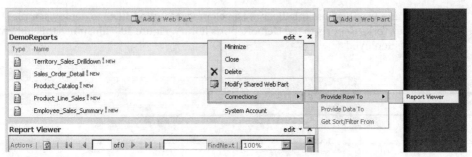

Figure 10-10

Immediately after the connection is established between two Web Parts, you will notice a change in the current View associated with the DemoReports list view Web Part, and next to each report definition item, an option box appears. This gives you the ability to select a report definition and the Report Viewer Web Part renders it, as shown in the Figure 10-11.

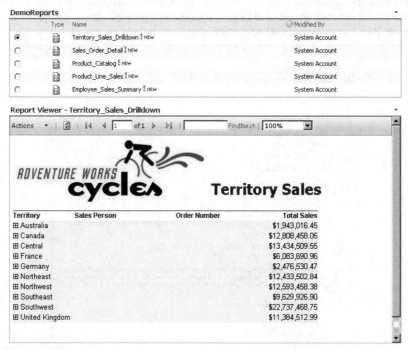

Figure 10-11

Master/Detail Filtering Across Two Pages via a Query String

Although the approach you utilized for passing report definitions in the previous section is a great way to interact with the Report Viewer Web Part, for those reports with parameters you still need to manually enter the parameter value or let your reports use the default values embedded in the report definition file. In this section, you will learn how to pass parameters to the Report Viewer Web Part from Web Parts that reside on the same page or other pages of the site.

1. Browse to Site Actions ⇨ Create Page.

2. In the Title text box, enter Sales Orders Master (SalesOrdersMaster.aspx).

3. Choose (Welcome Page) Blank Web Part Page from the available page layouts.

4. Click Create.

5. Repeat steps 1 through 4 and create another page called Sales Orders Details (SalesOrdersDetails.aspx).

6. Browse to the SalesOrdersDetails.aspx page and add a Report Viewer Web Part and Query String Filter Web Part to one of the available zones.

7. Configure the Report Viewer Web Part to render the Sales Order Details report, as discussed earlier in this chapter.

8. Configure the Query String Filter Web Part to read a query string parameter named SalesOrderNum as demonstrated in Figure 10-12.

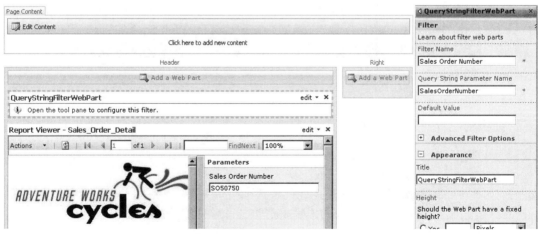

Figure 10-12

9. Click the Web Part Edit Menu for the Query String Filter Web Part, point to Connections, point to Send Filter Values To, and then click the name of the Report Viewer Web Part (Report Viewer – Sales_Order_Details) to which you want to link.

10. The Configure Connection dialog box appears. Select the field that you want to filter (SalesOrderNumer), and then click Finish, as shown in Figure 10-13.

Figure 10-13

11. Start SharePoint Designer.

12. Select the OpenSite option in the File menu and enter the site's URL in the Site Name text box.

13. Browse to the Pages folder and open `SalesOrdersMaster.aspx`. Select Edit Page Layout.

14. Select the Header zone and the Insert Data View option from the Data View menu. Click the link provided to open Data Source Library pane, as shown in Figure 10-14.

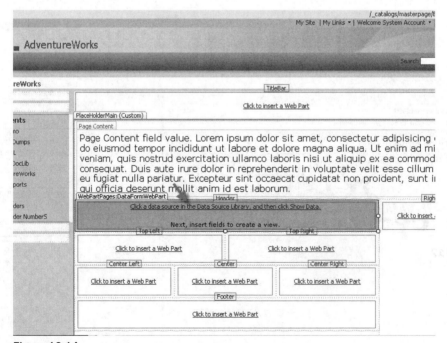

Figure 10-14

15. Expand Database Connections in the Data Source Library pane and click Connect to a database.

16. Click the Configure Database Connection.

17. Enter SQL Server name (or instance) in the Server Name box. Choose Microsoft .NET Framework Data Provider for SQL Server in the Provider Name dropdown. Under Authentication, choose the appropriate way of authenticating to the SQL Server (or instance) that hosts the Adventure Works database, as shown in Figure 10-15.

> Database connections in the Date Form Web Part can only use SQL authentication or Single Sign On Service. In this article, you will use SQL Authentication to connect to the Adventure Works database. Alternatively, you can use the SSO service shipped with Microsoft SharePoint Office Server 2007 Enterprise CAL.

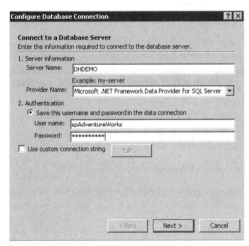

Figure 10-15

18. Choose Adventure Works from the Database dropdown. As you can see in Figure 10-16, instead of working with tables or view directly, you can also specify a SQL statement or stored procedure in the Configure Database Connection dialog box. Click Finish.

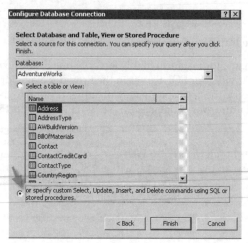

Figure 10-16

19. In the Edit Custom SQL Commands dialog box, click Edit Command and insert the following query in the SELECT Command text box, as shown in Listing 10-1.

Listing 10-1: Retrieving all of the Existing Distinct Sales Number

```
SELECT DISTINCT
      [SalesOrderNumber]
FROM [AdventureWorks].[Sales].[SalesOrderHeader]
```

20. Click on the OK button three times to close Data Source Properties dialog box.

21. Expand the Database Connections in the Data Source Library pane and click the connection you just built above.

22. Select the Show Data option and drag the SalesOrderNumber field into the Data View on the design surface.

23. SharePoint Designer inserts a Data Form Web Part onto the page that contains all the sales order numbers returned from the query in Listing 10-1.

24. Right-click one of the SalesOrderNumbers and select the FlyOut button, as shown in Figure 10-17.

25. Change the Format as section to HyperLink. This will open Edit HyperLink dialog box.

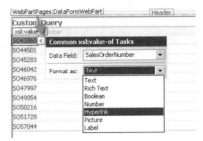

Figure 10-17

26. In the Edit HyperLink dialog box, type *{@SalesOrderNumber}* in the Text To Display text box. This ensures that each column in Data Form Web Part shows the sales order numbers. In the Address text box, enter */Pages/SalesOrdersDetails.aspx?SalesOrderNumber={@SalesOrderNumber}*, which is essentially a relative link to `SalesOrdersDetails.aspx` page created in step 4, passing in the required query string parameter for Query String Web Part on the destination page (*SalesOrdersDetails.aspx*). (See Figure 10-18.)

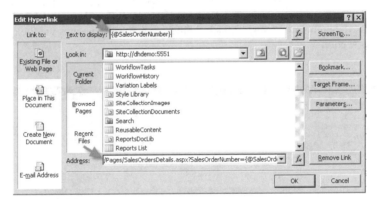

Figure 10-18

27. Click OK, save the page, and check it in.

28. Browse to the `SalesOrdersMaster.aspx` page. It should look like what is shown in Figure 10-19.

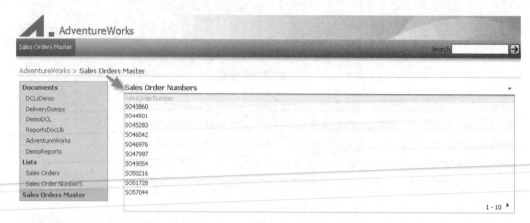

Figure 10-19

29. Click one of the available sales order numbers, and you should be redirected to the
SalesOrdersDetails.aspx page, where the sales order number is picked up by the Query
String Web Part and passed in to the Report Viewer Web Part through a Web Part Connection.
Figure 10-20 demonstrates Master/Detail Filtering across two pages via the query string you set
up in this section.

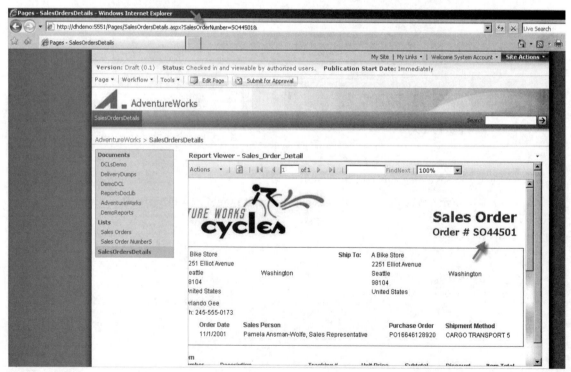

Figure 10-20

The Report Viewer Web Part Limitations

Now that you have a good understanding of what the Report Viewer Web Part's capabilities are, let's see what limitations this Web Part might impose on your reporting needs and applications.

While nitpicking the great work Microsoft has done in building the Report Viewer Web Part is certainly outside the scope of this book and is quite frankly not productive, some of the limitations that apply to this Web Part need to be highlighted.

❑ You cannot have multiple reports in your site that point to different instances of Report Server. This is due to the fact that Reporting Services integration with SharePoint is implemented and configured at the farm level and the Report Viewer Web Part or other integration citizens simply follow the same model at each site collection level.

❑ You cannot group multiple reports into a single instance of a Report Viewer Web Part. As alluded to earlier in this chapter, you should create a dashboard or a Web Part page that embeds multiple Report Viewer Web Part instances on a single page.

❑ You cannot open saved reports as an attachment to list items. The Report Viewer Web Part can only respond to reports that are in a document library or report history or are passed in either via a connectable Web Part scenario or as an incoming link from another Web Part (e.g., Library Web Part).

❑ You cannot customize the look and feel of the Report Viewer Web Part, but you can set properties to control its appearance to an extent. It's certainly sealed!

❑ Search functionality that comes with the Report Viewer Web Part is limited in terms of how you can construct your search phrases. First of all, you can only search for one term or value at a time. Second, famous search operators such as AND and OR and wildcards simply don't work. To overcome this problem, customers often use more sophisticated clickthrough reports and Report Builder or use the Microsoft Office SharePoint Server 2007 search facility to index snapshots or automatically generated reports via available delivery extensions.

❑ The URL you specify in the Report text box of the Report Viewer Web Part cannot be relative. Although current integration between Reporting Services and SharePoint supports rendering reports only in the default zone, in case the issue is fixed in the upcoming service packs or roll-ups, having to specify fully qualified URLs in the Report Viewer Web Part can cause issues in web applications with more than one zone.

❑ Last but certainly not least, unlike that of its predecessors, the Report Viewer Web Part code is not made available to the public. In case you need your own custom Report Viewer Web Part, you need to code it from scratch or put a wrapper around the Microsoft Report Viewer Control.

Reporting against SharePoint Lists

Lists are the building blocks of a SharePoint site, and many different types of lists are created automatically for every SharePoint site. SharePoint lists store information in pretty much the same way a relational database management system such as SQL Server stores data: in rows and columns. Lists provide a boatload of functionality already baked into the SharePoint platform such as UI elements for managing data, versioning, workflows, event handlers, and so on. These types of out-of-the-box functionality are tempting enough to make some customers wonder if they should keep all their data (or at least some portion of it) in lists and use it in the various out-of-the-box functionality contexts that SharePoint offers.

In this section, the end goals are to learn how to report against SharePoint lists and how to link the returned result sets in a drillthrough manner to other reports.

Choosing a Reporting Solution

Let's take a short break from the technical side of reporting against SharePoint lists and address an important question before you move on: What reporting solution should you choose? This surprisingly simple question can reveal a lot about where to store your data and what reporting solution you should adopt to extract what you need from your underlying data.

Although SharePoint lists can be easily created and managed (without requiring specialized skills in designing, implementing, and maintaining custom databases), they are only meant to be used for simple data structures where transactional operations and performance in interacting with such data is not a huge concern. If you require more advanced data models that carry complex relationships with high availability, a database is a more appropriate option when you decide where to store your data structures.

While small organizations may have their data span across a couple of lists, large, geographically distributed organizations often have their data stored in various places, so neither option discussed previously is the definite solution to all of their data-integration woes in Microsoft Office SharePoint Server 2007.

As a consultant, I have learned that sometimes when I get called to provide consultation to a customer, it's too late to implement things from scratch. I have also learned that business drives technology, not the other way around. With that being said, I often get my hands on projects where I need to design and implement reporting platforms against data that is already in place and distributed.

The bottom line is that it is not important that it makes sense to store structured data in SharePoint lists, and it doesn't matter whether combining such data with other types of data structures is the best practice. As long as the data scattered in various places can be interrelated, such requirements exist and must be satisfied. Be prepared to have solutions for such problems!

Avoiding Direct Reporting Off of the SharePoint Databases

No matter what reporting solution you choose, SharePoint configuration and content databases are not tuned and designed for direct reporting access, for a number of reasons:

❑ You can easily bring a well-architected SharePoint system to its knees by deadlocks that potentially lead to performance issues.

❑ A direct call into the SharePoint configuration and content databases is not supported.

❑ There can be multiple content databases per SharePoint application. They can be added later, so unless your reporting tool is smart enough to detect these additions, your reports may only cover a fraction of the data.

❑ There is always a chance that the underlying schema will be changed in future service packs and updates.

Instead, take advantage of alternative approaches such as:

❑ Use SharePoint or web service APIs in lieu of direct calls into the underlying SharePoint databases.

❑ Extract SharePoint data into a standalone database, flatten it, and run your reports against such databases.

Creating a Sales Order Numbers List

As you may know, one of the ways report parameters are used is to provide drillthrough functionality. In this section, you will use the parameter of the Adventure Works sample report "Sales Order Details" to pass a sales order number (from a report against a SharePoint list) to filter the report's data. The goal is to learn to report against SharePoint lists and link the result to other reports that point to other data sources. Assume that both data structures can be interrelated; otherwise, there is little point in merging them.

Before going any further, it makes sense to switch gears here and create a SharePoint list that stores some sales numbers. The goal is to build a report against this list and then link it into another report that shows more information about a specific sales number stored in the Adventure Works database.

1. Browse to Site Actions ⇨ View All Site Content.

2. Click Create.

3. On the Create Page, choose Custom List.

4. In the Title text box, enter SalesNumbers and hit the Create button.

5. Execute the query in Listing 10-2 in SQL Server Management Studio to get some sample sales numbers. Figure 10-21 shows the sample list after some sample sales numbers are added to it.

Listing 10-2 : Getting Top 10 Sales Numbers to Populate the Sample List

```
SELECT TOP 10
      [SalesOrderNumber]
FROM [AdventureWorks].[Sales].[SalesOrderHeader]
```

Figure 10-21

Creating the Report

First, you must create a Report Server project using Business Intelligence Development Studio. As you can see in Figure 10-22, when you create a new project, you have three templates to choose from for a report project: Report Server Project Wizard, Report Server Project, and Report Model Project.

The Report Server Project Wizard template simply saves a step and takes you straight to the Report Wizard. To meet specific requirements of this report, however, you will likely find it better to use the Report Server Project as you learn to do in this procedure. Click OK to create the solution and its only project, SPRSList.

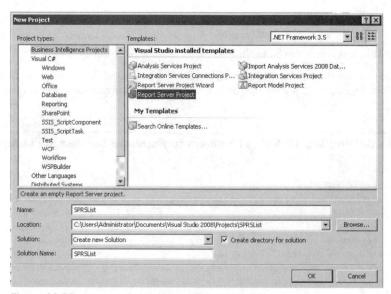

Figure 10-22

Since you have no data source created yet, add one. In Solution Explorer, right-click Shared Data Sources and select Add New Data Source. Make sure you specify the Type as XML and set a Web reference to `http://<Site_Url>/_vti_bin/lists.asmx`, replacing `<Site_Url>` with the path to the site with the SalesNumbers list you are trying to access, as shown in Figure 10-23.

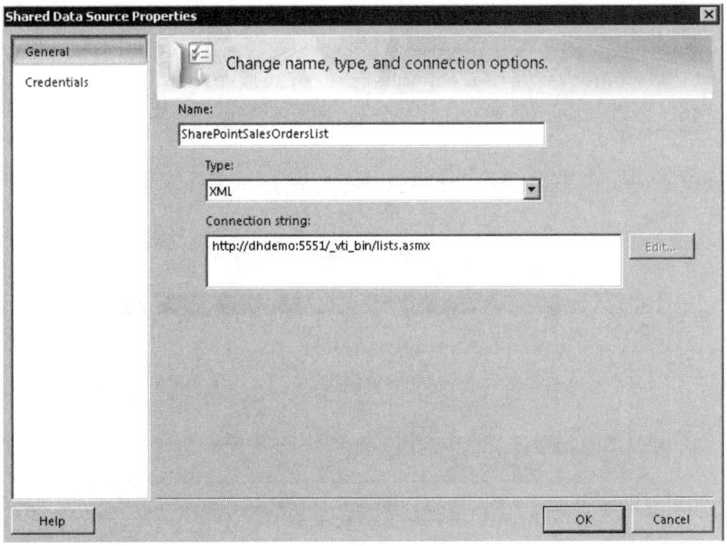

Figure 10-23

Click the Credentials tab and make sure you set it to Windows Authentication (Integrated Security) or No Credentials if anonymous access has been enabled in your SharePoint site. Now that you have the data source defined, you will need to author the report.

To do this, in Solution Explorer, right-click the Reports folder and select the Add New Report command on the context menu. This command starts the Report Project Wizard. Skip the Welcome screen and in the next screen, you need to choose the data source you created above. The next screen prompts you for a query string, as shown in Figure 10-24. Since you are using the `lists.asmx` web service as the data source, you need to pass in a valid query to retrieve the required data for your report. Add the XML shown in Listing 10-3 to the Query String text box.

Listing 10-3: Referencing GetListItems method in the Lists.asmx Web Service

```
<Query>
    <SoapAction>http://schemas.microsoft.com/sharepoint/soap/GetListItems
    </SoapAction>
    <Method Namespace="http://schemas.microsoft.com/sharepoint/soap/"
    Name="GetListItems">
        <Parameters>
            <Parameter Name="listName">
                <DefaultValue>SalesNumbers</DefaultValue>
            </Parameter>
        </Parameters>
    </Method>
    <ElementPath IgnoreNamespace="True">*</ElementPath>
</Query>
```

Figure 10-24

The GetListItems method of the lists.asmx web service returns information about items in the list based on the specified query. This method exposes different parameters, but in this example you are only using the listName parameter, which represents a string that contains either the display name or the GUID for the list. For more information on the GetListItems method, refer to the official documentation on MSDN: http://www.devhorizon.com/go/1.

Optionally, you can click Query Builder and examine the returned data from the web service, as shown in Figure 10-25. Click Next to continue.

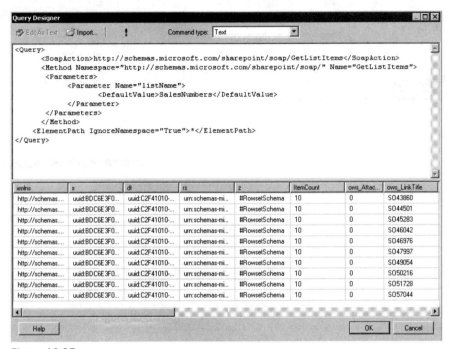

Figure 10-25

In the next wizard page, you select the report type. In an effort to keep things simple, let's specify a Tabular style. Click Next to go to the next page, which is used to design a table control that displays rows and columns of data. In this simple report, you will not be using any grouping, so only one column will be added to the Details section. Add `ows_Title` field to the Details section and click the Next button.

On the Choose the Table Layout page, simply choose a style for the table control and click the Next button to proceed to the last wizard page, where you need to specify a name for your report. When you click Finish, the report appears in the solution, and Report Designer displays in the document window, as in Figure 10-26.

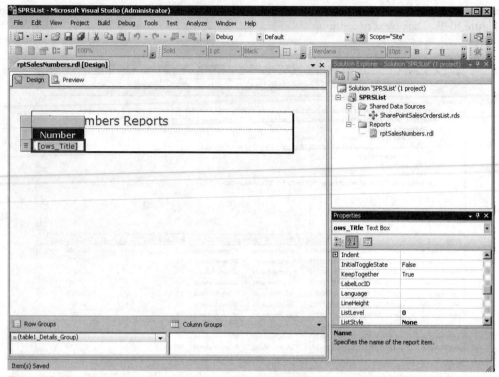

Figure 10-26

Everything is starting to come together, but you are not done yet! Recall the goals of this exercise:

❑   Reporting against the SalesNumbers SharePoint list.

❑   Building a drillthrough report by linking the preceding report to the AdventureWorks sample report "Sales Order Details" that filters its data based on the passed in parameter.

Next, you should import `Sales_Order_Detail.rdl` sample report definition file that installs with SQL Server Reporting Services 2008 and add it to the same Report folder in the solution you created above. Figure 10-27 shows your Report Server project after you add the Sales_Order_Detail.rdl report definition and its data-source file.

Figure 10-27

Open the rptSalesNumbers.rdl file in the Report Designer and select the `ows_Title` text box, as shown in Figure 10-28.

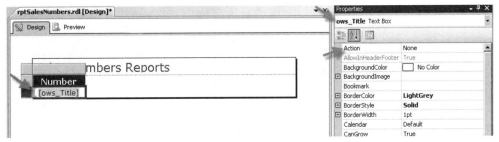

Figure 10-28

In the Action property pane, select "Go to Report" and choose the "Sales_Order_Detail" report from the available reports. Alternatively, you can type the URL of a report that's already published to your SharePoint site, but remember that you can only use a fully qualified URL, including the file name extension (for example, `http://dhdemo:5551/DemoReports/Sales_Order_Detail.rdl`). Relative paths are not supported. Click the Add button, define a new parameter, and set the Sales Order Detail report's only parameter to `ows_Title`. Figure 10-29 illustrates all the required settings to support a drillthough between these two reports.

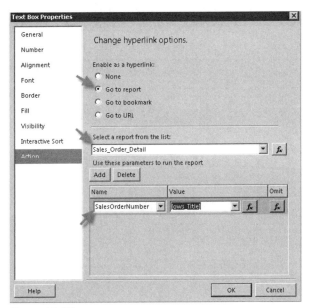

Figure 10-29

The last step to complete this section is to deploy the Sales Numbers report to the same folder where the Order Detail report is deployed. Figure 10-30 shows the new report deployed to the DemoReports library.

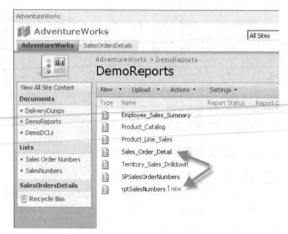

Figure 10-30

Point the Report Viewer Web Part in the `Dasboard.aspx` page to the new report (rptSalesNumbers). As shown in Figure 10-31, the report renders sample Sales Numbers stored in the SalesNumbers list.

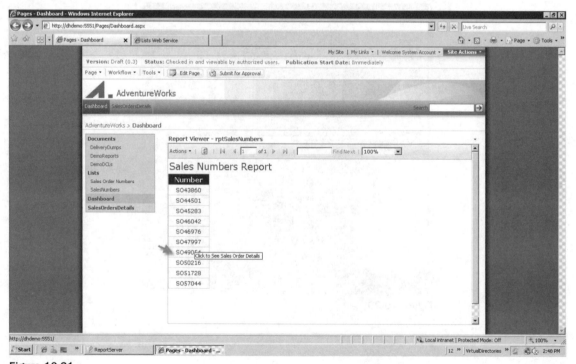

Figure 10-31

By clicking each sales number, you will be taken to the Details report to view more detailed information (stored in the Adventure Works database), as shown in Figure 10-32.

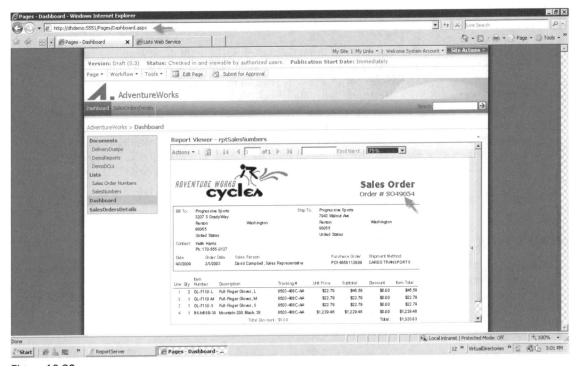

Figure 10-32

The goal of this exercise is to show you how to report off of lists in SharePoint and combine the report with other reports pointing to other data sources, given the fact the data you are reporting against can be interrelated. In addition, you've learned that you can add tremendous interactivity and depth to every single report you create by utilizing the drillthrough functionality of SQL Server Reporting Services 2008 across all your reports.

Displaying Your Reports Your Way

Earlier, you looked at the out-of-the-box options for incorporating reports in your SharePoint site pages. First, you looked at the out-of-the-box redirection to the `RSViewerPage.aspx` page when you click a report definition file. Second, you learned how a Report Viewer Web Part can be dragged and dropped onto a site page and further customized to meet an organization's reporting needs.

Having reports rendered on the SharePoint site pages and leveraging the innate ability of page customization works very well for many customers, but there are a number of scenarios in which customers simply don't want this level of customization. Instead, they want to have more control over the report rendition UI. Some other customers would like to have a single entry (or single version) to a specific page that contains their reports along with other content that is deployed once and shared among all sites across the farm and cannot be customized on a site-by-site basis. From here toward the end of the chapter, you will learn how to display reports your own way. You will start with lighter approaches, but later, you will see more customized solutions for rendering the reports onto your SharePoint pages.

> Most of the examples demonstrated throughout the remainder of the chapter are created using Visual Studio extensions for Windows SharePoint Services 3.0 (also referred to as VSeWSS in this book). VSeWSS is a tool for rapidly developing custom SharePoint applications. It provides developers with a familiar development environment that is completely integrated with Visual Studio IDE. This tool includes a collection of useful project and item templates for many of the most common development activities in SharePoint. VSeWSS will continue to be the recommended Microsoft tool for SharePoint development until the release of Visual Studio 2010. You can download the current Community Technology Preview (CTP) of VSeWSS 1.3 from http://www.devhorizon.com/go/2.

Displaying Reports in SharePoint Application Pages

Although the `RSViewerPage.aspx` page's current implementation is pretty close to satisfying most of BI business requirements, the challenge is that the behavior of this page cannot be modified using a supported approach. In this section, you create a page that runs within the SharePoint context and acts very similarly to the out-of-the-box `RSViewerPage.aspx` page. The difference is that you can control the behavior using code, and, of course, no hacking into the Report Server system pages is required!

You can create custom application pages to add your reporting components and come up with a custom solution. Application pages (also known as _layouts pages) are based in the virtual _layouts directory. They are compiled into a single assembly DLL, cached on each web front-end server, and loaded into memory once for each web application. Furthermore, application pages are not subject to attacks from users who have permissions to customize site pages.

> One thing that is unique about a secure application page compared to an unsecured one is that the secure application page derives from the `Microsoft.SharePoint.WebControls.LayoutsPageBase` class. The security model implemented in this class restricts pages to viewing by authenticated users only (`NTAuthority\Authenticated`). To open your application pages to everyone, for example FBA users, you should write application pages to inherit from the `Microsoft.SharePoint.WebControls.UnsecuredLayoutsPageBase` class (see http://www.devhorizon.com/go/4) or override the default behavior using custom code, as shown in Listing 10-4. In publishing sites, you should also be aware of the Lockdown mode feature (see http://www.devhorizon.com/go/5).

The first step is to create an empty project using the VSeWSS tool. Next, add two references to the `Microsoft.ReportingServices.SharePoint.UI.ServerPages` and `Microsoft.ReportingServices.SharePoint.UI.WebParts` assemblies.

Right click the project and choose Add ⇨ New Item from the context menu. From the available templates underneath Visual C# ⇨ SharePoint, choose Template and in the Name text box, type `WroxRSViewerPage.aspx`. This will create a folder called Templates and add the `WroxRSViewerPage.aspx` page to that folder. Go ahead and create a subfolder underneath the Templates folder called LAYOUTS and another folder called WroxSsrsMoss underneath the LAYOUTS folder. Move the `WroxRSViewerPage.aspx` page to this folder.

Create a new C# class named `WroxRSViewerPage.cs` in a folder called Code in the project. Make the class inherit from `BaseRSLayoutPage`. Next, provide an overridden implementation of the `OnInit` method, and `RequireSiteAdministrator` property as shown in Listing 10-4. Now that the files are in the right folders in the project, the next step is to modify them, as shown in Listing 10-4.

Listing 10-4: WroxRSViewerPage.aspx and WroxRSViewerPage.cs

WroxRSViewerPage.aspx :

```
<%@ Page Language="C#" Inherits="Wrox.ProSsrsMoss.Chapter10.WroxRSViewerPage"
EnableViewState="true" EnableViewStateMac="false" %>
<!--Extra Code Omitted for brevity-->
<html>
    <!-- Extra Code Omitted for brevity -->
    <body>
        <form id="Form1" runat="server">
            <!-- Extra Code Omitted for brevity -->
            <SharePoint:FormDigest runat="server"/>
            <RSWP:ReportViewerWebPart id="m_sqlRsWebPart" runat="server"
            ChromeType="None" Height="100%" Width="100%" />
            <!-- Extra Code Omitted for brevity-->
        </form>
    </body>
</html>
```

WroxRSViewerPage.cs :

```
namespace Wrox.ProSsrsMoss.Chapter10
{
    public class WroxRSViewerPage : BaseRSLayoutPage
    {
        protected ReportViewerWebPart m_sqlRsWebPart;
        protected string m_relativeReportUrl;
        private string GetPageUrlParameter(string parameter)
        {
            string str = this.Page.Request.QueryString["RV:" + parameter];
            if (string.IsNullOrEmpty(str))
            {
                str = this.Page.Request.QueryString[parameter];
            }
```

(continued)

Listing 10-4: (Continued)

```
        return str;
    }
    private void SetWebPartSettings()
    {
        this.m_sqlRsWebPart.ToolBarMode = ToolBarDisplayMode.Full;
        this.m_sqlRsWebPart.PromptAreaMode = CollapsibleDisplayMode.Displayed;
        this.m_sqlRsWebPart.DocumentMapMode = CollapsibleDisplayMode.Displayed;
        this.m_sqlRsWebPart.AsyncRendering = true;
        this.m_sqlRsWebPart.Height = "100%";
        this.m_sqlRsWebPart.Width = "100%";
    }

    protected override bool RequireSiteAdministrator
    {
        get
        {
            return false;
        }
    }


    protected override void OnInit(EventArgs e)
    {
        string m_relativeReportUrl =
        this.GetPageUrlParameter("RelativeReportUrl");
        if (!string.IsNullOrEmpty(m_relativeReportUrl))
        {
            SPSite site = SPContext.Current.Site;
            SPAlternateUrl defaultZone = site.WebApplication.AlternateUrls[0];
            String path = defaultZone.Uri.AbsoluteUri.Substring(0,
            defaultZone.Uri.AbsoluteUri.Length - 1) + m_relativeReportUrl;
            this.m_sqlRsWebPart.ReportPath = path;
        }
        this.SetWebPartSettings();
        base.OnInit(e);
    }
}
}
```

The complete code for both the ASPX page and the code-behind file can be found in the code download for this book at www.wrox.com.

Figure 10-33 demonstrates the new folder structure of your project.

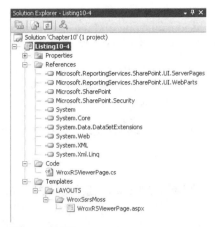

Figure 10-33

All the presentation code is self contained within the `WroxRSViewerPage.aspx` file, and there is the related code-behind file represented in `WroxRSViewerPage.cs`. Notice the highlighted lines in Listing 10-4: `WroxRSViewerPage.aspx`.

The inline code used in this example is almost identical to the out-of-the-box `RSViewerPage.aspx`, with only two exceptions:

❏ **Page Directive:** The ASPX file that is wired up to the code-behind containing the type for this page would contain a page directive like the one highlighted on the top of Listing 10-4. Additionally, `ViewState` has been set to True at the page level because the Report Viewer Web Part requires that it be enabled.

❏ **FormDigest Element:** This markup inserts a security validation within the form of the page. This element is necessary to be there to make posts from a SharePoint web application.

The `WroxRSViewerPage` class inherits from the `Microsoft.ReportingServices.SharePoint.UI .BaseRSLayoutPage` class, which in turn inherits from the `Microsoft.SharePoint.WebControls .LayoutsPageBase` class. This class handles some of the preliminary checks to ensure that the connection to the `ReportService2006.asmx` proxy endpoint is valid and can be properly established.

The code-behind starts with a method called `GetPageUrlParameter()`, that simply returns a parameter that it reads from the query string. Keep in mind that the `GetPageUrlParameter()` method is only used to extract the relative path to the report in Listing 10-4, but it can be used to pull in other parameters from the query string as long as they are prefixed by "RV:". Next, `SetWebPartSettings()` is needed to set some of the properties of `ReportViewerWebPart` control such as parameter prompt area, tool bar, and so on. The `RequireSiteAdministrator()` method, as the name implies, sets a value (in this case false) that indicates that the page can be accessed by everyone, not only site collection administrators. The `OnInit()` method performs the initialization and set-up steps required to create an instance of the page such as reading the parameter from the query string. Next, in the highlighted section, an `SPSite` object is returned from the current context, and the first alternate request URL of the Web application that site collection belongs to is stored in the `defaultZone` variable. In this example, it's assumed that `site.WebApplication.AlternateUrls[0]` represents the default zone, where reports are deployed.

Regardless of what zone this code is executed in, the `ReportPath` property of the Report Viewer Web Part is set to point to the URL of the default zone, and this fixes reports not being rendered in the non-default zone in the out-of-the-box implementation of the `RSViewerPage.aspx` page.

At this point, everything is handled except for the final piece: building and deploying your custom application page. Right click the project and click Deploy from the context menu. Go ahead and browse to the Windows zone (default) of your application, and access the page by typing the following URL, as shown in Figure 10-34: `http://<Site_Collection_url>/_layouts/WroxSsrsMoss/WroxRSViewerPage.aspx?RV%3aRelativeReportUrl=%2fdemoreports%2fsales_order_detail.rdl`.

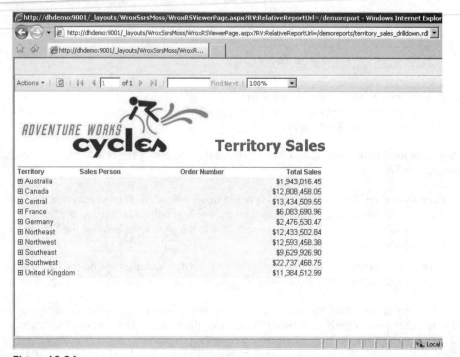

Figure 10-34

Now, let's access the report from the FBA zone. As you can see, as far as displaying reports is concerned, everything works in the FBA zone. Figure 10-35 shows the Territory Sales report in an FBA zone.

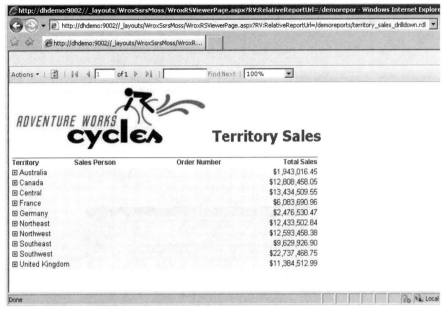

Figure 10-35

Several important things need to be highlighted here:

❑ FBA users should have enough permission (View and Execution) to access the requested report and its data source. If FBA users lack sufficient permission, an access-denied error will be thrown, as shown in Figures 10-36 and 10-37.

❑ FBA users should have enough permission to see the application page. To address this issue, you can override the RequireSiteAdministrator property and return true (of the LayoutsPageBase class), as shown in Listing 10-4.

❑ If you want FBA users to be able to view a report, you must configure the report to use stored credentials or an unattended report processing account in its data source. You learn about unattended report processing accounts in Chapter 12.

❑ The sample code provided in Listing 10-4 doesn't support subscribing to reports for FBA users. You can hide the toolbar for FBA users or create your own toolbar that derives from the Microsoft.ReportingServices.SharePoint.UI.WebParts.ReportViewerToolBar class, which, in turn, inherits from the System.Web.UI.WebControls.CompositeControl class.

❑ The code snippet in Listing 10-4 assumes that the default zone is where reports are deployed.

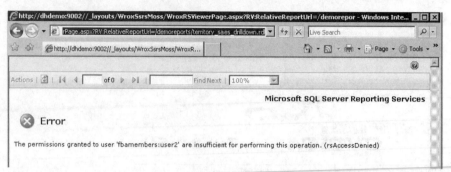

Figure 10-36

Figure 10-37

Displaying Reports to Anonymous Users

With the increasing popularity of SharePoint and its growth in delivering Internet-facing web sites, one of the most common questions I get when working with clients is how to use Reporting Services if you want to display reports to SharePoint anonymous users. Suppose that when a user enters the Adventure Works portal site, they can use a page to browse the catalog of products without logging in to an account. The initial view of the product catalog shows the featured products that the site wishes to promote and gives viewers access to the full catalog of items. Products are presented as images along with the name of the product, and browsing the catalog of products can be completely open to everyone without having to authenticate.

Many organizations have mixed environments based on their own authentication and authorization mechanisms, and often they have their entire site open to anonymous users. Unfortunately, Reporting Services requires you to connect to reports by using a valid security context and does not support anonymous access to reports, right out of the box. Anonymous users do not represent a true security context in SharePoint; therefore, when they try to access reports, they get the error message shown in Figure 10-38.

Figure 10-38

Deploying Reporting Services in environments with custom authentication and authorization infrastructure often calls for either creating your own custom implementation of displaying reports and passing the right security context to them or hiding custom security implementations from Reporting Services.

> Although Microsoft highly recommends that you not expose the Report Server over the Internet to anonymous users, you can employ some techniques to wrap anonymous users in a valid security context and open your reports to them (not the entire Report Server instance). A proof-of-concept implementation of wrapping anonymous users in a dummy FBA account can be found at `http://www.devhorizon.com/go/6`.

Boxing the Report Viewer Web Part

You have likely faced the situation where you need to build a custom display for your report, perhaps to enable you to perform user-specific validation for input parameters or to match the look and feel of your current SharePoint application. In a nutshell, the Report Viewer Web Part is a server control that derives from `Microsoft.SharePoint.WebPartPages.WebPart` class and handles interactions with the Report Server instance. The Report Viewer Web Part instantiates a ReportViewer control (`Microsoft.Reporting.WebForms.ReportViewer`) to access reports from your Report Server.

As stated earlier in this chapter, there is a great deal more that Report Viewer Web Part brings to the table, but its code has not been released to the public, and this has caused some problems for customers when it comes to customizing look and feel or controlling its behavior. Although you can always create your own Report Viewer Web Part from scratch, you can use an alternative approach by putting a wrapper around the Web Part. This approach makes sense if you need to interact with the Report Viewer Web Part programmatically right before a report gets rendered.

This section guides you through the process of wrapping the out-of-the-box Report Viewer Web Part inside a custom Web Part extender that acts as a container. Figure 10-39 shows the completed `WroxRSViewer` Web Part at runtime.

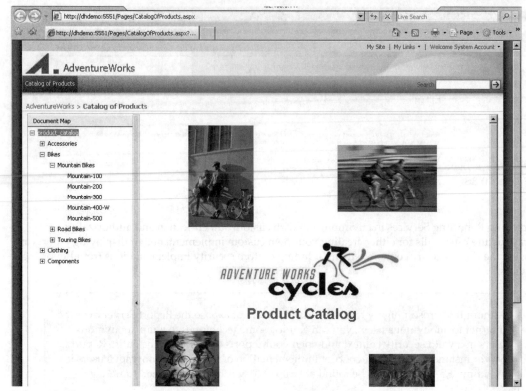

Figure 10-39

The first step is to create a Web Part project from Web Part template using the VSeWSS tool, as shown in Figure 10-40.

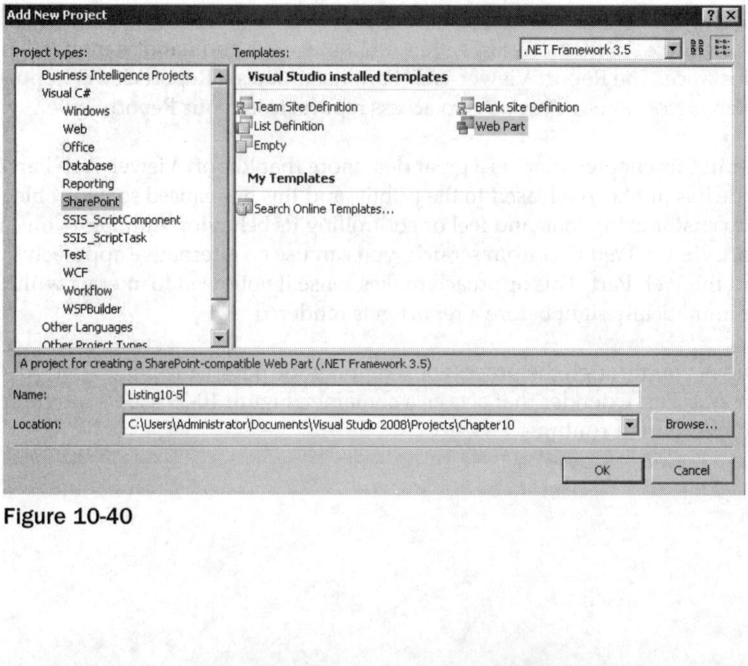

Figure 10-40

Next, add a reference to the `Microsoft.ReportingServices.SharePoint.UI.WebParts` assembly. As you may notice, the VSeWSS tool makes your new Web Part class derives from the `System.Web.UI.WebControls.WebParts.WebPart` base class, which is located in `System.Web.dll`. This means your Web Part is compiled by making use of the .Net Framework 2.0.

Users of the Web Part need a way to manage the relative URL of the report rendered in the Web Part. This is done by exposing a local field (`m_ReportUrl`) as public property. If this property is decorated with the `WebBrowsable` attribute, it would appear in the generic Tool Part in the Web Part's property pane, as shown in Figure 10-41.

```
public string ReportUrl
{
    get
    {
        return m_ReportUrl;
    }
    set
    {
        m_ReportUrl = value;
    }
}
```

Figure 10-41

The `ReportViewerWebPart` class provides a set of default properties that allow you to change the appearance and behavior of the Web Part. These properties contain basic customization properties such as height, width, chrome type, and much more, as illustrated in the following `SetWebPartSettings()` method.

```
private void SetWebPartSettings()
{
    this.m_sqlRsWebPart.ToolBarMode = ToolBarDisplayMode.None;
    this.m_sqlRsWebPart.PromptAreaMode =  CollapsibleDisplayMode.Displayed;
    this.m_sqlRsWebPart.DocumentMapMode =  CollapsibleDisplayMode.Collapsed;
    this.m_sqlRsWebPart.AsyncRendering = true;
    this.m_sqlRsWebPart.Height = this.Height.ToString();
    this.m_sqlRsWebPart.Width = this.Width.ToString();
    this.m_sqlRsWebPart.ChromeType = PartChromeType.None;
}
```

Although most of the properties used in the `SetWebPartSettings()` method are explained in Listing 10-4, one property needs to be highlighted here: `AsyncRendering`. This property indicates whether the hosted Report Viewer Web Part in your custom Web Part renders reports asynchronously. Since you have no clue what is going to be on the page or how many instances of your custom Web Part you will have on the page, it is good practice to utilize the asynchronous facility of the Report Viewer Part to minimize the impact on the rest of the page.

All the work of the `WroxRSViewer` class happens in the `CreateChildControl()` method as shown in the following code snippet.

```
protected override void CreateChildControls()
{
    base.CreateChildControls();
    if (!string.IsNullOrEmpty(this.ReportUrl))
    {
        SPSite site = SPContext.Current.Site;
        SPAlternateUrl defaultZone = site.WebApplication.AlternateUrls[0];
        String path = defaultZone.Uri.AbsoluteUri.Substring(0,
        defaultZone.Uri.AbsoluteUri.Length - 1)+this.ReportUrl;
        this.m_sqlRsWebPart = new ReportViewerWebPart();
        this.m_sqlRsWebPart.ReportPath = path;
        SetWebPartSettings();
        this.Controls.Add(this.m_sqlRsWebPart);
    }
}
```

In the `CreateChildControl()` method, an `SPSite` object is returned from the current context, and the first alternate request URL of the Web application that the site collection belongs to is stored in the `defaultZone` variable. In this example, it's assumed that `site.WebApplication.AlternateUrls[0]` represents the default zone and the default zone is where reports are deployed. Right after determining the appropriate path to the report, a new instance of the `ReportViewerWebPart` class is created and assigned to the `m_sqlRsWebPart` local field. Next, no matter what zone this code is executed in, the `ReportPath` property of the Report Viewer Web Part is set to point to the URL of the default zone, and this fixes the reports not being rendered in the non-default zone issue.

That's it! The custom Wrox RS Viewer Web Part is now complete. At this point, the Web Part can be used in a Web Part Page. Let's go ahead and build and deploy the solution. Once the solution is deployed, VSeWSS adds a site-scoped feature that should be activated. Now, if you look at the site collection's Web Part gallery, you should see that the new Web Part has been imported, as shown in Figure 10-42. This means you can add your custom Web Part to a Web Part zone, as shown in Figure 10-43.

	ReportViewer.dwp		3/13/2009 9:10 PM	System Account
	SummaryLink.webpart		3/13/2009 8:44 PM	System Account
	TableOfContents.webpart		3/13/2009 8:44 PM	System Account
	WroxRSViewer.webpart ! NEW		4/10/2009 8:33 PM	System Account

Figure 10-42

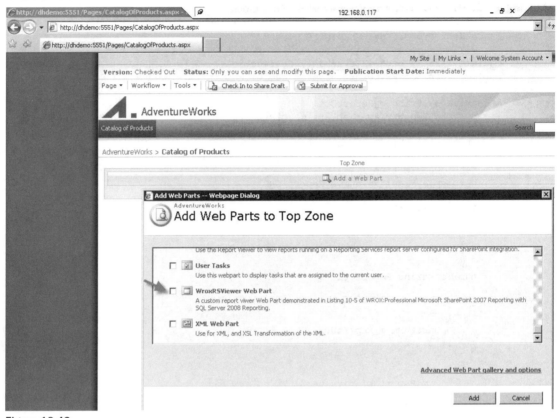

Figure 10-43

Listing 10-5 shows the full Web Part code. When the Web Part's properties are set, your custom Web Part renders the specified report, as shown in Figure 10-39.

Listing 10-5: The Full WroxRSViewer Web Part Code

```
namespace Wrox.ProSsrsMoss.Chapter10
{
    [Guid("54126b35-efce-427f-a693-776d61f4cc79")]
    public class WroxRSViewer : System.Web.UI.WebControls.WebParts.WebPart
    {
        private string m_ReportUrl;
        private ReportViewerWebPart m_sqlRsWebPart;

        [Personalizable(PersonalizationScope.User),
        DefaultValue("/DemoReports/Sales_Order_Detail.rdl"),
        WebBrowsable(true),
        WebDisplayName("Relative Report URL"),
        WebDescription("Specify a relative path to the report you intend to show
        in this Web Part.")]



        public string ReportUrl
        {
            get
            {
                return m_ReportUrl;
            }
            set
            {
                m_ReportUrl = value;
            }
        }

        public WroxRSViewer(){}
        private void SetWebPartSettings()
        {
            this.m_sqlRsWebPart.ToolBarMode = ToolBarDisplayMode.None;
            this.m_sqlRsWebPart.PromptAreaMode = CollapsibleDisplayMode.Displayed;
            this.m_sqlRsWebPart.DocumentMapMode = CollapsibleDisplayMode.Collapsed;
            this.m_sqlRsWebPart.AsyncRendering = true;
            this.m_sqlRsWebPart.Height = this.Height.ToString();
            this.m_sqlRsWebPart.Width = this.Width.ToString();
            this.m_sqlRsWebPart.ChromeType = PartChromeType.None;
        }

        protected override void CreateChildControls()
        {
            base.CreateChildControls();

            if (!string.IsNullOrEmpty(this.ReportUrl))
            {
                SPSite site = SPContext.Current.Site;
                SPAlternateUrl defaultZone = site.WebApplication.AlternateUrls[0];
                String path = defaultZone.Uri.AbsoluteUri.Substring(0,
                defaultZone.Uri.AbsoluteUri.Length - 1) + this.ReportUrl;
```

```
            this.m_sqlRsWebPart = new ReportViewerWebPart();
            this.m_sqlRsWebPart.ReportPath = path;
            SetWebPartSettings();
            this.Controls.Add(this.m_sqlRsWebPart);
        }
    }
  }
}
```

Building the Interactive Dashboard

In Chapter 9, you learned about foundational Reporting Service API calls via Report Server proxy endpoints. You also learned about how you may deploy your reports and associated data sources by calling into such APIs. In this section, you are going to dive deeper into coding against Reporting Services APIs when Reporting Services is configured in SharePoint integrated mode. You will create an interactive dashboard that is wrapped in a SharePoint Web Part and communicates via jQuery Ajax calls with a Windows Communication Foundation (WCF) endpoint that acts as an Ajax backend.

Windows Communication Foundation is part of the .NET Framework and provides a unified programming model for rapidly building service-oriented applications that communicate across the enterprise. jQuery is a fast and lightweight JavaScript library that simplifies and emphasizes interaction between JavaScript and HTML. jQuery is written with the mindset to change the way that you write JavaScript and your Ajax interactions for rapid web development.

While the WCF programming model, jQuery, and Ajax development can't be fully explained in this chapter, I will provide a brief overview in the following sections with the emphasis on the Reporting Services and SharePoint related topics. If you are a seasoned WCF or Ajax developer, you may want to skip over some parts of the remaining sections of this chapter.

Creating the WCF Service

The interactive dashboard Web Part which you are going to build in this chapter needs to take into account that communication with the backend Report Server may not be done in a timely manner. If that's the case, the Web Part should not hold up the processing of the entire page. This requires services for building the back end of the system that can handle Ajax communication.

SQL Server Reporting Services 2008 includes a relatively complete coverage of Reporting Services APIs via its proxy endpoint, but unfortunately such endpoints are neither Ajax-enabled nor JavaScript-friendly. In order to overcome this shortcoming, you need to build an Ajax backend service that consumes Report Server proxy endpoints and, more importantly, is Ajax enabled. In ASP.NET, there are just three ways to build such a service: ASMX Web services, HTTP handlers, and WCF services. In this book, you will use the WCF approach, and for more portability for cross domain Ajax requests, JavaScript Object Notation (JSON) data strings to move data back and forth between the interactive dashboard and Report Server APIs in an asynchronous manner. Because JSON is a based on a subset of the JavaScript programming language and is a lightweight data-interchange format, it's a perfect serialization format for browser-server communication.

In the future, if you decide to host your WCF service in the SharePoint's _layouts or _vti_bin virtual directories, you need to consider two important things right up front. First of all, it is only possible in ASP.NET 3.5 that you can build your AJAX back end of services using WCF. Although SharePoint is fully supported on machines that have .NET Framework 3.5, not every customer has it on their production servers. Also, to support WCF services additional configuration must be deployed to the SharePoint runtime environment through a custom virtual path provider. However, this approach may not be an option in multi-tenanted, hosted environments or in situations where you don't know what environment would host your code.

Daniel Larson in his book titled *Developing Service-Oriented AJAX Applications on the Microsoft Platform* (see `http://www.devhorizon.com/go/10`), demonstrates a future-proof solution and an alternative approach to hosting the WCF service in SharePoint by wrapping the service implementation in an ASP. NET handler. Using this technique you can safely move from an HTTP handler to a full fledged WCF endpoint when WCF is fully supported in SharePoint without any workarounds in the way SharePoint internally works.

Enough talking about WCF. Let's start building something here! First, you need to build an AJAX-enabled WCF service that returns JSON data. Start Visual Studio 2008, and create a new WCF Service Application project called `Wrox.InteractiveDashboard.ServiceEndPoint`, as shown in Figure 10-44.

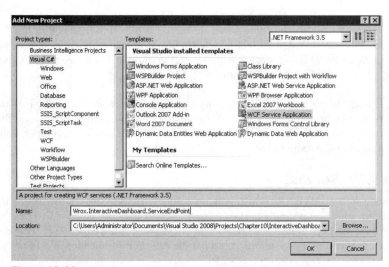

Figure 10-44

When you click on the OK button in Figure 10-44, this generates one class, one interface, and a Web. Config (or App.config when running outside of IIS) file. Because you are not ready to dive into these out of the box files yet, just go ahead and do some clean up. Right click on the classes and delete the files. Then, clean your App.Config so it looks like Listing 10-6.

Listing 10-6: Modified App.Config file

```xml
<?xml version="1.0" encoding="utf-8" ?>
<configuration>
  <system.web>
      <compilation debug="true" />
  </system.web>
  <system.serviceModel>
      <services>
      </services>
      <behaviors>
         <serviceBehaviors>
         </serviceBehaviors>
      </behaviors>
  </system.serviceModel>
</configuration>
```

Before going any further, it makes much sense to switch gears here and put the backend plumbing to the Report Server Web Service in place. First, you need to add a class to represent a business object that captures basic information about a report. The `Report` class has six supplied properties, as shown in Listing 10-7.

Listing 10-7: Report business entity

```csharp
namespace Wrox.InteractiveDashboard.ServiceEndPoint
{
    public class Report
    {
        public string Name { get;set; }
        public string Path { get; set; }
        public string UrlAccess { get; set; }
        public string Description { get; set; }
        public string PublishedDate { get; set; }
        public string PublishedBy { get;set; }


    }
}
```

The interactive dashboard you are going to build in this section must have a means to communicate with the Report Server Web Service and to locate the Web service at run time. Therefore, add a Web reference to the project that points to `http://Site_URL/_vti_bin/ReportServer/ReportService2006.asmx` and name it `ReportServer`. This generates a proxy class that interfaces with the Web service and provides a local representation of that service to the WCF endpoint you are going to build in just a moment.

Once you add a reference for the Web service to your project, the next step is to create a repository class that provides access to the backend service, as demonstrated in Listing 10-8. First, you create an instance of the Web service's proxy class, `ReportingService2006`. Notice the highlighted lines in Listing 10-8. These lines are used to make a call to the Web service's `ListChildren` method using the proxy class to get a collection of all the reports in a specified report library. Later, you create an array of Report business entities and return it to the caller. For demonstration purposes, the following example has three `const` variables and assigns them the hard-coded strings as value. In the real world, these configuration settings must be either stored in the WCF endpoint `Web.config` or passed from the dashboard (which is the consumer of the service).

Listing 10-8: Repository class

```
using System;
using System.Collections;
using System.Collections.Generic;
using System.Linq;
using System.Web.Services.Protocols;
using Wrox.InteractiveDashboard.ServiceEndPoint.ReportServer;
using System.Diagnostics;
namespace Wrox.InteractiveDashboard.ServiceEndPoint
{
    public class ReportRepository

    {
        //Note: the following URLs should be changed to reflect your own environment.
        private const string serviceUrl=
        "http://dhdemo:5551/_vti_bin/ReportServer/ReportService2006.asmx";
        private const string serverUrl= "http://dhdemo/ReportServer";
        private const string reportLibrary= "http://dhdemo:5551/ReportsDemo";

        public static Report[] GetReports()
        {
            ReportingService2006 reportingService =
            new ReportingService2006();
            reportingService.Url = serviceUrl;
            reportingService.Credentials =
            System.Net.CredentialCache.DefaultCredentials;
            IList<Report> reports = new List<Report>();
            CatalogItem[] catalogItems =
            reportingService.ListChildren(reportLibrary);
            foreach (CatalogItem item in catalogItems)
            {
                if (item.Type == ItemTypeEnum.Report)
                {
                    Report report = new Report();
                    report.Name = item.Name;
                    report.Path = item.Path;
                    if (item.Description == null)
                      report.Description = "No Description is provided for
                      this report.";
                    else
                      report.Description = item.Description;

                    report.UrlAccess = String.Concat(serverUrl, "?",  item.Path);

                    report.PublishedBy = item.CreatedBy;
                    report.PublishedDate = item.CreationDate.ToString();
                    reports.Add(report);
                }
            }
        }
```

```
            return reports.ToArray();
        }
    }
}
```

With the backend coding finished, it now needs to be wired up to the actual WCF Service. Right click on the project, and choose "Add New Item" from the context menu. Choose to add an AJAX-enabled WCF Service and call it "ReportService", as shown in Figure 10-45.

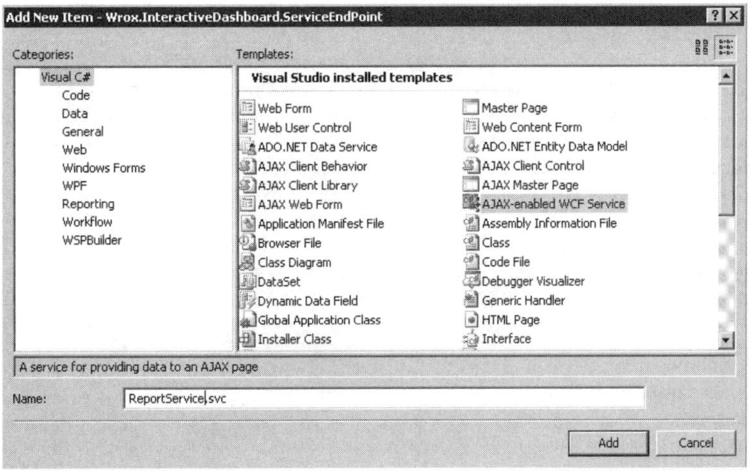

Figure 10-45

This adds the `ReportService.svc` file and changes the existing `Web.config` file, as shown in Listing 10-9. Look at the new `Web.config` file. Most of the elements in the modified `Web.config` file are basic WCF settings.

Note that the default configuration for a WCF service is side-by-side execution with ASP.NET, so you need to set an application-level flag called `aspNetCompatibilityEnabled` and set it to `true` to indicate that you want your WCF service to run and behave just as native ASP.NET code.

The body style that is the response type used in the operation in the ReportServices file (see Listing 10-10) is set to Bare. The Bare setting is not supported by the `WebScriptEnablingBehavior`. You need to specify the `WebHttpBehavior` on the endpoint by changing `<enableWebScript />` to `<webHttp/>`. Bare messages are more lightweight and easier to work with comparing to wrapped response messages, but they are limited to a single input parameter. Because our service has no complexity we will skip the use of wrapped messages as the response type.

These changes in the configuration file in conjunction with the `<webHttpBinding>` standard binding gives a `WebHttpBehavior` to your endpoint that exposes your WCF service through HTTP requests and responses that use JSON style messaging instead of SOAP. This is ideal for jQuery/Ajax calls that you will incorporate into the dashboard later in this section.

Listing 10-9: Modified Web.config file

```xml
<?xml version="1.0" encoding="utf-8" ?>
<configuration>
  <system.web>
    <compilation debug="true" />
  </system.web>
  <system.serviceModel>
    <serviceHostingEnvironment aspNetCompatibilityEnabled="true" />
    <services>
      <service name="Wrox.InteractiveDashboard.ServiceEndPoint.ReportService">
        <endpoint address=""
              behaviorConfiguration="Wrox.InteractiveDashboard.
              ServiceEndPoint.ReportServiceAspNetAjaxBehavior"
              binding="webHttpBinding" contract="Wrox.InteractiveDashboard.
        ServiceEndPoint.ReportService" />
      </service>
    </services>
    <behaviors>
      <endpointBehaviors>
        <behavior name="Wrox.InteractiveDashboard.ServiceEndPoint.
        ReportServiceAspNetAjaxBehavior">
          <webHttp/>
        </behavior>
      </endpointBehaviors>
    </behaviors>
  </system.serviceModel>
</configuration>
```

The `ReportService.svc` file contains the markup and code-behind for the service. `ReportService.cs` is where the actual logic of your service will go, so go ahead and change it to what is shown in Listing 10-10.

For the sake of simplicity, no interface is used to define the contract, so the `ReportService` class implicitly represents the contract of the service and its explicit implementation, which is pretty straightforward except for a call into the `GetReports()` method of the `ReportRepository` class. Note that the `ServiceContract` and `OperationContract` attributes are the attributes that you may have used previously in your other WCF programming exposures, so I will skip explaining them here.

In addition to setting the `aspNetCompatibilityEnabled` `Web.config` flag to `true`, you need to explicitly opt-in for the compatibility mode on the WCF service by decorating the `ReportService` class with the `AspNetCompatibilityRequirements` attribute and setting it to either `Required` or `Allowed`. In the following example, you won't use any ASP.NET intrinsic objects (for example, the `HttpContext` object), so `Allowed` should work fine. Arguably, `Required` is a better choice, because if `Allowed` is specified, you can still run your service side-by-side even if `Web.config` says `false`. However, if you do this, you could have a hard time finding out why the `HttpContext.Current` is null!

Note that the `BodyStyle` property is set to `WebMessageBodyStyle.Bare`, as you don't want the service to write extra XML elements and return a `Wrapped` response message, only bare un-wrapped JSON. Unlike ASMX, the ability to return raw non-ASP.NET AJAX formatted data in a bare unwrapped format is a bonus that the WCF Web programming model offers. Because you will be using jQuery to call the service, this helps you avoid using the Microsoft Ajax client libraries and ScriptManager.

Listing 10-10: WCF service code behind

```
namespace Wrox.InteractiveDashboard.ServiceEndPoint
{
    [ServiceContract(Namespace = "")]
    [AspNetCompatibilityRequirements(RequirementsMode =
    AspNetCompatibilityRequirementsMode.Allowed)]
    public class ReportService
    {
        [OperationContract]
        [WebGet(BodyStyle = WebMessageBodyStyle.Bare, ResponseFormat =
        WebMessageFormat.Json)]
        public Report[] GetReports()
        {
            return ReportRepository.GetReports();
        }
    }
}
```

The endpoint to reach the method on the implicit interface is defined in the `ReportService.svc` file (see Listing 10-11). Although, you could define your service inline in the .svc file, this approach is not as flexible as the code-behind service residing in an assembly. Assembly-based services can be shared across several service-host applications and are more maintainable.

The `@ServiceHost` directive indicates the language being used to implement the service along with the fact that the WCF service should be compiled with debug symbols and the name of the code-behind file. Finally, through the `Service` attribute, the markup indicates the CLR type name of the hosted service. This should be a fully qualified name that equals to the `Wrox.InteractiveDashboard.ServiceEndPoint.ReportService` type, which in turn implements your service contract.

Listing 10-11: WCF service markup

```
<%@ ServiceHost Language="C#" Debug="true"
    Service="Wrox.InteractiveDashboard.ServiceEndPoint.ReportService"
CodeBehind="ReportService.svc.cs" %>
```

At this point, the WCF service is pretty much all done. To host the service that you have just created and test it right inside of Visual Studio, all you need to do is hit F5. That's it! This launches the Cassini server, which in turn uses the `Web.config` file to expose the appropriate endpoint, as shown in Figure 10-46.

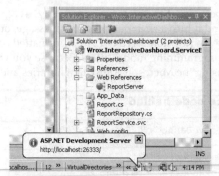

Figure 10-46

At this point, you should be able to browse to the service at `http://localhost:<PortNumber>/ReportService.svc`, as shown in Figure 10-47. As you can see, metadata publishing for this service is disabled. If you follow the instructions on the page, you should be able to get the publishing metadata feature up and working after completing three easy steps that require modifying the `Web.config` file. Publishing metadata allows clients to retrieve the metadata using an HTTP/GET request using the `?wsdl` query string.

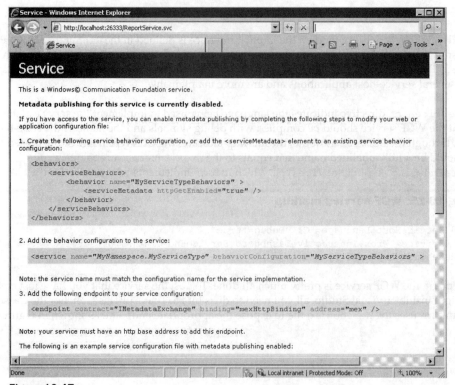

Figure 10-47

Building the Interactive Dashboard Web Part

With the backend WCF service created, the question is how you can use it in an interactive dashboard wrapped in a SharePoint Web part. The steps required by a developer to accomplish this task aren't much different from those required to create an Ajax enabled Web Part.

First, create a C# class library project and call it `Wrox.InteractiveDashboard.SharePoint`. Next, add a user control to the project and name it `ssrsDashboardUI.ascx`. The user control comes with no code-behind and should be deployed to the `[..]\12\TEMPLATE\CONTROLTEMPLATES` folder on the server. This file will contain the user interface (UI) representation of the interactive dashboard that can be dynamically loaded into a Web Part. The HTML markup for your control should look like Listing 10-12.

Notice the first section of highlighted code. There are several placeholders surrounded with $ signs that will be replaced at runtime with appropriate information returned from the service.

At the very end of the user control's HTML markup, there are two references to a jQuery runtime script and a custom JavaScript file used in this project called `dashboard.js`. You can get the jQuery runtime at `http://www.devhorizon.com/go/11`. Custom JavaScript dashboard.js is also included in the code download of this chapter.

Listing 10-12: ssrsDashboardUI user control HTML markup

```
<%@ Control Language="C#" %>
<div id="wrapper">
    <div id="header">
        <img src="/_layouts/images/SSRSInerativeDashboard/aw_logo.png"/>
    </div>

    <div id="content">
        <!--DIV: Ajax Loading Icon-->
        <div id="reports">
          <div class="loader">
            <img alt="Loading" src="/_layouts/images
            /SSRSInerativeDashboard/loading.gif" /> Please wait...
          </div>
          <div id="reportsContainer"></div>
          <div style="clear:both"></div>
        </div>

        <!--DIV:Content-->
          <div id="templates" class="off">
            <div id="report_template">
              <div class="dashboard_item">
                  <div class="dashboard_header">
                    <h2>$name$</h2>
                    <a href=$hideAction$>Hide</a>
                  </div>
                  <div class="dashboard_body">
                    <p>
                      <b>Published By</b>:$publishedby$<br />
                      <b>Published Date</b>:$publisheddate$<br />
```

(continued)

Listing 10-12: (Continued)

```
                <b>Description</b>:$description$
            </p>
        </div>
        <div class="dashboard_footer">
            <a href="$urlAccess$">View Report</a>
            <a class="withParams" href="$urlAccessWithParameters$">
            View Report without filters</a>
        </div>
    </div>
</div>
</div>


    <script type="text/javascript" src="/_layouts/
    SSRSInerativeDashboard/jquery-1.3.1.js"></script>
    <script type="text/javascript" src="/_layouts/
    SSRSInerativeDashboard/dashboard.js"></script>
    </div>
</div>
```

The `dashboard.js` file contains the core JavaScript functionality for the interactive dashboard to function, as shown in Listing 10-13. This file must be deployed to the `[..]\12\TEMPLATE\LAYOUTS\ SSRSInerativeDashboard` folder to be successfully referenced by the user control.

The `initGrid()` JavaScript method will be called from the Interactive Dashboard Web Part. This method simply calls into another method called `refreshGrid()` which is responsible for making an Ajax call to the backend WCF service.

In the `refreshGrid()` method, first, you declare a $() function – a very powerful function in jQuery. You use this function to select elements from the document by passing a string containing CSS syntax. This function returns a jQuery object that contains all the elements that match the CSS selector. If you know the basics of CSS selectors, this syntax should look familiar. Once the matching element ("#reports") is returned, the script calls the `addClass()` function to add the specified class ("loading") to the matched element. This line renders a loading Ajax icon when the page is requested, which informs the visitors that there is more information to be displayed or still to be loaded on the page.

The complete code for the CSS file used in this section can be found in the code download for this book.

Next, you need to make the Ajax call. Thankfully, making Ajax calls with jQuery is relatively easy through a handful of ready to use functions. To connect to the backend service using jQuery, you should use the `$.ajax()` function — jQuery's low-level AJAX implementation. This function connects to the service and sends arguments to the service using GET and JSON. When you specify JSON as the data type, jQuery automatically prepares the result for your callback function so that you can use it right away. As you can see, `error`, `success`, and `complete` callbacks are also specified to give the developer more information about the Ajax call.

Finally, you pass the returned JSON object to the `bindReportsData()` function which in turn iterates through the returned Report objects, reads the metadata about each report, and binds it to the HTML portion of the user control. As you will see later in this chapter, when users click on the VIEW REPORT link on the dashboard, they will be redirected to a custom SharePoint Application page called `RSViewer.aspx`. This page is used to render the reports using the URL Access method. The URL address of the custom `RSViewer.aspx` page is passed to the `dashboard.js` script from the Web Part (via the `report_viewUrl` variable). Then it is concatenated with the URL of the actual report from the service, and finally it is written to the HTML portion of the link in the user control.

For more information on rendering reports using URL Access, see the official documentation at `http://www.devhorizon.com/go/12`.

Listing 10-13: dashboard.js

```
function initGrid() {
    refreshGrid();
}

function refreshGrid() {

    $("#reports").addClass("loading");

    $.ajax(
    {
        type: "GET",
        dataType: "json",
        async: true,
        url: report_serviceBaseUrl.replace('$op$',
        'GetReports').replace('$params$', ''),
        cache: false,
        complete: function(object, status) {
            $("#reports").removeClass("loading");
        },
        error: function(obj, error, args) {
          alert('An exception was thrown in the backend WCF service:' +
          obj.responseText);
        },
        success: function(json, status) {
            if (json) {
                bindReportsData(json);
            }
        }
    });
}

function bindReportsData(data) {
    var container = $("#reportsContainer").empty();
    if (data) {
        var template = $("#report_template").html();

        for (var i = 0; i < data.length; i++) {
            var reportUrlAccess = report_viewUrl.replace('$reportUrl$',
```

(continued)

Listing 10-13: (Continued)

```
                "reportUrl=" + data[i]["UrlAccess"]);
                var reportUrlAccessWithParameters = "";
                var hasReportWithParams = false;

    // Code Omitted for brevity

                var html = template.replace("$name$", data[i]["Name"])
                    .replace("$description$", data[i]["Description"])
                    .replace("$publishedby$", data[i]["PublishedBy"])
                    .replace("$publisheddate$", data[i]["PublishedDate"])
                    .replace("$urlAccess$", reportUrlAccess)
                    .replace("$urlAccessWithParameters$",
                    reportUrlAccessWithParameters)
                    .replace("$hideAction$", "javascript:alert('Write code to
                    close this report.');");
                var item = $(html);
                if (hasReportWithParams) {
                    item.addClass("withParams");
                }
                container.append(item);
            }
        }
    }
```

Now that the rendering portion of the interactive dashboard has been created, it is time to jump to the Web Part and add the necessary code to wire everything up. In this section you create a custom Web Part that hosts the interactive dashboard. The Web Part will be an ASP.NET 2.0 Web Part that inherits directly from the `System.Web.UI.WebControls.WebParts.WebPart` class, but it will be deployed to a SharePoint site.

The first step is to add a new C# Class named `SSRSInerativeDashboard.cs` to the existing project in Visual Studio. Because the requirements of the interactive dashboard dictate that it should not hold up the page rendering while it retrieves reports metadata, the Web Part needs to load its content asynchronously.

As previously covered, the user interface (UI) of the dashboard is fully encapsulated in a user control named `ssrsDashboardUI.ascx`, so you need to load the user control into your Web Part. This is done in the overridden `CreateChildControls()` method for the Web Part by calling the `LoadControl()` method, as shown in Listing 10-14.

After the user control is dynamically loaded and the UI portion of the Web Part is rendered, there is still one thing missing, and that is referencing the cascading style sheets. To put together all the UI elements and complete the appearance of the dashboard, you need to reference a custom CSS file. Although you can directly reference a CSS file in many UI artifacts in SharePoint such as master pages or application pages, referencing a custom CSS file that is unique to a Web Part requires a little bit of more work.

There are a couple of ways to accomplish this. The following example uses a helper method to register the custom CSS file in the `OnPreRender()` method of the Web Part. The helper method uses the `CssRegistration` class (inheriting from the `Microsoft.SharePoint.WebControls` class) to register the external CSS file. The result of this call is a `<link/>` element that is inserted into the resulting HTML page with the external CSS file applied, as shown below.

```
<link rel="stylesheet" type="text/css" href="/_layouts/SSRSInerativeDashboard/
dashboard.css"/>
```

The complete code for both the CSS file and the helper method used in this section can be found in the code download for this book.

Although the user control contains all the dashboard's UI elements, it certainly doesn't include the required code to emit client side JavaScript Ajax call to the WCF backend service. Therefore, you need to include this logic in the Web Part code. This is done in the `Render()` method and after the user control's `RenderControl()` method is called.

First, in the JavaScript code the path to the WCF service is specified and stored in the `report_serviceBaseUrl` variable. In order to keep the example simple, the path to the WCF service is hard coded. Ideally, this should be either exposed as a Web Part property or if the service is hosted in SharePoint's _layouts or _vti_bin virtual directories, the path should construct at runtime.

Next, the URL of the `RSViewer.aspx` page that is responsible for rendering the report is passed to the `dashboard.js` script. Each variable in the JavaScript code contains a bunch of placeholders surrounded with $ signs that will be replaced with appropriate operations and parameters in the `dashboard.js` script.

Finally, a call into the `initGrid()` method is made, which in turn prepares the Ajax call and takes care of the rest of the rendering tasks as discussed previously.

Listing 10-14: Interactive Dashboard Web Part

```
namespace Wrox.InteractiveDashboard.SharePoint
{
    [Guid("28df167c-7587-4ef4-b17f-1f8920a6b15a")]
    public class SSRSInerativeDashboard : WebPart
    {
        UserControl dashUI = null;
        public SSRSInerativeDashboard()
        {
            this.ExportMode = WebPartExportMode.All;
        }
        protected override void CreateChildControls()
        {
            dashUI=(UserControl)Page.LoadControl("/_controltemplates/
ssrsDashboardUI.ascx");
            dashUI.ID = "DashUI";
            this.Controls.Add(dashUI);
        }
```

(continued)

351

Listing 10-14: (Continued)

```
        protected override void OnPreRender(EventArgs e)
        {
            Utility.RegisterWebPartCSS("/_layouts/SSRSInerativeDashboard/
            dashboard.css", this);
            base.OnPreRender(e);
        }
    protected override void Render(HtmlTextWriter writer)
        {
            dashUI.RenderControl(writer);
            writer.Write(@"<script type=""text/javascript""
            language=""javascript"">");
            string wcfUrl =
            "http://localhost:26333/ReportService.svc/$op$?$params$";
            writer.Write(string.Format(@" var report_serviceBaseUrl =
            ""{0}"";",wcfUrl));
            writer.Write(@" var report_viewUrl =
            ""/_layouts/SSRSInerativeDashboard/RSViewer.aspx?$reportUrl$"";");
            writer.Write("$(initGrid);");
            writer.Write(@"</script>");
        }
    }
}
```

With the Web Part implementation finished, the last step is to create a custom `RSViewer.aspx` application page with code-behind to render the requested reports. Although you can redirect the requests to the out of the box `RSViewerPage.aspx` page or your own custom report viewer page (see the "Displaying Your Reports Your Way" section), in the following example you will learn another technique for accessing reports in Reporting Services other than the popular out of the box Report Viewer Web Part. This approach is known as accessing reports using URL access.

Begin by adding an ASPX page to your project and name it `RSViewer.aspx`. The idea here is that the page is deployed to `[..]\12\TEMPLATE\LAYOUTS\SSRSInerativeDashboard` folder and the code-behind is going to be contained in a C# class, which will be deployed to the GAC.

Listing 10-15 shows the complete code for `RSViewer.aspx`. Notice that the first line of the `RSViewer` page references the `Wrox.InteractiveDashboard.SharePoint` assembly. At this point the assembly does not yet exist, but it will when the project is deployed. Next, look at the `@Page` directive. Notice how it indicates that the `RSViewer` page inherits from the `Wrox.InteractiveDashboard.SharePoint.RSViewer` class. Finally, notice that the `RSViewer` page uses a master page named `application.master`. This master page lives in the SharePoint's _layouts virtual directory with the rest of SharePoint's system pages to provide a consistent look and feel across all such pages.

Because the requirement of the interactive dashboard dictates that the dashboard page that hosts the interactive dashboard Web Part and RSViewer page must use the same master page, you need to write extra code to satisfy such a requirement. When the page renders, you will need to flip the default master page used in the RSViewer.aspx page with the site's master page in the OnPreInit() method of the code behind file.

In addition to a code-behind file, the RSViewer page comes with some inline code and a JavaScript function. Notice the second highlighted block in Listing 10-15. The inline code reads the reportUrl from the query string, appends appropriate parameters, and renders the requested report in an iframe using the URL access technique. It also uses the adjustIframe() JavaScript function to adjust the height of iframe to the rendered report.

Listing 10-15: RSViewer.aspx page HTML markup

```
<%@ Assembly Name="Wrox.InteractiveDashboard.SharePoint,
Version=1.0.0.0, Culture=neutral, PublicKeyToken=4668604e0bfeca67"%>
<%@ Page Language="C#" EnableSessionState="true" ValidateRequest="False"
Inherits="Wrox.InteractiveDashboard.SharePoint.RSViewer"
MasterPageFile="~/_layouts/application.master" %>
// Code Omitted for brevity
<asp:Content ID="Content6" ContentPlaceHolderID="PlaceHolderMain" runat="server">
<div id="wrapper">
  <div id="content">
    <div id="report">
      <% string accessUrl = Request["reportUrl"];
        if (accessUrl != null){
          accessUrl = String.Concat(accessUrl,"&rc:Stylesheet=ssrsreport");
          if (!String.IsNullOrEmpty(Request["reportParameters"]))
          {
            string reportParameters = Request["reportParameters"].Replace(",",
            "&");accessUrl = String.Concat(accessUrl, "&" + reportParameters);
          }
          Response.Write("<iframe src='" + accessUrl + "' id='reportIframe'
          frameborder='0' height='400'></iframe>");
        }
      %>
  </div>
</div>
<script type="text/javascript">
  function adjustIframe() {
    var e = document.getElementById('reportIframe');
    if (e){
      var h = 0;
      if (!e.contentDocument){
        if(e.contentWindow.document.getElementById
          ("ReportFrameReportViewerControl"))
          {
          var f = e.contentWindow.document.getElementById
           ("ReportFrameReportViewerControl");
          if (f){
```

(continued)

Listing 10-15: (Continued)

```
                          f = f.contentWindow.document.getElementById("report");
                          if (f){
                            f = f.contentWindow.document.getElementById("oReportDiv")
                            if (f){
                              f.style.overflow = "hidden";
                              h = f.scrollHeight;
                            }
                          }
                        }
                        f = e.contentWindow.document.getElementById
                          ("ParametersRowReportViewerControl")
                        if (f){
                          h += f.offsetHeight;
                          if (f.parentNode.childNodes.length == 3){
                            h += f.parentNode.childNodes[1].offsetHeight;
                          }
                        }
                      } else if (e.contentWindow.document.body){
                        h = e.contentWindow.document.body.scrollHeight;
                        e.contentWindow.document.body.style.overflow = "hidden";
                      }
                      if (h < 400) h = 400;
                      e.style.height = h + "px";
                    }
                  }
                }
                setInterval("adjustIframe()", 250);
              </script>
              </div>
          </asp:Content>
```

The code-behind for the RSViewer page is a C# class that inherits from Microsoft.SharePoint.
WebControls.LayoutsPageBase, as shown in Listing 10-16. The LayoutsPageBase class provides
everything you need to create a page that lives in SharePoint's _layouts virtual directory. Along with
inheriting from the LayoutsPageBase class, you must also override the OnPreInit() and
OnPreRender() methods. First, you need to flip the master page dynamically and set it to the master
page of the current SPWeb object. Next, you need to register the CSS file that is referenced in the page's
HTML elements using pretty much the same technique as in the interactive dashboard Web Part.

Listing 10-16: RSViewer.aspx code-behind

```
public partial class RSViewer : LayoutsPageBase
    {
    protected override void OnPreInit(EventArgs e){
        base.OnPreInit(e);
        SPWeb curWeb = SPContext.Current.Web;
        this.MasterPageFile = curWeb.MasterUrl;
    }
    protected override void OnPreRender(EventArgs e){
    Utility.RegisterPageCSS("/_layouts/SSRSInerativeDashboard/dashboard.css",
    this.Page);
        base.OnPreRender(e);
    }
    }
```

That's it! The interactive dashboard and associated parts are now complete. Let's go ahead and deploy everything to a SharePoint site. At this point the Web Part can be used within a SharePoint site and dropped onto one of the available zones of a Web Part page. If the WCF service is up and running and the Web Part is pointing to the right URL, you should see a rendering icon while the Web Part communicates with the backend service to retrieve information about the reports, as shown in Figure 10-48.

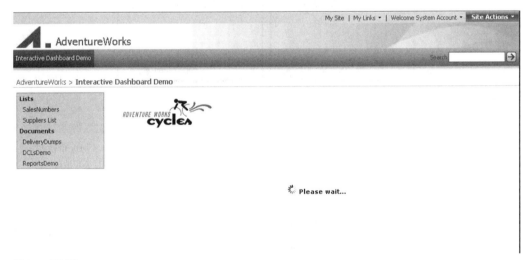

Figure 10-48

After the Ajax call is made successfully, the interactive dashboard is rendered, as shown in Figure 10-49.

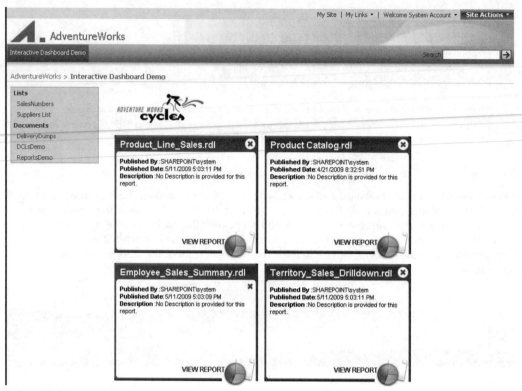

Figure 10-49

As demonstrated in Figure 10-49, for each report in the destination Report Library , a box is created that has the name of the report (which in this example is the name of the `.rdl` file) on the top bar, a VIEW REPORT link at the bottom, and bunch of metadata inside. Hover over the VIEW REPORT link and examine the link to the `RSViewer.aspx` page.

When you click on the link to view a report, you will be taken to the `RSViewer.aspx` page, which in turn renders the report, as shown in Figure 10-50. Notice that how the height of the rendering area will be adjusted based on the height of the report through the `adjustIframe()` JavaScript function.

Adjusting the height of an `iframe` that renders a report is one of the most frequently asked questions in Reporting Services forums. It can be easily accomplished using the script provided in this example.

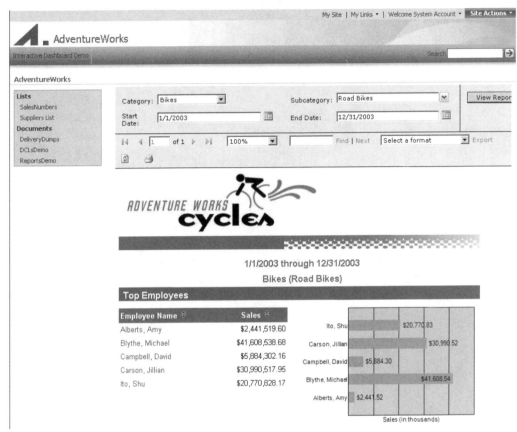

Figure 10-50

Summary

When you put together all the pieces presented in this chapter, you have a powerful array of options for displaying and interacting with your reports deployed in a Report Server in integrated mode. This chapter began with an overview of the out-of-the-box ways of putting reports onto SharePoint pages and then moved into more custom approaches of displaying reports.

The discussion described several realistic business scenarios based on experience in field. The chapter also offered guidance on why you should stay away from live reporting against SharePoint content and configuration databases. As a report developer, you have many options available to you, such as using SharePoint web services and the object model to extract what you need from SharePoint.

If you have completed all the procedures in the earlier chapters of this book, you're ready to test your skills by learning how to use Reporting Services features to manage your reports and take things to the next level. That's what Chapter 11 covers.

11

Managing Reports

Once a collection of reports and other content is out there on a SharePoint site, it will need to be managed. One thing that is often misunderstood is the difference between content and report server administration management. A Reporting Services installation consists of several server side administration tasks at the farm level, which typically falls within the responsibilities of the farm administration role.

On the other hand, site collection administrators and content managers can perform various tasks to control access to reports and data sources, automate report generation, and create historical archives. All these items can be managed independently of each other through a series of interfaces installed by Reporting Services Add-in for SharePoint. To manage items effectively, you need to know which tasks site collection administrators and content managers perform and where they should apply such settings.

The Reporting Services management story in SharePoint integrated mode revolves around the following topics, which will be covered throughout this chapter.

- ❑ Client tools for management
- ❑ Scalability planning
- ❑ Managing data sources
- ❑ Demystifying unattended report-processing account
- ❑ Understanding on-demand report execution
- ❑ Report-processing options
- ❑ Static and data-driven subscriptions

Client Tools for Management

New users are often confused by which configuration tools are available when Reporting Services is installed in SharePoint integrated mode. There are three tools for managing your report server instance in SharePoint integrated mode: SQL Server Management Studio (SSMS), Reporting Services Configuration Manager and SharePoint itself! In most cases, there is no overlap in functionality among the tools; for example, the Reporting Services Configuration Manager tool is used to configure a Reporting Services installation and does not help you manage report server content. Content management is performed through various functionalities installed by the Reporting Services Add-in and enables you to take advantage of report processing and management capabilities within SharePoint.

In previous chapters, you learned how to use the Reporting Services Configuration Manager tool, so you won't be walked through that tool once again. One thing needs to be highlighted, though: Report Manager, which is one of the available configuration tools in native mode, is not supported for a report server that you configure for SharePoint integrated mode, as shown in Figure 11-1. Remember, in integrated mode, SharePoint is the new web interface to manage many tasks related to your report server instance.

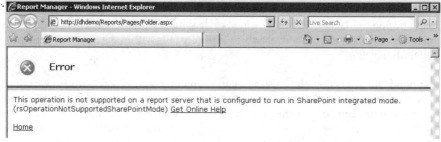

Figure 11-1

When you use SSMS to connect to an instance of report server that runs in SharePoint integrated mode, it's recommended that you enter a URL to a SharePoint site rather than the URL of report server instance, as shown in Figure 11-2. Also notice that if you are using Windows Authentication, you must connect using your credentials. If you select Basic Authentication or Forms Authentication, type the account and password (see Figure 11-3).

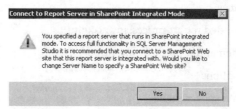

Figure 11-2

Figure 11-3

Once you choose the proper authentication method and based on the URL you entered (SharePoint site URL or SharePoint integrated mode report server URL) you will see two different views in the SSMS console. Figure 11-4 shows the SSMS console when you specify the URL of a SharePoint Web site in which the Reporting Services integration feature is activated. Figure 11-5 demonstrates the second view of the SSMS console when you directly enter the URL of the report server configured in SharePoint integrated mode.

Figure 11-4

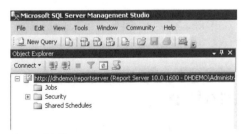

FIGURE 11-5

Notice that when you connect to the report server instead of the SharePoint site, there are a limited number of tasks that you can perform using SSMS. This is because the report server can only return application data stored or managed in the report server catalog, not from the SharePoint configuration and content databases. If you have the required permissions, there are two common tasks that you will get in both views. First, you can view and set server properties and defaults by right-clicking the site to which you are connected. Second, you can view and cancel jobs. However, there are two additional tasks you will get when connecting to a SharePoint site, as shown in Figure 11-6. First, you can create and manage shared schedules defined for the site to which you are connected. Second, you can view the permission levels defined for the site to which you are connected.

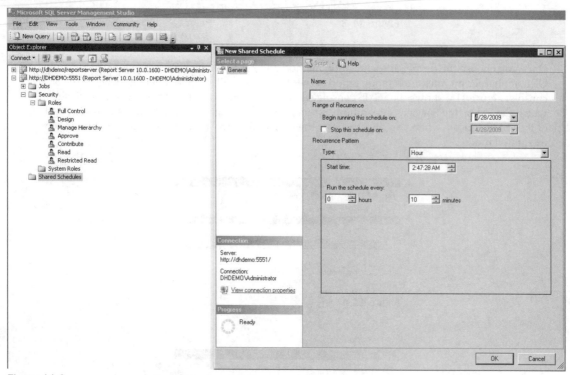

Figure 11-6

Scalability Planning

One way to manage Reporting Services content on a SharePoint site is to store all reports in a single report library and all data sources in a single data connection library, but before long, you'll find that the number of reports and related files become so large that it is difficult to manage security, to find content, or even to browse through them using built-in display methods such as out-of-the-box SharePoint list views. It is common in the early stage of designing a business intelligence application to wonder how many reports or data sources can exist in a single document library.

This surprisingly simple question can reveal a lot about the scalability considerations of your Business Intelligence solutions deployed to SharePoint. A while ago Microsoft, published a white paper titled *Working with Large Lists in Office SharePoint Server 2007* (http://www.devhorizon.com/go/8), which is one of the best papers published with regard to best practices in scaling your SharePoint lists without an adverse impact on farm performance. The test results in this white paper demonstrate the best practices for accessing and working with extremely large lists. The whitepaper also evaluates the performance characteristics of large SharePoint lists under various loads and modes of operation. Although this white paper appears to be focused exclusively on SharePoint lists, report and data connection libraries are special document libraries, and document libraries, in turn, are just specialized lists. That being said, the capacity and scalability best practices that apply to SharePoint lists also apply to document libraries that contain your reports and data sources.

The conclusion of this paper is that the maximum number of items supported in a list with recursive folders is 5 million, and a 2000 items per list limitation can be mitigated by grouping items within containers (folders). There is one question that needs to be answered here: Does this mean that you can store 5 million reports in a report library as well?

The answer is certainly not! If you read the paper to the end, you will find out that if the rows in a SharePoint list exceed 5000, the SQL Server lock that affects those rows is escalated from a row lock to a table lock on the Lists table within the SharePoint content database. There is one important thing to note regarding the lock escalation: This is a SQL Server behavior and the scope is to the content DB, not the site collection. Since all the lists within the same site collection are stored in a single table in the underlying content database, lock escalation can severely affect operations in other lists.

Structuring your reports and related files using folders not only helps you come up with a more scalable solution; it is also useful for organizing content into logical groups by subject matter, target audience, security, or any combination of all. Folders can be nested into a hierarchical structure, and you can provide a description for a folder to supply users with more information about the folder contents.

Managing Data Sources

A data source contains all the connection information for a dataset used in a report. As you have seen in several chapters of this book, data sources can be created for a specific data set or may be shared and repurposed among different reports. Typically, most of the reports in a Business Intelligence application get their data from a common data repository; hence, they can leverage a common set of connectivity characteristics. In Chapter 9, you learned how shared data sources can be advantageous by minimizing administrative overhead and by simplifying the deployment process.

By introducing data connection libraries in Microsoft Office SharePoint Server 2007, Microsoft introduced another feature with a reusability goal in mind. Data connection libraries were designed with one primary objective: to abstract data connection settings from the dependant files. Although a data connection library is not required for publishing your Reporting Services data sources, it is always a good idea to have all of your connection files grouped in one place.

Note that a data connection library not only can contain Reporting Services data sources; it can also contain an Office Data Connection (ODC) file or an Universal Data Connection (UDC) file used by Microsoft Office InfoPath 2007 and Excel Services, as shown in Figure 11-7. For example, InfoPath 2007 uses data connections that conform to the Universal Data Connection (UDC) file schema and typically have either a *.udcx or *.xml file extension. The goal is to have a central entry point to the underlying data so when your reports, InfoPath forms, and Excel files transition from development machines to test and finally production farms, their connection information is managed separately and can be easily updated to match new environmental settings. Remember, it is all about reusability, right?

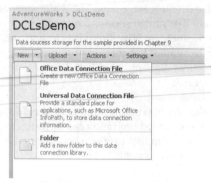

Figure 11-7

Security in a Data Source

Most likely when you design and test your reports in an authoring tool such as BIDS, you use a local database that represents only a subset of production data. Since everything exists in a standalone setup, chances are that you won't face any security issues. However, when your reports are deployed to production, the underlying data used to provide content to your reports are usually hosted on remote servers. To retrieve data for a report, a report server must connect to the remote server using a set of credentials you provide in advance or the ones obtained at runtime.

A data source is the last stop before the security context under which underlying data is accessed is evaluated. For example, if you store credentials in a data source, the underlying data is always accessed under the security context of the stored account. That being said, it is very important that you understand how you should configure security settings in your data sources. Typically, the network policies implemented in your organization dictate the kinds of security settings you can use in your data sources.

For example, if SharePoint web application's authentication provider is set to Kerberos and the Reporting Services authentication mode is configured to Windows Authentication (Central Administration ⇨ Application Management ⇨ Configure Reporting Services Integration), the simplest type of security to implement in your data source is Windows Authentication (see the first option in Figure 11-8). This way, the user's credentials would be delegated across multiple computers all the way to the underlying data source. Windows Authentication (integrated security) option must only be selected when Kerberos is supported or when SharePoint web front end server, report server, and underlying data sources all coexist in the same machine (that is, standalone installation).

> To fully understand various security implications involved in the overall report execution process, it is important to differentiate among the following three security contexts:

> **a) Security context for network connection to a computer that hosts a data source or resource.**
>
> **b) Security context used in authenticating to a data source (not applicable for some data sources).**
>
> **c) Security context used to retrieve data from a data source (not applicable for some data sources).**

If your network does not support Kerberos or when you create reports against data sources that don't use Windows credentials for authentication, you will need to work around connection constraints, because soon you will find yourself getting trapped into an issue called *double hop*. Simply put, Windows credentials can be passed across one computer connection before they expire. A user connection to a SharePoint web application counts as the first connection (one hop). If the user opens a report that retrieves data from a remote server, that login counts as a second connection (second hop) and will fail if you specified the connection to use Windows Authentication (integrated security) without using Kerberos. If multiple connections are required to complete a round trip from the SharePoint user's computer to an external report data source, your best solution is either of the following options:

❑   Prompt the user for credentials

❑   Stored credentials

When you right-click a published data source and choose Edit Data Source Definition from the ECB (Edit Control box) menu, the page demonstrated in Figure 11-8 is shown. There are three settings in this page that deserve more attention. The first is Prompt the user for credentials, the second is Stored Credentials, and the third is Unattended report processing account. Before we dive into the last two settings, let's walk through the Prompt the user for credentials option.

When you configure a report data source to use prompted credentials, each time a user accesses the report that uses this data source, the Login dialog box pops up, asking for the user's name and password to retrieve the data. This is an ideal security precaution that makes sure only those who have enough permission will get to see the underlying data, but it only works for on demand access to reports. We will discuss on-demand report execution later in this chapter. Also note that prompted credentials can be a Windows account or a database login. Just select the Use as Windows credentials option in case you opt in for Windows accounts and that will do it.

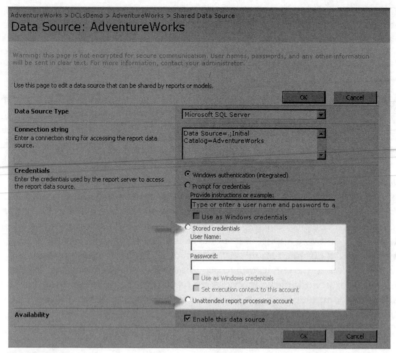

AdventureWorks > DCLsDemo > AdventureWorks > Shared Data Source

Data Source: AdventureWorks

Warning: this page is not encrypted for secure communication. User names, passwords, and any other information will be sent in clear text. For more information, contact your administrator.

Use this page to edit a data source that can be shared by reports or models.

	OK Cancel

Data Source Type	Microsoft SQL Server

Connection string Enter a connection string for accessing the report data source.	Data Source=.;Initial Catalog=AdventureWorks

Credentials
Enter the credentials used by the report server to access the report data source.

- Windows authentication (integrated)
- Prompt for credentials
  Provide instructions or example:
  Type or enter a user name and password to a
  ☐ Use as Windows credentials
- Stored credentials
  User Name:

  Password:

  ☐ Use as Windows credentials
  ☐ Set execution context to this account
- Unattended report processing account

Availability   ☑ Enable this data source

	Ok Cancel

Figure 11-8

Stored Credentials

Several features in Reporting Services such as subscriptions or scheduled report history generation require that you hard code the credentials in the data source. As previously mentioned, stored credentials are also recommended as part of a strategy for accessing remote database servers when Kerberos is not an option. Obviously, this account must also be granted read permission at minimum to access the underlying data. You have probably heard repeatedly that you must not enter the credentials in the connection string field, where it appears in clear text to any user who has Edit Items permission in the document library that contains your data source.

By storing credentials, they are encrypted and stored in the report server catalog. In addition to encrypting the credentials, the password that you enter is not visible like all other password fields in various SharePoint user interfaces. However, as you can see on the top of the page shown in Figure 11-8, SharePoint warns you if you are not using a secure communication channel when setting up stored credentials.

You can select options that determine how the stored credentials are authenticated. If you select Use as Windows credentials, the stored credentials should be a Windows user account, because it is passed to Windows for subsequent authentication. Otherwise, the credentials are passed to the database server for authentication.

There are two important tips to remember with regard to Use as Windows credentials. First, do not check this box if your data source is using database authentication (for example, SQL Server authentication). In case you want to log in and retrieve data using SQL account, note that for SQL Server, Oracle, ODBC, or

OLE DB data sources, the user name and password get appended to the connection string. For Analysis Services, the connection succeeds only if you are using the TCP/IP protocol; otherwise it fails. Finally, in XML data sources, connection fails on the report server if SQL logins are used.

Second, the Windows domain user account must also have permission to log on locally. This permission allows the report server to impersonate the user on the report server box and send the connection request to the external data source as that impersonated user.

The next option is Set execution context to this account. You should select this option only if you want to set the execution context on the database server by impersonating the account that represents the stored credentials. For example, in SQL Server databases, think of this option as Transact-SQL SETUSER function. There are two important tips to remember when selecting this check box. First, for SQL Server databases, this option is not supported with Windows users; use SQL Server users instead. Second, do not use this option for reports initialized by subscriptions, report history, or snapshots, because these processes need a valid Windows user context to function.

Demystifying Unattended Report Processing Account

Report server never allows its service account (with its administrator permissions) to be delegated or impersonated when connecting to other computers, so if no other credentials are stored in a given data source, report server must use an account to access the data source, right? Well, in the Reporting Services world, this liaison account is referred to as an unattended execution account. Simply put, unattended execution accounts can be used by report server in the following two scenarios:

❑ **Security context for network connection:** Sends connection requests over the network to connect to external report data sources such as an XML file. Another example would be when connecting to SQL Server using a SQL account stored in the data source. In this case, the network connection context is made under the unattended execution account because Windows has no knowledge of what to do with a SQL account. If the unattended execution account is not specified, report server impersonates its service account but removes all administrator permissions when sending the connection request.

❑ **Access to external resource:** Retrieves external resources used in a report for anonymous users. For example, when you are authoring a report in BIDS that links to an external image, in preview mode your credentials will be used to display the image. Once the report is deployed and viewed on the SharePoint site, report server uses its unattended execution account to retrieve the image. If the unattended execution account is not specified, the image is retrieved using no credentials (i.e., anonymous access). Obviously, if neither of these two accounts has sufficient rights to access the image, it won't be displayed in your report. This is very important when deploying reports to SharePoint, because images used in your report may or may not be in the same site collection that the current report viewer has permission to access.

You can use any Windows user account as the unattended execution account. For security purposes, avoid using the report server service account, to ensure that you do not compromise security on your report server instance. Give the unattended execution account only read and network logon permissions so it can connect to other computers. It must also have read permissions on any external resources (such as images) that you want to use in your report. Remember, local accounts are not suitable for the unattended execution account, except for standalone installations where everything coexists in the same server. The simplest way to set up an unattended execution account is to specify it in the Execution Account page in Reporting Services Configuration tool, as shown in Figure 11-9.

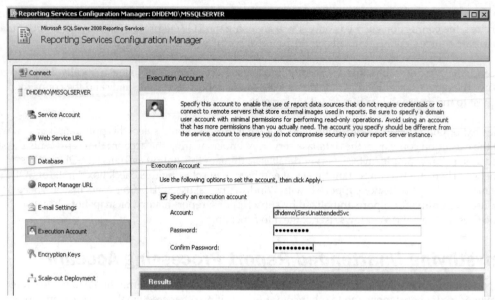

Figure 11-9

The unattended execution account is encrypted and stored in the `RSReportServer.config` file, as shown in Figure 11-10. If you have installed Reporting Services using a scale-out topology, you must run the configuration tool on each report server and use the same set of credentials for unattended execution account.

```
C:\Program Files\Microsoft SQL Server\MSRS10.MSSQLSERVER\Reporting Services\ReportServer\rsreportserver.config - Notepad++
File  Edit  Search  View  Format  Language  Settings  Macro  Run  TextFX  Plugins  Window  ?

rsreportserver.config
76        <UrlRoot>
77        </UrlRoot>
78        <UnattendedExecutionAccount>
79            <UserName>AQAAANCMnd8BFdERjHoAwE/C1+sBAAAA5hOOdHf5/OmBkr1YFgincgQAAAAiAAAAUgB1AHAAbwBy
80  AHQAaQBuAGcAIABTAGUAcgB2AGUAcgAAAANmAAACoAAAAEAAAAPjEaOTQiR7WcSSGX1gTmDQAAAAA
81  BIAAAKAAAAAQAAAADbsIAN2M3SwmJRPZMoe9rCAAAAqTd2L7bZWg1/E1XoOdKiH9MVuKM9oInuk
82  3bs6cOf3IxQAAADdF8+qGGLwwW/Jo1xycSQB8OQMSQ==</UserName>
83            <Password>AQAAANCMnd8BFdERjHoAwE/C1+sBAAAA5hOOdHf5/OmBkr1YFgincgQAAAAiAAAAUgB1AHAAbwBy
84  AHQAaQBuAGcAIABTAGUAcgB2AGUAcgAAAANmAAACoAAAAEAAAADsktyrqxHi5Gf7Lj6O+VakAAAAA
85  BIAAAKAAAAAQAAAA1thAr61eVoFvttEDGebjkhgAAACiKCHBLTTxm6nuM31FZzcFiGvZ/TljfJ4U
86  AAAAkbt/Uphime5eYVn0VxL+i1KNI2E=</Password>
87            <Domain>AQAAANCMnd8BFdERjHoAwE/C1+sBAAAA5hOOdHf5/OmBkr1YFgincgQAAAAiAAAAUgB1AHAAbwBy
88  AHQAaQBuAGcAIABTAGUAcgB2AGUAcgAAAANmAAACoAAAAEAAAAEyDle/J4F32/DhLVR4EyTgAAAAA
89  BIAAAKAAAAAQAAAAEKnwwov8huzuhQZrdtZUoRAAAAB9LnbbKEfUh1EUD41YuKhgFAAAAKoQazH1
90  ewbyhRQOrOtP8U8x23Te
91        </Domain>
92        </UnattendedExecutionAccount>
93        <PolicyLevel>rssrvpolicy.config</PolicyLevel>
```

Figure 11-10

An unattended execution account must be used only for specific functions. Microsoft has made it crystal clear that an unattended execution account is only meant to be used to connect to external servers, not as a login mechanism to database servers nor to retrieve data after the authentication is passed successfully. Although you can select Unattended report processing account in your data source and specify `Integrated Security=SSPI` in the connection string to log in and retrieve data from your database server on behalf of the unattended execution account (see Figure 11-11), this is not a recommended approach.

For more information, see the official statement in the "How to Use the Unattended Report Processing Account" section in Books Online at `http://www.devhorizon .com/go/9`.

Figure 11-11 (a)

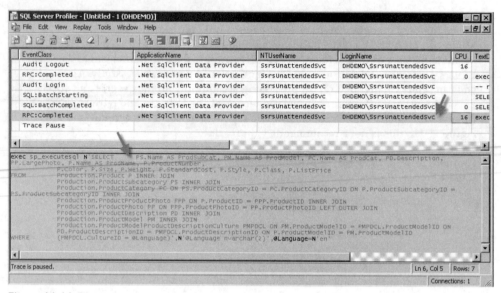

Figure 11-11 (b)

Understanding On-Demand Report Execution

Simply put, when a user clicks a report in a report library, the datasets defined in that report execute and return data to the report server from the underlying data source. Next, the report execution engine uses the report definition file stored in the SharePoint content database to determine how to create the report from the retrieved data, transform it into HTML, and finally push it down through the HTTP pipeline to the user's browser.

Truth to be told, there is more to the report execution process than stated above. The report execution process can be broken into smaller discrete operations. It is important to understand how much processing is required to produce a report, because this helps you make better decisions regarding how reports should be delivered to the end users. For example, if the users don't need to view the most updated version of a specific report, why do they have to go through the report execution process each time they request to view that report? Why not leverage one of the available execution options to generate the report in advance of the user viewing it?

From here on, the goal of this chapter is to introduce techniques to optimize report server capabilities and improve the performance of your reports, which altogether results in a better user experience.

What Goes Where?

The first step in your dive into the report execution process is to understand the set of databases used when you configure your report server deployment in SharePoint integrated mode. As you may know, report server integrates with SharePoint at three different storage levels:

1. SharePoint farm configuration database
2. SharePoint content database
3. Report server catalog

Microsoft Windows SharePoint Services 3.0 uses a database, known as the configuration database, to store configuration settings that apply to the entire farm. When you set up Reporting Services in SharePoint integrated mode, some configuration settings must be specified in the SharePoint Central Administration site. These settings are necessary for integration between products and apply globally; hence, they are stored in the configuration database. Global settings in the configuration database include settings such as the report server URL, integration authentication model, and default settings to limit or enable report history, logging, and so on.

In addition to farm-level settings kept in the configuration database, some content needs to be stored in SharePoint web application content databases. As you may know, each SharePoint web application maps to one or more content databases that are provisioned when creating site collections. Report server uses SharePoint content databases as storage repositories for published reports, models, shared data sources, resources, properties, and permissions. Two things need to be highlighted here.

First, Reporting Services is not meant to be replaced by SharePoint; it is supposed to be integrated with SharePoint. That being said, it wouldn't make much sense for the Reporting Services team to store everything in SharePoint. Second, as part of the integration requirements, the WSS 3 object model must be available on the Report Server. If you are not running a single server SharePoint/Reporting Services, you must install the Windows SharePoint Services 3.0 object model on the report server. The WSS 3 object model provides access to content and configuration databases via the object model and under the security context of its service identity, as shown in Figure 11-12.

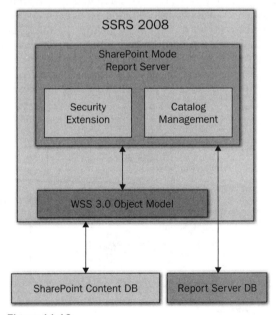

Figure 11-12

No matter what mode Reporting Services is in (native or integrated), report server uses two SQL Server databases to store persistent data. One database is used for primary storage (`ReportServer`), and the other one is used for temporary storage (`reportservertempdb`). Collectively, the two databases are referred to as the report server catalog. In the Reporting Services world, the terms report server database and report server catalog are interchangeable, referring to the primary and temporary storage that report server uses to accomplish various tasks.

> Recall from Chapter 10 that direct reporting against SharePoint databases is a bad
> idea. Steer away from directly reporting against the report server catalog as well.
> Instead, use the proxy endpoints or Reporting Services APIs.

The data kept in a Report Server catalog is used by all heavy-duty operations that Reporting Services is solely responsible to handle such as schedules, subscriptions, and snapshots. Besides storing data for specific Reporting Services operations, the report server catalog plays a very important role in boosting the overall performance factor when Reporting Services is deployed in SharePoint integrated mode.

The report server primary database keeps an internal replication of the report content files that exist in the SharePoint content databases. The replication decision was made by the Reporting Services team to produce less exchange of content and fewer round trips between two products for processing. Additionally, report server temporary storage is used to store session data and temporary snapshots that are stored for subscription, interactive report processing, or report caching. After reading this section, you might ask the following question: If data is kept in two databases, what validation checks are in place to ensure there is no risk of information inconsistency? You'll find the answer in the next section.

On-Demand Synchronization Process

The report server catalog keeps a copy of the reports stored in the SharePoint content database to facilitate faster report processing. When you publish, update, or even open a report in the browser, the report server compares the timestamp (UTC format) of the copy in the `ReportServer` database with the timestamp of the report definition file stored in SharePoint content database. If the timestamps are different, report server copies the newer version to the `ReportServer` database. These synchronization and item verification steps are often referred to as the *synchronization process*, and the rule of thumb is that SharePoint is the master and report server plays the slave role in the overall process. Figure 11-13 demonstrates this process.

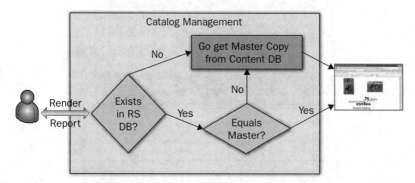

Figure 11-13

Note that synchronization service is only for content. For example, there is no synchronization of report-level (item-level) permissions between SharePoint and a report server instance. Those settings remain in the document library that hosts report content and are managed merely by SharePoint.

Publishing a report is a key process to activating the synchronization process. The important thing to keep in mind is that if you directly upload a legacy report definition file (`*.rdl`) to a document library instead of publishing it, this will delay the creation of the internal (slave) copy. If a report is not published to a document library, when a report is requested, the report definition file will have to be upgraded to a new version first; then the synchronization process can kick in. Recall from Chapter 9 that direct uploading action bypasses the initial validation checks performed by the authoring tool (BIDS) when opening the legacy files or during the publishing process.

Controlling Report Execution Timeout

One of the new features that ships with SQL Server Reporting Services 2008 is that long-running reports are penalized in favor of smaller reports, but there are still times when you may want to control the amount of time that your report server instance uses to process a report. In addition to the `<Timeout>` element in the report definition that controls the report query execution limit (30 seconds by default), there are two ways that you control report execution timeout values. One way is to apply it globally across the farm, and the other is to override the global value for each report. For the globally applied timeout value, browse to Central Administration ⇨ Application Management ⇨ Reporting Services Server Defaults page and change the value on this page (1800 seconds by default), as shown in Figure 11-14.

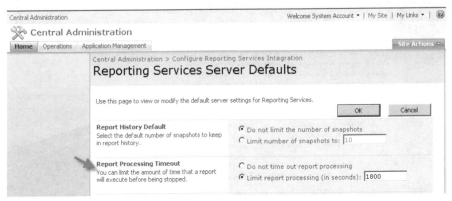

Figure 11-14

You can also override the global value for each report by clicking the ECB menu, which appears to the right of the report title, and selecting the Managing Processing Options item, as shown in Figure 11-15.

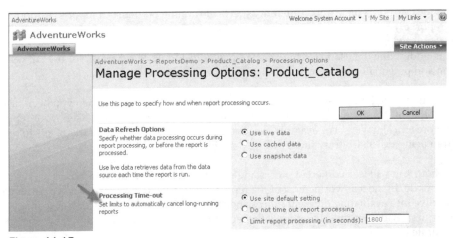

Figure 11-15

The report server also allows the administrator to configure at what interval to check for long running reports in the RSReportServer.config file located in the \Reporting Services\ReportServer folder. Open RSReportServer.config file and locate the RunningRequestsDbCycle element. The value specified in this element is the interval that the report server checks active report executions and decides whether long running ones should be timed out. This value is set to 60 seconds by default, as shown in Figure 11-16. The decision to timeout or not to timeout a report is made by comparing the actual process time versus the report execution timeout value that you specify. You can just go ahead and change this frequency to override how often Report Server should evaluate report execution processes.

Note that if the timeout value you specify for your reports is smaller than what is specified in the RSReportServer.config file, the timeout operation may never happen. For example, if you set a timeout value of 30 seconds for your report, and the RunningRequestsDbCycle value is set to the default value of 60, then there is a possibility that your report takes 40 seconds to execute and the report server's long-running report detection job never starts in time to kill that report.

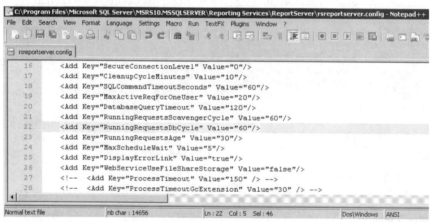

Figure 11-16

Report Processing Options

In the previous section, you learned different aspects of running on-demand reports. Although on-demand report execution always results in the most up-to-date data returned to users, each time the report is requested, a new instance of the report is created, which in turn results in a new query issued against the underlying data source. This can exponentially add up to report server overall resource utilization and potentially can bring a well-designed deployment to its knees.

When users don't need the most up-to-date data from the data source, and when you need fast report performance, there are some other processing options available to help you manage your report delivery needs in more efficient ways. For example, you can run a report from cache or snapshots to prevent the report from being run at arbitrary times during peak hours.

In this section, you will learn different processing options for configuring your report server instance in integrated mode. In the real world, most of the reports you develop have one or more parameters, so before we dive into evaluating different processing options, it makes sense to look at managing report parameters first. Without properly setting your report parameters, the results shown in such reports may not be accurate.

Managing Report Parameters

Unlike when you run parameterized reports in an on-demand way, end users won't get a chance to specify parameter values for reports delivered to them via background processes such as caching, subscriptions, and so on. The culprit is that in processes such as snapshots, caches, or subscriptions, choosing a different parameter value at runtime would result in a new processing request, which is simply not allowed.

You can manage the default values configured for the report parameters when authoring reports. In addition, you can manage report parameters after they are published to a SharePoint document library. Browse to the document library for the report. Click the ECB menu, which appears to the right of the report title, and select Manage Parameters. If the report contains any parameters, they will be listed in the prompt order. Click one of the available parameters, and you should be looking at a page similar to the one shown in Figure 11-17.

In this page, you can override the default value for the selected parameter as well as specify how the parameter value should be provided to the report. Available options are:

❑ **Prompt:** Parameter appears as a text box (for single-valued parameters) or combo box (for multi-valued parameters) in the parameter input area next to the rendered report. Users can specify a new value or select from the available options.

❑ **Hidden:** By selecting this option, the parameter will be hidden in the parameter input area, but its value can be set in background processes such as subscriptions, caching, and so on.

❑ **Internal:** An internal parameter is not exposed to end users or background processes but is still available in the report definition file.

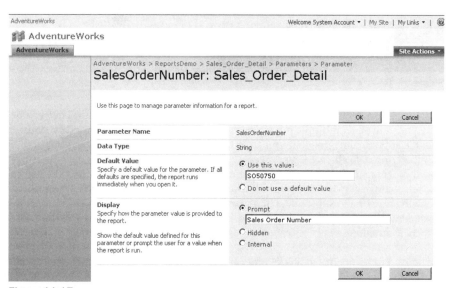

Figure 11-17

Creating Schedules

One of the more common requirements for enterprise reporting is the ability to deliver reports to end users through some sort of schedule. Thankfully, SQL Server Reporting Services 2008 has some sophisticated scheduling capabilities that give you the flexibility to design and implement various schedule-based background operations. Schedules are the heart of background processes in Reporting Services and come in two flavors: operation-specific or shared schedules.

Operation-specific schedules are for exclusive use with a particular report or operation and can't be repurposed by other reports or operations. Figure 11-18 demonstrates an operation-specific schedule used for invalidating the cache version of a report every Monday at 8:00 a.m. This means the cached report is expired every Monday at 8:00 a.m. and replaced with a newer version when a user requests the report. We will cover caching reports in great detail later in this chapter, so let's stay focused on the scheduling part for now.

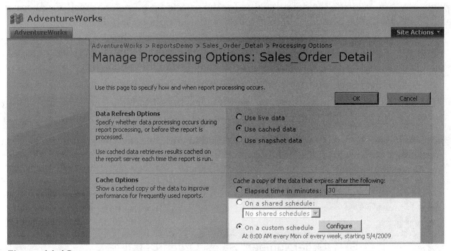

Figure 11-18

Compared to operation-specific schedules, shared schedules are more powerful. They can be defined once and then referenced by multiple reports and operations. You can create, modify, pause, or rerun a shared schedule anytime. Imagine that you are working on a bunch of reports in your organization that have their underlying data changed every weekend and must be available to subscribers first thing every Monday morning. Using the scheduling framework in Reporting Services 2008, you can create a shared schedule that triggers the operations linked to it on a weekly basis, and certain use cases are executed to deliver reports to subscribers. If a mandate comes in that the delivery interval must be changed to a monthly basis instead, all you need to do is to change one shared schedule, not all operation-specific schedules.

Most of the built-in functionality in SharePoint can't go beyond site collection, as does a shared schedule. You can configure site-collection schedules on Site settings page. Click the Site Actions menu at the top of the page. Click Site Settings ⇨ Modify All Site Settings ⇨ Manage Shared Schedules in the Reporting Services section, and click Add Schedule. In the page demonstrated in Figure 11-19, you can specify schedule details. Most of the settings on this page are quite straightforward and do not require further explanation, with the following exceptions:

❑ **Pause selected schedules:** Anytime you decide to pause a schedule or a group of schedules, you can select them on Manage Shared Schedules page and hit Pause Selected Schedules. Obviously, operations triggered by the last execution of the selected schedule won't be paused. They will continue until they complete, timeout, or result in errors.

❑ **Run selected schedules:** Use this option if you want to run a shared schedule (or a group of shared schedules) no matter when its kick-in time is scheduled. You can even run paused schedules! This is a great option for troubleshooting, development, and warm-up operations.

❑ **Modifying a shared schedule:** When modifying a shared schedule, note that if a schedule kicks in before you have completed your modifications, the earlier version of the schedule applies to the processes bound to that schedule. The modified version only takes effect when you complete the new changes and save the shared schedule.

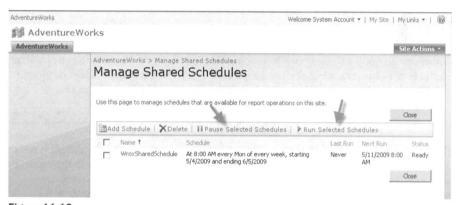

Figure 11-19

Note that when creating schedules in SharePoint, you may get the following error if the SQL Agent service is not started in the Report Server box.

The SQL Agent service is not running. This operation requires the SQL Agent service (rsSchedulerNotResponding).

The Report Execution Cache

Let's move on to a very important performance-enhancement technique in Reporting Services called caching! Reporting Services provides a powerful, easy-to-use caching mechanism that helps you keep a balance between having current data in your reports and having faster access to them.

To prepare a report (and data) for caching purposes, you need to do your homework and planning first. Figure out how your design may best utilize the caching facility provided by Reporting Services and what risks you need to be aware of. Then come back to the SharePoint side of the design to see how the two can be used to complement each other.

Next, you need to ensure that the data source used by the report uses stored credentials and has no user-profile dependencies. Again, don't worry about hard coding stored credentials in the data source, as this information is stored in an encrypted form in the `ReportServer` database.

From a server-side resource utilization and execution-time perspective, the first time a cached report is requested, everything is identical to the on-demand process. In fact, the first user who hits a cached instance pays the price for everyone else who requests the same instance. Once the report turns into a cached instance, it is stored in the `reportservertempdb` database as an intermediate format image until the cache is invalidated by the timestamp specified in the cache expiration settings. At this point, if any user requests that report with the same combination of parameter values (for parameterized reports), the report server retrieves the image from the `reportservertempdb` database and translates it into a rendering format using designated rendering extensions.

> **Like many other heavy-duty reporting operations, caching capability is managed by report server, not by SharePoint. Reporting Services caching facility does not utilize SharePoint's object caching or disk-based caching. In Reporting Services deployed in integrated mode, cached instances are still stored and retrieved from the `reportservertempdb` database and solely managed by report server.**

The final step of your planning and preparation is to come up with a cache invalidation policy. The key question you should ask yourself in this step is: How frequently must the data in the report be refreshed? The answer to this surprisingly simple question reveals a lot about the schedule you need to associate to your report's cache expiration time, as shown in Figure 11-18. Remember in a transactional data source that underlying data may change often; keeping an in-memory representation of data for a long time may not be a good idea. If your users are constantly requesting different parameter combinations for a report, caching that report is not really helpful. Of course, caching comes at a cost and can be destructive if used in inappropriate ways.

After you have completed the preparatory steps, the final piece of puzzle is the most obvious one: caching the report! In your report library, click the Edit button, which is located to the right of the report title, and then select Manage Processing Options, as shown in Figure 11-20. From the Data Refresh Option section, Select Use Cached Data, and then select an appropriate cache expiration schedule, as shown in Figure 11-21. Click OK to inform report server that your report is ready to be cached.

Figure 11-20

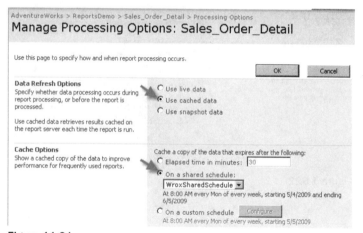

Figure 11-21

Snapshots and History

As discussed earlier, the report execution cache is a great way of boosting performance on the report server while giving users a reasonable balance between having current data in reports and having them access reports faster than typical on-demand report execution. Reporting Services 2008 offers report snapshots that can be used as an alternative approach to the report execution cache for delivering reports to end users.

In your report library, click the Edit button, which is located to the right of the report title, and then select Manage Processing Options, as shown in Figure 11-20. From the Data Refresh Option section, Select Use snapshot data, as shown in Figure 11-22.

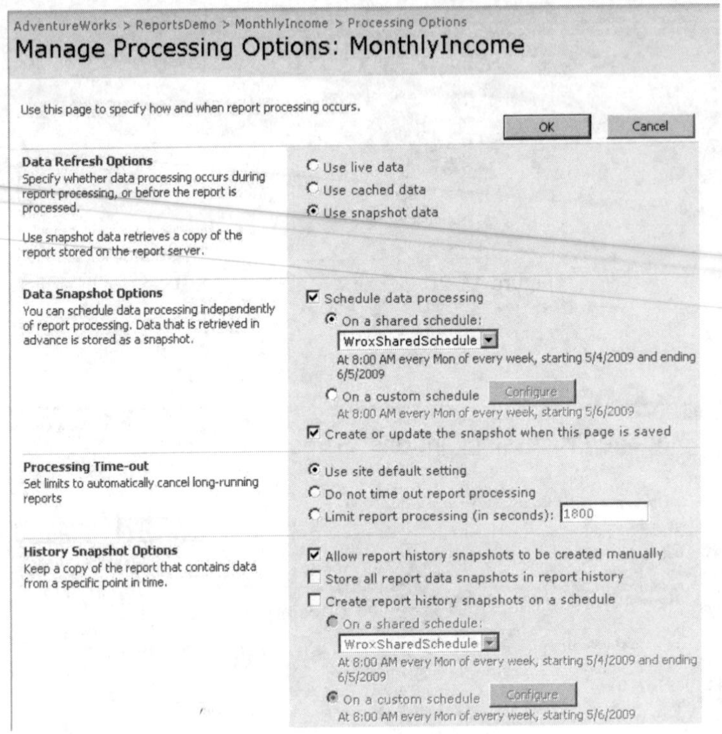

Figure 11-22

In concept, report snapshots and the report execution cache are used for a single purpose: delivering reports faster while lowering on-demand execution costs. Report snapshots can be used for the following two purposes:

❑ Creating report histories

❑ Controlling report processing

Functionality wise, report snapshots differ from a cached instance in the following ways:

❑ Snapshots offer more control over when and where reports should be cached.

❑ In snapshots, a report's data processing occurs independently of its execution.

❑ Snapshots are lightweight and do not contain rendering information.

❑ Snapshots are static and offer less interaction with reports.

Now, let's take a look at each difference in more detail.

The first obvious difference is that you have full control over how often a cached instance must be invalidated (using an expiration schedule), but you certainly cannot control when the new cached instance should kick in. This is because cache refreshment depends on when the first request is received after a cached instance expires. In addition, Report execution caching lacks the ability to produce a persistent copy of a report that contains the layout (and data) from a specific point in time. In contrast, report snapshots can be placed into history without overwriting previous snapshots. Remember that when report execution is persisted, end users will have the ability to compare it at various points in time as well. This is a very important feature and often a common business requirement.

For example, imagine that the finance department of Adventure Works wants to maintain an income report at the end of each month in their intranet portal. They would like to allow the Adventure Works executive team to view and compare the results presented in each report against other months of the current fiscal year or even earlier fiscal years. In addition to allowing the executive team to have access to various snapshots of the report for comparison purposes, such results must be presented in the fastest way possible. Let's imagine that they typically look for such reports starting from the first week of each month. So why not just generate report snapshots prior to midnight on the last day of each month and keep them as report histories?

The ability to target and select a precise time of cache refreshment can be done in two ways: manually or on a scheduled basis. If you click the Edit button, which is located to the right of the report title, and then select Report History, you will see the report history shown in Figure 11-23. On this page, you can take manual snapshots of a report and store them as part of report history log.

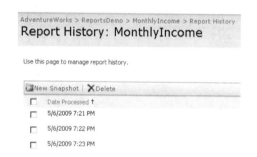

Figure 11-23

You can also create and manage snapshots in the Manage Processing Options page shown in Figure 11-22. If you look at the bottom of the page, there is a section called History Snapshot Options (see Figure 11-24). This section allows you to configure the following options:

❑ **Allow report history snapshots to be created manually:** If you clear this check box, when creating manual snapshots, users will get the error shown in Figure 11-25.

❑ **Store all report data snapshots in report history:** Stores snapshot data in the report history log.

❑ **Create report history snapshots on a schedule:** Creates history snapshots at a predefined interval based on a shared or custom schedule.

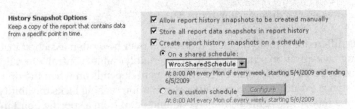

Figure 11-24

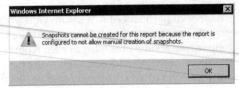

Figure 11-25

The second difference between snapshots and caching is that in snapshots you can schedule data processing independently of report processing (see Figure 11-26), though in the report execution cache you get everything all together. This way, data can be retrieved in advance and stored as a snapshot, which makes snapshots a more lightweight report processing option compared to report execution cache.

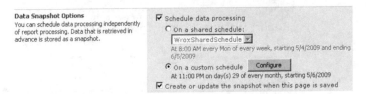

Figure 11-26

The third difference is that rendering information is not tied and stored with the snapshot. Instead, the final viewing format is adjusted based on what is appropriate for a user or an application requesting it. This functionality makes snapshots a much more portable solution.

The fourth difference is that report snapshots offer less flexibility when compared to the report execution cache. Snapshot reports lack interactivity with the users to an extent. They are like pictures and can be modified, but a cached report allows users to interact with the reports at the same level that on-demand report execution offers. For example, they provide different parameters, which may result in calling a different cached instance or on-demand execution from live data. In other words, snapshots are always taken using default parameter values (if applicable), and there is no way to change them when the snapshot is retrieved from the report server catalog. Figure 11-27 demonstrates a snapshot report. Notice how the parameter input area is disabled, making it impossible to interact with the report.

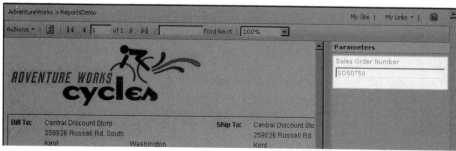

Figure 11-27

Static and Data-Driven Subscriptions

Rather than allowing users to connect to a SharePoint site to view reports, it is often required that reports be delivered to them in various ways other than browser-based access. None of the report-processing techniques (cached instances and snapshots) covered in this chapter so far offer an automated way of delivering a report to end users.

As previously discussed, on-demand report execution requires that users actively request reports each time they want to view them, which may introduce some performance overhead. Thankfully, Reporting Services offers subscriptions that can be used to schedule and then automate the delivery of reports via email, to a network folder, or even through periodic dumps in a SharePoint document library where users have set up alerts to get notified when a new item is added.

In this section, you learn how to work with static and data-driven subscriptions to provide a more flexible report-delivery mechanism that runs in the background.

Understanding Delivery Extensions

Once a report is published to SharePoint, it can be executed on demand, or the execution output can be delivered to various locations on a designated schedule. A report server instance configured for SharePoint integration includes four delivery extensions that enable you to distribute reports within your organization to various locations. Delivery extensions are the heart of subscription. For now, let's just take a brief look at what comes out of the box and then dive into each extension.

- ❏ **Email:** Used to e-mail a report to individual users or groups.

- ❏ **Windows file share:** Provides the ability to automatically copy a report to a file share on a scheduled basis.

- ❏ **Null delivery:** Used in conjunction with a data-driven subscription to preload the cache with several instances of the same report with different combinations of parameter values.

- ❏ **SharePoint document library**: Uses a SharePoint library document library.

> Before configuring a parameterized report to be delivered using any of the
> out-of-the-box delivery extensions, make sure that your report doesn't use default
> parameter values. Report parameters that have default values can't be overridden in
> the delivery configuration page when creating a subscription. Select Do not use a
> *default value* when setting report parameters (see Figure 11-17). For more
> information, see the "Managing Report Parameters" section, earlier in this chapter.

The Email Delivery Extension

These days, we manage our lives through our inbox, and it's always cool to receive identical copies of
the reports via email rather than having to go hunting all over the company's Internet or intranet sites to
find what we need. Thankfully, in Reporting Services, recipients of a report don't necessarily have to be
online users who hit reports via their browsers. By utilizing email delivery extensions in conjunction
with subscriptions, you can provide a fixed or fluctuating list of recipients and specify how you would
like content to be presented to them.

For example, in emails sent to end users, you can specify whether emails should include reports as
attachments or, at a minimum, a link that points to the actual reports in a SharePoint site. You then
establish a custom or shared schedule for emails to be distributed among users. If you want, you can
override reports' default parameter values for the emails sent to users or, in a more dynamic way,
provide parameter values at runtime when a subscription runs.

Report server sends email notifications by using a Simple Mail Transport Protocol (SMTP) server mail
server. You can specify which SMTP server to use and set the sender email address by using the
Reporting Services Configuration Manager tool, as shown in Figure 11-28. Once the SMTP settings are
specified, the e-mail delivery extension shows up when creating subscriptions using the Manage
Subscription page, as shown in Figure 11-29. Note that if you skip setting the SMTP configuration, the
email delivery option is not available when you try to create a subscription, as shown in Figure 11-30.

In addition to SMTP settings in the Reporting Services Configuration Manager tool, the SQL Server
Agent service must be running before you start using the e-mail delivery extension. As a matter of fact, if
this service is stopped, you can't create subscriptions, let alone using a delivery extension! Figure 11-31
demonstrates an error message that is thrown when you attempt to save the subscription settings
without having SQL Server Agent service running in advance.

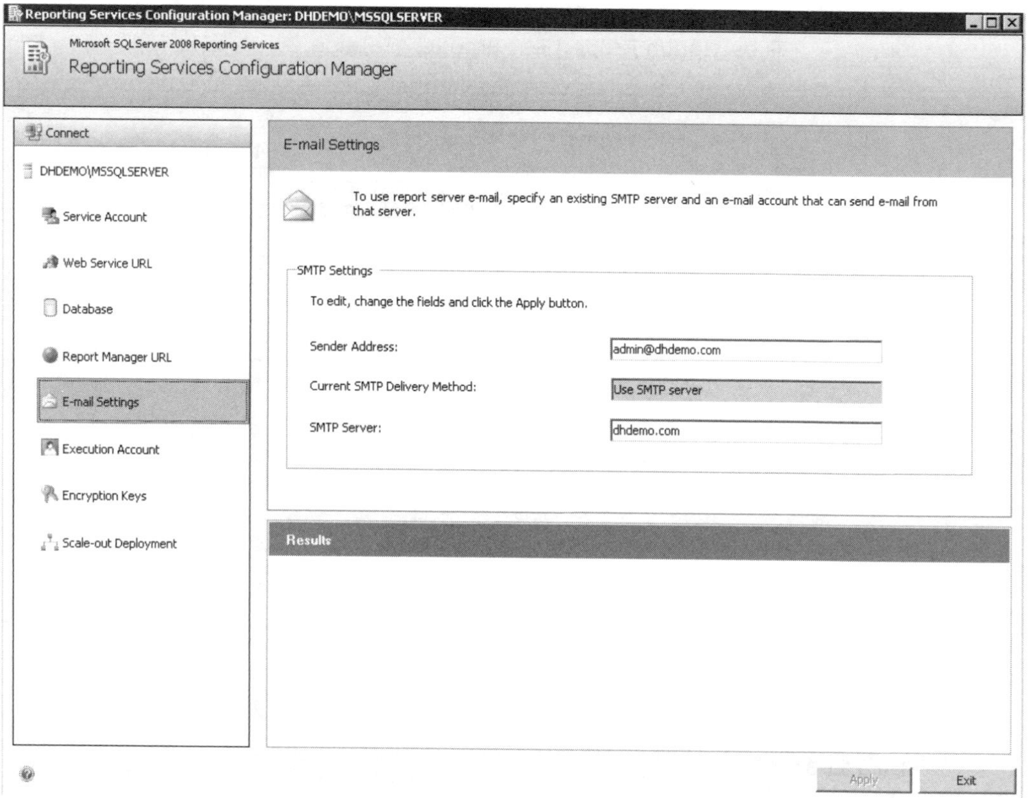

Figure 11-28

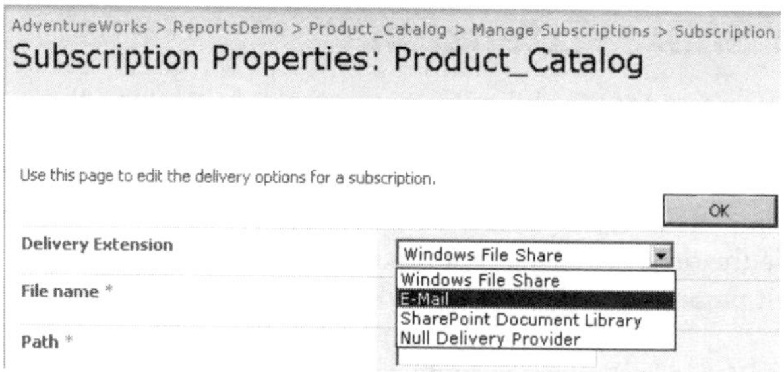

Figure 11-29

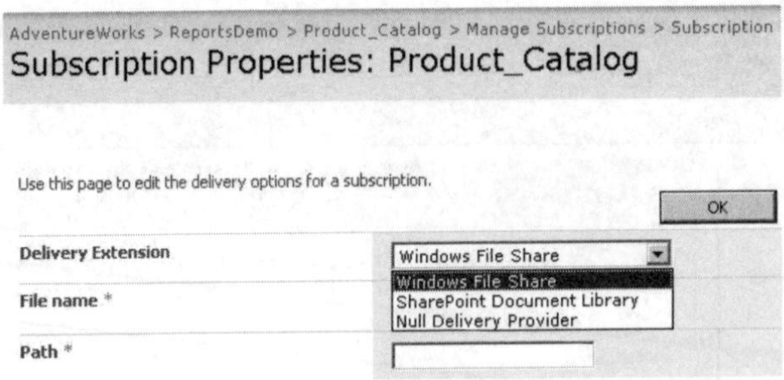

AdventureWorks > ReportsDemo > Product_Catalog > Manage Subscriptions > Subscription

Subscription Properties: Product_Catalog

Use this page to edit the delivery options for a subscription.

OK

Delivery Extension   Windows File Share

Windows File Share
SharePoint Document Library
Null Delivery Provider

File name *

Path *

Figure 11-30

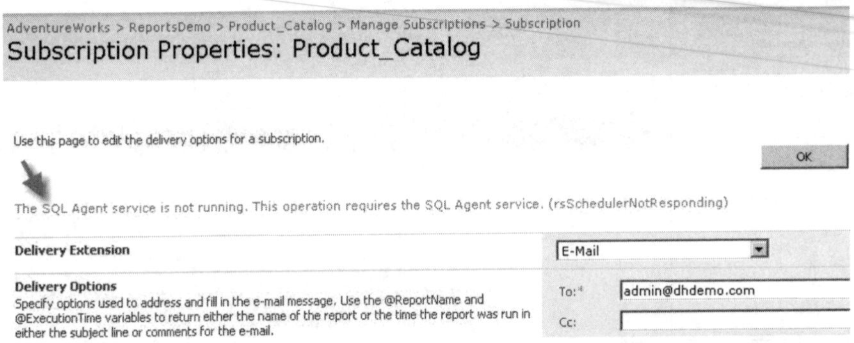

AdventureWorks > ReportsDemo > Product_Catalog > Manage Subscriptions > Subscription

Subscription Properties: Product_Catalog

Use this page to edit the delivery options for a subscription.

OK

The SQL Agent service is not running. This operation requires the SQL Agent service. (rsSchedulerNotResponding)

Delivery Extension   E-Mail

Delivery Options
Specify options used to address and fill in the e-mail message. Use the @ReportName and @ExecutionTime variables to return either the name of the report or the time the report was run in either the subject line or comments for the e-mail.

To: *   admin@dhdemo.com

Cc:

Figure 11-31

You will learn more about e-mail delivery extension later in this chapter.

The Windows File Share Extension

Windows file share extension provides the ability to share reports by making them accessible on a Windows file share on a scheduled basis. For example, you might store an Excel version of reports on one of the web front end servers for access by other applications for which you don't want their direct access to either the SharePoint site or report server instance. Using Windows file share delivery extension, you can schedule the delivery of the reports using a custom or shared schedule. You can also override the report's default parameter values, if you wish.

One important thing to consider is that when copying reports into a file share (or SharePoint document libraries), reports become static files with no sense of interactivity. For example, if you deliver a drillthrough report, the drillthrough functionality doesn't work. Additionally, if the report includes matrix, tablix, or charts, the default presentation is used. If you wish to retain interactive features in a delivered report to folder share, you must use another delivery extension. There are some workarounds such as selecting *Web Page* as the rendering format to preserve some of the interactive features, but because the delivered report is not a true .rdl file, users will not experience the full features they get when executing a live report.

Another issue that tips a lot of people over the edge when using Windows file share delivery extension is that the Windows account used by the designated subscription often doesn't have sufficient permissions to write to the target folder; you need to give it all the required ACL permissions. On another note, you can define a schedule for Windows file share subscription using a custom schedule or a shared schedule as you do with all other report-processing options we have discussed so far.

Figure 11-32 demonstrates how to use Windows file share delivery extension in a static subscription. We will cover static subscriptions in great details in the next section. Once the subscription is created, reports are delivered in Excel format to the specified path. As you can see, the path must conform to the Uniform Naming Convention (UNC) format; otherwise, you will receive an rsInvalidExtensionParameter exception.

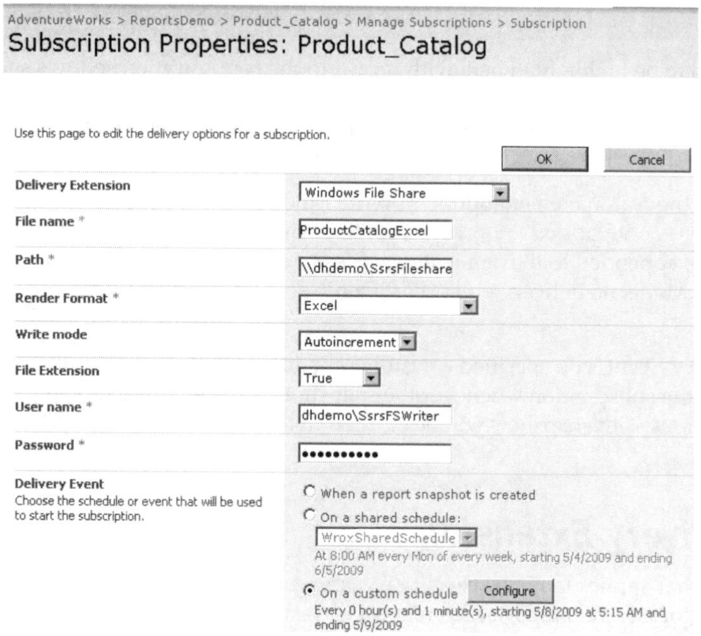

Figure 11-32

After the subscription runs, you should be able to see that the static files are delivered to the UNC path specified in the subscription as shown in Figure 11-33.

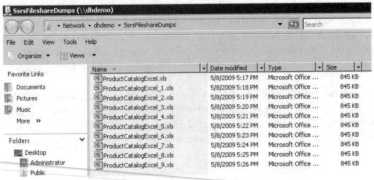

Figure 11-33

Three things need to be highlighted here with regard to the configuration settings shown in Figure 11-32:

❑ When using Windows file share delivery, the target folder must exist prior to the subscription execution. The report server does not create folders on the file system.

❑ Selecting the Autoincrement option in Write Mode preserves previous deliveries and avoids the initial file (`ProductCatalogExcel.xls`) to be overridden by other generated files. As such, a number is appended to the name of new files to create a unique file name. If you select None for the Write Mode, no delivery will occur if a file of the same name already exists in the destination folder.

❑ In Delivery Event, you specified a custom schedule that triggers the subscription to run. You can also pair the subscription whenever the snapshot is created for that report. More about pairing subscriptions with snapshots will be covered in the "Static Subscription" section later in this chapter.

The Null Delivery Extension

There is a caveat that applies to report execution caching. When users request different combinations of parameter values for a cached report, each request is treated separately for creating a new cached instance. Because each unique combination of parameters results in a new unique cached report, caching is not as effective. More users will pay the price for the initial caching of the parameter combination.

To improve the cache hit rate for cached reports with parameters, Microsoft introduced the null delivery extension in Reporting Services, which is available in both native and SharePoint integrated modes. This delivery extension doesn't actually deliver a report; instead, it preloads the cache on a designated schedule to improve server performance and report execution time.

Cache expiration settings in the report execution properties must match the cache preloads process by null delivery extension. If new cached instances are delivered to the cache, before the old instances have expired, newer instances are ignored. For example, if you create a subscription that runs every Monday at 8:00 A.M. and prepopulates the cache using the null delivery extension, the old copies in the cache should expire prior to Monday, say, every Monday at 7:59 A.M.

To preload the cache with a series of parameterized report instances using the null delivery extension, you need to create a subscription. Creating a subscription with the null delivery extension is identical to creating any other delivery extensions but with fewer configuration settings.

Figure 11-34 demonstrates the Sales Order Detail report configured to be preloaded to the cache with a parameter value equal to SO50750. This is scheduled to run every Monday at 8:00 A.M.

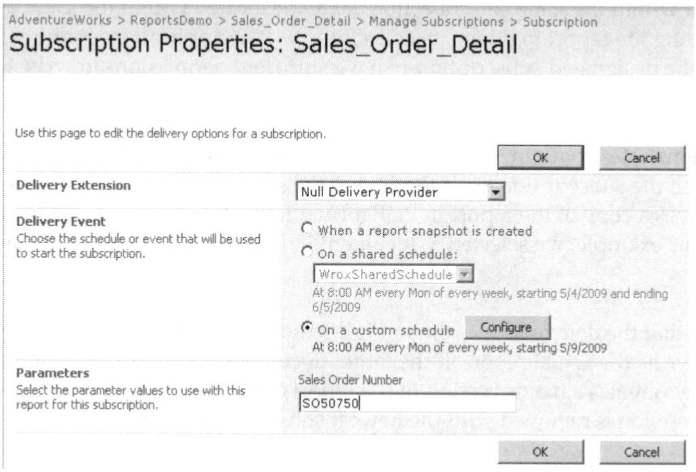

Figure 11-34

To have an effective preloading process in cache, old copies must expire in advance. Figure 11-35 demonstrates the execution properties for the Sales Order Detail report. Notice how the cached instances are configured to be invalidated at 7:59 A.M. every Monday.

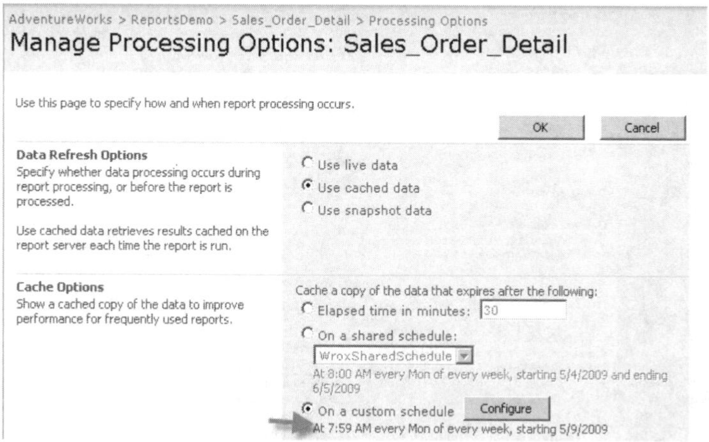

Figure 11-35

The SharePoint Document Library

The SharePoint document library delivery extension is somewhat similar to Windows file share delivery extension, with two major differences. First, the target location is a SharePoint document library, not a folder in a file system. Second, this delivery extension is available only in SharePoint integrated mode.

The SharePoint document library delivery extension delivers a copy of the report to the specified document library. The document library can be any document library in a SharePoint farm. It does not have to be located within the same site collection. It can be located within the same or a different Web application. Copying the report to other site collections or Web applications requires the Windows account used by the designated subscription to have sufficient permissions to write to the target document library.

Figure 11-36 demonstrates configuring a SharePoint document library extension configuration in a static subscription. When the subscription executes, it uses the specified SharePoint document library delivery extensions and saves a copy of the report in PDF format to the target document library, as shown in Figure 11-37. In this example, we selected a document library located in another SharePoint web application.

Again, remember that the delivered files are not full-featured .rdl files, so the user experience might not be as interactive as the actual report. If the target document library has versioning enabled, the subscription always creates a major version of the report copy. If you limit the retention of versions, the oldest report version is removed with the newest subscription delivery.

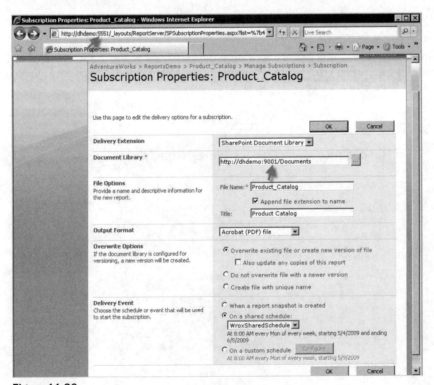

Figure 11-36

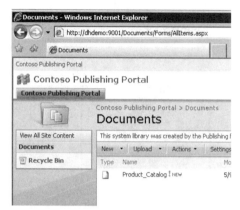

Figure 11-37

Static Subscriptions

We covered many concepts and ideas with regard to subscriptions without actually seeing subscriptions in practice. Unfortunately, it is difficult to explain the concepts without at least covering the supporting concepts. Now we can look into creating subscriptions.

In Reporting Services, subscriptions come in two flavors: static (that is, standard) and data-driven. They are used to deliver reports to end users on a scheduled basis and heavily rely on the underlying delivery extension for the delivery part. Static subscriptions are created and managed by individual users (with enough permissions) to deliver content tailored to them. A static subscription consists of fixed values that cannot be varied during subscription execution. Everything is fixed and needs to be determined up front when the subscription is created. For example, there is only one rendering format, delivery option, and report parameter value in static subscriptions.

In this section, you create an email subscription for the Product Catalog report to send the report to yourself on a custom schedule as a PDF file. Before you can define a subscription, the report must have a data source that stores credentials or uses no credentials. For more information about stored credentials, see the "Stored Credentials" section, earlier in this chapter. It's also assumed that you have enough permission to view the report and create a subscription.

1. Browse to the report library containing the Product Catalog report.

2. Point to the Product Catalog report, click the Edit button from the ECB menu that appears to the right of the report title, and select Manage Subscriptions, as shown in Figure 11-38.

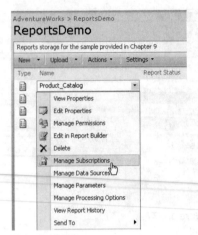

Figure 11-38

3. Selecting Manage Subscriptions from the ECB menu opens the subscriptions page of the Product Catalog report, where you can see all available static and data-driven subscriptions created for the Product Catalog report. At this stage, the Manage Subscriptions for Product Catalog page contains no subscription, as shown in Figure 11-39.

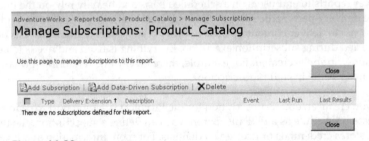

Figure 11-39

4. Click Add Subscription to create a new static subscription. This opens Subscription Properties page.

5. In the Subscription Properties page (already covered in this chapter; see the "Email Delivery Extension" section), open the Delivery Extension dropdown list and select the default value of e-mail.

6. Fill out the required fields (To and Subject) with appropriate values. Clear the Include a link to the report option, which includes a link to the report in the body of the email.

7. In the Report Contents section, Choose PDF as your preferred delivery format.

8. Specify a custom or shared schedule for the report to execute. For more information about schedules, see the "Creating Schedules" section, earlier in this chapter. For the sake of simplicity, let's create a report-specific schedule that runs once and only three minutes from now.

9. Click the OK button. You will be redirected to the Subscription Properties page, where you need to hit the OK button one more time to get back to Manage Subscription page. This time around, your static subscription is listed, and you can visually confirm its status.

10. Wait three minutes, and then click the Refresh button to view the status of the subscription, as shown in Figure 11-40. If the subscription runs successfully, the Last Run column displays the timestamp of the subscription execution, and the Last Results column shows the action taken or an error message. At this point, the email should have been delivered to the specified recipients, as shown in Figure 11-41.

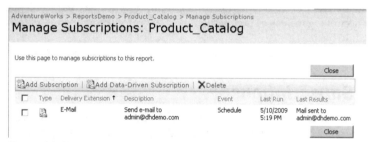

Figure 11-40

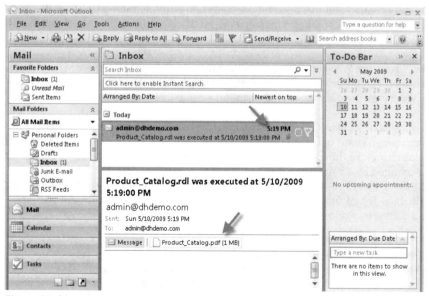

Figure 11-41

If you want to send only a link to the report on the SharePoint site, you should select the Include a link to the report check box and clear the Show report inside message check box. If you select these two check boxes simultaneously, the delivered email will include both the report (as an attachment) and the link, which is the default configuration for the email delivery extension.

> All of the out-of-the-box delivery extensions that ship with Reporting Services deployment (in integrated mode) can be triggered by report snapshots. For example, when you create a subscription that uses the Windows file share delivery extension, if you select *When a report snapshot is created* (see Figure 11-32), every time a snapshot is created, it will trigger the subscription, which in turn uses the underlying delivery extension to deliver the report to the specified UNC path. This behavior occurs regardless of the method used to create the snapshot, manually or on a schedule basis.

Data-Driven Subscriptions

When users create static subscriptions, they set the subscription settings manually, and such settings become fixed in the subscription definition. While at this point static subscriptions can certainly be used in many real-world scenarios, what if you have a large recipient list and want to vary report delivery settings for each recipient?

Microsoft provided a capability in SQL Server Reporting Services 2008 called data-driven subscriptions that are typically created and managed by site collection administrators. Unlike static subscriptions, data-driven subscriptions contain settings that are set dynamically and might change for each row retrieved from the subscriber table.

Because the Adventure Works database (sample database in this book) does not include a table to store data-driven subscription delivery information, you must create that subscriber table before diving into the intricacies of creating data-driven subscriptions.

For the purpose of demonstration, this chapter features a simple data-driven scenario with a single table that contains four columns of email addresses, output format, include report, and include link Boolean conditions. You can take things to the next level by defining other columns for every subscription setting that can be changed by a value from this table such as parameter values. You can also create a totally separate database that stores the subscription data used in various reports. Much flexibility comes out of the box with data-driven subscriptions that allows you to design and implement customized background delivery solutions that may vary for every user.

> In Internet facing sites that authenticate users against a custom membership provider, you can also store subscription data in the underlying membership repository and combine it with roles rather than individual users. This way, you can even offer more flexibility compared to linking subscription data to individual users.

In this section, you use SQL Server Management Studio to run a script that creates the ProductCatalogSubscriptionDelivery table in the Adventure Works database. Then you review and enter the contents in the new table.

1. Start SQL Server Management Studio and connect to the SQL Server instance that hosts Adventure Works database.

2. On the toolbar, select New Query. Make sure the Available Databases dropdown list is pointing to the Adventure Works database.

3. Copy and paste Listing 11-1 in the T-SQL windows; on the toolbar, click Execute.

4. This script adds three email accounts to the ProductCatalogSubscriptionDelivery table in the Adventure Works database, in addition to the corresponding subscription settings such as render format type, include report, and include link Boolean conditions.

5. Use a SELECT statement to verify that you have three rows of data, as shown in Figure 11-42. For example: Select * From ProductCatalogSubscriptionDelivery.

Listing 11-1: A sample subscriber table

```
Use AdventureWorks
CREATE TABLE [dbo].[ProductCatalogSubscriptionDelivery] (

        [SubscriptionID] [int] NOT NULL PRIMARY KEY ,
        [Format]         [nvarchar] (20) NOT NULL ,
        [IncludeLink]    [bit] NULL,
        [IncludeReport]  [bit] NULL

) ON [PRIMARY]
GO

INSERT INTO [dbo].[ProductCatalogSubscriptionDelivery]
      VALUES
            (1,'user1@dhdemo.com','IMAGE',1,1)

INSERT INTO [dbo].[ProductCatalogSubscriptionDelivery]
      VALUES
            (2,'user2@dhdemo.com','EXCEL',0,1)

INSERT INTO [dbo].[ProductCatalogSubscriptionDelivery]
      VALUES
            (3,'user3@dhdemo.com', 'MHTML'1,1)
GO
```

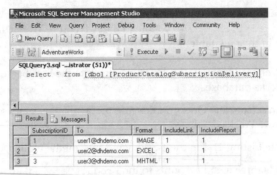

Figure 11-42

When creating a data-driven subscription, it is important to ensure that the report for which you want to create the subscription uses stored credentials or no credentials. Begin from exactly where you started creating a static subscription, as shown in Figure 11-43. In the Manage Subscriptions page, click Add Data-Driven Subscription, which opens step 1 of the "Create a Data-Driven Subscription" wizard.

Figure 11-43

In step 1, you must specify a query that retrieves subscription information from the subscriber table you set up in the previous section. The query should use a shared or custom data source. Because you created the subscriber table in the Adventure Works database, you can reuse the same data source you use for your reports, but if you have created the table in another database, it's obvious that you need a second data source. In addition, the query specified in this step should produce only one row for each subscriber. For example, if you are using the e-mail delivery extension, the query should return a minimum valid e-mail address per row. Optionally, the query can return more fields used to vary delivery settings and report parameter values for each recipient.

Before you move on to the step 2, the query must be validated. At this stage, validation is more than just processing the query. It returns the schema of all the columns from the underlying subscriber table, which can be referenced in subsequent selections in other steps of the Create a Data-Driven Subscription wizard. As you can see in Figure 11-44, you can also specify a query timeout value for data-driven subscriptions, which determines how long query processing can take to complete when extracting data from the subscriber table. Note that this timeout value only applies to the subscription query time and is different from the report execution timeout. For more information about the report execution timeout, see the "Controlling Report Execution Timeout" section earlier in this chapter.

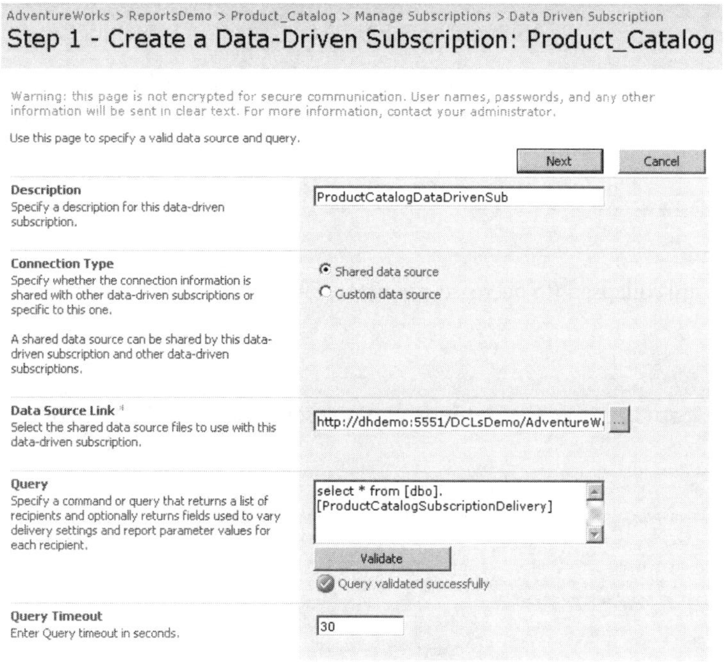

Figure 11-44

In step 2, you select parameter values to use with the subscription. Because the Product Catalog report does not have any parameters, you can safely proceed to step 3. If you happen to be using a parameterized report, in stage 2, you must specify parameter values, or you can get the values at runtime from the subscribers table to vary report output and other settings.

Step 3 is where you select delivery options to use with your data-driven subscription. First, you select a delivery extension and configure its delivery options for the data-driven subscription. Let's select the e-mail delivery extension. For more information on various delivery extensions when Reporting Services is deployed in SharePoint integrated mode, see the "Understanding Delivery Extensions" section in this chapter. Upon selection of the e-mail delivery extension, the page posts back to itself and new settings are again rendered.

You are required to complete the three fields in this page: To, Include Report, and Subject. Configure the delivery extension settings according to the following table:

Delivery Setting	Source	Value
To	Subscriber Table	To
Include Report	Subscriber Table	IncludeReport
Render Format	Subscriber Table	Format
Subject	Static Value	Product Catalog Update
Include Link	Subscriber Table	IncludeReport

When all regions are collapsed (to decrease page real state), your page should look like the Figure 11-45.

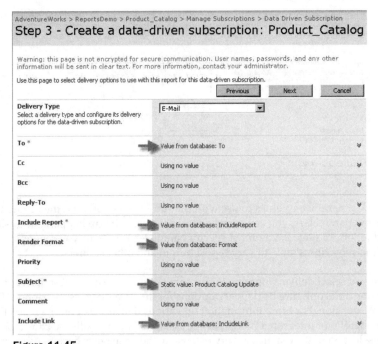

Figure 11-45

Step 4 schedules properties for this data-driven subscription. To keep things simple, let's just specify a report-specific schedule. Click Finish to complete the wizard. Upon completion of the wizard, you will be redirected back to the Manage Subscriptions page for the Product Catalog report. Wait until the custom schedule you setup in step 4 triggers, which in turn triggers the data-driven subscription. If you click the Refresh button while the subscription is in progress, you should see the counter of rows returned from the subscriber table and processed by the subscription. Once all three records are processed, the Manage Subscriptions page should be similar to Figure 11-46.

Figure 11-46

Figure 11-47 shows the email sent to user 1 in the format of an image (.TIF), including a link to the actual report on the SharePoint site.

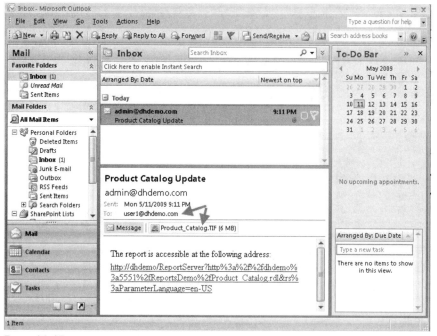

FIGURE 11-47

One thing needs to be highlighted here: The Product Catalog report that comes with the Reporting Services sample has two references to `User!Language` in its report definition file (`.rdl`) which is used to determine the primary language of the text in the rendered report. When creating a subscription, this element is detected as a user profile dependency and you get the following exception:

```
System.Web.Services.Protocols.SoapException: The 'http://dhdemo:5551/ReportsDemo/
Product_Catalog.rdl' report has user profile dependencies and cannot be run
unattended. --->
```

As discussed previously, reports that have no stored credentials or have dependencies on user profiles can't be used as report snapshots or cached instances and can't be delivered via subscriptions. For the sake of demonstration, these two references have been replaced in the Product Catalog report definition file with the word *English*. In reality, when users hit your reports with different browser locals, report server uses this parameter to detect their language and adjust the report accordingly based on the user's preferred language, so you shouldn't touch this element for multilingual reports.

Figure 11-48 shows the delivered report to user 2 in Excel format without having a link to the actual report on the SharePoint site.

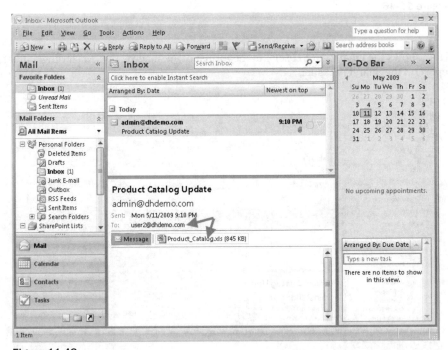

Figure 11-48

Finally, Figure 11-49 demonstrates the final delivery to user 3 as an inline MHTML format that renders in the body of the email.

Figure 11-49

Summary

To ensure a successful enterprise implementation of your Business Intelligence solutions, you need to have an efficient mechanism for delivering information through reports to end users. As such, reporting performance must be consistent and balanced.

Microsoft elected to take report execution options to the next level in SQL Server Reporting Services 2008 configured in SharePoint integrated mode by providing many functionalities such as subscriptions, report snapshots, and caching techniques. In this chapter, you learned how to use these functionalities rather than having users access the reports in an on-demand manner.

Most of the techniques discussed in this chapter have the advantage of being scheduled and run in the background, giving you greater control over when and where execution occurs. The goal is to enhance the performance of the report server and the user experience when viewing reports.

12

Using Gauges in SharePoint Dashboards

Dashboards have been a very important part of and will continue to be among the most important features of any application. Earlier in this book, you learned about dashboards and how to make them perform better in SharePoint. In this chapter, you will examine another aspect of dashboards: the visualization techniques of aggregated data.

The word *dashboard* gets thrown out there a lot in almost any conversation about accessing information. It has become the buzz word for accessing information quickly in today's IT world. Similar to car dashboards, dashboards in the IT world allow you to get information quickly. You can think of a dashboard as the visual representation of data that allows the end user to interpret data within seconds to make fast and accurate business decisions.

How do you visually represent rows and rows of data that will allow end users to make fast business decisions? You probably know the saying "A picture is worth a thousand words." The same idea applies here as well. Can you think of a way to represent the data in an image? An image that can quickly tell you what you need to know? You guessed it; gauges can help you display aggregated data in such a way that the end user can immediately get key points of the data in split seconds.

Gauges are a new addition to the SQL Reporting Services family and are one of the most important graphical data regions that allow you to create visually advanced digital dashboards. The gauge data region allows you to display aggregated data and is one of the most popular forms of displaying data in dashboards. This chapter covers adding gauges to existing reports and also addresses creating a gauge that can be added to a SharePoint site as a visual representation of data stored in SharePoint.

In the examples you'll encounter in this chapter, you will have a chance to apply the knowledge you've accumulated from previous chapters. So this chapter assumes that you already know your way around BIDS, you have a basic understanding of publishing reports to SharePoint, and you know how to access data from a SharePoint list. Since dashboards are mostly used by managers or higher executives for viewing aggregated data, these reports give anyone who works on them great visibility. So let's start creating dashboards that will get you that promotion you've deserved for a long time.

Adding a Gauge to an Existing Report

Now with SSRS 2008 you have the capability to add gauges to your reports, and your first step should be to see if you can enhance existing reports in your environment. Several reports that you currently use in your environment might benefit from visual enhancement, and with gauges you can give your reports the improvement they need.

One of the examples of this situation can be easily demonstrated using the AdventureWorks Sales by Sales Territory report, as shown in Figure 12-1. The report shows the total numbers for each sales territory, but by looking at this there is no easy way to tell whether Adventure Works is doing well or not. The best way to measure performance of an organization or a business unit is to have Key Performance Indicators (KPIs). KPIs are the business metrics that help you measure the success of an organization or a business unit based on that organization or business unit's goals.

Territory Sales Drilldown 2008

Sales by
Sales Territory

Sales Territory	Sales Person	Sales Order Number	Total Due
⊞ Australia			$1,943,016.45
⊞ Canada			$12,808,458.05
⊟ Central			$13,434,509.55
	⊞ Jillian Carson		$13,434,509.55
⊞ France			$6,083,690.96
⊞ Germany			$2,476,530.47
⊞ Northeast			$12,433,502.84
⊞ Northwest			$12,593,458.38
⊞ Southeast			$9,629,926.90
⊞ Southwest			$22,737,468.75
⊞ United Kingdom			$11,384,512.99

Figure 12-1

So to get a better understanding of where the sales organization is with its goals, you need KPIs. For this example's sake, assume that Adventure Works has a set a KPI for the Australia, Canada, and Central sales territories as follows:

Sales Territory	Target	Bad	Good	Very Good
Australia	$3MM	$0MM to $1.5MM	$1.5MM to $2.5MM	$3.5MM to $5MM
Canada	$12MM	$0MM to $6MM	$6MM to $12MM	$12MM to $15MM
Central	$15MM	$0MM to $8MM	$8MM to $16MM	$16MM to $20MM

By having access to the KPI table for the sales territories, you can tell whether the sales organization is in good shape or not. Looking at the numbers presented in the table, you see that Australia falls under the Good range, since the total is around $1.95MM, and both Canada and Central fall under the Very Good range. With the help of the KPI table, you can easily tell whether the sales territories are on target or need more work. Although you are able to use the KPI table as a legend, since you access the information manually, this takes a lot more than a few seconds.

Your goal is to give the user this information at a single glance. The user should be able to tell whether the territory is doing well or not without having to look at a table. To accomplish this, you will create gauges that tell how these sales territories are doing against their sales goals based on the KPI table. Instead of creating a new report for the gauges, you will directly put the gauges on the Sales by Sales Territory report. This way, the KPIs will sit on top of the information presented by the tablix, helping the sales executive make accurate and fast decisions.

Before you add your gauge, your first step is to open the Sales by Sales Territory report in BIDS. Once you have the report open, go ahead and add some space to the top of the report so that you can add a gauge. Once you have pushed things down and added some whitespace at the top of the report, add a gauge to your report design region in BIDS and select the 180 Degrees North radial gauge from the list of gauges, as shown in Figure 12-2.

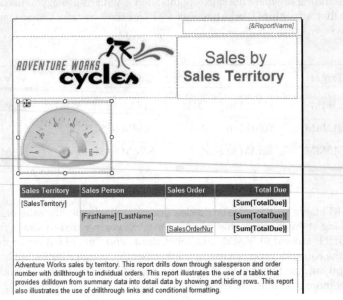

Figure 12-2

Binding the Pointer to a Data Field

At this point, you have added the radial gauge to the top of the tablix that displays the total sales. Now what you need to do is bind the pointer to an aggregated data field. Pointers in gauges are what you bind to an aggregated field. In this example, you will use the TotalDue column from the TerritorySales dataset, since this column shows the total sales in dollars. To bind the TotalDue column to the pointer, all you need to do is drag and drop the field on to the gauge, as shown in Figure 12-3. Once you've brought over the TotalDue field, you have hooked up the total dollar amount for ALL sales for all sales territories. Your goal is to be more specific, so how do you get only Australia data? The answer is by using expressions!

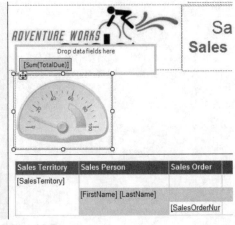

Figure 12-3

To modify the data field, right-click the pointer and click the Pointer Properties. On the Radial Pointer Properties dialog box, click the Expression button next to the Value option, as shown in Figure 12-4.

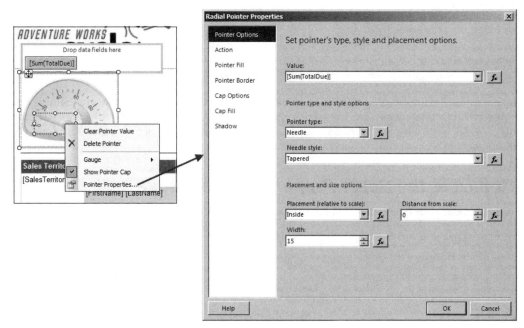

Figure 12-4

What you need to do with the expression is filter out the data you do not need. So you need to write an expression that will add all values for Australia. The gauge data region will show only aggregated data and in Figure 12-4 the expressions is set to sum all values, so by using expressions you can easily filter out everything that is not Australia.

The expression you will use to filter out the other territories is the IIF statement. With the IIF statement, you'll check the SalesTerritory value. If the value is equal to Australia, you will add the value TotalDue. If the value is not equal to Australia, it will add a 0. Since adding the 0 is not going to affect the total, you'll get the total for Australia. The expression will look similar to the following code:

```
=Sum(IIF(Fields!SalesTerritory.Value = "Australia",
CDbl(Fields!TotalDue.Value),CDbl(0)))
```

When you look at the expression, you will see that you also wrapped the values TotalDue and 0 inside the conversion function CDbl (convert to double). The reason you do this is that Reporting Services does not understand that the 0 used in the expression string is a number and it parses it as a string. If you don't convert both values to the same type, Reporting Services will give you the following error when aggregating data:

```
[rsAggregateOfMixedDataTypes] The Value expression for the gauge panel
'GaugePanel1' uses an aggregate function on data of varying data types.
Aggregate functions other than First, Last, Previous, Count, and
CountDistinct can only aggregate data of a single data type.
```

The error message informs you that the two types don't match by letting you know that SUM is trying to aggregate varying data types. The easy workaround is to convert the TotalDue field and the 0 both to double, as shown in the preceding code. Although there are other types of conversion functions, you selected double because you are dealing with currency.

Customizing the Scale Properties of a Gauge

Once you create your expression, you have bound the gauge to the data you wish to report on, and the next step is to modify the scale properties of the gauge. Now you'll right-click the scale and modify its settings as follows:

General Properties	Value	Description
Minimum	0	This is the lowest value in the KPI range for the Australia Sales Territory.
Maximum	5000000	This is the highest value in the KPI range for the Australia Sales Territory.
Interval	Auto	By default, the gauge equally distributes the tick marks. Using this value, you can customize the intervals. In this case, you'll use Auto, which sets the interval to $1MM.
Interval Offset	Auto	This value pushes the starting point of the scale to the number. The Auto value starts the scale at $1MM, but you can start your intervals at $2MM or $3MM based on your requirements.

When you complete adding the above values into the General Properties of the radial gauge, click the Number section to modify the values as follows. This section allows you to customize the look and feel of the values displayed on the gauge.

Number Properties	Value	Description
Category	Currency	This will format our values to look like $12345.
Decimal Places	0	Change the value to 0 here, since your report is in Millions range. If you want, you can set the value to 2 to get the cents for the dollar.
Use 1000 Separator (,)	True	Check this checkbox to add the comma to separate the thousands of your value ($12,345).
Show values in	Millions	This value represents your data in millions, so if you have a value that is $1,943,016.45, it will show this as $1.9MM. You can also choose to display your value in thousands and billions.
Negative Numbers	($1,234)	This value allows you to customize how you will display negative numbers on your gauge. You can select any of the formats listed in the list box. For this example, you will use the number in parentheses.
Symbol	$ English (United States)	This is the currency your value will be displayed as on the gauge. In this example, you select the US Dollar, but if you click the dropdown, you will see all of the other currencies available to choose from.
Show symbol after value	False	This shows the currency symbol after the value if set to True. Since each currency has its own way of displaying its symbol, this property allows you to customize the location of the symbol based on the currency you're using. For example, for the Turkish YTL, you put your symbol after the value as 1,000 YTL. In this case, you choose False so that your symbol stays in front of the value.
Include a space	True	This places a space between the currency symbol and the value if the value is set to True ($12,345).

Once you complete updating all of the values listed in the preceding tables, click the Preview tab to see the preview of your gauge. The gauge will point to a value that is close to $2MM, as shown in Figure 12-5, since the total value for Australia Territory Sales is to $1,943,016.45.

Sales Territory	Sales Person	Sales Order Number	Total Due
⊞ Australia			$1,943,016.45
⊞ Canada			$12,808,458.05
⊞ Central			$13,434,509.55

Figure 12-5

Setting Layout Properties on a Radial Scale

Once you have your scale configured the way you want it to display the values, you can also modify the layout properties of the scale by modifying its radius, start angle, sweep angle, or bar width, as shown in Figure 12-6.

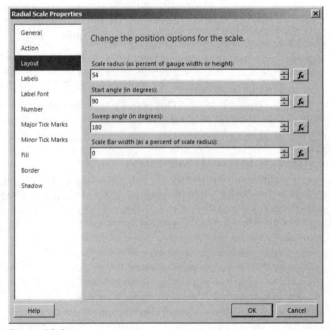

Figure 12-6

Although in this example you will not be modifying the layout properties of your gauge, the layout properties come in handy when you have specific requirements for your gauge. For example, if you change the position of your scale labels, you will probably need to resize the Scale Radius property so that your labels are displayed correctly.

The scale radius is the distance that starts from the center of the gauge and ends at the middle of the scale bar. This value is measured as a percentage of the gauge diameter, which is why in 180 Degree gauges the value is closer to 55 and in 360 Degree gauges the value is closer to 35.

In this example, you are using a 180 Degrees North gauge, so the radius and the angle calculations will be slightly different from those of a 360 radial gauge. The start angle and the sweep angles are based on values between 0 and 360, so when working with 180 Degree gauges, you will need to modify these numbers to get the scale where you want it to be positioned.

Customizing the Appearance of a Gauge

Binding the pointer to a data field and changing the value's appearance will get your gauge working, but it still needs some work, since at this point it's not telling us anything different from the tablix below it. In the next sections, you will customize the appearance of the gauge to enhance its look and feel, which will result in getting the information across to the end user much faster. The steps for customizing the look and feel of a gauge are as follows:

1. Adding a range to a gauge
2. Adding a marker pointer to a gauge
3. Adding a label to a gauge
4. Configuring snapping intervals on a gauge
5. Using a custom image as a Pointer on a Radial Gauge

Adding a Range to a Gauge

One of the things that make a gauge very powerful is that it can easily display the ranges of a KPI. Your first step in customizing the appearance of the gauge will be adding the ranges defined earlier in this chapter. To add a range to your gauge, right-click the gauge surface, click the Add Range option, and then right-click the added range and click the Range Properties option to get the Range Properties dialog box, as shown in Figure 12-7.

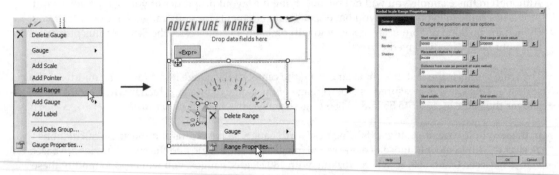

Figure 12-7

Since the Sales Territory KPI has three ranges (Bad, Good, and Very Good), you will create three ranges for your gauge. Once you add your first range to the gauge, open the properties of the range, as demonstrated in Figure 12-7. Once you have the range properties open, go configure its properties with the values shown in the following table.

Range Properties	Category	Value	Description
Start range at scale value	General	0	This is the value where the range will start from.
End range at scale value	General	1500000	This is the value where the range will end. This will be your first range, so according to your KPI table, you know that for Australia the first range ends at $1.5MM.
Start width	General	5	This is the starting width of the range. And by default this value comes as 15px. You can change this to any value you want but it makes sense when the range is initially thinner and gets thicker as the values grow higher.
End width	General	22	This value is the ending width of the range in the gauge. In this example, you will use the number 30, but you can change this value based on your requirements.
Fill Style	Fill	Gradient	Under the Fill category, the Fill style is the first thing you select. In this example, you will select Gradient, but you can also select a solid color or a pattern overlay.
Color	Fill	Red	This is the first color of the gradient.
Secondary Color	Fill	Orange	This is the second color in the gradient color option. Here you will select Red as the color to represent the range Bad.

Once you have completed setting the values for the range, click OK and save your changes. Now you will repeat the same steps for the remaining two ranges, Good and Very Good. At this point, go ahead and add a new range to the gauge, and change its properties as follows:

Range Properties for the "Good" Range	Category	Value
Start range at scale value	General	1500000
End range at scale value	General	2500000
Start width	General	20
End width	General	30
Fill Style	Fill	Solid
Color	Fill	Orange

After you're done configuring the preceding range's properties, add a new range with the following values.

Range Properties for the "Very Good" Range	Category	Value
Start range at scale value	General	2500000
End range at scale value	General	5000000
Start width	General	30
End width	General	40
Fill Style	Fill	Gradient
Color	Fill	Orange
Secondary Color	Fill	Green

Adding a Marker Pointer to a Gauge

With the completion of the third range, you have added three ranges that allow the user to understand the sales performance for Australia. Save your report as Territory Sales Drilldown 2008 With Gauge.rdl and click Preview. At this point, by looking at the preview shown in Figure 12-8, although $1.9MM sounds like a big number, you can tell that it's still in the lower part of the (Good) orange range, which tells the end user Australia is not doing so great as a Sales Territory after all. By adding a gauge to this report, you've immediately improved what the user is able to understand by looking at the KPI. The executive sales office will be able to take action based on this report. They'll probably ask their Australian team why they are performing very close to Bad, since they are barely in the Good range.

Territory Sales Drilldown 2008

Sales by
Sales Territory

Sales Territory	Sales Person	Sales Order Number	Total Due
⊞ Australia			$1,943,016.45
⊞ Canada			$12,808,458.05
⊞ Central			$13,434,509.55

Figure 12-8

Although the Australia sales territory seems to be in the Good range, you need to know how far it is from meeting its goal. Now that you've added ranges to your gauge to identify how well a territory is performing, the next step is to display the target sales goal for the territory. You can display these target numbers is by using pointers, but this time, instead of using the needle- type pointer, you will use the marker type for the pointer.

Since a gauge can have more than one pointer, you will add another pointer to the gauge that points to the target sales goal for the Australian territory, which is $3MM. To add a new pointer to the gauge, right-click the gauge and click the Add Pointer option. Once the Pointer Properties dialog box appears, configure the pointer using the following values:

Pointer Properties	Category	Value
Value	Pointer Options	3000000
Pointer type	Pointer Options	Marker
Marker style	Pointer Options	Wedge
Placement	Pointer Options	Outside
Distance from scale	Pointer Options	10
Width	Pointer Options	20
Length	Pointer Options	25

To make the pointers stand out more, change their Fill settings. Apply the following settings to both of the pointers by right-clicking the pointer and clicking the pointer properties. On the Properties dialog box, update the look and feel settings with the following values for both pointers:

Pointer Properties	Category	Value
Fill style	Pointer Fill	Solid
Color	Pointer Fill	Gold
Line style	Pointer Border	Solid
Line width	Pointer Border	1pt
Line color	Pointer Border	Black

After you finish updating both of the pointers, save your project and click Preview. As shown in Figure 12-9, you will now have a marker that points to $3MM, and both pointers stand out and catch the eye. As sales executives now look at this gauge, they can see several things at a quick glance.

Figure 12-9

By looking at the gauge shown in Figure 12-9, you can see the following:

❑ The performance for the Australia sales territory is Good, but it is on the border and very close to being bad.

❑ Its target sales goal is $3MM, and it's sold approximately $2MM.

Adding a Label to a Gauge

The final step in the appearance of the gauge is to add a label to the gauge that will indicate what the KPI is representing. Adding a label is also very similar to adding a range or a pointer; all you need to do is right-click the gauge and select the Add Label option. Find the label you added, right-click it, and select the Label Properties option to open the Properties dialog box for the label and apply the following values to the label:

Label Properties	Category	Value
Text	General	Australia Sales (USD in Millions)
Anchor label to	General	RadialGauges.RadialGuage1
Text alignment	General	Center
Vertical Alignment	General	Middle
Top	General	100
Left	General	−22
Width	General	145
Height	General	14
Angle	General	0
Auto resize text to fit label	Font	False
Font size is a percentage of gauge size	Font	False
Font	Font	Arial
Size	Font	8pt
Style	Font	Bold
Color	Font	White
Fill Style	Fill	Solid
Color	Fill	Brown
Line style	Border	Solid
Line width	Border	1pt
Line color	Border	Black
Shadow offset	Shadow	1pt

When you complete all of the settings, click OK and save your changes by saving the report file. If the label is not showing fully, go ahead and select your gauge and resize it by changing its height. With the addition of the label to the gauge, you have completed creating your gauge. To see your gauge with the label, click the Preview tab.

The completed gauge now gives the end user of this report a dashboard look and feel, as shown in Figure 12-10.

Figure 12-10

When a manager looks at the report shown in Figure 12-10, he or she can instantly get an understanding of where things stand with Australia sales performance and its target status.

Snapping Intervals on a Gauge

Although the following items will not be applied to the example, it's still something you might have to use in a report that you're building. Before you move on to adding gauges into a tablix region, let's go over some of the other ways to customize the look and feel of the gauge.

A snapping interval is the value that your pointer will use to calculate where it should snap or point to. The term *snapping* is used because the pointer will be snapped to the rounded multiple of the snapping interval value. For example, for Australia the total sales value is $1.93 MM, and if you set the snapping interval to 1,000,000, the value will immediately snap to the $2MM major tick instead of snapping to the closest minor tick. If the value is $3.1MM, it will then snap to $3 MM. So the pointer will snap to the rounded multiple value, based on your snap interval value.

> If you leave the default value for the snapping interval, the pointer will point to the nearest tick to the exact value of the data field.

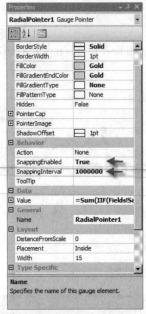

Figure 12-11

To set the snapping interval for a gauge's pointer, you use the Properties pane of the pointer. So to set the snapping interval, go ahead and click the pointer. Once the pointer is highlighted, on the Properties pane search for the Snapping Enabled property and set it to True, as shown in Figure 12-11. Then set the Snapping Interval property by typing the interval you want the pointer to snap to.

Using a Custom Image as a Pointer on a Radial Gauge

In addition to the pointers available to you with the gauge, you also have the ability to create your own pointer image and tell the gauge to use that image as a pointer.

To use a custom image as a pointer, follow these steps:

1. Select the pointer you wish to change by clicking it.

2. On the Properties pane, expand the PointerImage node.

3. Assuming that you will embed your image to the project, under the Source property, select the Embedded option.

4. For the Value property, select the name of the image you wish to choose, as shown in Figure 12-12.

5. For the TransparentColor, pick the color value that you want to remove from the image. In most cases, No Color will do the trick.

Figure 12-12

Creating Multiple Gauges in the Same Report

Let's continue to enhance the report by adding more sales territories. Go ahead and add Canada and the Central sales territories to the report. To add the gauges for Canada and Central, you can easily copy the gauge you create and paste it to the report design region twice.

Select the gauge, copy it, and paste two copies of it to the report design area. Place them where you would like to see them; in this example, you will place them horizontally. Once you have the two new gauges, which are copies of what you did for Australia, update the label, the expression on the needle pointer, and the sales goal number on the marker pointer using the KPI table.

Following is the table introduced at the beginning of the chapter. Use these numbers to customize the two new gauges you added to your report.

Sales Territory	Target	Bad	Good	Very Good
Australia	$3MM	$0MM to $1.5MM	$1.5MM to $2.5MM	$3.5MM to $5MM
Canada	$12MM	$0MM to $6MM	$6MM to $12MM	$12MM to $15MM
Central	$15MM	$0MM to $8MM	$8MM to $16MM	$16MM to $20MM

Just to summarize again, let's go over the steps to update the second gauge so that it displays data for Canada.

1. Right-click the pointer properties and modify the expression to say Canada instead of Australia.

2. Right-click the scale properties and update the Minimum and Maximum values using the values listed in the above table. (For Canada, this would be Minimum=0 and Maximum=1,500,0000.)

3. Update the intervals value in the scale properties to be 3,000,0000 instead of 1,000,0000.

4. Then right-click on the marker and from the pointer properties dialog and update the value. (For Canada this would be to 12,000,0000.)

5. Update the label to state Canada instead of Australia.

Follow these steps for the Central sales territory gauge using the Central numbers listed above.

Once you've completed these steps, save your report. When you click the Preview tab, you will see all three gauges, giving you a lot of information that you initially didn't have with this report, as shown in Figure 12-13.

Territory Sales Drilldown 2008 With Gauge

Sales Territory	Sales Person	Sales Order Number	Total Due
⊞ Australia			$1,943,016.45
⊞ Canada			$12,808,458.05
⊞ Central			$13,434,509.55

Figure 12-13

Adding a Gauge to a Tablix Data Region

You now have a good understanding of how to add a gauge to a report and update its settings so it displays information accurately. In your walkthrough you created gauges for three territories, but there might be times when you want to automate the process of creating gauges. With the help of a tablix, you can now create nested data regions. You can put a gauge inside a tablix cell, and the tablix will automatically create the gauge for each of the rows that have that cell.

To better understand nested data regions, let's add a gauge to the report you were working on earlier. Now that you have the report open, go ahead and add a gauge. But wait; where do you put the gauge? Adding a gauge to a tablix is no different from adding a gauge to a report design area. Once you determine where you would like to add your gauge, you simply drag and drop it to the tablix cell. Now that you're ready to add a gauge to your tablix, prepare your tablix for a gauge. Although you could place the gauge anywhere you would like in the tablix, for this example, display the gauge in its own column, right next to the Total Due column.

To do this, you will add a new column on the tablix by right-clicking the Total Due column and selecting the Insert Column ⇨ Right option, as shown in Figure 12-14. This will create a new column to the right of the Total Due column, which you will use to place your gauge.

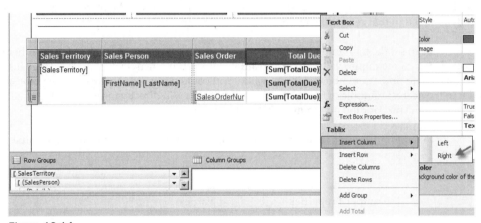

Figure 12-14

Once you add the column, add a 180 Degrees North radial gauge to the new column by dragging and dropping it to the cell that applies to the Sales Territory group (the first cell under the header). You will add the gauge to this specific cell, because in this cell the data is already grouped by sales territory. Since that's what you need for the gauge, this is the cell you will add the gauge to.

After adding the gauge to the tablix cell, you will see that the gauge will automatically change its size so that it fits the cell. To make the gauge readable, you will need to resize the column width and height.

The next step is to bind the pointer to a data field. This is going to be a little different from the example you did earlier. Since the data is already grouped by the sales territory in the cell where the gauge resides, all you have to do is display the total of the TotalDue data field. Drag and drop the TotalDue data field into the gauge, as shown in Figure 12-15.

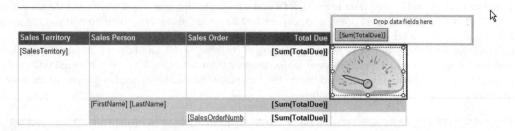

Figure 12-15

This will automatically add the =Sum(TotalDue) expression to the gauge. Note that you don't have to use the IIF statement to filter out the other territories as you had to do in the other gauges, since the data is already grouped in that cell for the tablix.

The next step is to set the minimum and maximum values on the scale of the gauge. In the other gauges, you created custom maximum values for each sales territory, but when displaying the gauge inside the tablix, you have to find a common maximum value. You could easily find the maximum value and round it to the nearest multiple of $5MM, but in this case you will directly insert the value of 20,000,000 for the maximum and 0 for the minimum value on the gauge.

After setting the minimum and maximum values, format the number properties with the values listed below.

Number Properties	Value
Category	Currency
Decimal Places	0
Use 1000 Separator (,)	True
Show values in	Millions
Negative Numbers	($1,234)
Symbol	$ English (United States)
Show symbol after value	False
Include a space	True

Once you've completed configuring the scale properties, click OK and save your report. After you save the report, click the Preview tab. In the preview you will see that multiple gauges were created, one for each sales territory, as shown in Figure 12-16.

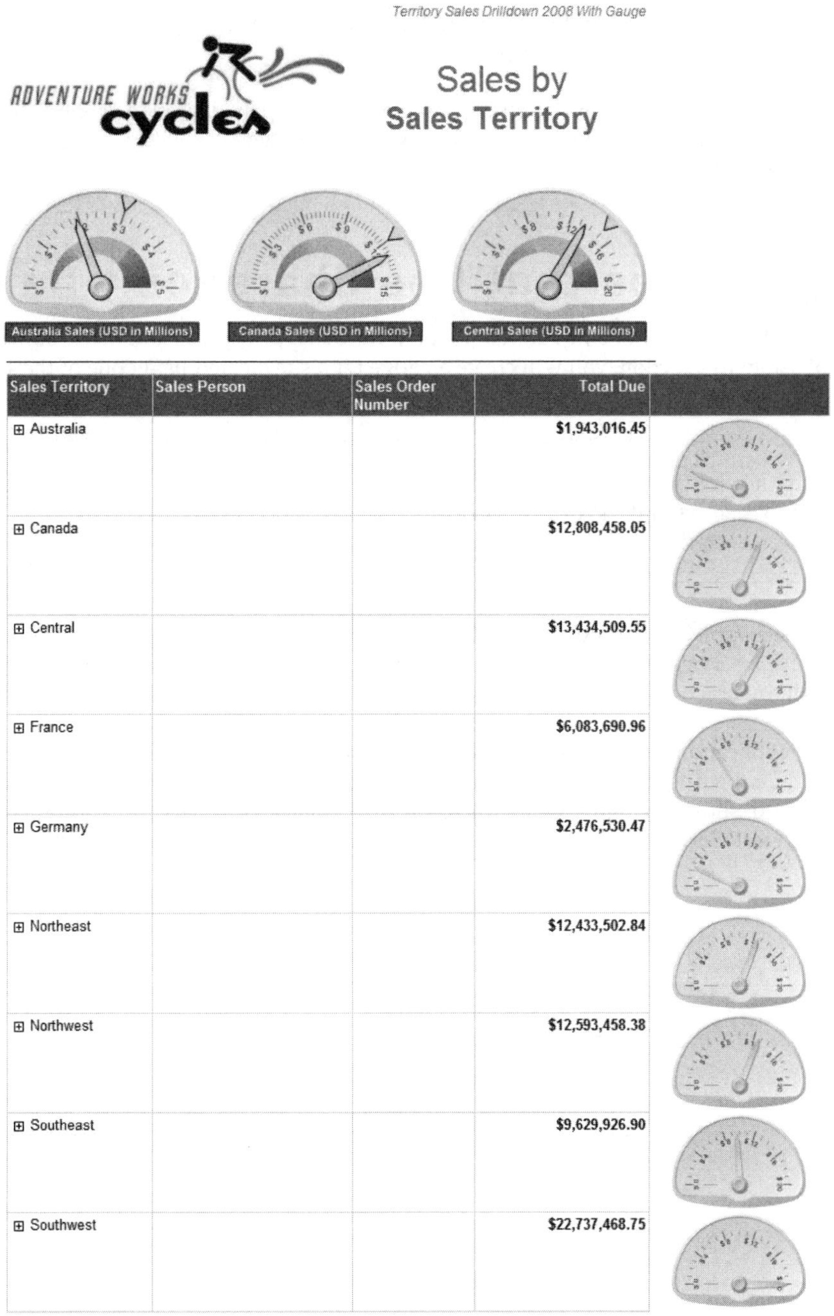

Territory Sales Drilldown 2008 With Gauge

Sales by
Sales Territory

Sales Territory	Sales Person	Sales Order Number	Total Due	
⊞ Australia			$1,943,016.45	
⊞ Canada			$12,808,458.05	
⊞ Central			$13,434,509.55	
⊞ France			$6,083,690.96	
⊞ Germany			$2,476,530.47	
⊞ Northeast			$12,433,502.84	
⊞ Northwest			$12,593,458.38	
⊞ Southeast			$9,629,926.90	
⊞ Southwest			$22,737,468.75	

Figure 12-16

Now that you have enhanced your report, deploy it to SharePoint. Make sure that the report's deployment properties are set to where you want to deploy your report. In this case, you will deploy them to the `http://host/Reports` site. After validating that the report deployment settings are set correctly, right-click the report and click Deploy.

So with a couple of gauges you've enhanced the way information is displayed in a report stored in SharePoint. Now that you've published your report to SharePoint, you can start talking about reporting data stored in SharePoint.

Creating Gauges that Use SharePoint Data

Creating a gauge that uses SharePoint data can involve various types of lists, but here you will use a special type of list. In this section, you will create a gauge for a site created using one of the 40 Application Templates provided by Microsoft.

> The 40 Application Templates are out-of-the-box templates that are custom sites created for specific scenarios and can be downloaded from `http://technet.microsoft.com/en-us/windowsserver/sharepoint/bb407286.aspx`.

The Call Center site application template, which can be downloaded at `http://tinyurl.com/mrl3du`, allows users to track service requests. When a service request is created, the template tracks several things, such as the average resolution time and knowledge base articles that help resolve open issues.

The Call Center application also comes with role-based dashboards. It includes a dashboard for the Service Rep, one for the Knowledge Manager, and one for the Service Rep Manager. The Service Rep Manager dashboard, shown in Figure 12-17, tracks the performance of service representatives by displaying the Overall Service Request Status chart and the Average Resolution Time KPI.

In the next walkthrough, you will enhance the look and feel of the Service Rep Manager dashboard by using gauges. First, create a gauge that will replace the Average Resolution Time Web Part, shown in Figure 12-17.

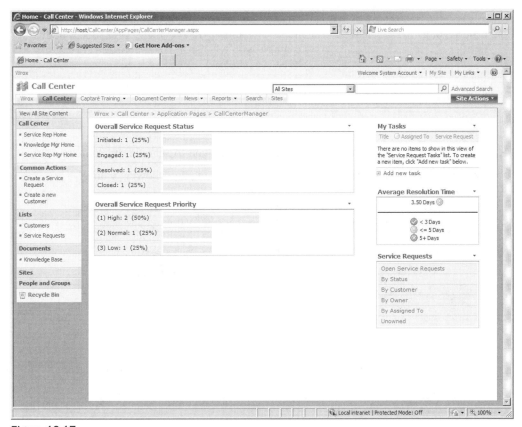

Figure 12-17

The following steps walk you through creating a gauge that will display the Average Resolution Time:

1. Create a new project called Call Center Reports.

2. Add a report named AverageResolutionTime.rdl to your project.

3. Add a new data source from the Report Data tool window using the following values.

Data Source Property	Category	Value
Name	General	dsSharePoint
Type	General	XML
Connection String	General	`http://yoursite/_vti_bin/lists.asmx`. In this example, you will use `http://host/CallCenter/_vti_bin/lists.asmx`.
Credentials	Credentials	Use Windows Authentication

4. Right-click the data source you created and click Convert to Shared Data Source.

5. Right-click the data source and add a new data set using the following values:

Dataset Property	Category	Value
Name	Query	ServiceRequest
Data source	Query	dsSharePoint

For the query, use the following select statement:

```
<Query>
    <SoapAction>http://schemas.microsoft.com/sharepoint/soap/GetListItems
    </SoapAction>
    <Method Namespace="http://schemas.microsoft.com/sharepoint/soap/"
      Name="GetListItems">
        <Parameters>
            <Parameter Name="listName">
                <DefaultValue>Service Requests</DefaultValue>
            </Parameter>
        </Parameters>
    </Method>
    <ElementPath IgnoreNamespaces="True">*</ElementPath>
</Query>
```

The preceding query will bring back columns from the default view. If the column you will report on is not in your default view, add that column to the default view. In this case, you added the Resolved Time to your default view to get that column back with the preceding query.

6. Add a Bullet Graph gauge to the report design area.

7. Bind the pointer to the following expression:

```
=AVG(CDbl(RIGHT(Fields!ows_ResolveTime.Value, LEN(Fields!ows_ResolveTime.Value) -
INSTR(Fields!ows_ResolveTime.Value, "#"))))
```

The ResolveTime column brings back the value of the Resolve time as a string (float;#2.000000). The preceding expression will use the expression you created in Chapter 6. You then convert the value to a double and calculate the average value using the AVG function.

8. Update the Scale to use the following values:

Scale Property	Category	Value
Maximum	General	9
Interval	General	1.5
Style	Font	Bold
Color	Font	Black
Size	Font	14

9. Add a ranges using the following values.

Range Property	Range #1	Range #	Range # 3
Fill Color	Green	Orange	Red
Placement relative to scale	Cross	Cross	Cross
Start range at scale value	0	3	5
End Range at scale value	3	5	9
Start width	30	30	30
End width	30	30	30

10. Right-click the gauge and click Show Minor Tick Marks.

11. Right-click the gauge and create a new label. Right-click the label and configure the label with the following values:

Label Property	Category	Value
Text	General	Average Resolution Time (Days)
Top	General	19
Left	General	8
Width	General	80
Auto resize text to fit label	Font	False
Font size is a percentage of gauge size	Font	False
Font	Font	Arial
Size	Font	8
Style	Font	Bold, Italic
Color	Font	Black

12. On the report project properties, set the deployment properties as follows:

Deployment Properties	Value
Overwrite Data Sources	True
Target Data Source Folder	`http://yoursite/Data Sources`. (In this example, `http://host`/CallCenter/Data Sources.)
Target Report Folder	`http://yoursite/Reports`. (In this example, `http://host`/CallCenter/Reports.)
Target Server URL	`http://yoursite`. (In this case, `http://host/CallCenter`.)

13. Deploy your report to SharePoint by right-clicking the report and clicking Deploy.

14. Go to the Service Rep Manager Home page and click `Site Actions` ⇨ `Edit Page`.

15. On the page, click the Add a Web Part link under the Right zone and select the SQL Server Reporting Services Report Viewer Web Part.

16. Modify the shared Web Part properties of the SQL Server Reporting Services Report Viewer Web Part using the following values:

Web part Properties	Value
Report	`http://yoursite/Reports/ AverageResolutionTime.rdl` (In this example, `http://host/CallCenter/Reports /AverageResolutionTime.rdl`.)
Toolbar	None
Prompt Area	Hidden
Document Map	Hidden
Asynchronous Rendering	False
Height	150
Width	250
Chrome	None

17. Click OK close the Web Part settings.

18. Click the Exit Edit Mode.

Once you exit the edit mode and save your changes, at this point you have created an enhanced version of the Average Resolution Time KPI, as shown in Figure 12-18.

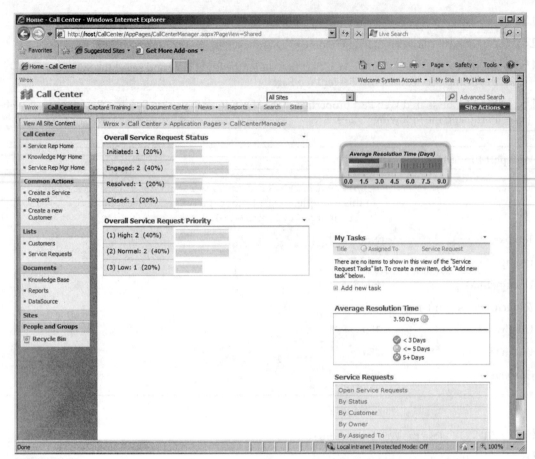

Figure 12-18

Summary

If you've made it this far in the book, congratulations! You've created a report, deployed it to SharePoint, and finally displayed your report on a SharePoint site. You went over requirements gathering, report development basics, and the different methods of deploying reports by creating a custom PowerShell script and custom SharePoint Features. You created dashboard and enhanced them using AJAX and jQuery and also created a custom web service that allowed you to create custom joins on LOB databases and SharePoint lists.

In the final chapter of the book, you worked with gauges and enhanced your existing reports and SharePoint sites with them. We hope you enjoyed this journey as much we have enjoyed writing about it. In today's world, SharePoint and Business Intelligence are two very important topics, and if you're working on bringing them together, welcome on board!

The power of Business Intelligence using SQL Reporting Services 2008 in SharePoint integrated mode hopefully came out in this book, and we hope that what you've learned has inspired you to create solutions that will solve critical business needs.

Index